Changing Money

Changing Money

Financial Innovation in Developed Countries

Edited by

MARCELLO DE CECCO

Published in cooperation with
the European University Institute, Florence

Basil Blackwell

Copyright © European University Institute 1987

First published 1987

Basil Blackwell Ltd
108 Cowley Road, Oxford, OX4 1JF, UK

Basil Blackwell Inc.
432 Park Avenue South, Suite 1503
New York, NY 10016, USA

British Library Cataloguing in Publication Data

Changing money: Financial Innovation in Developed Countries

1. Finance
I. De Cecco, Marcello
332   HG173
ISBN 0-631-155015

Library of Congress Cataloging in Publication Data

Changing money: financial innovation in developed countries

Bibliography: p.
Includes index.
1. Finance. I. De Cecco, Marcello.
HG175.F545   1987   332   86-28317
ISBN 0-631-15501-5

Typeset in 10½ on 11½pt CG Times by
System 4 Associates, Gerrards Cross, Buckinghamshire
Printed in Great Britain by
T J Press Ltd, Padstow

Contents

Contributors

Marcello de Cecco is Professor of Monetary Economics at the University of Siena, and Professor of Economics at the European University Institute.

Albert M. Wojnilower is Managing Director and Chief Economist at the First Boston Corporation.

Meyer Eisenberg is Director of the National Center on Financial Services, and Professor of Law at the University of California, Berkeley.

Donald D. Hester is Professor of Economics at the University of Wisconsin, Madison.

Meghnad Desai is Professor of Economics at the London School of Economics.

William Low is Professor of Economics at the London School of Economics and the University of Essex.

John H. Forsyth is Director of Morgan Grenfell Ltd.

Hermann-Josef Dudler is Director of the Deutsche Bundesbank.

Cesare Caranza is Director of the Monetary Section, Research Department at the Banca d'Italia.

Carlo Cottarelli is an Economist in the Monetary Section, Research Department at the Banca d'Italia.

Christian de Boissieu is Professor of Economics at the University of Paris I (Panthéon-Sorbonne).

Yoshio Suzuki is Director of the Institute for Monetary and Economic Studies at the Bank of Japan.

Enrica Guglielmotto works in the Department of Study and Planning at the Istituto Bancario San Paolo di Torino.

Giuseppe Passatore works in the Department of Study and Planning at the Istituto Bancario San Paulo di Torino.

Preface

This book contains a series of essays, written by national specialists, on the changing face of money and credit in developed countries. After a theoretical introduction by the editor, which tries to assess the position of financial innovation in monetary theory, the origins and diffusion of financial innovation are analysed with respect to several national contexts. Government inspired innovations are distinguished from market determined ones, the former being more prevalent in countries with a dirigiste tradition, like those of continental Europe and Japan, while the latter seem to have characterized the Anglo-American financial scene. The authors attempt to identify the permissive agents of innovation, as well as the repressive ones, to describe the present state of affairs in their countries, and to make educated guesses about future trends. The book is the result of a conference held at the European University Institute in October 1985. The conference convenor, who also edited the book, tried to assemble a mix of lawyers, academic economists, central commercial and merchant bankers, whose opinions may usefully portray the many faceted world of financial innovation. Jacqueline Bourgonje was very efficient in helping me in the organization of the conference and Jessica Spataro provided excellent assistance during the event, while Fiona Cameron edited the first draft of the conference papers.

1

Financial Innovations and Monetary Theory

MARCELLO DE CECCO

Modern monetary theory coincides, in its development, with the development of deposit banks, and with the development of what can be defined as modern banking systems.

There is, indeed, a very large body of monetary theory which precedes the phenomenon of modern deposit banking; and that theory includes extremely sophisticated analyses of the monetary phenomena. Monetary theory as we know it, however, is fundamentally based on the analysis of the implications for economic theory of the series of stupendous financial innovations, which, in the last 150 years, have given rise to contemporary banking systems. Compared to recent financial innovations, the rise of deposit banking systems in the nineteenth century was a veritable revolution. It was a true *technical* revolution, as cheques, discounts, giros, clearing houses and telegraphic transfers developed very rapidly throughout the advanced world. It also implied a true revolution in economic theory. If we except the work of a few visionaries, monetary theory before the rise of deposit banking was almost exclusively concerned with the fiscal aspects of money. Money was seen, as Sir John Hicks has put it, as 'the finances of the sovereign'. Only the sovereign, through his tax collection system and his expenses, was provided with an extensive network which would make his coins 'current'.

This technical prerogative was, of course, reinforced by the legal one of monetary sovereignty. But it is hardly believable that monetary sovereignty might have meant much had the sovereign not been, almost everywhere, such a large and extended collector of taxes and spender of their proceeds. Once the sovereign had established himself as a credible money supplier, he would almost inevitably transform his service to the community into an 'exorbitant privilege' faced with mounting expenses. He would debase his own currency rather than increase taxation. Monetary theory, in the more than two thousand years of European monetary history, is thus almost exclusively dedicated to the analysis of the effects on economic life of the monetary deeds, and misdeeds, of the sovereign.

With the rise of modern deposit banking, however, the sovereign's monetary privilege comes to be shared by the banking system. Banks, in developed countries, establish a network of branches as pervasive and diffuse as the sovereign's tax collection system. Banks, moreover, since they make money by giving credit, mix two activities that had hitherto tended to remain separate. Since they create money, i.e. by extending loans to their clients, they come to compete with the sovereign in one of his most jealously guarded prerogatives. But, in addition to that, they intermediate between savers and borrowers, something the sovereign did not do. For the economic life of modern countries, banks thus become the real planning centres. They soon become more economically important than the sovereign himself.

Modern monetary theory is thus dedicated to analysing how banks create money and intermediate between savers and borrowers, and how the sovereign and the banking system stand, in relation to one another, as they perform what are basically the same functions. A large part of modern monetary theory is dedicated, in analogy to older monetary theory, to studying the ways in which the sovereign and the public can reign in the banking system. It soon becomes apparent that, by linking money creation to credit creation, banks have found the philosopher's stone. They can expand credit at will and without bounds, as long as the sovereign, and the public, do not devise ways to constrain and constitutionalize their powers.

Studying what exactly are the powers that banks wield over the economy and how they use them constitutes the field of modern monetary theory. How to constrain and to make the best use of the powers the banking system wields on the economy, is what modern monetary policy debates are about.

A considerable part of modern monetary theory is dedicated to the study of the unique phenomenon of financial intermediation (which often involves maturity transformation), conducted via money creation. An equally important part of it is dedicated to the study of the uneasy, but basic, mix of industry and banking – of the tendency that *Spätskapitalismus* has of becoming *finanz-Kapitalismus* – but also of the possibility that exists to start a process of industrial development by mobilizing capital through banks.

Like the state, banking is essentially a macrophenomenon. It is worthy of analysis as a system. Taken individually, banks, if there are a large number of them in existence and they are not large, are hardly able to create credit. They can hardly create deposits. Like the telephone system, the whole constitutes a phenomenon qualitatively different from its component parts. However, classical economic theory has tended to approach and study banking as it had approached other relevant actors in economic life, for instance, producers and consumers, by considering them individually and studying their profit and welfare maximizing behaviour as individuals.

Several of the shortcomings of modern monetary theory stem from this failure to realize that banking is a relevant phenomenon only if banks are studied as a system, a macrostructure. But what for some economists is myopia, for other economists is a subtler normative stand. A whole school of monetary economists, led by Edward Shaw, has developed a monetary theory whose main role is that of negating the peculiar functions that banking performs, as a macrostructure. Moreover the same prerogative of monetary sovereignty is negated to the state. All money, including bank deposits, is taken to be somebody's debt and somebody else's credit. No special social or economic functions are attributed by this theory to money, so that every act of money creation must, by definition, all other things remaining equal, diminish the borrowing capacity of either the state or the banking system.

The 'inside money' school's solution to bring money back into the microeconomic fold is only the last attempt to exorcise the 'demonic' features of money, a man-made phenomenon which has played havoc with the economic theorists' attempts to give economic life a unitary explanation, based on natural laws.

If the old economists tried to exorcise the monetary sovereignty of the state, modern economists have tried to do the same with the banking system. That is to say, to devise either monetary theories or institutional reforms which would do away with the banking system's embarrassing ability to create money by giving credit, thus becoming the pivot of the capitalist economic system. The 'inside money' attempt has already been mentioned. Other attempts to reduce money to the nature of the 'veil', which may in no way hide or distort the true relations between relative prices established by natural laws, have been more numerous. The best known among them is that of linking money creation to the production of a natural commodity, gold or silver. This would – so economists hoped – bring back money from the alchemist's crucible to the scientist's laboratory. Other attempts have been aimed more at institutional reform than at hitting the theoretical nail on the head. Suffice it here to remember the 'one hundred per cent' banking reserves proposal of Henry Simons, or the Banking Reform of 1844 in England, which tried to legislate the separation of money from credit. More recent attempts have been the great banking reforms of the 1930s, whose effects are still with us, and have been the cause of much recent financial innovation.

If we consider the recent history of institutional financial reforms, we notice that, very often, these reforms attempt to turn the traditional poacher of monetary history, the sovereign (the state, in modern parlance), into the gamekeeper, who should control a more important poacher, the banking system. Of course, for a model like that to function effectively, one has to be certain that the gamekeeper will stick to his new role, and will not relapse into his old bad habit of debasing the currency. To make that outcome less likely, central banks have been put between the state and the banking system, and have been given the task of restraining, as far as they can, the inflationary tendencies of the state, and of controlling the banking system.

The triad on which modern monetary systems are built is thus composed of the state, the original repository of monetary sovereignty; the central bank, to which the state sometimes gives the direct task of issuing money; and the deposit banks system. More often than not, the banking system has come to be formed by a core – a few very large banks – and a periphery – a multiplicity of small banks and of financial institutions other than banks.

This configuration of a financial system is far removed from the ideal financial system as modelled by neo-classical economic theory. It is a configuration based on monopoly or oligopoly, where each financial institution performs most of the functions required by the modern economy. 'Omnibus banking' clearly prevails over specialization. In this configuration, credit is administered according to what has come to be called in the literature 'equilibrium rationing', which contradicts the basic tenet of neo-classical theory, that credit must be allocated only by interest rates rising or falling according to the movements of demand and supply.

The configuration of financial structure which has prevailed in most capitalist economies thus sees finance as being administered mainly by contractual, clientele-type relations between bankers and borrowers, bankers and savers. Auction markets in the financial system tend to be the exception rather than the rule.

Large banks thus seem to be linked by long-term contractual obligations to their best clients. Interest rate policy administered by the monetary authorities through open market operations only works because banks, when their available funds are decreased by open market bond sales operated by the central bank, tend to ration credit to their clients, and do that by starving the core of their clientele less than its periphery. Hence the inverse selectiveness of monetary policy, which tends to preserve what already exists, and to discourage what is new.

In a context like this, financial innovations can only come about if they are induced by technological change. Engineers and electronic firms, for instance, perfect electronic wire transfer systems or automated teller machines, and banks adopt them, in an attempt to keep up with the times or in an attempt to compete with other banks without touching the price of loans or deposits. In such a context, innovations are often introduced by the monetary authorities and foisted upon the banking system. The central bank operates as the impartial umpire, to prevent the outbreak of competitive wars. A recent inquiry conducted by auditors Touche Ross among bankers in the main industrial countries has found that this is indeed how electronic banking innovations have come about. They are technology-induced, much more than market-orientated.

The model of financial system we have just depicted, however, contains a contradiction within itself. Monetary policy operated by achieving financial programming through equilibrium rationing, which works mainly through the large deposit banks allocating scarcer or more abundant credit according to their priority list of clients. The large banks try – as was said above – to reconcile the central bank's will with their long-standing customary obligations to their clients. This model of financial programming, however, cannot be subjected to very severe strains without giving rise to important structural changes.

It cannot stand either a protracted budget deficit policy or a protracted dear money policy. Both policies are made effective by the central bank's special action on the large banks. If the government wants to impose a protracted budget deficit policy by issuing large quantities of bonds, it must sooner or later disintermediate the banks and sell its bonds directly to the public, who will go out of deposits and buy bonds. The fear that the government will have to put up taxes in the future to repay its debt comes into play only very late in the day, perhaps never in countries with governments that enjoy sufficient legitimacy with their citizens. An easy money policy of this kind may thus have the effect of disintermediating the banks and of transforming them into *rentiers*. Firms may also have to face the option of either going out of business or of becoming *rentiers* themselves.

A policy of protracted dear money will also operate through the banks. Faced with the unpleasant task of cutting credit even to their best customers, banks will react by starting side-shows which will allow them to carry on lending to their clientele.

The internal inconsistency is thus apparent: monetary policy operates via the large banks, but it operates, beyond certain boundaries, by making the banks weaker, or by changing the structure of the financial system. Banks are asked to cooperate to make effective measures which will, by their very effectiveness, make the banks weaker.

If one wanted to model this complex relationship between the three elements of the triad, one would need to use non-linear analysis. Within the bounds of fiscal and monetary moderation,[1] the system is not internally inconsistent. It operates for its own institutional perpetuation. Outside these boundaries, the internal consistency we have noticed manifests itself; and the system, by its very functioning, leads to its own structural transformation.

We can now turn to consider the process of financial innovation from the intellectual viewpoint we have constructed. Financial innovation, not of the technological kind we considered above, but more of the organizational kind, will be inversely correlated to the specialization of the financial system under scrutiny. Since, even in specialized financial systems, monetary policy is essentially a policy of equilibrium credit rationing, and makes itself effective through large banks, its exceeding the boundaries of moderation spells, after a while, disaster for the latter, who cannot remain wed to a collusive behaviour with the central bank. As a result, the banks will start evading the prescriptions of the central bank by creating other lending agencies through which they will continue to supply credit to their core clients. They will also turn

---

1 The term 'moderation', of course, rather evades the problem, as it would definitely not be easy to quantify moderation in a real world situation. Moreover, what is moderate in one context may be excessive in another.

themselves into money brokers, matching demand for, and supply of, loanable funds without intermediation. There will thus be an increase in off-books, primary financial operations, a forced transformation of contract markets into auction markets. Since these other functions, in specialized financial systems, are performed by distinct financial institutions, the banks will invade their preserves, in an attempt not to lose their market share. Thus immoderate behaviour by the monetary authorities will result in specialized systems, in a gradual, but inevitable, breakdown of demarcation lines, in competition in all markets by all financial intermediaries, which will, if it is left free to work itself out, eventually result in a financial structure where large, all-purpose, financial institutions will dominate. The final outcome of financial innovation for specialized financial markets will thus be a drastic decrease of specialization, and a drastic increase of concentration levels.

From the point of view of efficient financial structures this outcome may not be at all negative. The theoretical foundations on which financial specialization rests are not very firm ones. The theories according to which financial development leads to specialization are more normative than positive. They rest on the assumption that markets are always more efficient than hierarchical structures, and that specialization, by reducing power concentration, will exorcise the threat a concentrated financial structure exerts over the freedom of action of the 'real' sector of the economy.

A streamlined financial structure, consisting of a few large, all-purpose institutions, is supposed to be somewhat conducive – to use Edward Shaw's parlance – to 'financial repression'. At least, it ought to be the point of departure, rather than the point of arrival, of 'financial deepening'. There is, however, an intermediate stage, when the immoderate behaviour of the monetary authorities (which will usually be induced by external shocks or by the government's decision to finance its deficit through the bond market) will lead to a financial structure where primary financial instruments will prevail over indirect finance, and there will be a rise of brokerage and a decline of intermediation.

This intermediate stage may superficially vindicate the Gurley–Shaw school and its model of financial development. But, when the stage is reached where the very consumer behaves – as Sir John Hicks wrote 50 years ago – as a little bank, being present on both sides of the financial market, and auction pricing prevails over contractual financial operations, at that very time the need of the industrial structure for financial intermediation will reassert itself. As a result, a yawning gap will open between the needs of individuals and the needs of firms. It is doubtful, in fact, whether the 'securitization' of credits can proceed too far and whether the whole gamut of financial requirements of the business sector can be serviced by auction markets. Banks came into being because of the 'lumpiness' of the debtor–creditor relationship, because of its contractual, customary nature. A banker's relationship with his clients is, an anthropologist would say, a deeply 'embedded' one; it can hardly be reconciled with an 'arm's length' relationship. This is apparent when one reads George Ackerlof's splendid article on 'lemons'.[2] The less the bankers know their clients and the context in which they operate, the less they will risk. Embeddedness means to be part of a sensitive information network, one of whose centres is the bank.

Thus, on balance, we see that the reduction of the financial structure to either a few large 'omnibus' banks or to a system of securities markets will induce the needs of savers to diverge from those of borrowers. One may venture to foresee that either solution will induce the rise in concentration levels in the non-financial business sector. We can further venture to say that perhaps branch banking will be more 'embedded' into the productive sector of the economy than a system of financial markets where auction methods prevail, and where demand and supply are reconciled by price movements.

The forecast is, therefore, that the stage of 'securitization' and the prevalence of auction markets will be a passing one for the United States and Great Britain. In both these countries, regulation[3] crystallized a financial structure based on a temporary division of functions and market shares. To some of the less sophisticated financial economists, this artificial solution appeared as the epitome of modernity, the stage of financial development towards which less advanced countries would, or ought to, move. In fact, the regulation of the British and US financial markets had stopped in mid-course a process of financial rationalization which, if left to grind to its final conclusion, would have meant the disappearance of many politically powerful financial institutions.

The financial structure based on a plurality of financial institutions and markets was thus 'frozen' by political action, and remained frozen until the political power of the institutions threatened with extinction diminished.

John Hicks wrote that capitalism requires, for its progress, that a large part of economic relations be allowed to remain of a contractual, customary nature. Only a top layer of economic relations must be allowed to be of an auction, arm's length nature. If this layer becomes thicker, the shocks which auction markets, by their working, communicate to the rest of the economy (which works to its best advantage on a long-term contractual basis) will result in deep and continuous fluctuations in investment and employment, which will, in turn, cause continuous intervention by governments, with economic policies that, by superimposing themselves on the already existing fluctuations, will very often achieve results opposite to those desired.

The 'unfreezing' of the institutional set-up in the financial system of the United States which has occurred in the last 30 years, and which has given rise to a spate of 'financial innovations', has been originated by a diminution of the relative political power of the financial sectors protected by the regulatory 'freeze' of the 1930s and by the corresponding increase of the political power

---

2   G. A. Ackerlof, 'The Market for "Lemons"', in *Quarterly Journal of Economics*, 1969.
3   Which in the United States was written in law, while in Britain was exercised by the authority of the central bank.

of their competitors. This has not been a bloodless fight and has gone on by fits and starts, but the trend has been clear. For the groups penalized by the Roosevelt Reforms to reacquire a market share, a mainly fix-price system has had to be transformed into a mainly flex-price system. But monetary policy had adapted itself to being managed in a fix-price environment and with the move, by the financial system, to a mainly flex-price environment, monetary policy has lost its bearings. It still works, as far as it does, because the system is *still* partly a fix-price one. As Stiglitz and Blinder have observed,[4] open market operations transmit a message from the Federal Reserve (the Fed) to the economy *only* because banks give credit according to equilibrium rationing procedures. Once banks are disintermediated, and most of the credit market becomes an auction market, how will monetary policy messages be transmitted to the economy? If the only means will be interest rate changes, as seems inevitable in the new flex-price environment, the instability of the economy must certainly increase, if we accept Hicks's classic conclusions.

It was noted above, however, that this is a necessary phase through which specialized financial systems must go once the fetters of regulation are removed and a new competitive structure develops, which entails a drastic redistribution of market shares. The fix-price financial system, in other words, must become a flex-price system to allow the profound reshuffle of market shares which will in turn allow it to become a fix-price system again. The danger, of course, is that in the intermediate phase, when the system has become a mainly flex-price one, instability may become so great, and interest rates may have to oscillate so much, that the system may get out of control altogether. In that case, one may easily envisage a return, after a few wild gyrations, to a drastic fix-price system. The fear is that the dynamics of the transition from one fix-price system to the other may involve a severe loss of welfare and resources for the United States and Britain.

The fear is also, for the Europeans and Japanese, and even more for the developing countries, that their largely fix-price financial systems may be subjected to shocks emanating from the US and British financial systems, under the form, for instance, of deep interest rate oscillations. This fear has become reality in the past five years. The result has been that the European financial systems – some more than others – have been dragged by these shocks into institutional transformations which are not altogether welcome, as they probably represent, for the more rational European financial systems, a retrogression into a previous and less efficiently organized phase of their development.

Will the European and Japanese systems be able to take the best from the 'financial revolution' now going on in the United States and Britain, and keep the negative impacts at bay? It is essential that they will be able to do so, *before* the US and British financial systems get re-regulated according to the

---

4 Blinder, A. S. and Stiglitz, J. E., 'Money Credit Constraints and Economic Activity', in *American Economic Review*, May 1983.

rules dictated by the new power structure which emerges from the flex-price phase.

The fear is that the shocks imparted by the 'fall-out' of the flex-price phase in the United States and Britain to the European and Japanese systems may dislocate the latter, so that a penalty is paid by the European economies in terms of growth. This seems to have been the case in the past five years. But a penalty can be also a longer-term one, if the Europeans become convinced that the flex-price system is a more advanced stage of financial development. In that case, they will move into a phase which is totally unnecessary for them, as they have already been where the United States and Britain want to go. Once they move into a flex-price system, they will have lost all their institutional advantages *vis-à-vis* the United States and Britain. The consequences of such a *faux pas* may be momentous. It is only to be hoped that such a blunder may be avoided.

2

Financial Change in the United States

ALBERT M. WOJNILOWER

During the past 20 years the US financial system has been undergoing a dramatic transformation. A new structure is emerging better suited to the modern temperament. As befits the 'me' and the 'now' generation, it is less regulated and less disciplined, but also much more dependent on governmental support. If not for the hugely expanded role – far beyond anything ever contemplated – played by US government guarantees, deposit insurance and lending of last resort, the financial system would not function. Government is expected to replace the safety net that private associations and families no longer consider themselves obligated (and probably would be unable) to provide for their members.

Concurrently, the US financial culture is being revolutionized by the application of new electronic technology originally invented for other purposes. The resulting mixture of radically cheapened and speeded-up transactions, coupled with reduced discipline and increased dependence on governmental bail-outs, is a volatile brew.

Some observers have been inclined to view financial change in the United States as primarily stimulated by a desire to overcome and outwit governmental intervention. That is much too narrow a view. The effort has been to capitalize on the advantages of regulation and to escape the restraints. If the governmental safety net had not been widely extended, many new features of the US financial system would not have been tried, or would have failed in the attempt. To be sure, each competing financial interest has expended a great deal of effort in trying to obtain, in the name of deregulation, the legislative enactment of a so-called 'level playing field' (as if there ever was or could be such a thing) that slopes in its particular direction. For a time, their efforts were supported by the supervisory authorities, which, like the rest of society, for a while lost faith in the legitimacy of any other than market constraints. Because of the preoccupation with deregulation on the part of academics, practitioners, and regulators, many have been late in recognizing that technological change is overtaking many of the issues. While the traditional institutions contest their jurisdictional disputes, the advances in computation and communication are rendering both the institutions and their quarrels obsolete.

Removing the pricing restrictions from a market is certain to increase the quantities bought and sold; deregulation of US financial markets has already spurred a major surge in securities turnover and private indebtedness. What is questionable is whether, without regulation, these increases will be self-limiting other than by disaster. Not every novelty is good or permanent; that is why I much prefer the term 'change' to the value-laden label of 'innovation' that is often indiscriminately used to describe the financial turmoil of recent years.

While financial structure and technology have changed greatly in a few years, human nature presumably remains much the same. The biological and historical evidence is that undue optimism – the propensity to gamble, speculate, and borrow too much and to overvalue near-term gain – is somehow engrained within our species. That is why most (perhaps all) societies which have left a written record were impelled to regulate their money and credit systems.

Perfection has its price. Market perfection has its drawbacks as well as its advantages. Competition brings out the best but also the worst in people, as every sports fan knows. As with fixed foreign exchange rates, regulated financial markets seemed unbearable and were overthrown. Now we are discovering that unregulated markets (like floating exchange rates) may also seem unliveable. In the United States, I believe, fragility of the financial structure is already prompting a return to regulatory intervention, perhaps of a more intrusive and arbitrary nature than its forebears.

SOME PECULIARITIES OF US FINANCIAL STRUCTURE

The financial structure of the United States, like its history and political and social institutions, differs from the rest of the world in some very important respects. Most notably, the United States is served by tens of thousands of independent financial organizations, most of them quite small. Their interests for the most part are local and parochial. As a result, they have little political cohesiveness or influence on the national scene. The fragmented banking system reflects the US public's innate suspicion of concentrations of power. It is as though every community had been deemed entitled to at least one bank: a locally owned financial public utility that enabled the locality to control its own financial destiny. But if a community warranted one such independent utility, then it should have at least two, to forestall any opportunity for monopolistic exploitation. Although the interlinking of our communities by automobile and telephone has largely destroyed the logic of such localism, the concept maintains a strong nostalgic and political appeal.

Americans' desire for both strong central government and profound local autonomy is reflected in the anomaly of 'dual' banking: banks and certain other financial institutions may be chartered by the federal government *or* by the state government, each of which have their own supervisory law and authorities. To complicate matters further, the Federal Reserve System (the central bank, the Fed), the Federal Home Loan Bank Board, and the federal deposit insurance system (the FDIC, FSLIC, and NCUA)[1] maintain extensive supervisory organizations alongside the federal and state authorities. The Securities and Exchange Commission (SEC) also enters significantly in certain instances. In some ways the multiple regulation is stultifying, but it also offers an opportunity to play the regulators off against each other, since it is possible to switch from one form of charter to another.

Another unusual aspect of the US depository system is that small deposits have long been regarded as withdrawable on demand, even if the legal terms of the deposit may require notice. Of late, to be sure, federal regulations have laid down penalties for early withdrawal of fixed-maturity time deposits, but the penalties are essentially limited to a loss of interest. A bank or savings institution that does not routinely allow immediate, no-notice withdrawal might as well close its doors. To an important extent, this privilege was generalized to large deposits at large banks through the invention of marketable certificates of deposit in 1962. Should the unmatured large certificates of deposit or commercial paper of a major bank or bank holding company lose easy saleability on the open market, that entity would find it extraordinarily difficult to raise funds to roll over maturing paper and would be threatened with insolvency. Official support is virtually certain to be mobilized at an early stage. As a result, partly by law and partly through case-by-case response, the coverage of the deposit insurance system at large banks is in practice nearly universal.

THE BREAKDOWN OF THE COMPARTMENTS

An environment in which thousands of institutions, most of whose liabilities are *de facto* federally insured, compete for the public's financial business, would seem made to order for cut-throat rate competition and high-risk lending. And so it is proving – but only lately. The reason problems did not multiply sooner is that, until the recent wave of deregulation, such competition in effect was prohibited. In addition, partly as a consequence (both deliberate and accidental) of regulation, the various financial markets had become rather nicely compartmentalized. Competition, to the extent permitted by the rules,

1   Federal Deposit Insurance Corporation, Federal Savings and Loan Insurance Corporation and National Credit Union Administration.

was active within but not much between the specialized compartments.

Recently, however, the changes in technology and in the ideology of the rule-makers have been breaking down the walls separating the various compartments. Almost by definition each sheltered precinct already contained a more than optimal number of competitors. Under the new rules and technology, each type of institution must now seek predatory survival throughout the whole overcrowded financial city. In addition, the established institutions are coming into unexpected collision with novel types of firms spawned by the new environment, organizations that are unencumbered by left-over baggage from a previous existence in a regulated, low interest rate environment. When conservative speed limits on a road are suddenly removed, the casualties mount, both among the fast drivers and the slow. Or, to use a different but also apt analogy, freeing pets by releasing them into the jungle is not liberation, but murder.

Geographic Boundaries

One prominent type of financial compartmentalization in the United States has been geographic. From the outset, and to a considerable extent still, financial institutions have been restricted in their branching and other operations within their own states or even narrower boundaries. For example, savings banks used to be allowed to make mortgage loans only within a 50 mile radius of their offices. Until quite recently New York City banks were restricted in branching into the suburbs and the rest of the state, and Texas banks are still prohibited by the state constitution from having any branches whatsoever. As already mentioned, the cosmopolitanization of business, and the ability and willingness of virtually all Americans to drive their cars many miles for work and shopping has removed any justification for these restrictions. Nevertheless, the restrictions are valued by local institutions (not necessarily only the small ones) for the protection they afford, however leaky, against presumed powerful invaders.

In reality, since the postal service and the telephone now enable institutions to solicit funds and clients all over the country and indeed the world, the physical location of offices is of rapidly diminishing relevance. Also the legal barriers are breaking down. The desire to lure (or retain) financial firms who are large employers is gradually forcing the more restrictive jurisdictions to lower their 'immigration requirements'. In other cases, outsiders have been admitted because only they were willing to put up the capital to save shaky local institutions. While major battles over 'turf' remain to be fought in Congress and the state legislatures about these boundary disputes, these should be viewed as rearguard actions. Only by national legislation can these jurisdictional squabbles be fully decided, but outside the context of a national crisis such legislation can be passed only in the unlikely event that the various interests reach a substantial consensus. In effect, a peace treaty can be reached only after the war has been resolved on the battleground. In the meanwhile institutions continue to expend energy and attention in trying to surmount geographical barriers they find restraining, or bolstering those they regard as protective. Often they find that success in escaping one's cage turns out to be unrewarding or even dangerous, but that staying in it may afford even less protection.

Functional Compartmentalization

While the geographical constraints, though remaining important to particular financial entities, no longer have much fundamental significance, functional compartmentalization still plays a meaningful, though also waning role. Some of the compartmentalization reflects natural specialization, some the intentional or accidental effects of regulation. What follows is a selective review of the rise and fall of the functional compartmentalization of US financial intermediaries, as seen from the standpoint of some of the major types of financial organizations, old and new. Some have been able to take advantage of these changes, others have been injured. At the conclusion of this survey, we shall step back once more to assess briefly the performance of the system as a whole.

Until about ten years ago, US *commercial banks* had a legal monopoly on the issuance of cheque book (checking) accounts and, indeed, on the entire private money and payments function. After 1933 and until very recently, moreover, interest payment on cheque account deposits was prohibited (although it is not clear that such payments were widespread or large before that). Ceilings also were mandated on the rates payable on time and savings accounts, but for many years these remained well above market rates and had little impact. After they started to become 'binding', during the 1960s, they were set at slightly lower levels for commercial banks than for other, more mortgage market orientated savings institutions.

Thus, until quite recently, the function of commercial banks was mainly to process local cheque accounts, to make loans to medium-sized and smaller businesses (large ones had access to the commercial paper and securities markets) and to buy government securities. Purchase of stocks or other equity positions and the underwriting of private securities was (and remains) forbidden. What a confined role in a rapidly growing economy!

Obviously, the banks have managed to enlarge their scope. Beginning in the early 1960s – with the tacit connivance of the regulators who could have nipped these efforts in the bud – the larger banks gained access to the national and international deposit markets, first by inventing negotiable certificates of deposit and then through massive participation in the Eurodollar market. These new instruments undermined and eventually led to the abolition of most of the interest rate ceilings. In the political bargaining, the banks managed to achieve regulatory parity with thrift institutions in the bidding for savings accounts. As access to funds grew and became more assured, not only the sourcing but also the lending of bank funds quickly became national and then global in scope. Now banks had the resources to service the credit needs of even giant companies. The growth of their time and savings deposits also enabled banks to become aggressive consumer and mortgage lenders, as well as the dominant buyers of the obligations of state and local governments (interest on which, in the United States, is exempt from federal income tax). In both retail and wholesale credit markets, their share of the total business grew substantially.

Nevertheless, as is also obvious, this growth did not prove to be an unmixed private or social blessing. Profit margins in lending were squeezed, so more loans of poorer quality had to be made to maintain earnings. Interest rates fluctuated more. Although banks soon learned how to shift the rate risk to borrowers through floating rate loans, this further weakened the quality of the loans. The lending of funds in massive quantities to replace earnings lost through reduced margins led to gigantic misadventures with real estate investment trusts (REITs) and then with foreign loans. Nor is the book closed on the huge merger and acquisition loans of recent years, which have taken the place of REIT and foreign loans as the principal volume outlet.

It is ironic but true that the deregulated banking system has survived its mistakes only because of the explicit and implicit support provided by the governmental regulators. Even with that support, however, as will be shown below, the future of commercial banks is threatened by newer institutions that are technologically more suited to the times and less encumbered by past mistakes. The fact that some major banks have made virtually open declaration of their intent to focus on investment banking rather than commercial banking shows that they see the handwriting on the wall.

The *thrift institution* 'compartment' is another illustration of a group of restricted but sheltered institutions that managed to rid themselves of detested regulatory restrictions only to find themselves, with a few notable exceptions, fighting a losing battle in the open market. Traditionally, savings banks and savings and loan associations, originally founded to provide a safe haven for small depositors as contrasted with the unstable commercial banks, have been closely associated with mortgage finance. For many years, they were assured preferred and profitable access to funds by being allowed to pay interest rates up to a ceiling that, while a little higher than for commercial banks, was substantially below mortgage rates. The rate ceilings prevented price competition for deposits, but the existence of a large number of institutions assured vigorous competition in the provision of mortgage loans and various customer services. Such competition grew especially intense at times of monetary ease, when other lenders such as commercial banks and life insurance companies also would become aggressive mortgage market lenders.

The thrift institutions' idyll was rudely shattered when, in 1959, for the first time, interest rates on short-term marketable Treasury securities developed the habit of rising above the deposit interest ceilings during episodes of monetary tightness. Suddenly thrift institutions would lose deposits ('disintermediation') – as with commercial banks, their deposits were and are *de facto* withdrawable on demand – but they could not liquidate their largely non-marketable mortgage holdings. Because they were threatened with insolvency, housing finance would grind to a halt, and soon the whole economy would follow into recession.

This seemed to all a deplorable state of affairs. Conservatives blamed the governmental interest rate regulations, while liberals were upset with the declines in homebuilding and rises in unemployment. All agreed on the self-evident solution: (a) let the institutions freely compete as to rate; and (b) promote new facilities to make mortgages marketable just like securities.

For the thrift institutions (and, I would maintain, for the economy as a whole) the consequences were disastrous. Whether or not interest rates were regulated, of course short-term Treasury securities would have to challenge the thrifts for funds when money was tight; but with the rates freed to move up, the escalation of rates became much steeper and costlier to all concerned. Still worse, it now became possible for short-term deposit rates to approach and exceed the long-term rates the institutions were earning on their assets, so that the earlier sharp but short disintermediation squeezes were replaced by a chronic earnings shortfall. Meanwhile, the thrifts gradually lost their regulatory advantage over commercial banks in types of accounts and rates they could use to attract funds. In return, they received the right to accept cheque book accounts and make consumer and other loans, but these were expensive new privileges to exercise in markets that were already overcrowded.

Gradually, also, major strides were made towards making mortgages marketable – 'securitization' in today's jargon. New governmental programmes spearheaded the standardization of mortgages, increased the scope of governmental guarantees and established procedures for assembling and marketing mortgage packages and securities collateralized by such packages. To the extent, however, that mortgages now had a market price, balance sheets could be 'marked to market', exposing clearly the destruction of capital wrought by the upward revision in the interest rate level. In addition, institutional buyers of securities, including pension funds, which enjoyed better tax treatment and did not have to carry the costly burden of operating consumer banking offices, became a competitive source of cheap mortgage money. As the private market has built its 'innovations' on the base created by federal agencies, nearly half of new home mortgage generation has now become securitized, and the lessons learned are being applied to other types of lending in ways that probably will transform completely the lending business.

Securitization has also weakened the erstwhile alliance between, and reduced the political influence of, homebuilders and savings institutions. Nevertheless, their stronger base of popular support – as contrasted, for example, with the hostile political environment faced by the larger banks – did enable the thrifts and small banks to mobilize significant governmental help once their problems were recognized as endangering the country's entire deposit structure. Whereas governmental (including Federal Reserve) intervention in large bank crises has been orientated chiefly to the protection of depositors, measures on behalf of the thrift industry and small banks have also included the subsidization of capital and earning power. Supervisory accounting rules have been altered to permit gradual rather than abrupt write-offs of losses, governmental 'income certificates' have been issued that are countable as capital and mergers have been subsidized among failing institutions so that some might survive. As a result, the competitive tone of the thrift industry – and, to a degree, of the entire financial system – is set to some extent by deposit insured firms operating essentially on the government's capital, which in taking big risks have everything to gain and nothing to lose.

A large proportion of the new home mortgages that are not being securitized – because the technical problems have not been overcome – are adjustable rate mortgages. These only become feasible after state interest ceilings were overridden by federal law in 1980. Because of the 'overbanked' nature of the mortgage market, the great majority of such loans carry substantial concessions below prevailing long-term rates in the initial years, and future upward adjustments are 'capped' as to timing and total increase. If the 1980–2 interest rate peaks were to be repeated, or if short-term rates were to rise sharply, many of the recent problems of thrift institutions would recur.

The firms that seem to have adapted best to the new environment are those that sell rather than hold the mortgages they originate. They have become, in effect, mortgage underwriters and traders, rather than lenders or investors. Like banks, the thrift industry senses that fees, trading and turnover rather than deposit taking and lending are today's profit opportunities.

Still another financial compartment that has lost its shelter is the *life insurance* industry. So long as regulatory ceilings limited deposit interest rates, the life insurance companies – investors in long-term, relatively higher–risk assets – were able to offer insurance savers higher yields (including a tax-deferment feature) than they could safely obtain elsewhere. Following deregulation, however, attractive rates became available on liquid governmentally insured assets and on Treasury securities as such. In addition, adoption of the new tax reform proposals now under consideration would do away with the tax incentives to life insurance saving. Thus, life insurance companies may be left largely with the low-profit group term insurance market. They have responded by diversifying more actively into various forms of other insurance, as well as money and pension management, but this, like the reactions of the banks and thrift institutions, is a forced relocation from a profitable sheltered preserve into an already crowded competitive arena.

Insurance companies have become particularly alert to new opportunities in the field of credit insurance. Many types of debt obligations that are not federally guaranteed, prominently including certain types of mortgages and municipal bonds, now carry private insurance. The history of private credit and deposit insurance in the United States is not encouraging. Developments in Ohio and Maryland serve to remind us that in times of difficulty the acid test of such insurance is its ability to enlist federal support.

This nexus was highlighted recently when insurance companies undertook to insure part of a major bank's loans to Latin America. Clearly such insurance had no actuarial properties. Rather, the intent seemed directed at rendering more certain the helpful involvement of federal authorities in the event of a default; if the authorities failed to bail out the situation, not only might the bank collapse, but also its insurers. In the event, this particular insurance transaction was ultimately rescinded, but it provides a useful illustration of the deeply embedded role of official insurance in US financial practice.

A brief word may be appropriate about the role of *pension funds*. An individual's pension fund contributions remain, of course, unwithdrawable before retirement. The preferential tax treatment has not changed, nor is it being seriously challenged. Investment options for pension funds have broadened greatly. One of the greatest new opportunities is the purchase of long-term Treasury bonds, large-scale issuance of which is a relatively recent phenomenon (partly because it was blocked earlier by a legal interest rate ceiling). However, such securities can also be safely bought by individuals directly and, to a limited extent, placed in tax-benefited 'individual retirement accounts'. Thus, even pension funds are in some long-term jeopardy from 'do-it-yourselfers'.

THE INTERNATIONAL ASPECT

In passing, it may be mentioned that the various laws and regulations inhibited foreign as well as domestic competition and also limited the role of US institutions in the international financial markets. In important respects, the US market was insulated from the rest of the world. Particularly noteworthy is the effect of the interest rate ceilings on domestic time deposits, which eventually played a major part in the genesis of the Eurodollar market, where interest rates on dollar funds were unregulated. The rise in US rates relative to the rest of the world after the ceilings became inoperative has contributed to raising the foreign exchange value of the dollar. So, too, has the sense that individual US institutions and instruments are more likely than their counterparts in other countries to receive government backing in case of trouble. Although too big a subject for discussion here, clearly such matters as financial change, structure, insurance and regulation in any one country have vital international dimensions.

WINNERS AND LOSERS

Thus far we have been dealing with institutions that seemed destined, on the whole, to be losers in the upheaval of the US financial structure. Now we turn to two major classes of winners, the mutual funds and the securities industry. They happened to be in the right place at the right time: able to exploit the changing regulatory framework and, more importantly, able to exploit new technology without being held back by inflexible and depreciated investments, whether in securities, buildings or human organization.

Money market mutual funds were originally organized during the 1970s to take advantage of the fact that interest rates payable on small time and savings accounts were restricted, but rates payable on deposits of $100,000 and over were not. The new funds amalgamated small individual investments into amounts over $100,000, invested the proceeds in major bank certificates of deposit (CDs), took a fee, but still were able to pay the public a much higher return than banks and thrifts were permitted. Immediate withdrawal privileges were granted and, indeed, advertised. Accounting devices were invented that fixed the dollar value of the 'deposits' at par regardless of changes in the market value of the funds' investments. Although money market mutual fund balances were not insured, the fact that they were redeposited in the giant banks imparted a quasi-insured character. Later the funds diversified into commercial paper, Eurodollars and other short-term instruments. By then they had grown so large that it became tacitly understood by all that the authorities would have to regard a run on a major fund as equivalent to a run on the banking system. The vulnerability of the financial system was also intensified by the likelihood that the funds would withdraw deposits *en masse* from any bank they came to perceive, rightly or wrongly, as questionable.

Why did not the authorities from the outset prohibit (or obtain legislation to outlaw) this flagrant evasion of their regulations? Several short-term political reasons loomed large at the time, but the major reason for the official failure to act was, I believe, that officialdom itself no longer believed in the usefulness or survivability of interest rate regulation, and was therefore quite pleased to see its own responsibilities eroded. In this, as in other similar instances, the authorities did not foresee the rapid growth and evolution of the new instruments and their potential for insinuating themselves under the deposit insurance umbrella.

The larger money market funds quickly learned how to make their 'deposits' into instruments far more versatile than the individual time or savings deposit they initially replaced. They exploited innovations in telephone service to place their customer relationships on a telephone basis. Thus they avoided the need for buildings or branches and sidestepped constraints of geography. By paying commercial banks to handle most of the accounting transfers, they minimized the need to build up large and inflexible organizations. Soon they were able to perfect arrangements that allowed their customers to write cheques (generally limited to amounts of $500 and over) on money market fund accounts.

Computerization of the accounts rendered transfers among accounts virtually costless. It was only a small step to link the many old and new types of mutual funds – invested in bonds, equities, mortgage-backed securities, tax-exempt securities, even gold – in such a way that the public could make telephone transfers among different funds at no explicit cost. When fully utilized, today's money market fund holding offers the individual an immediately withdrawable cheque account – but one that also pays a time deposit interest rate and is instantly and costlessly convertible by telephone into diversified portfolios of other kinds of assets. In July 1985 net purchases of all mutual funds set a record of $8.4 billion, of which only $0.7 billion was in money market funds.

Recognizing this competition, banks and thrifts in late 1982 obtained the right to offer, free of interest rate restrictions, the money market deposit account (MMDA), an instrument very similar to, though less versatile than, a money market fund. Emphasizing heavily the fact that such accounts up to $100,000 are explicitly federally insured, they have promoted MMDAs very successfully. This means, however, that depository institutions now must pay market interest rates on large balances which in the regulated environment they had been able to attract at below market rates. Furthermore, they still need to maintain physical branches to attract the funds and remain, as a practical matter, largely confined to local depositors for their intake.

Other non-traditional participants are also entering banking markets and trying to become financial institutions. Of course, some large manufacturers and retailers have long been active lenders to their consumer and business customers. Now others are joining them. Consumer credit remains perhaps the only major financial sector in which, despite rapid credit growth, default rates have not increased substantially and profit margins remain attractive – suggesting that more expansions are yet to come. For decades the depository institutions have been encroaching on the lending territory of the stores (partly by utilizing affiliations with VISA and Mastercard). For the stores and other nonbank lenders, it seems only natural to respond by challenging the banks on their home grounds.

Whether this response will be successful remains to be seen. As suggested above in regard to mutual funds, the trend seems to be towards centralization of financial services via telephone and computer, and away from the more expensive face-to-face kind of service in which bankers and retailers are experienced. Critical to the success or failure of the nonbank entrants is whether or not they will find a way – over the resistance of the now more vigilant authorities – to hook their liabilities into the federal deposit insurance system, as the money market funds have effectively accomplished. Whether or not the nonbank newcomers prosper, however, they are actively intensifying the 'overbanking' that already prevails.

Finally, in this catalogue of financial institutions, we turn to the securities industry, probably the principal gainer from all these changes in financial structure. The post-1933 environment created a large, new niche for the securities industry. It was the beginning of chronic sizeable federal budget deficits which necessitated active underwriting, distribution and secondary markets for Treasury securities. At the same time, the prohibition of bank interest on short-term deposits quite unintentionally gave security dealers a cheap and protected source of short-term finance for their positions. They were able to offer corporations a rate of return on safe under-30 day (and, indeed, overnight) funds when no one else was allowed to. Since the collateral was essentially Treasury securities, and since the Federal Reserve monitors and lends to the major government security dealers, private funds lent to such dealers are *de facto* insured. Reliable functioning of the government securities market is at least as essential to the avoidance of financial panic as is confidence in the banks. Should a serious question arise, as most notably in the aftermath of the 1982 failure of a small dealer, Drysdale and Co., official intervention is prompt.

When interest rate and other deregulation opened the door for banks to compete effectively for short-term funds and began to erode the prohibitions on bank underwriting of securities, some in the securities industry feared for their own future. Ironically, however, the outcome has been the opposite – to favour the securities business and to disadvantage banks. One important reason for this has been the enormous advance in computer and communications facilities, which securities firms with their smaller and more flexible organizations proved faster at adapting to their needs. The same technological advances made it possible to invent an endless flow of new investment instruments and techniques, again a process that bureaucratic and closely regulated organizations found cumbersome.

The cheapening of transactions revealed (as was to be anticipated) an enormously elastic demand for turnover and speculation. The growth of deposits and credit is constrained by anti-inflationary monetary policy targets, but growth of turnover is subject to no limit. In the latter 1960s, the New York stock exchange viewed itself as optimistic in planning for occasional 10-million share days, but after the fixed high commission system was abolished in 1975 under pressure from the antitrust authorities, trading volume multiplied. Now average volume is approaching 100 million shares daily. Volume in debt securities has also soared. The average holding period of over ten-year Treasury bonds (outstandings divided by trading volume at major dealers) has shortened to about 20 days in recent years; two decades ago it was measured in years. In 1984 The First Boston Corporation, one of the leading securities dealers, transacted a total face value of $4.1 trillion, an amount exceeding the total GNP of the United States!

Meanwhile, as described earlier, the banking type intermediaries were stubbing their toes in expanding into unfamiliar lending territory. As interest rate volatility increased, banking type institutions felt compelled to try to insulate themselves through resort to floating rate lending. Thereby, however, they conceded the business of taking interest risk to the new and enormously successful financial futures and options markets. In these markets the securities industry has played a much more active and profitable role than the banks. In addition to the more familiar contracts, such as those for Treasury bonds, bills and Eurodollars, various futures and option contracts have been created, of course dependent on computerization, that represent whole classes of instruments, such as stock index futures. The service rendered is analogous to the 'bundling' performed by mutual funds. Moreover, the easier it becomes for investors (individual or institutional) to buy and sell instruments that represent bundles of securities, the greater the volume of trading generated among the professionals who hold the options and securities underlying these bundles. It may be added that these innovations also attract substantial trading volume from abroad where, with a few exceptions, such facilities are largely non-existent. Because of these facilities, New York and Chicago would probably be international financial centres even if the dollar were not the leading world currency.[2]

Another dramatic result of computerization is the ability to create novel security forms by dismembering existing securities or synthesizing new ones. An important but rapidly waning advantage of banks and insurance companies over securities markets is their ability to tailor loans, small or large, to particular situations. Such loans, almost by their very definition, are non-marketable. However, the process of 'securitization' – repackaging such instruments into marketable form – is well under way. Reference has already been made to mortgage backed securities, but the concept is being rapidly extended to consumer loans, business equipment loans and even ordinary business loans. Currency and interest rate swaps, as well as the 'stripping' of securities – the sale of bond coupons (not necessarily all from the same issue) separate from the principal – may be viewed as falling in a similar category. A particularly fascinating invention is the 'collateralized mortgage obligation' (CMO) which rearranges a collection of relatively homogeneous home mortgages into several classes of marketable securities with widely differing maturity, income and risk attributes.

THE CHANGING NATURE OF FINANCIAL INTERMEDIATION

Traditionally the US financial system has featured 'indirect' finance. Only on a relatively limited scale have small savers lent directly to investors or purchased their obligations. Rather they have lent to intermediaries that amalgamated the funds, substituted their own more reliable liabilities and assumed the credit, interest rate and other risks and costs.

Now, however, as already mentioned, the nature of intermediation is changing to bring savers and borrowers closer together. Knowingly or unknowingly, the savers are assuming more of the risks, although the government turns out to be an ever more prominent partner when things go wrong. In competition with the traditional forms of liquid deposits, newer types of high-grade liquid instruments, notably various kinds of mutual fund shares and short-term US Treasury obligations, now allow smaller savers to approach the securities market more safely and directly. Individuals and mutual funds have become major buyers in all bond markets. Other securities markets, too, have become much more open and active as transactions charges have plummeted. The actual and tacit extensions of official guarantees and insurance

---

2 It may be noted that the financial futures and related markets apparently have drawn away a substantial amount of speculative interest from the commodity markets, thereby contributing to the reduction in commodity prices.

have played an important role in attracting all kinds of investors, foreign and domestic.

Through securitization, the markets increasingly are able to place loans at lower cost to the borrower than charged by the traditional lenders, while offering higher returns to the investor. The enormous competitive advantages the traditional intermediaries used to derive from their position as assemblers and fiduciaries of low-cost funds is disappearing. This loss of primacy opens the door for newcomers into the more profitable credit origination, monitoring and insurance business, which the traditional intermediaries would have liked to preserve for themselves.

At the same time that their financial intermediation function is shrinking, the monopoly held by banks over the cheque payment system also is eroding and in some cases perhaps even becoming a burden. It has already been described how money market mutual funds have become 'middlemen' between banks and the upper-income public with respect to cheques over $500. More importantly, the major charge card companies have done the same for a vast range of middle-sized and small transactions. Stores and consumers are paying VISA and Mastercard for guaranteeing customer credit. In principle, banks could have been earning all this revenue and attracting larger balances by developing a method for guaranteeing store customers' cheques, but they could not organize a national network able to monitor individual customer transactions. How many would have predicted 20 years ago that a handful of credit cards could bestride the world?

This development carries an important message about the global village. Following the same pattern as credit cards, only a few futures and options contracts have been genuinely successful. Having a headstart can turn out to confer an insurmountable advantage. Perhaps the predominance of IBM in the computer field or the dominance enjoyed by certain telephone or TV systems illustrates the same technological force. On a more local note, major New York banks have recently linked their automated teller machines to accept each other's identification cards. From the customer's view, the bank name on any particular station is becoming quite inconsequential. All this suggests a force of electronics that eventually will have us doing virtually all our payments and financial asset management over our telephones (or perhaps nearby 'financial telephone booths'), using a national or even international telephone book and at marginal transaction costs that only trivially inhibit addictive use of the system.

Recently I suggested to a computer expert that soon all of us would, every time we came home, push a telephone button to display on our video screen the rates and prices offered on various deposit-type instruments throughout the country (or even the world). Then a few more button pushes would rearrange our portfolio in response to the slightest detectable or presumed advantage. 'You are wrong,' he replied, 'by the time you come home this already will have been done for you automatically on the basis of the program you have chosen.'

THE CENTRAL ROLE OF OFFICIAL INSURANCE

The displacement of traditional financial intermediaries by direct, securities market finance would be much slower if the public were more concerned about the liquidity or creditworthiness of the newer instruments. When interest rates were low and stable, defaults were not much of a problem. Only the top risks were able to borrow in the public market, while interest rate controls and lender compartmentalization among financial intermediaries resulted in credit rationing which screened out weak borrowers. In today's world, default frequency is a good deal higher, yet there has been little damage to the general public.

One way in which the market has responded to the heightened credit risks is by proliferating various types of private credit insurance to enhance the marketability of securities. Banks have jumped into the credit insurance business through a multiplicity of guarantee and credit back-up devices, and various new assurance ventures insure mortgage loans, bond issues and other credits. Some rude surprises have already occurred and more seem likely. There is not much relevant history by which to make the required credit judgements. Some loans will go sour no matter how earnest the scrutiny at their origination. This may not be so serious in the case of mortgage-backed obligations where, as soon as payments are overdue, the trustee responsible for the collections normally will have little difficulty in locating the property (and probably the owner) and going to foreclosure and substantial recovery. Things may not be so simple with packages of consumer loans or business loans. With business loans in particular, lenders in the past routinely monitored borrowers to make sure that the funds were used as promised, and that no undue new obligations were undertaken that might impair the soundness of the loan. Under securitization, the loan originator no longer has a monitoring interest once the loan 'leaves the nest', and it is doubtful whether the current marketing structure includes adequate incentive or payment for anyone to perform this costly function.

It is not the microproblems *per se* that warrant the serious concern, however. Even in the most antiseptic conditions, microproblems can snowball into a systemic threat, and today's conditions far from being antiseptic are rather infection-prone. In addition, macroproblems such as war, depression, inflation, major changes in key prices etc. can infect large masses of seemingly unlinked credits. Private insurance is helpless against such crises. Indeed, concern about the safety of the guarantors can deepen the problems.

Each default crisis of the past 15 years or so has led to a broadening of *de jure* or *de facto* official insurance against default and/or illiquidity. A vast range of instruments far beyond anything ever envisaged is now protected, or deemed by the market to be protected. A partial list of the additions would include most deposits in excess of the federal $100,000 per account insurance limit, small state-insured deposits, much commercial paper, repurchase agreements against Treasury securities, customers' assets held by stock exchange firms, pension liabilities and some life insurance liabilities. Add to this the endless expansion and diversification of US Treasury securities and guarantees, as well as of the issues and guarantees of Federal agencies (for which the government cannot escape responsibility despite the lack of a legal obligation), and it is easy to see why the public assumes that most of its claims are fully insured.

These developments underscore the importance of the relationship, however accidental and unintentional, between deposit insurance and financial regulation. From the public's point of view, all instruments perceived to be insured are equally secure against default. Consequently, the choice of which to hold is properly based solely on yield. In the prevailing fiercely competitive environment, pressures become irresistible for financial intermediaries to take greater credit risks in order to be able to pay the yields the market demands. The situation is aggravated by the many institutions that are operating without any genuine net worth, whose managements therefore have little or nothing to lose by taking greater chances. When regulation restrained the rates management could offer and charge, such risk-taking was neither necessary nor feasible.

The systemic risks of the present condition are so awesome that a return to closer governmental regulation is not only necessary but inevitable, and indeed already underway. As long ago as its 1957 report, the FDIC noted that had an FDIC been functioning, according to modern rules, in the 1920s, it would have run out of both its own funds and borrowing authority in 1930, long before the worst of that banking crisis. Today the adequacy of the deposit insurance reserves has become a subject for justifiable concern. A breakdown of the insurance machinery would be the financial equivalent of nuclear catastrophe, and surely can and will be averted by official action. An unfortunate corollary of the nuclear analogy, however, is that no individual acting alone can do anything to prevent such a disaster or to protect himself against the destruction. Thus there are no private incentives to take precautionary measures, although if enough people could be persuaded to take such steps, the disaster might be mitigated or even prevented.

It is therefore understandable – but deliciously ironic – that even bank supervisors with extreme libertarian views have been intervening forcefully in individual banking situations in ways their liberal predecessors would not have dared. The emphasis currently is on making institutions strengthen their capital bases. This might cushion the drain on the insurance funds, but does not deal with the fundamental problems. The only way for most intermediaries to earn a competitive return on a higher capital base is by raising the average lending margin, and this can be accomplished only by making riskier loans. Any apparent gain to the soundness of the financial structure as a whole is illusory.

Proposals to charge risk-related insurance premiums are more to the point. Of course, any institution stigmatized by a high insurance premium will lose its large (uninsured) deposits and be forced to bid high rates to attract small (insured) deposits from distant places. Its survival then would be dependent on taking still greater risks than before. But even if the insurance rating could somehow be kept secret, on what experience are the risk differentials to be established? If the penalties are large enough to bite, they will be tantamount to a selective credit control. The Home Loan Bank Board is trying to stop California savings and loan associations, which are virtually unrestricted by state law, from using federally insured deposits to finance race horses, among other ventures. What insurance premium should they charge, if that premium were the only available deterrent? And if the penalties are large, then it would take a large new force of inspectors to make sure that loans are honestly assigned to the correct risk categories.

Can any insurance company survive without the right to refuse or cancel coverage? But should or will any government agency exercise such life-or-death power? Governmental efforts are already in evidence to side-step the need for such decisions by compelling standardization of various loan instruments and setting minimum standards for inclusion in the 'insured' universe. As in the tax system, social and political considerations will no doubt intermix with the insurance considerations.

Furthermore, it is no longer a matter of protecting only the depository institutions. Deregulation has allowed all institutions, instruments and markets to intermesh in such a way that a serious leak anywhere can threaten a system-wide failure, as in a ship whose hold is not divided into compartments. This means that every inch of the system needs the safeguard of stringent prudential regulation. Our new financial structure is more technologically advanced, but it is also more dependent than ever on official lenders and insurers of last resort. These must break down eventually unless they are empowered to limit the potentially infinite moral hazard and adverse selection to which normal market processes subject them. To put fuses and circuit breakers on electric wiring promotes rather than hampers the freedom of electricity.

COUNTING THE BLESSINGS

The present turbulence in the US financial structure should make us more appreciative – as we ought to have been all along – of how well the system of 20 years ago worked. It provided the benefits of widespread competition among financial firms, while preventing the Gresham's Law kind of competition that has developed more recently in which profligacy drives out prudence. The old system also produced a kind of credit rationing, along quality rather than price dimensions, that rendered default panics virtually inconceivable and the deposit insurance system unassailable.

Financial institutions under the old system could quickly be subjected to a liquidity crunch by a tight monetary policy. As a result, surges in inflation and interest rates did not become intense or long-lasting, and were nipped in the bud before they became embedded in behaviour and expectations. The liquidity crunches themselves were promptly reversible by an easing of general monetary policy, so that recessions were mild. Nor were the authorities continually entangled in precedent-setting bail-outs. Because inflation and interest rates could not get out of hand, and credit could not collapse, it was literally true that a great depression was impossible.

Those happy circumstances no longer prevail. The combination of technological advance and deregulation has given free rein to the ingrained human propensities to borrow, lend, speculate and gamble too much, and substantially reduced the transactions costs of doing so. A daily trading volume of perhaps $250 billion (excluding foreign exchange), representing a thirty-fold or so increase in a decade, can hardly be essential to the efficient allocation of the country's resources.[3] Indeed, the electronically mobilized tidal waves of crowd psychology can be quite destructive. The reason there is so much trading is that people enjoy trading; for many, it has a narcotic attraction. As with gambling, we enjoy trading particularly when the price of admission is low, there are many winners and some of the prizes are prodigious.

Even more to the point, deregulation is stimulating a marked increase in the debt ratios of all sectors – household, business and government. In the earlier interest rate regulated environment, people could not borrow nor lenders lend as much as they preferred. Now that consumer sovereignty rules in the credit market, the quantities bought and sold are larger, just as the textbook stipulates. The stories of organized crime suggest that people will pay very high rates for the privilege of borrowing, even when the default penalties are drastic. And as for companies that have less than maximal indebtedness, they had better quickly borrow to the limit, unless they wish to risk takeover by a buyer who will in effect use the target company's unused borrowing power as his purchase money.

But all this leaves the system much more vulnerable to economic downdrafts. No matter how conscientious the borrowers, any lapse in the economy's aggregate income growth will trigger many more defaults than before. The economy's minimum flying speed has been increased, but do the flight controllers, pilots and passengers know?

To invent aeroplanes is to invent plane crashes. I would not want aircraft disinvented (though the argument is close). The advance of financial technology is presumably similarly irreversible, but its benefits for the human soul are less clear-cut. Suppose new technology made alcoholic beverages both better-tasting and nearly costless. Would that be good? How would a free market handle this? Virtually all the cars the free market builds and sells will travel at 100 mph or faster, but there are few places where it is permitted (or safe) to drive at that speed. Let us not count the 'blessings' of financial innovation until we have learned to enjoy them in moderation.

---

3 This does not include over $350 billion daily in repurchase agreements, as contrasted with some $7 billion ten years ago.

3

The Current Status of the Regulation of Financial Services and Products in the United States: Developments and Trends

MEYER EISENBERG

INTRODUCTION

The Evolution of a Financial Services Industry and its Problems

A mere decade ago the fields of banking, investment companies, thrifts, insurance, brokerage and retailing were largely separate. Only visionaries spoke of a 'financial services industry'. Now the term is commonplace.

The entry of large retailers into the financial services area, with enormous credit card bases, interstate networks of stores or offices, a high degree of consumer recognition and experience in advertising and customer relations, are among the more recent and highly visible symptoms of this development. For example, the controversy about interstate banking, which used to be discussed in terms of whether automated teller machines (ATMs) were branches, has now been eclipsed by developments such as the use by retailers and financial institutions of 'nonbank banks' to provide expanded interstate banking capability. The proliferation of money market mutual funds and the linkage of those funds with other financial services, the acquisition of limited service (nonbank) banks by non-banking organizations such as brokerage firms and retailers, and the offering of brokerage and investment advisory services by banks, illustrate the degree to which 'homogenization' has become more and more of a reality than merely a cliché invoked at industry meetings, along with the well worn 'level playing field' and 'functional regulation'.

In any event, technology, innovation and deregulation have made possible the emergence of new products and the linkage of existing services and products. Money market mutual funds compete with bank offerings. Banks have developed money market deposit accounts (MMDAs) as a response. Thrifts have their own version of the MMDA. These accounts are linked with 'sweeps', credit and debit cards, brokerage accounts, pre-authorized payments and other bank accounts. Insurance companies have developed their own string of new 'flexible annuity', variable annuity and 'universal life' products, with various savings, conversion and insurance features. Insurance companies have bought brokers, as well as nonbank banks to help sell their products and services.

These developments have occurred against a background of law and regulation which was designed in the 1930s, or earlier. The banking system is regulated by multiple federal and state agencies – the Federal Reserve, (the Fed), the Comptroller of the Currency (OCC) and the Federal Deposit Insurance Corporation (FDIC), as well as state banking agencies. The thrifts have their own regulator and deposit insurance agency, as do the credit unions. Insurance is regulated (more or less) by the states, except when they offer securities products, which involve the Securities and Exchange Commission (SEC) and state 'blue-sky' protection. Investment companies are regulated by the SEC and the states, as are broker dealers and investment advisers. Pension funds are separately regulated under the Employee Retirement Income Security Act (ERISA), while antitrust is the responsibility of the Justice Department. The Bush Task Group on the Regulation of Financial Services reported in 1984, and yet a year later no administration bill encompassing its recommendations had yet been sent to the Congress.

The Congress remains at an impasse on interstate banking, nonbank banks and bank powers (e.g., revision of the Glass–Steagall Act). The courts, however, are acting and have become the instruments through which national banking policy is made – district by district, circuit by circuit and ultimately by the Supreme Court. We have regulation by loophole, not a rational national policy on the development of financial services. Banking agencies, often at odds with each other, authorize certain powers for banks and are immediately challenged by other agencies and state regulators or they are sued by the various trade associations representing particular industry groups. States authorize banks to sell certain types of insurance; the insurance agents sue. Large banks want interstate banking; small banks and regional banks sue. That is how the pattern of financial services structure and regulation is evolving. In addition, the depository insurance issues exemplified by the recent problems experienced by savings and loan institutions in Ohio and Maryland, not to mention the failure of Continental Illinois bank, raise policy questions of major proportions and involve issues that may well affect the confidence of Americans in their financial system. And all the while, the world watches.

The consumer is bewildered. Corporate strategists and lawyers devise ways in which to exploit a new loophole or widen an old one, but they are unsure of what the rules will be next month or next year.

If we add to this complex structure of business developments and regulation the likely advances in technology, 'smart cards', point-of-sale (POS) terminals (shared and captive), ATMs (shared and captive), interactive cables, home banking and brokerage (a PC in every home), we have – a mess. A mess that must be sorted out and rationalized if these industries are to survive and prosper and continue to serve the legitimate interests of consumers and business, fulfil the need for savings and capital formation, facilitate money transfers and credit functions and, in general, provide the financial services the United States needs to function well.

Current Regulatory Overview and Context

Only a few years ago, the word 'deregulation' was generally used to describe the changes that were rapidly occurring in the financial services industry. The word was used loosely and referred to everything from actions that were clearly deregulatory (like uncapping interest rates) to the rearrangement of agency jurisdiction and the simplification of government forms. Anything deregulatory was good; anything that was re-regulatory or increased regulation was bad. With the arrival of the Reagan administration in 1980, there was an atmosphere in the capital which reflected the view that it was Washington which was responsible for creating various problems for business through 'overregulation' and government intrusion in business matters. The administration was going to lift the burdens of government regulation from the backs of business and the public. Vice President Bush was put in charge of 'deregulation' and task forces on paper work reduction and financial regulation were set up and staffed. There had indeed been instances of real deregulation in the past ten years: abolition of the minimum commission rate for stock exchange listed securities in 1975 and the more recent lifting of regulatory restraints on interest which may be paid to depositors by banks and savings and loans institutions (S&Ls). In other industries, like airlines, haulage and communications, deregulation has indeed proceeded at a rapid pace. But it now seems that the deregulatory cycle in some of the areas of financial services, although not ended, has at least stalled. Indeed, the financial services industry appears likely to face a new round of regulatory changes which will look curiously like re-regulation in several major areas. And, while the thrust to interstate banking has achieved partial success in the approval earlier this year of regional banking by the Supreme Court in the *Northeast* case,[1] other devices like the approval by federal regulators of nonbank banks have been successfully challenged in the courts.[2] In other words, in the

1 *Northeast Bancorp Inc.* v. *Board of Governors*, 105 S. Ct 2545 (1985).
2 *Florida Department of Banking* v. *Board of Governors*, 760 F.2d 1135 (11th Cir., 20 May 1985), pet. for cert., pending; *Independent Bankers Association of America* v. *Conover*, 44 BNA Wash. Fin. Rep. 344, No. 84–1403 (M.D. Fla, 1985).

financial services area the picture is mixed at best and sorting out the trends and issues is a difficult exercise. That, however, is what this paper will attempt to do.

The failure and government rescue of the Continental Illinois bank and the recent crises among state chartered S&Ls in Ohio, Maryland and elsewhere have raised serious questions about the adequacy of current depository insurance schemes, both state and federal. The Maryland and Ohio experiences indicate that state sponsored depository insurance is almost certainly going to be phased out. The resolution of questions regarding the revision and strengthening of the current federal scheme of depository insurance and guarantees remains a top priority issue. The continuing failures of agricultural banks, particularly in the Midwest, and the severe problems in the Farm Credit System only add to the atmosphere of urgency.

The battle over the authority of federal regulatory agencies to extend interstate banking through the limited approval of nonbank banks and the interstate acquisition of failing banks or thrifts are symptoms of a still unresolved, decades-old battle over the territorial restrictions on branch banking imposed by the McFadden Act in 1927. Major bank issues relating to the restrictions on bank powers, imposed by the Glass–Steagall Act in 1933, are also unsettled. The recent failure of several dealers in government securities (e.g., E.S.M., Bevil, Bressler and the earlier failures of Lumbard, Wall and Drysdale) seems certain to lead to the imposition of federal regulation on that segment of the industry, despite the reluctance of the Fed and the SEC to undertake such jurisdiction. All of this points to a revised regulatory structure with a larger, rather than a smaller, role for government.

The ideological arguments made by some academics and government policy-makers that the 'market place' is the ultimate regulator and that the role of government will continue to be diminished and ultimately phased out in many areas of financial services, cannot be given much credit in the light of recent events. Certainly some deregulation will occur, but most financial regulatory agencies, even though led by conservatives, consider some additional regulation necessary. The deregulation in financial services that has taken place in recent years, in the commission rate area and in the lifting of restrictions on interest rates, was followed by the efforts of certain federal regulators to grant banks extended powers, such as the ability to engage in securities underwriting, brokerage, real estate and insurance ventures. Those who thought they saw a resolution of the 'powers' and territorial (interstate banking) controversies following the lifting of interest rate restrictions, the spread of automated teller machines (ATMs) and loan production offices (LPOs) and the changes in state banking laws have, in the light of recent events, had to revise their predictions. The situation is now more muddied and less likely to be quickly and easily resolved than it was 12 months ago, because the problems faced by the various components of the financial services industry have proved too difficult to be left to the industry, to self-regulatory groups or even to the states. Nor can the issues be left for resolution by federal agencies. Unless there is a disaster, it will take a concerted effort by the administration and Congress, with the assistance and cooperation of the various industry segments, to produce and implement a rational, workable financial services policy. So far there is no sign of such a resolution.

Accordingly, over the next few years we can expect an extended debate and re-evaluation of what distinctions need to be maintained between types of financial institutions; how depository institutions can be effectively insured; whether some restrictions on nationwide banking will remain in place; and whether the Glass–Steagall restrictions on bank powers should be maintained, revised or repealed. Recent developments indicate that, despite rapid acceleration of technological capabilities and development of new products, we can expect tougher regulatory responses in certain areas like deposit insurance, the regulation of government securities dealers and the maintenance of bank viability. Solutions in these areas are likely to rely more on the federal government than on the states (e.g., deposit insurance); more on extended monitoring of the industry than on 'free market' solutions; and more on slower development of additional bank powers (Glass–Steagall revisions) and territorial developments (going beyond regional banking) than on the immediate elimination of existing legal barriers.

As of now, the Bush Task Group recommendations have not yet been submitted to the Congress. Currently those recommendations are being reviewed at the Treasury Department and the Office of Management and Budget (OMB). The failure to move forward on the Bush proposals is just one indication of the lack of agreement on a comprehensive approach to the resolution of these difficult financial services issues. It would not be surprising if these issues continue to be addressed on an *ad hoc* basis in continued disputes among the various regulators (federal and state) and in court actions involving these agencies and the various contending trade associations. Congressional action does not appear to be imminent. Congress, for example, was pre-empted by the courts, who have resolved, at least temporarily, major arguments among the contending parties in the nonbank bank and the interstate banking controversies. Congressional failure to agree on a comprehensive bill left the door open to a case-by-case, agency-by-agency and rule-by-rule approach.

In addition to court actions, which have for the present effectively halted the spread of the nonbank bank loophole, states have proceeded, without further Congressional action, to expand their regional interstate (reciprocal) banking compacts; competitive industry members have accelerated their development of new products and services; and institutions, government and the public have watched warily as problem after problem arose indicating weaknesses in savings and loans, banks, insurance, government securities dealers and other areas of the complex and varied components of the financial services industry. Many problems could be traced to bad management. Others resulted from inadequate regulation, just plain bad luck, bad investment judgements, incredible lapses and the pressures for greater returns created by a more competitive and less protected industry environment.

None the less, a major crisis, or the confluence of current forces not now in agreement, could result in the adoption by Congress of some important financial services measures, particularly on regulatory reorganization and interstate banking. We will begin with a review of the Bush proposals for change in the regulatory scheme on the theory that the Report provides a *reference or starting point* for generation of more definitive administration proposals.

The administration has appointed George Gould as a consultant to the Treasury Department and the President has nominated him as Under-Secretary of the Treasury with responsibility for financial services policies. He is reported to be conducting a full review of the administration's policy in this area, presumably including the Bush proposals.[3] His recommendations will provide a new (or revised) reference point for consideration and discussion. Although there will be some differences, it is likely that his review and recommendations will embrace major segments of previous administration policy developed by then Treasury Secretary Regan. Mr Gould's report to Secretary Baker, who has publicly supported interstate banking and expansion of bank powers, may, however, contain some surprises, reflecting more recent developments, e.g., the Maryland and Ohio savings and loan failures. But he is unlikely to chart a completely new course on the major issues. Nor should we forget that Mr Regan, who as Secretary of the Treasury pushed hard for abolition of the interstate banking barriers and for expansion of bank powers, is now White House Chief of Staff and is in a powerful position, in terms of both his office and background, to influence administration policy in this area. It is unlikely that Mr Regan's previously articulated positions will be easily altered. Moreover, the role to be played by the OMB is unclear. If OMB staff are more deregulatory minded than some of the regulators think appropriate, then an interesting situation will develop, which may delay even further the implementation of any administration programme in this area.

THE BUSH TASK GROUP RECOMMENDATIONS

Assuming that part of the Bush Task Group Report will survive the Treasury and OMB review and that Messrs Gould, Baker, Regan and Miller (Director of OMB) will agree on a legislative package resembling the previous administration plan with modifications, what does that mean for the financial services industry?

We should begin then with a discussion of the Bush recommendations, even though the promised legislative package is not likely to arrive until the Gould–Baker–Regan review is completed.

3 See *American Banker*, 17 July 1985, 'New No. 3 man at Treasury will review Glass–Steagall Act', by Nina Easton.

The Bush Report

On 15 November 1984 the Vice President's office released the long-delayed report of the Task Group on the Regulation of Financial Services, 'Blueprint for Reform'. That report sets out a number of major recommendations on the restructuring of the federal financial regulatory system. The report, signed by the group's chairman, Vice President Bush, its vice chairman, then Treasury Secretary Regan, and the heads of the major regulatory agencies, executive branch agencies and policy makers,[4] was approved by the President as the basis for the administration's legislative programme in the 99th Congress.[5]

In dealing with regulatory reform, the administration has not abandoned its previous position on the expansion of powers for financial institutions (e.g., the modification of Glass–Steagall restrictions) along the lines previously proposed by then Secretary Regan. Since, as we have noted, former Secretary Regan, now White House Chief of Staff, will have a continuing interest in implementing the deregulatory programme he supported as Treasury Secretary, the policy adopted by the new Secretary, Mr Baker, and his staff, including Mr Gould, will probably support interstate banking and removal of many of the Glass–Steagall barriers in the area of bank powers. The former Comptroller of the Currency, C. Todd Conover, was aggressive in pushing the administration's position on interstate banking, particularly in his determination to process over 400 nonbank bank applications, helping major bank holding companies to avoid, in so far as the courts would permit, the interstate branching restrictions of the McFadden Act and Douglas Amendment.[6] It appears that the new Comptroller, nominated by the President, Robert Clarke of Texas,

---

4 In addition to the Vice President as chairman and Secretary Regan as vice chairman, the members of the Task Group included: the Attorney General, the Director of the Office of Management and Budget, the Chairman of the Council of Economic Advisers, the Assistant to the President for Policy Development, the chairman of the Federal Reserve Board, the Federal Deposit Insurance Corporation, the Federal Home Loan Bank Board, the Securities and Exchange Commission, the Commodity Futures Trading Commission and National Credit Union Administration, and the Comptroller of the Currency. Richard C. Breeden, Deputy Counsel to the Vice President, was staff director of the Task Group.

5 As the time of writing (October 1985) that legislative package had not yet been submitted to the Congress by the administration.

6 The nonbank bank approvals made by the then Comptroller have been challenged in court and a US District Court in Florida has enjoined Conover's actions while he was still in office. *See, IBAA/Fla Bankers Assn* v. *Conover*, No. 84–1403 (M.D. Fla), 44 *BNA Wash. Fin. Rep.* 344, 2/15/85. Conover said that he was considering an appeal, but none was taken. Since his resignation in April 1985, the Court of Appeals in Atlanta held that the Fed acted beyond its power in approving the US Trust's nonbank bank application for Palm Beach, Florida. *Fla Dept of Banking* v. *Bd of Govs*, slip opinion, Nos. 84–3269, 84–3270 (11th Cir., May 20, 1985), *US Trust* pet. for cert., No. 85–193, filed 8/5/85, pending. See below.

will continue to support generally the Administration's position. He will face new developments, however, which may make it difficult to support the full elimination of the interstate branching restrictions and the unqualified removal of Glass–Steagall barriers on bank powers.

Summary of the Bush Report

(1) The report explores the overlap and duplication among federal bank regulatory agencies, particularly the Comptroller of the Currency, the Federal Reserve and the FDIC. Other agencies also regulate financial services in such matters as securities (SEC) and antitrust (Justice Department Antitrust Division). Other agencies deal with various aspects of financial institution regulation. Supervision of bank holding company activities by the Comptroller and the Fed are referred to as an example of 'fragmentation' or layering of regulation.

(2) The report discusses artificial advantages (and disadvantages) for particular entities resulting from differential regulation. Banks, insurance companies, savings and loans (S&Ls), brokers and investment companies offer some similar products, but differential regulation in some cases gives certain products advantages over others, based on the applicable regulatory scheme, rather than on relevant product differences.

(3) Dual federal and state systems for depository institutions. The report lauds states as laboratories for experimentation and innovation and refers to duplication of state and federal regulation. There is, however, no critical evaluation of the effectiveness or the adequacy of state regulation. Developments in Ohio and Maryland do not indicate that the role of the states in the regulation of depository institutions will be expanded. Indeed, the failure of the state depository insurance mechanisms and the imposition of federal standards to achieve FDIC or FSLIC insurance and restore depositor confidence indicate that proposals to expand dependence on state regulation are unlikely to generate much support. Nor is there any criticism in the Bush Report of the duplicating structures and the problems caused by complying with 50 different state requirements and the interpretations of 50 state administrative bureaucracies. The continued necessity for redundant state regulation in securities or banking is open to some question. Nor is the recent failure of Baldwin–United in the insurance area evaluated in terms of the effectiveness of state insurance regulation.

The key recommendations and points (as summarized in the Bush Report itself, at pp. 11–12) are:

(1) The three existing federal bank regulatory agencies would be reduced to two by eliminating the FDIC's role in examining, supervising and regulating state non-member banks. A new 'Federal Banking Agency' (FBA) would created within the Treasury Department, in operating and upgrading the existing OCC. This agency would regulate all national banks, while the Federal Reserve Board would be responsible for federal regulation of all state-chartered banks.

[*Comment*: In effect, the power of the OCC is expanded significantly. There is no indication that this change can be achieved under the present political circumstances in the Congress. There does not seem to be a willingness to grant more power to a cabinet agency, controlled by the administration.]

(2) The regulation of bank holding companies would be substantially reorganized. At present, the Fed regulates all bank holding companies, even though a different agency usually regulates the subsidiary bank(s) of the holding company. Under the new system, in almost all cases, the agency that regulates a bank would also supervise its parent holding company. This would make it possible for most banking organizations to have a single federal regulator rather than two.

(3) The Fed would transfer its authority to establish the permissible activities of bank holding companies to the new FBA, although it would maintain a limited veto right over new activities. [*Comment*: As a practical matter, what activities banks can participate in will, under the proposal, be left to the FBA. Even the activities of the 50 top bank holding companies will effectively be in the hands of the FBA, since the expectation is that the veto will never be used by the Fed. There is little likelihood that such a proposal would again receive the Fed's support. The Fed has repeatedly indicated its concern over the nonbank activities approved for banks. Recent developments have heightened rather than lessened this concern.]

(4) The FDIC would be refocused exclusively on providing deposit insurance and administering the deposit insurance system. All its current responsibilities for environmental, consumer, antitrust and other laws not directly related to the solvency of insured banks would be transferred to other agencies, as would its responsibilities for routine examination, supervision and regulation of state non-member banks. At the same time, the FDIC would assume new authority to review issuance of insurance to all institutions and sample nontroubled firms in conjunction with the primary supervisor. The FDIC would also have new authority to take enforcement action against violations of federal law concerning unsafe banking practices in any bank examined by it, where the primary regulator failed to take such action upon prior request of the FDIC. [*Comment*: There is a significant potential for a more active and powerful FDIC in these recommendations. Given recent developments, proposals for dealing with depository insurance problems may well result in the inclusion of a number of these proposals.]

(5) A new programme would transfer current federal supervision of many state-chartered banks and S&Ls (and their holding companies) to the *better state regulatory agencies*, creating new incentives for states to assume a stronger role in supervision. [*Emphasis added*] [*Comment*: The standards for transfer are unclear. Whether this proposal is workable or provides a constructive incentive remains to be seen. How will a 'better state regulatory agency' be defined? And who will make that determination? Given recent developments, this proposal would seem to be dead.]

(6) The special regulatory system for thrifts would be maintained, but

eligibility would be based on whether an institution is actually competing as a thrift, rather than on its type of charter. [*Comment*: S&Ls want to become more like banks, but continue to be regulated by the Federal Home Loan Bank Board (FHLBB). How these lines are drawn ('whether an institution is actually competing as a thrift') will be crucial. Most thrifts will resist reclassification.]

(7) The FDIC and Federal Savings and Loans Insurance Corporation (FSLIC) would be required to establish common minimum capital requirements and accounting standards for insurance purposes. [*Comment*: Action along these lines is likely.]

(8) Antitrust and securities matters would each be handled by a single agency. [*Comment*: 'Functional regulation' is accepted as a desirable approach. However, when the SEC recently proposed that bank personnel selling securities be registered as brokers under the Securities Exchange Act, banks protested vigorously. Functional regulation may be more acceptable in theory than in practice.]

(9) Some specific regulatory provisions would be simplified to eliminate unnecessary burden. These include existing legislative provisions that encourage 'wasteful litigation', as well as outdated application requirements in various areas that result in substantial unnecessary paperwork. [*Comment*: This would involve translation – elimination of RICO litigation, modification of S.36(b) shareholder litigation standards relating to excessive mutual fund advisory fees, repeal of the Public Utility Holding Company Act, etc.]

Essentially, there would be an expanded Comptroller's office with a new name – the Federal Banking Agency (FBA), within the Treasury. (Placing the new FBA in the Treasury is a politically important move, one which indicates the unwillingness of the executive branch to give additional powers over financial matters to an independent agency.) The FDIC will be confined to insurance concerns. It will shed any regulatory responsibilities that are not related to 'safety and soundness'.

The Fed would continue to regulate the 50 largest bank holding companies. The 1,400 other bank holding companies would go to the new FBA. The Bush Report encourages the increase, rather than decrease, of state involvement, which may not be very deregulatory, (nor, after the Ohio and Maryland S&L crises, very likely). The S&Ls continue under the FHLBB, but the report suggests new minimum capital requirements for the FDIC and FSLIC, and uniform accounting standards are suggested. The FDIC does get the power to act to remove bank management in cases involving safety and soundness. It also is given joint examining power with the problem bank's primary supervisor.

Context and Prospects for Consideration of the Bush Recommendations

The Bush Task Group Report is the latest attempt (and there have been over 20 such reports in US history) to deal with regulatory reorganization. How the regulatory structure, at least at the federal level, will be maintained or revised, given the changing nature of the financial services industry, will become an increasingly important issue over the next few years. It is unlikely, at this point, that Congress will adopt any major reorganization of the federal agencies. Some specific areas of jurisdiction and authority, however, might be rearranged. Functional regulation at least in the antitrust, deposit insurance and securities areas may, for example, be adopted in some form. Recent protests by bankers and the filing of a court action by the American Bankers' Association seeking to enjoin the enforcement of a newly adopted SEC rule regulating bank personnel engaged in brokerage activities[7] raises questions over whether even a minimal amount of functional regulation, which was readily accepted in theory, will be accepted in practice. The Bush Report indicates in an important way the ideological position of the current administration. There is, however, no agreement among the agencies. (Some of the signatories to the Bush Report quietly abandoned it shortly after it was published and the infighting among the agencies has reflected further disagreement.) Nor is there agreement in Congress or among the concerned industry groups – the Investment Company Institute (ICI) and the Securities Industry Association (SIA) both oppose expanded securities powers for banks and the real estate agents want to keep the banks out of the real estate business, as do the insurance agents with respect to bank entry into their business, and so on. Each industry, including the banks, wants to enter the others' territories without opening itself up to competition. The acceptable tilt of the 'level playing field' differs for each group.

INTERSTATE BANKING LEGISLATION

In addition to legislation on regulatory restructuring, Congress may consider some form of interstate banking legislation. Several bills have been submitted proposing an eventual phase-in date ('trigger') for nationwide banking. Although the administration has favoured the extension of interstate banking, Senate Banking Committee Chairman Jake Garn (Republican, Utah), has openly opposed 'trigger-date' proposals. House Banking Chairman Fernand St Germain (Democrat, Rhode Island), has indicated that his first priority is the closing of banking loopholes, particularly the nonbank bank mechanism (which has been halted for the present by court actions) and the South Dakota type

---

7   See discussion of *American Bankers Association* v. *SEC*, No. 85–2482, (D.D.C., August 1985) and SEC Rule 3b–9, adopted July 1985, infra. at pp. 74–75. The District Court rejected the ABA's request for relief and the ABA said it would appeal.

of insurance loophole,[8] which permits banks to enter the insurance business in certain states.

Any loophole or interstate legislation will predictably face a tough battle in Congress. However, many believe that Congress should revise the statutory McFadden and Douglas territorial restrictions on interstate banking, in the light of the extensive development of *de facto* interstate banking in recent years. The Chairman of the Board of Governors of the Federal Reserve System, Paul Volcker, for example, has openly advocated immediate revision of the existing law. In testimony before the House Banking Subcommittee on Financial Institutions, Supervision, and Regulation,[9] Mr Volcker indicated the many ways in which interstate banking has spread, despite Congressional inaction. He urged that Congress adopt legislation liberalizing interstate banking. He also urged that the legislation include a variety of safeguards to encourage continuing diversification of banking resources.

Mr Volcker's concern was that the movement toward interstate banking, while desirable, was going forward without protection against certain risks to the dual (state and federal) banking system and the traditional fears regarding excessive competition. He recommended, first, that limitations be placed on the nation's largest banking institutions, preventing them from acquiring other banks and that states set limitations on the proportion of banking assets within their own borders that could be acquired through acquisitions or mergers of institutions of significant size. Secondly, Volcker urged a requirement that interstate acquisitions generally take the form of a holding company affiliate so that states could retain authority over the in-state operations of the holding company. Third, he suggested a number of transitional frameworks, short of full nationwide banking, through regional arrangements.

Despite Mr Volcker's and others' urging, it is unlikely that Congress will feel sufficient pressure to act quickly. In *Northeast Bancorp*[10] the Supreme Court upheld the legality of Connecticut and Massachusetts statutes allowing out-of-state bank holding companies in the New England region to acquire in-state banks, if the states where the institutions have their principal place of business accorded reciprocal privileges to Connecticut and Massachusetts institutions. In accordance with that decision, states may, in effect, legislate

8 See, for example, *American Banker*, 3 May 1985, 'Garn: no chance Congress will back national phase-in', by Bartlett Naylor; and see *American Banker*, 26 April 1985, 'Odds change daily on interstate bill', by Naylor and Nina Easton. Currently there is some speculation on an attempt to tack bank territorial and powers reforms on to more popular measures to limit bank cheque holding practices. Whether this tactic will work is doubtful at present.

9 See Statement by Paul A. Volcker before the Subcommittee on Financial Institutions, Supervision, and Regulation of the Committee on banking, Finance and Urban Affairs, House of Representatives, 24 April 1985.

10 *Northeast Bancorp Inc.* v. *Board of Governors*, 105 S. Ct 2545 [1985]. See discussion later in the text.

exemptions to the McFadden and Douglas prohibitions within their own boundaries. Regional banking compacts between states are currently viewed as legal means by which to meet the Douglas Amendment prohibitions. A number of those compacts have already been concluded.[11]

Additionally, changes brought about through technological advances may have the effect of further pre-empting the field, i.e., foreclosing Congressional action. Since the regional pacts are now legal, the lifting of the cloud by the Supreme Court makes Congressional action on nationwide interstate banking less necessary. In effect, part of the pressure for interstate banking has been relieved by the Court's approval of the limited interstate reciprocal regional compacts. This type of interstate banking satisfies a number of regional banks, even if money centre banks like Citibank and Chase Manhattan remain unhappy with the result. There are, on the other hand, some major national banks who are relieved that the 'trigger' that has been pulled thus far includes only regional interstate banking, rather than a full nationwide lifting of restrictions. This is not the right time for some of these banks, who have loan repayment and other problems, to go nationwide. Accordingly, the national interstate 'trigger' is not likely to be pulled in the immediate future and the development of regional compacts is likely to grow.

CURRENT DEVELOPMENTS – SOME FAILURES, MORE PRODUCTS
AND LOOPHOLES

*Institutional Failure – a Crisis in Supervision and Problems
with the Depository Insurance Scheme*

Institutional failures and related problems in supervision, as well as perceived inadequacies in the depository insurance scheme, have been more visible in 1984/5. Concerns have focused on the soundness of certain depository institutions, the effectiveness of regulatory supervision and the adequacy of the insurance system.

Since June 1984 we have seen the federal bank agencies rescue Continental Illinois, several significant failures among state chartered savings and loans – specifically, major runs in Ohio and Maryland – and substantial loan losses at major banks. All of these events raise issues regarding the quality of supervision and the capability of our current depository insurance scheme to prevent and cope with disasters.

The Continental Illinois situation was a dramatic example of the failure of management to monitor loan commitments, properly to assess risks and to take basic steps to assure the application of appropriate standards to its loan officers. Questions regarding the failure of bank managements and

11 See *American Banker Weekly Review and Outlook*, 29 April 1985, 'Interstate banking makes waves', by Jeffrey Marshall.

regulators to detect the problems earlier have been the subjects of Congressional and public scrutiny.[12]

Clearly, the Continental Illinois case will place new pressure on federal regulators to extend the scope and quality of the bank examination process. Indeed, the Comptroller's Office and the FDIC have both taken further regulatory steps in response to events related to Continental Illinois. An additional issue has been raised, given recent substantial bank losses, by the cancellation or failure to renew directors' and officers' liability insurance. Insurance that was previously widely available is now much harder to find and costs much more than previously.[13]

Continental Illinois raises questions regarding the capability of federal regulators to prevent a run on a large institution and to protect the federal depository insurance fund. The administration's initial tough position, that banks should be allowed to bear the consequences of the risks they take and fail if necessary, was abandoned in the face of a large institutional failure that might have produced a ripple effect of failures spreading to smaller institutions, who held Continental Illinois paper on deposits in excess of the insurable limits.

The federal rescue of Continental Illinois raises the question of whether, in effect, the government insures all deposits and obligations of failing banks, if the bank and the projected crisis is large enough. Do we have one insurance programme for smaller bank failures (let them go) and another for the largest of banks – even if they take outrageous risks, have poor management and controls that do not work? If so, can the system stand another Continental Illinois? Two or three more? Further, the failure to detect Penn Square's

---

12 See 'Inquiry into Continental Illinois Corp. and Continental Illinois National Bank', Serial No. 98–111, 18, 19 September and 4 October 1984, Hearings before the Subcommittee on Financial Institutions Supervision, Regulation and Insurance of the Committee on Banking, Finance and Urban Affairs, House of Representatives, 98th Congress, 2nd Session. Also, see 'Continental Illinois National Bank: Report of an Inquiry into its Federal Supervision and Assistance', Staff Report, Subcommittee on Financial Institutions Supervision, Regulation and Insurance, House Banking Committee, House of Representatives, 4 August 1985.

13 A number of banking institution directors and officers have resigned in the face of huge bank losses and uncertain insurance protection. See *San Francisco Chronicle*, Monday, 9th September 1985, 'Directors resigning over lost insurance'. Some insurance companies have refused to renew liability policies and others have markedly increased the premiums. In response to the directors' and officers' liability crisis, banking institutions have begun to devise new ways to provide coverage. These measures have included proposals to bolster provisions in the institution's bylaws to indemnify directors; self-insurance through the establishment of a subsidiary; pooling resources through an insurance company established through bank trade organizations; and requesting policies with higher deductibles from insurance companies.

imprudent loan practices[14] raises questions regarding the regulatory safeguards – where was everyone? Continental Illinois succeeded in focusing the minds of Congressional committees, regulators and the public on the necessity for reorganizing and strengthening the depository insurance system and further specializing the activities of the FDIC. It also raised questions about supervision and the ability to prevent such financial disasters in the future.

New regulatory proposals inevitably followed. The Chief of the FDIC Liquidation Division, James A. Davis, has been preparing for submission a contingency plan to handle large bank failures.[15] The new large-bank pay-out system would enable the insurance fund to pay off depositors of a large failed bank over a weekend. The system will rely heavily on computerized systems to estimate which depositors are eligible for insurance. Further, Federal Reserve System chairman Paul Volcker has proposed some changes in the Fed's regulation of banks, including a boost in capital requirements from 6 to 9 per cent and setting more restrictive guidelines for bank dividend policies.[16] Mr Volcker explained that the increase in the minimum capital requirement would impose market discipline on banks 'by requiring banks to find a large market for debt, or equity, that would have no insurance protection'. We can expect to see more proposals that augment existing regulatory constraints on large bank operations in response to Continental Illinois and other bank problems.

The ripple effect of bad banking practices, speculative real estate activity and trading with undercapitalized and irresponsibly run government securities dealers was evident in other situations that gained wide attention in 1985. In Ohio, the failure of an unregulated Florida government securities dealer (ESM Securities) brought down one of the state's largest savings and loan institutions and resulted in the closing of all state-chartered S&Ls for a period of time.[17] In Maryland, real estate and other speculative activities, alleged violation of self-dealing prohibitions and the failure of state regulators to detect or investigate symptoms of problems in several state-chartered S&Ls resulted in similar depository institution problems for them. A state-wide moratorium was required and state legislative action was necessary to restore confidence. The recent failure of EPIC (Equity Property Investment Corp.), a mortgage securities company in Virginia, affiliated with another Maryland S&L, portends more problems of substance and public perception for state-chartered S&Ls.[18]

14   See 'Failure of Penn Square Bank', No. 97–777, 10 December 1982, GPO printing 1983, Hearing Before the Committee on Banking, Housing, and Urban Affairs, US Senate, 97th Congress, 2nd Session.
15   See *American Banker*, 9 September 1985, 'Overseers of banks that live and die'.
16   See *Wall Street Journal*, 10 September 1985, 'Fed chairman proposes major changes in several areas of banking regulation'.
17   See *Wall Street Journal*, Monday, 15 April 1985, p. 14, 'ESM's auditor given favor in '81, records indicate', by Martha Brannigan.
18   See *American Banker*, Monday, 26 August 1985, 'Officials study plan to rescue EPIC companies', by David LeGesse.

The crises in Ohio[19] and Maryland[20] have raised serious questions about the ability of state and private depository guarantee funds to cope with the failure of even a modest sized institution. Even the failure of moderate size institutions appears to have broad effects on the confidence of depositors and the ability of other institutions to cope with a financial crisis. The erosion of confidence in state-chartered S&Ls and the spread of panic regarding the safety of deposits was dramatically demonstrated by the long lines of shocked depositors in Ohio and Maryland, who were intent on withdrawing their funds from the troubled institutions as quickly as possible. It is likely that proposals to reorganize the depository insurance scheme, which call for the creation of private insurance plans and the extension of state insurance programmes, died with the Maryland and Ohio failures. A more likely course is the transformation of non-federally insured depository institutions into federally insured entities. The Ohio and Maryland failures cast doubt on the ability of state regulation to prevent and cope with the types of serious problems presented by the Maryland and Ohio situations. These failures also cast some doubt on the ability, under present circumstances, of the federal government to provide effective assistance if significant failures continue to occur. Given the massive size of current S&L losses, such failures are certainly possible.[21]

In September 1985 members of the Federal Savings and Loan Advisory Council announced recommendations for the formation of a Federal Savings and Loan Insurance Corporation (FSLIC) liquidation firm.[22] The Council is considering creating a corporation to buy the bad assets of failed S&Ls in order to shore up the FSLIC. The proposed corporation would liquidate the bad loans and foreclosed properties which the FSLIC has had difficulty in managing. Other proposals to strengthen federal depository insurance programmes can be expected. It is clear that some action must be taken soon.

Federally based insurance solutions will predominate since recent events made clear that there is no public confidence that state or private schemes will work. Moreover, it seems unlikely that regulatory proposals which call for treating S&Ls more like commercial banks and giving them considerable additional powers will gain substantial support. Indeed, a tightening of S&L regulations is likely – increasing the quality of regulation, examination and oversight. Closer scrutiny of affiliated transactions and speculative investments may also result from the recent crises. Further, public awareness of the

19 See *Wall Street Journal*, 2 April 1985, 'Bank board chairman's cool initial response to Ohio...'
20 See *New York Times*, 20 May 1985, 'Old Court; fast growth, by high risk-taking', by Gary Klott.
21 See the letter of Edward Gray, Chairman of the FHLBB, to Senate Banking Committee Chairman Garn, 25 July 1985, reported in 45 *BNA Wash. Fin. Rep.*, 302 (8/26/85).
22 See *San Francisco Chronicle*, Tuesday 10 September 1985, 'US may sell bad assets of failed S&Ls'.

importance of federal insurance is now greater than ever. We are not likely
to hear again a state governor admit that he did not know the difference
between FSLIC and state insurance for depository institutions. The detailed
story leading to the failures in Ohio and Maryland, which are the subject of
legislative and judicial proceedings, does not augur well for further 'deregulation' of S&Ls, or, as we have noted, the addition of broader powers. FHLBB
chairman Gray blames the current failures on the quality of investments and
undue risks undertaken by S&Ls with expanded powers granted by state
legislatures.

Nonbank Banks – Closing a Loophole

Among the major 'loophole' issues relating to the territorial limitations placed
on banks by the McFadden and Douglas constraints, the continued controversy
over nonbank banks is perhaps the most visible, at least for the present. These
developments indicate again that, as was the case in the ATM controversy
in the mid-1970s,[23] the courts will not permit the regulatory agencies to
avoid (or evade – depending on your point of view) the McFadden Act
prohibitions on interstate banking by administrative action. The recent finding
that authorization by the Comptroller and the Fed of the formation of nonbank banks (or banks exercising limited banking powers) was illegal, is another
example of the independence exhibited by the courts on these issues.[24]

The controversy took shape in mid-1984 when the then Comptroller,
C. Todd Conover, announced that, barring the enactment of federal legislation
closing the loophole by the end of the 1984 legislative session, he would open
the regulatory gates for the consideration of more than 300 nonbank bank
applications that had previously been filed. The applications were filed in

---

23　See, for example, *Independent Bankers Association of America* v. *Smith*,
534 F.2d. 921 (D.C.Cir., 1976). There the Comptroller ruled that ATMs, which
accepted deposits, were not branches and therefore not subject to the restrictions
of the McFadden Act, that banks could not branch interstate or beyond the
boundaries set for state banks by state law. The Court of Appeals ruled that the
ATMs were indeed branches under S.36 of the Act, in that they performed branch
bank functions (like accepting deposits). The fact that the machines were automatic
and not staffed with live bank personnel made no difference. The court observed
that if the Comptroller wanted to change the law he must go to Congress and
not seek to exercise regulatory authority which he did not have. Congress has
not changed the McFadden Act provisions. Recently, the Court of Appeals for
the Second Circuit ruled that point-of-sale/ATM systems, installed in a supermarket and not owned by the bank, were not branches of the bank. *Independent
Bankers Association* v. *Marine Midland Bank*, 757 F.2d 453 (2d Cir., 1985).
Whether the supermarket becomes a bank is unclear. See, Symons and White,
'Shared ATMs', *Banking Law*, pt 2 (West Pub., 1982).
24　See *US Trust (Florida Dept of Banking* v. *Bd of Govs)* and *IBAA* v. *Conover*,
n.2 above.

anticipation of quick approval and in order to take advantage of the broad gap this type of bank would create in the McFadden restrictions. By early February 1985 the number of applications had reached 400.[25]

Nonbank banks, as we have noted, are entities that are limited service banks – that is, they either do not make commercial loans or do not accept demand deposits. A loophole in the Bank Holding Company Act (BHCA) was said to permit bank holding companies to acquire limited purpose banks in states outside the state where the bank holding company has its headquarters. Thus, among the applications gaining early preliminary approval by the Comptroller were those from Citicorp, Security Pacific and Chase Manhattan, large money centre banks who had for years been seeking to break through the barriers to interstate banking.

The Comptroller's position did not go unchallenged. As the Comptroller's office accepted more and more nonbank bank applications, court actions by state-chartered and smaller national banks and their trade associations were instituted to block the spread of the nonbank banks, at least on a federal level. As noted, recent court rulings have succeeded in stopping the expansion of nonbank banks for the present. However, some perspective on the development of the issue may be of interest in terms of the numbers of banks involved and the degree to which interstate banking was becoming a reality, before the courts acted. It also indicates the degree of pressure present in the drive to eliminate the interstate restrictions and the counter-pressure of forces resisting change.

The 29 nonbank banks approved in the first group by the Comptroller's office were owned by 13 bank holding companies in nine states. The majority of the 300 applications then pending before the Comptroller were processed in batches. (The Fed must also grant approval and that agency exhibited much more reluctance than did the Comptroller in granting approvals.) Of the 29 initial approvals, 17 would not offer commercial loans; 12 would not accept demand deposits. By February 1985 the Comptroller had approved 215 applications;[26] the Fed had approved only ten. By April 1985, the Comptroller's office had preliminarily approved 277 applications.[27]

During the same period (February–March 1985), the Fed had pending applications to aquire nonbank banks in 16 states, and ten of those states had statutes which raised questions as to whether these acquisitions were valid under state law (North Carolina, Florida, Pennsylvania, Maryland, Connecticut, Texas, New Hampshire, New Jersey, Colorado and South Carolina). Meanwhile, the Community Bankers of Florida, the Independent Bankers Association of America (IBAA), the Florida Bankers Association and Barnett Bank of Jacksonville were successful in obtaining a federal court injunction against

25 *American Banker*, 18 April 1985.
26 *New York Times*, 20 February 1985.
27 *American Banker*, 18 April 1985.
28 See IBAA case cited in n.2 above.

the Comptroller on the ground that he had exceeded his authority by chartering entities that were not real banks.[28] (See discussion of Fed proposed rules on nonbank banks below.)

State legislative action against nonbank banks has also had some effect. At the end of January 1985, the Comptroller had preliminarily approved 26 nonbank banks in Texas for, among others, Citicorp, Chase, Chemical, Irving, Mellon, First Interstate and Security Pacific. Similarly, moves to outlaw nonbank banks in a dozen states had yielded new restrictions. By early February, seven states had enacted legislation; by 20 February, the number had grown to ten, as listed above. A number of banks had argued to the Fed that the restrictive state laws were invalid.[29] Citicorp, for example, had asked the Fed to override laws in Florida and North Carolina restricting the ability of banks to open nonbank bank entities in those states.[30]

Early reports predicted that the Fed would probably uphold the Florida prohibitions. The *American Banker* reported an informal meeting at the Fed where the state/federal issue was discussed, including questions over the validity of the state restrictive statutes.[31] All of this flowed from the Fed's original approval of US Trust's application for a nonbank bank in Florida in April 1984, which was eventually reversed by the Court of Appeals (see below). Presumably the Fed, in the light of the US Trust case, would not want states to authorize nonbank banks for state chartered institutions.

The question remains whether or not the states' restrictive laws are constitutional. The Fed did not formally reverse its original approval of US Trust's application in Florida, but, in a highly unusual move, welcomed the Court of Appeal's decision that it lacked the power to grant US Trust's applications. The final outcome in that suit awaits the Supreme Court's determination of whether to hear the appeal taken by US Trust (see below). Other states, for the time being, have avoided passing nonbank bank legislation until the results of the suits filed during 1984 are clear. States have been actively engaged in other protective measures, such as reciprocal agreements with other states (see below).

The challenge to nonbank banks during 1984 had thus proceeded on two fronts: (a) state legislative and court actions and (b) federal court actions. The judicial disposition of these challenges is still not final, pending resolution of *US Trust* and *Dimension Financial* in the Supreme Court. The developments to date are reviewed below.

As the situation now stands, despite the active support of the Comptroller's office and the Fed's initial reluctant support (which has now turned to an

---

28   See IBAA case cited in n.2 above
29   See *American Banker*, 14 February 1985.
30   For a summary of 1984 state actions relating to limiting nonbank banks and their activities, see 44 *Wash. Fin. Rep.*, 1/14/85 at 37–39, 'State nonbank bank prohibitions under study: legal issues raised'.)
31   *American Banker*, 2 August 1985.

embrace of the court decision it lost), the federal court actions have, at least for the time being, put a halt to the federal regulatory approvals of nonbank banks by those agencies. However, the FDIC seems willing to permit such banks under its jurisdiction. Both Merrill Lynch and Sears have received clearances to acquire and set up limited service state-chartered banks. FDIC will confront the issue again when Franklin Resources' proposed purchase of Pacific Union Bank comes before it.

Action Against the Comptroller: the Jacksonville Case

In *Independent Bankers Association of America* v. *Conover*[32] a federal district court in Jacksonville, Florida enjoined the Comptroller from chartering any more nonbank banks. The ruling stopped the national chartering of *de novo* nonbank banks, but did not apply to state-chartered institutions. Thus, under this ruling, states willing to charter nonbank banks could do so, but the Comptroller's office could not.

Clearly, the nonbank bank is a device which takes advantage of a perceived loophole in the Bank Holding Company Act to avoid the restrictions on inter-state banking which would otherwise apply to banking operations. The court in the *IBAA* case pointed to the absence of Congressional authority for the Comptroller's action.

This decision[33] put an effective halt to the approval of nonbank banks by the Comptroller. Although the Comptroller originally argued that the case applied only to Florida, he later agreed not to pursue the issue, particularly since an appeal would go to the same court of appeals in Atlanta that decided the *US Trust* case. As already noted, by April 1985 the OCC had preliminarily approved 277 nonbank bank applications, but within two months after the *IBAA* ruling, 19 applications had been withdrawn.[34] In the meantime, the Fed was reluctantly engaged in defending its approval of the US Trust's application for a nonbank bank in Palm Beach, Florida. In response to the *IBAA* ruling, Federal Reserve chairman Paul Volcker called for prompt Congressional action to close the controversial nonbank bank loophole.[35] Congressional action was not forthcoming and the effect of the *IBAA* ruling and the *US Trust* decision was to make Congressional action less necessary, since the nonbank bank route to interstate banking had been largely blocked, except for possible FDIC action.

None the less, Congressional committee chairmen Garn (Senate Banking) and St Germain (House Banking) have renewed their pledge to pass legislation outlawing these entities and forcing those who entered into operation after 30 June 1983 (or some other agreed upon date) to cease operations. There is, however, considerable doubt as to whether the committee chairmen will

32 *IBAA* v. *Conover*, see n.2 above.
33 See n.6 above.
34 *American Banker*, 18 April 1985.
35 Ibid.

be able to make good their threat given the court actions. The closing of the nonbank bank loophole, which seemed to be quite likely in 1984, may now have to await more comprehensive legislation. The Comptroller's office is, for now, not accepting any new nonbank bank applications and has not approved any of these applications since the *IBAA* federal court ruling.

Action against the Fed: the US Trust Nonbank Bank Application

In February 1984 the Fed approved US Trust's application to convert its Florida trust company into a limited purpose bank that would accept deposits, but would not make commercial loans.[36] The Florida Banking Department challenged the Fed's action in court and won a striking victory in the Court of Appeals for the Eleventh Circuit in Atlanta which held the Fed's approval to be unwarranted. The Fed, in an unusual move, welcomed the loss and refused to appeal. It was US Trust, which had previously intervened in the proceeding, that filed the petition for *certoriari* in the Supreme Court. The background to the Fed's unusual posture as the delighted loser is important in understanding its position.

The Fed was never in a rush to approve the applications for nonbank banks. The Fed approved these applications only because it thought that it had no other legal option and it imposed certain conditions on the applicants which limited the attractiveness of the limited (nonbank) bank device. In letters to Suburban Bancorp of Bethesda, Maryland, Bankers Trust and Bank of Boston, the Fed ruled that bank holding companies could not perform such services as cheque clearing, cheque cashing and data processing for their nonbank banks.[37] The new limitations put the Fed at odds with the Comptroller, who had actively encouraged the nonbank bank development. (The *Wall Street Journal* of 11 November 1984 reported that the Fed's move was really aimed at keeping non-banking companies such as Sears and Merrill Lynch out of the banking business. Sears is already in the S&L business and Merrill Lynch now operates a state-chartered bank in Princeton, NJ, which it renamed Merrill Lynch Bank and Trust Co.) The Fed's letter to Suburban Trust and the other bank holding companies required almost total separation between the bank holding companies and their affiliated limited service banks.[38]

The Fed's order prohibited transactions by bank holding companies with these affiliates without its approval. The Fed stated:

> This prohibition was intended to be broad in scope and to cover all transactions with affiliates. In particular, and without limitation, we would like to bring to your attention that the following transactions would be inconsistent with this prohibition: the provision to or receipt from, affiliates of Suburban Bank/ Washington or the customers of its affiliates of services such as check clearing,

36 US Trust Corp., New York, 70 *Fed. Res. Bull.* 371 (April 1984).
37 *Wall Street Journal*, 22 November 1984.
38 See criticism of Fed move by bankers as costly and inhibiting the growth of these banks in *American Banker*, 23 November 1984.

loan payments, loan balance inquiries, receipt of deposits, trust administration services, advice to trust customers, courier services, or check cashing unless such check cashing or other customer services are provided on the same basis to customers of unaffiliated depository institutions.

On 9 January 1985, the Fed agreed to seek public comment to a liberalization of the Suburban Trust type of restrictions. It proposed to permit the holding company to perform back-office services for the nonbank subsidiary or affiliate, including cheque clearing and record keeping.[39] The proposal would roll back the Fed's policy to its pre-November 1984 position (prior to the Suburban Trust letter restrictions).[40] The loosening of the Fed's revisions resulted from criticism that the Suburban Trust restrictions were too constraining, making the nonbank bank almost useless.[41]

The comment file on the proposed relaxation of requirements is summarized in *American Banker* (19 February 1985, p. 22). Most interesting is the Department of Justice comment endorsing the proposed liberalization. The Justice Department's comments are said to have 'surprised many banking industry executives, who suggested it signals that the Reagan Administration now openly supports nonbank banks'. Why anyone should be surprised is in itself surprising, given the Comptroller's historic active support of nationwide interstate banking, a policy which was not initiated by Mr Conover. Moreover, the Comptroller had the backing of the Treasury and Secretary Regan himself had been active and vocal in his support of not only interstate banking, but additional bank powers. The more recent court developments have largely pre-empted this development for the present, but the difference in attitude between the Fed and the Comptroller is worth noting and explains the Fed's gallant acceptance of defeat in the *US Trust* case and the Department of Justice's position in opposition to the Fed.

Returning to the US Trust matter in more detail, several months after the Fed's proposed relaxation of its nonbank bank requirements, the Court of Appeals for the Eleventh Circuit decided *Florida Department of Banking* v. *Board of Governors* – the *US Trust* case.[42] As noted previously, the Federal Reserve had approved the application of a New York bank holding company, US Trust, to expand the nonbanking activities of its wholly owned Florida trust company subsidiary. The Florida Department of Banking, the Florida Bankers' Association and a Florida bank petitioned for review of the Fed's order. The Court of Appeals held that the Fed should have used its authority under the Bank Holding Company Act (BHCA) to deny US Trust's application to expand its activities. US Trust had received approval from the Fed to

39 See, 44 *BNA Wash. Fin. Rep.*, 1/14/85 at 40.
40 43 *Wash. Fin. Rep.*, at 930, 701.
41 See 44 *BNA Wash. Fin. Rep.*, at 40–1.
42 *Florida Department of Banking* v. *Board of Governors*, 760 F.2d 1135 (11th Cir., 20 May 1985), pet. for cert. pending sub nom. *US Trust Corp.* v. *Board of Governors*.

expand its wholly owned subsidiary's activities to include acceptance of time and demand deposits and the making of consumer loans. The subsidiary would not engage in the business of making commercial loans, and thus would arguably not literally fall within the statutory definition of 'bank'.

The Court of Appeals rejected such a literal interpretation of the statute. The court found that despite a superficial compliance with the BHCA, the Fed should not have approved the application. The court found that approval of US Trust's application violated the policy of the BHCA to allow states to choose for themselves whether to open their borders to out-of-state banks. The court dismissed US Trust's attempt to avoid the interstate restrictions by limiting its activities to the literal requirements of the statute (accept deposits or make loans, but not both). The court said it was effectuating the Congressional intent to leave such decisions to the states and not to a federal regulatory agency. With the Eleventh Circuit's opinion in *US Trust* and the injunctive action against the Comptroller in Jacksonville, regulatory approval of nonbank banks was halted. These cases, however, do not prohibit states from granting such applications, nor do they necessarily apply to the FDIC.

After the Eleventh Circuit ruling, US Trust filed a petition for *certiorari* with the Supreme Court seeking review of the decision.[43] US Trust's argument is that the Court of Appeals had refused to defer to 'Congress' clear statutory definition of "bank"', which requires that the entity accept deposits *and* make loans. The Fed will probably oppose review, but the Comptroller through the Department of Justice will probably support US Trust's petition. If the Court accepts the case for review, a major ruling on interstate banking could be the result.

Dimension Financial: More Nonbank Bank Issues

The Supreme Court has already agreed to hear another case involving nonbank banks. In *Dimension Financial Corporation* v. *Board of Governors*,[44] the Court of Appeals for the Tenth Circuit ruled that changes made by the Fed in its regulation defining 'bank' within the meaning of the Bank Holding Company Act were beyond its jurisdiction. The Court of Appeals held that the Fed's Regulation Y, defining 'commercial loan' to include money market and interbank transactions, thus expanding the jurisdiction of the Fed under the Act, was invalid. The court argued that the Fed's regulation, which considerably expanded its own jurisdiction, exceeded its rule-making authority under the Act. By broadening the definition of a 'demand deposit' and 'commercial loan', the Fed tried to bring more nonbank banks under the BHCA and the Douglas Amendment. When the Supreme Court hears the Fed's appeal, the Department of Justice is set to oppose the Fed's position.

---

43 *US Trust Corp.* v. *Board of Governors*, No. 85–193, US S. Ct, pet. for cert. filed 8/5/85.
44 *Dimension Financial Corporation* v. *Board of Governors*, 744 F. 2d 1402 (10th Cir., 1984), pet. for cert. granted.

The line of recent cases discussed here has effectively barred the proliferation of nonbank banks through federal agency approval.[45] Not all the legal issues at the federal level have been settled, however. The 'loophole' in the BHCA which defines a bank as an institution which makes commercial loans *and* accepts deposits still exists and the appeals in the *US Trust* and *Dimension* cases are pending in the Supreme Court. *Dimension*, at least, will be heard on the merits. One question that will be put to the court in *Dimension* is: if we take the Florida District Court decision (*IBAA* v. *Conover*) at its word and the Comptroller's office has no authority to charter an institution that does *not* engage in both loan and deposit activity, because it is not a bank, and the Court of Appeals in *Dimension* is also correct that the Fed has no authority to broaden the definition of 'commercial loan' and demand deposits so as to cover a larger number of nonbank banks, then neither federal regulator would appear to have primary jurisdiction over these institutions. Peter Wallison, former general counsel of the Treasury Department, raised some interesting questions on the legal controversy:

> If the Court (the Tenth Circuit in *Dimension*) is correct, and the nonbank banks are not engaged in the core business normally associated with banking, it can hardly be contended that the policy behind the Bank Holding Company Act – if not its words – would support the divestiture of nonbank banks by non-banking 'commercial firms' such as American Express, Sears, or Merrill Lynch . . . Second, if nonbank banks are not engaged in the business of banking, how can it be contended that the acquisition of nonbank banks by bank holding companies across state lines is in fact interstate banking?[46]

Some of the legal confusion may be settled when the Supreme Court decides in *Dimension Financial*. If the Supreme Court decides to hear US Trust's appeal, that decision may clarify the law further. However, it would still be left for Congress to resolve the issues relating to interstate banking. If Congress does nothing and the nonbank bank loophole remains closed by court rulings, then interstate banking developments will centre on the reciprocal state compacts authorized in *Northeast*. Chairman Volcker wants the nonbank bank loophole closed, as does House Banking Committee chairman St Germain. The Comptroller and the Treasury want the loophole widened.[47]

Recent Developments: Control Data and Mark Twain

Recent events indicate that the Fed will be extremely reluctant to retreat from its own policy positions. In an agreement of 26 July 1985, the Fed gave

45 See, *Washington Post*, May 1985, 'Nonbank banks may soon be extinct', by James Rowe Jr.
46 See *American Banker*, 11 April 1985, quote from commentary by Peter Wallison on *IBAA* v. *Conover*. Wallison has now filed a brief *amicus curiae* in the Supreme Court on behalf of Sears in the *Dimension Financial* case, raising similar questions.
47 See *American Banker*, 15 April 1985, 'Volcker says Congress should close nonbank–bank loophole, by Bartlett Naylor.

permission to Control Data Corporation to continue to operate a nonbank bank, City Loan Bank of Lima, Ohio – but only for two years. Control Data Corporation will operate the institution through its subsidiary, Commercial Credit Corporation, but both Control Data and its subsidiary agreed to conform their activities to those permissible for bank holding companies under S.4 of the BHCA within the two years, unless the dispute over nonbank banks were resolved either by the Supreme Court or by Congress. Control Data's institution is a former state-chartered, privately insured thrift that was converted to a nonbank bank, following the collapse of the Ohio Deposit Guarantee Fund. Control Data and its subsidiary promised the Fed that City Loan would not engage in the business of making commercial loans, thereby avoiding the formal definition of the term 'bank' contained in the BHCA.[48] (The Fed here, however, appears to be adopting the court's position in *US Trust* that an institution taking deposits but not making commercial loans is still a bank under the BHCA and that, therefore, the Fed had jurisdiction under the Act.)

In another move, the Fed again sought to enforce the legal restrictions on interstate banking. On 12 August 1985 the Fed ruled that it must approve any relocations to another state of subsidiary banks owned by bank holding companies. The Fed's ruling was a response to a decision by Mark Twain Bancshares of St Louis to move one of its subsidiary banks from Independence, Missouri to nearby Overland Park, Kansas. In its ruling the Fed stated that Mark Twain's move was illegal, since such relocations require the Fed's approval. Moreover, the Fed indicated that any bank holding company that retains control of a bank outside its home state – while simultaneously controlling a bank inside its home state – is in violation of the Douglas Amendment's prohibitions against interstate banking.[49]

Mark Twain Bancshares had received initial approval from the Comptroller's office for its move. We can expect a bank holding company to challenge the legality of the Fed's relocation ruling. (Mark Twain may file suit, or another case may come from New Jersey's Horizon Bancorp, if the Fed also bars the relocation of its subsidiary bank.) This and other developments in the nonbank bank controversy indicate that when there is no fully articulated Administration policy, and where federal regulators cannot agree and Congress does not act to resolve the issues, the courts will act on the cases before them, with the resulting policy being formed on a case-by-case basis by courts which are looking to effectuate the intention of Congress in statutes passed in 1927, 1933 and 1956.

48 See *BNA Wash. Fin. Rep.*, vol. 45, 8/26/1985 at 311.
49 See, *American Banker*, 13 August 1985, 'Fed prohibits cross-border relocations', by Nina Easton.

Regional Compacts: Pulling the Regional Trigger

The Northeast Litigation

Another important part of the interstate banking controversy involves regional compact arrangements, whereby several states agree to reciprocal interstate banking privileges for each member of the compact. Some states have been waiting for court resolution of the nonbank bank issues before passing prohibitions against nonbank bank formation within their states, but many states have gone forward with protecting and enhancing the banking community within their boundaries through the conclusion of reciprocal interstate banking compacts with other states.

These regional agreements initially evoked challenges from banks in states adjacent to, but excluded from, the states in the compact. Thus, the New York banks, excluded from the New England compact, brought the action in *Northeast Bancorp*[50] to void their exclusion. In *Northeast*, the court was asked to review orders of the Fed approving applications for the acquisition of bank holding companies in Massachusetts and Connecticut. The Second Circuit held that the state statutes in question did not violate the commerce, interstate compact of equal protection clauses of the Constitution. Massachusetts and Connecticut had passed statutes authorizing bank holding companies, located in other New England states, to make acquisitions within their states, provided that the New England home state of the bank holding company had granted reciprocal privileges to Massachusetts- and Connecticut-based bank holding companies. The Supreme Court affirmed the Second Circuit's decision. Thus, both *Northeast* opinions recognized the role of the states establishing the rules under which they could choose to permit out-of-state banking institutions within their borders.

Litigation instituted by excluded money centre banks from adjacent states has not been the only result of the regional compacts. Some of the larger US banking companies face financial constraints on their ability to expand nationwide through acquisition.[51] When the purchase of other banks becomes too costly and nonbanking subsidiaries are legally barred from conversion to commercial banks at the federal level, these large institutions would like to be able to rely on regional compacts as an option for expansion.

The Federal Reserve Bank of New York found that banks in areas with strong regional pacts fared better than the largest national institutions in expansion. The result may be that well-managed, profitable regional bank holding companies will be able to compete and serve as a sort of balance against the largest national institutions. New York banking institutions will

---

50 *Northeast Bancorp Inc.* v. *Board of Governors*, 740 F.2d 303 (2d Cir., 1984), affirmed, 105 S.Ct 2545 (1985).
51 See report from the Federal Reserve Bank of New York in *American Banker*, 29 August 1985.

continue to compete with the institutions in the strongest regional pacts (New England, the Southeast, Western and Midwestern compacts).[52] Merger activity is currently high among the institutions within these regions, and more mergers may bring stronger regional firms, but possibly more difficult regulatory problems as well. The Supreme Court's decision in *Northeast* clears the way for a good deal of bank merger and acquisition activity in the various regional reciprocal banking configurations. This important step towards interstate banking is a middle course between McFadden–Douglas and nationwide banking. It provides a period for testing and realignment, the results of which cannot now be predicted.

State Legislative Activity

The formation of new regional agreements was a feature of 1985. Some highlights of state legislative activity involving regional and interstate banking issues will assist in putting judicial and other developments into clearer focus.

(1) In June, the California State Senate passed a bill that would allow reciprocal interstate banking between California and the eight other Western states in the 12th Federal Reserve District. The state assembly passed a rival bill, which would permit any out-of-state bank holding company and its subsidiaries to buy any established state-chartered California bank with assets of $200 million or less. The final legislation may be a compromise providing for both out-of-state acquisitions of failing institutions and less broad regional interstate privileges.[53]

(2) Governor Babbitt of Arizona signed a measure in April 1985 permitting out-of-state banks to merge with, or acquire, Arizona financial institutions. The legislation was hailed as a compromise supported by both large and small Arizona institutions.[54] Two California banks, Security Pacific and Great American First Savings Bank, agreed in August 1985 to each buy a large Arizona savings institution. Arizona's current banking and economic policy includes pursuit of capital infusions from out-of-state institutions. One of the agreements may be thwarted if the Federal Home Loan Bank Board disapproves the acquisition. In the past, the FHLBB only allowed thrifts to expand into new states through the acquisition of an insolvent institution. The FHLBB allowed interstate acquisitions of healthy thrifts only if the buyer has paid the 'entry fee' of taking over a failing institution.[55] The FHLBB announced in August 1985 that its old policy would be re-evaluated. The announcement came after the Federal Savings and Loan Advisory Council passed a resolution

---

52   See *American Banker* Special Report, 27 June 1985, 'Interstate banking: merger waters are already boiling' by Fraust and Sudo.
53   See *American Banker*, 1 July 1985.
54   See *American Banker*, 19 April 1985.
55   *American Banker*, 16–22 August 1985.

calling for a change in the FHLBB policy which blocks interstate mergers between healthy thrifts.[56]

(3) The Illinois Senate Finance Committee passed in May 1985 a regional interstate banking bill which had received Governor Thompson's endorsement. The bill approved by the Senate committee allows regional interstate banking with six states contiguous to Illinois – Indiana, Iowa, Kentucky, Michigan, Missouri and Wisconsin. (Indiana and Kentucky already have laws allowing reciprocal banking.) The Illinois bill would also allow state-wide multibank holding companies, eliminating the current division of Illinois into five regions.[57] A state task force on financial services announced its recommendations that September. The task force recommended opening Illinois to nationwide interstate banking in two to five years. Governor Thompson indicated his interest in such 'trigger' legislation.[58]

(4) In contrast, Iowa has not passed any form of interstate banking legislation. In May 1985 the state House of Representatives deleted an amendment to a farm aid bill that would have allowed out-of-state holding companies to acquire troubled and other Iowa institutions.[59] While Iowa institutions may need infusions of capital, out-of-state bank control is politically difficult in a state where voters fear bank seizure of farm property.

(5) In Washington State, a reciprocal interstate banking bill passed both houses of the state legislature in April 1985. Under the legislation, an out-of-state bank would be allowed to acquire a Washington financial institution that was at least three years old, as long as the acquirer's home state had similar legislation.[60]

(6) The District of Columbia tentatively approved a bill in June 1985 that will permit regional interstate banking between DC and 11 Southern states.[61] The final vote was expected some time in the autumn.

(7) In Maryland, Citicorp and Chase Manhattan announced agreements to buy troubled state savings and loans to get into the Maryland banking business. The Maryland General Assembly (the Legislature), in the aftermath of the thrift crisis, is considering a bill that would allow privately insured thrifts to convert to banks in order to allow out-of-state banks to buy the S&Ls.[62] These and other states have been active on the regional and interstate banking front. The legislation passed has mostly fallen into two categories: provisions that authorize the state banking agency to enter into reciprocal agreements with other states; and provisions that allow out-of-state institutions to acquire failing or other state institutions. There has been some tension in getting

56 *American Banker*, 26 August 1985.
57 *American Banker*, 7 May 1985.
58 *American Banker*, 10 September 1985.
59 *American Banker*, 7 May 1985.
60 *American Banker*, 24 April 1985.
61 *American Banker*, 27 June 1985.
62 *BNA Wash. Fin. Rep.*, vol. 45, 8/26/85 at 304.

legislatures to pass both types of provisions. States that have had problems with troubled institutions (e.g., Maryland) have tended to enact out-of-state acquisition legislation. States with healthy, diverse institutions have tended to enact regional compact legislation (e.g., Connecticut).

Although interstate banking has met strong opposition in every state, the opponents are losing the fight to the interstate compacts and to the failed institution acquisitions by out-of-state banks. The House Banking Committee released in June 1985 a study on bank chains. Chain banks are two or more banks controlled by an individual or group. They are not considered to be bank holding companies because they are not controlled by a parent; hence, chain banks escape a great deal of federal regulation. The House study revealed that, contrary to the conventional industry wisdom, chain banks are not limited to *intra*state networks. The report found 128 *inter*state networks, constituting 24 per cent of total US bank chains.[63]

The extent of interstate bank chains may be surprising to some, but few members of the financial services industry are unaware of the creeping statistics on the growth of interstate banking. In a special report in June 1985 the *American Banker* listed the following: 14 acquisitions of troubled institutions over state lines by bank holding companies from September 1982 to 1 May 1985; eight bank holding companies acquired institutions in states which allow nationwide entry; and 12 banks were 'grand-fathered' into states because their interstate operations began before the passage of state or federal laws banning those activities.[64]

No tally has yet been made of the number of reciprocal agreements reached between states. However, state legislative activity in regional and other interstate areas will surely be of major importance in the next few years. Barring Congressional action, the states have the burden of making interstate policy. Patterns set now, under court-determined policy, could last for years. Congressional ability to change the policy becomes more difficult as banks adapt to new business alliances and to the more competitive world of financial services.

Underwriting and Securities Activities of Banks

The FDIC: More Powers for State Non-member Banks

On 19 November 1984, the FDIC adopted a final rule permitting state non-member banks to engage in a broad range of securities activities.[65] The

---

63   See *American Banker*, 10 June 1985, 'Study finds 128 bank chains across state lines', by Bartlett Naylor.
64   *American Banker* Special Report, 27 June 1985, 'Interstate banking: merger waters are already boiling', by Fraust and Sudo.
65   See original solicitation of views by the FDIC, 47 Fed. Reg. 42121 (1982), the FDIC's proposed rule issued 9 May 1983 and its revised rule issued 1 May 1984; final rule issued 19 November 1984, 12 CFR Part 337; see, 43 *BNA Wash. Fin. Rep.*, 11/26/84 at 837.

FDIC said it would not be a violation of the Glass–Steagall Act for such a bank to establish *a securities subsidiary* – if adequately capitalized and physically separated from the bank, under a different name and logo, with different management – which would: underwrite investment quality debt and equity securities; underwrite and distribute mutual funds (which invest in investment quality securities); and underwrite money market funds. The banks may also apparently engage in brokerage activities, not limited to discount operations like Schwab & Co. The bank can advertise the relationship with the securities subsidiary, even though the name of the subsidiary and logo must be different.

The FDIC rules are similar to the FHLBB's rules regarding separation of the bank or S&L from their service corporation. FHLBB's rules permit S&L service corporations to offer certain brokerage and investment advisory services.

The Securities Industry Association (SIA) and the Investment Company Institute (ICI) challenged the FDIC's rule on the ground that the Glass–Steagall Act does indeed apply to state non-member banks. The FDIC read the Act to apply only to member and national banks. In *ICI* v. *FDIC*,[66] the Court of Appeals for the District of Columbia Circuit considered the FDIC's refusal to consider the ICI's petition protesting against Boston Five Cents Savings Bank's attempt to enter the mutual fund business. The petition requested that the FDIC declare unlawful Boston Five's plan to sell mutual fund shares through fully owned subsidiaries and that the FDIC prevent the bank from implementing the plan. The Court of Appeals held that the FDIC decision not to consider ICI's petition on the merits could not be reviewed under the Administrative Procedure Act. Such action, the court said, must be considered a matter committed to agency discretion. The court rejected the ICI's argument that the FDIC had the authority to prevent the savings bank from implementing its plan under the FDIC's statutory cease-and-desist powers. On this question, the court indicated that the statute requires a 'reasonable' showing that an institution may face insolvency before the FDIC may intervene. Finally, the Court of Appeals overturned the District Court's order to 'compel agency action unlawfully withheld', finding the order ambiguous, beyond the authority of the court and in effect an injunction, which was appealable.

After the ICI's initial action was filed in the District Court, the FDIC issued a 'Statement of Policy on the Applicability of the Glass–Steagall Act to Securities Activities of Subsidiaries of Non-Member Banks'.[67] The FDIC reassessed its view that the Glass–Steagall Act did not reach the securities activities of non-member banks if the activities were conducted through a

---

66   728 F.2d 518 (D.C. Cir., 1984).
67   47 Fed. Reg. 38984 (1982).

separate 'bona fide subsidiary' and complied with the FDIC's conditions effecting 'separation'.

The ICI after the issuance of the Policy Statement brought a second related suit against the FDIC in September 1982. In *ICI* v. *FDIC*,[68] the US District Court for the District of Columbia decided the case on the merits. The District Court sustained the FDIC's interpretation of s.21 of the Glass–Steagall Act. The FDIC had produced regulations on the basis of its interpretation that the Glass–Steagall Act does not prohibit controlled securities activities by state insured non-member banks when conducted through subsidiaries and affiliates. The District Court found that s.21 is silent as to the activities of bank subsidiaries and affiliates, and thus was not intended to bar securities activities by subsidiaries or affiliates of insured non-member state banks. Since Congress chose deliberately not to intrude upon state non-member banks, the District Court found the FDIC regulations within the FDIC's authority.

The practical effects of the loosening of the regulatory strings on non-member banks' securities activities on member banks seeking greater latitude in those areas remains unclear. The *New York Times* on 20 November 1984 quoted an FDIC official as saying 'We couldn't wait any longer' for Congress to act. Yet, there has been no rush by state non-member banks to try out their new powers and an evaluation of this initiative would be premature at this point.

The number of states that allow securities activities by state banks has been limited, but indications are that efforts to expand state-granted powers are being made in several states. Recent failures of state-chartered S&Ls may slow this development considerably, especially since the chairman of the FHLBB has blamed the quality of investments and speculation for the majority of the failures.

In another suit against the FDIC, the Securities Industry Association and FAIC Securities Inc. challenged the FDIC's new more restrictive rules on brokered deposits.[69] (These are deposits solicited from depositors by brokers, who then place them with depository institutions, who pay a fee to the broker. Sharp criticism of this practice has come from regulators, e.g., Mr Gray of the FHLBB, on the ground that banks and S&Ls obtaining these funds are often in a weak position to begin with and are put under increased pressure by the fees paid to the brokers. The practice is said to channel large amounts of money into speculative hands, all with federal agency insurance coverage, imposing even greater strains on the insurance system.) The FIDC and the FHLBB had changed the existing federal insurance coverage of $100,000 per depositor, per financial institution, by adding the qualification that a coverage of funds deposited by or through a deposit broker is limited to $100,000 *per broker*, per financial institution.

---

68   *ICI* v. *FDIC*, Civil Action No. 84–3875, slip opinion (D.D.C., 23 April 1985).
69   See *FAIC Securities Inc. and SIA* v. *FDIC and FHLBB*, No. 84–5408; No. 84–5409; No. 84–5411; No. 84–5412; slip opinion, 26 July 1985 (D.C. Cir., 1985).

The SIA's injury claim was based on the removal of insurance protection, if the brokers had more than $100,000 from their clients deposited at any one institution. The SIA and FAIC Securities brought the suit to protect the interests of brokers, who were in the business of placing these deposits for a fee. These brokers could, under the revised regulations, no longer have more than $100,000 in deposits insured at each bank or S&L. The effect of the revised regulations is to force deposit brokers to spread money received from clients to other institutions and to severely limit their operations.

The Court of Appeals for the District of Columbia heard arguments on whether the SIA and FAIC Securities had standing to sue to bring the action, and whether the revised regulations exceeded the FDIC's and FHLBB's statutory authority. The Court of Appeals found that the appellees had standing to sue because the impact of the regulations substantially affected the brokers' ability to sell insured certificates and depositors' capability to invest through brokers.

On the substantive issue, the Court of Appeals found the FDIC's and FHLBB's regulations to be outside their statutory authority. The court examined the Federal Deposit Insurance Act to determine whether the agencies' interpretation was based on a 'permissible construction' of the statute. The court of appeals found that the FDIC's and FHLBB's regulations amounted to a redefinition of the very terms which the statute itself had defined. To allow the revised regulations to stand, the court ruled, would permit the agencies effectively to repeal the Congressionally mandated definitions. Thus, the court declined to use the legislative history to justify a $100,000 limit for each broker's clients at each institution. On the basis of the plain language of the statute, the Court of Appeals affirmed the district court's ruling, finding the revised regulations limiting to $100,000 the amount of insurance available for each broker at each institution, to be beyond the agencies' authority. Thus, the FDIC's and the FHLBB's attempt to limit insurance available for 'brokered deposits' failed.

The Fed and Citicorp's Attempts to Move into Underwriting

While the brokers argued with the FDIC over insurance protection for their activities, and securities industry members tried to keep state non-member banks out of the investment business, larger banking institutions were devising programmes to further expand their investment activities. Notably, Citicorp throughout 1984/5 made significant efforts to circumvent the Glass–Steagall restrictions.

In 1984 Citicorp asserted its right to underwrite various municipal and corporate securities through a separate subsidiary, and applied to the Fed to consider its request. Citicorp Securities Inc. (CSI), a subsidiary of Citicorp, had been underwriting and dealing in US government securities since 1982. Citicorp, through its subsidiary, also wanted to deal in municipals, industrial development or revenue bonds, commercial paper and mortgage backed securities. Citicorp proposed that these activities would constitute a minor segment of CSI's activities. Citicorp could, thereby, take advantage of a perceived 'loophole' in the Glass–Steagall Act that had thus far been unused. Citicorp argued that s.20 of the Glass–Steagall Act allows a nonbank subsidiary of a bank holding company to engage in securities underwriting as long as the subsidiary *is not 'principally engaged'* in underwriting. Even if the activity is permitted under Glass–Steagall, the Fed also had to determine whether these underwriting activities were 'closely related to banking', under the provisions of the BHCA.[70]

The Fed delayed action on the Citicorp application until the end of February 1985. Citicorp had been engaged during January in responding to questions and in submitting memoranda supporting its position. Citicorp proposed a 20 per cent limitation on its subsidiaries' underwriting activities. Thus, CSI would arguably not be 'principally engaged' in underwriting.[71] S.20 applies to bank affiliates, while s.21 applies to banks. S.21 originally included the words 'principally engaged', as did s.20, but Congress struck 'principally' from s.21, but not from s.20. It was on that basis Citicorp argued that the proposed activity was permissible.[72]

In February 1985, the Fed, in a preliminary analysis, denied Citicorp's application to underwrite commercial paper through its subsidiary. The Fed took the position that Citicorp's proposal was inconsistent with the Glass–Steagall restrictions on banks. Although the Fed denied Citicorp's application, it has permitted bank holding companies to engage in other brokerage activities. For example, in 1983, the Fed approved Bank of America's acquisition of Charles Schwab & Co., the nation's largest discount brokerage firm. (Schwab executes agency orders from the public at discounted rates, but does not engage in underwriting or provide advisory services.) Other brokerage activities on the approved list include:

1 Execution and clearing of stock index futures.
2 Execution and clearing of futures contracts based on a municipal bond index.
3 Execution and clearing of orders in options and futures in gold bullion, foreign exchange and various financial instruments.
4 Offering investment advice and to buy and sell government securities.
5 The purchase and sale of municipal securities for other brokers.[73]

After the Fed had preliminarily denied Citicorp's application in February, Citicorp responded by withdrawing its application to underwrite a broad range of municipal and corporate securities. Major commercial banks viewed

70 *American Banker*, 30 January 1985.
71 The opponents of Citicorp's application point out that 20 per cent, or even 10 per cent, of CSI's business is a very substantial amount by any measure.
72 See discussion, 44 *BNA Wash. Fin. Rep.*, 2/4/85 at 165–6.
73 See 'Recent legislative and other developments impacting depository institutions', FDIC Report, July 1985.

Citicorp's withdrawal as a setback; members of the securities industry regarded it as a victory.[74] But both reactions now seem premature. Some observers expected Citicorp to submit a revised and more modest plan to the Fed.

There was nothing low-key about Citicorp's response. In a letter to the Fed in August 1985 Citicorp adopted its 'typically bold approach'.[75] The letter to the Fed accused the securities industry of trying to 'restrict the activities of bank affiliates and "protect its extraordinarily profitable oligopoly"'.[76] The August letter was prepared as a supplement to Citicorp's March scaled-down re-application to the Fed. As of August 1985 42 letters had been filed on Citicorp's most recent application. The Fed has not yet issued its final ruling.

Citicorp began its response to the comments by indicating that only five out of the 42 letters sent to the Fed were opposed to the bank's underwriting proposal. Among the five opponents were Salomon Brothers (a major underwriter), the SIA and the ICI. Citicorp urged the Fed to stick to the narrow question of whether its application was consistent with current law. That is, Citicorp requested that, in ruling on the application, the Fed should not attempt to determine the outer limits of which securities underwriting activities are permissible under the Glass–Steagall Act and the BHCA, but should only consider the legality of specific requests made by Citicorp.[77]

Despite Citicorp's urging that the Fed consider bank applications to engage in underwriting on a case-to-case basis, the Fed may, given the pressure from new applicants, want to determine its broad policy position on banks engaging in underwriting activities, including the limited menu proposed by Citicorp. Over the coming year (1986), the Fed will be continually pushed to consider 'the outer limits' of the Glass–Steagall Act and the BHCA insofar as bank underwriting and securities activities are concerned.

Another example of such pressure on the Fed is the recent application of Bankers Trust New York Corp. and J. P. Morgan and Co. Inc. to gain permission to place commercial paper through nonbanking subsidiaries, an activity in which they are already engaged through subsidiary banks. While federal law prohibits banks from engaging in securities activities, the statute has been interpreted to mean that *bank holding companies* cannot be 'principally engaged' in securities activities. Bankers Trust and J. P. Morgan have asked to place commercial paper through subsidiary-owned nonbanking subsidiaries. Thus, the Fed sought comments on how much commercial paper may be placed under the Glass–Steagall Act before the affiliate is 'principally engaged' in securities activities.[78]

Earlier, in June 1985, the Fed submitted a statement to the District Court

74 See *American Banker*, 27 February 1985.
75 See *American Banker*, 22 August 1985.
76 Ibid.
77 See *BNA Wash. Fin. Rep.*, vol. 45, 8/26/85 at 303.
78 See *BNA Wash. Fin. Rep.* 7/1/85.

of the District of Columbia in another suit brought by the SIA and the ICI.[79] The Fed's statement said, in response to the SIA's and the ICI's charges of violations, that the commercial paper activities carried on by Bankers Trust Co. did not violate the Glass–Steagall Act because the activities constituted only a limited percentage of Bankers Trust's business.[80]

If the Fed adopts this reasoning in its formal rulings, then Citicorp can expect at least a partial victory from the Fed, *if* the Fed also agrees that such activities are appropriate under the Bank Holding Company Act. However, in later requesting comments, the Fed indicated that its June 1985 statement applied to the Glass–Steagall restrictions, but not to the legality of commercial paper activity appropriate under the BHCA, thus leaving the final result in doubt. As responses to the Fed's call for further comments are filed, familiar sides will form. Larger banking institutions will support Bankers Trust's and

79 *A. G. Becker, Inc.* v. *Board of Governors, Securities Industry Assn.* v. *Board of Governors*, No. 80–2414, D.D.C, statement filed 6/4/85.

80 See *BNA Wash. Fin. Rep.*, 6/10/85. Earlier (in 1984) the Supreme Court ruled in *SIA* v. *Board of Governors*, 104 S. Ct 2979 (1984) that commercial paper is indeed a security within Glass–Steagall and that state member banks could not engage in underwriting or distributing such paper. This case involved A. G. Becker's attempt to halt Bankers Trust's commercial paper underwriting activities. The lower court decision, *A. G. Becker Inc.* v. *Bd of Govs*, 519 F. Supp. 602 (D.D.C., 1981), rejected the Fed's analysis, holding that the Glass–Steagall Act did not confer upon the Fed the type of administrative discretion it had under the BHCA to determine what activities were 'closely related' to banking: 519 F. Supp., at 613–14. The Court of Appeals reversed the District Court, 693 F. 2d. 136 (D.C. Cir., 1982), finding that the Fed could lawfully permit Bankers Trust to act as an agent in the sale of commercial paper. The appellate court gave the Fed the type of deference and room for interpretation that the District Court refused to find. The court also applied a functional analysis to the role of commercial paper and found it more like a loan than a security: 693 F. 2d at 149. (The court hedged on small denomination commercial paper issued to the general public, ibid., at 151.) Since the court found that no security was involved, it did not need to consider the definition of 'underwriting' in Glass–Steagall.

As indicated above, the Supreme Court reversed, 104 S. Ct 2979, finding that although the Fed's views were entitled to deference, that was so only if the Fed's view was reasonable and consistent with the Congressional intent (ibid., at 2983). The Court focused on the basis for Glass–Steagall, the risk inherent in the securities business and the conflict of interest position into which banks are cast when they assume the role of investment bankers in addition to their role as commercial lenders and creditors. The court found that the banks' activities in commercial paper involved securities and that Congress knew that it was including commercial paper in its use of the term 'security'. The court emphasized the banks' conflicting role and the objectives of Glass–Steagall to limit the effect of those conflicts (ibid., at 2990).

J. P. Morgan's applications;[81] the securities industry will vigorously assert that the proposed activity is illegal.

Other Bank and Securities Matters

The banking community has brought suits to protect its interest in expanded underwriting activity as frequently as the SIA and the ICI have filed suits to oppose such expansion. A recent example of the bankers' offensive measures is the suit filed by the ABA to stop the SEC from enforcing a new rule requiring banks engaged in securities brokerage to register as 'brokers' and 'dealers'.[82] The ABA claims the SEC had no authority to issue the new rule because banking institutions are governed by their own primary regulators. Compliance with the registration and reporting requirements applicable to broker–dealers would be unnecessarily costly for banks, the ABA claimed. Moreover, the securities reporting requirements would, according to the ABA, subject the banks to capital requirements inconsistent with those already imposed by bank regulators.[83]

The SEC's new Rule 3b–9 was adopted in July 1985; the ABA's suit was filed in August and the federal court in Washington, DC heard the case in October. The SEC defended its new rule, as being within its authority under the Securities Exchange Act. SEC chairman Shad has pointed out that the rule is in accord with the Administration's basic position favouring functional regulation.[84] After an initial hearing, the District Court ruled in favour of the SEC and the ABA has said that it will appeal.

Overall, these developments point to a continued testing of existing law by banks who want to engage in securities activities. The Fed has lobbied for federal legislation to lift current restrictions (subject to certain conditions) on banks engaging in underwriting and other activities. Much opposition can be expected from members of the securities industry to any such proposed legislation. Moreover, serious policy questions remain. As banks engage in more non-traditional activities, the degree to which they should be regulated as unique institutions, as the *American Bankers Association* suit against the SEC indicates, is open to question.

81 See also, application of Chemical New York Corp. for permission to engage in distributing 'best efforts' underwritings, primarily through private placements through a subsidiary of the holding company, Chemical Securities Distribution Inc. Chemical argues that 'best efforts' distribution is not the kind of underwriting prohibited by Glass–Steagall. The SIA disagreed. 44 *BNA Wash. Fin. Rep.* 898, 5/27/85.
82 See *American Bankers Assn* v. *SEC*, No. 85–2482, DDC, 8/5/85.
83 See *BNA Wash. Fin. Rep.*, vol. 45, 8/12/85 at 245.
84 See the earlier discussion of Bush Task Force recommendations. Indeed, this may be a test of whether functional regulation will be accepted in practice as well as in concept. If functional regulation could not be accepted in this context, the viability of the policy would appear to be significantly compromised. Indeed, the Comptroller's office reaction may not reflect broader Administration policy.

Banks in the Insurance Business

The 'South Dakota Loophole'[85]

Some states are adopting legislation that permits state banks and their subsidiaries to offer various types of insurance. These laws would put banks in the insurance business on a general basis. The first of these laws was passed in South Dakota (2 March 1983). Citicorp and other bank holding companies immediately applied to enter South Dakota to buy state banks and start insurance subsidiaries. Federal legislation, which would have closed the door to bank sales of insurance, died in the 98th Congress, along with the other bank powers legislation.

A number of states – including some major financial states – are now looking to follow in South Dakota's footsteps, including New York, New Jersey, Michigan and Minnesota, but the recent Fed decision denying the Citicorp[86] application throws real doubt on the viability of that course of action.

The three bank regulatory agencies initially supported expansion of bank insurance powers, as did the Administration. The Fed now, in denying the Citicorp application, appears to have joined the opposition, at least to this type of development.

The insurance industry is vehemently opposed, just as the securities industry is opposed, to modifying Glass–Steagall in the securities area. Meanwhile, arrangements between banks and insurance companies permit the sale of insurance by independent agents stationed in banks. The bank rents the space for a flat fee or a percentage of the insurance sold. Bank of America has announced an arrangement with Capital Holding Corporation to permit insurance agents to offer insurance in space rented by the insurance company at Bank of America branches. Bank of America is getting a flat fee rather than a percentage. Citibank has an arrangement with American International Life to staff six 'Personal Insurance Centers' at selected Citibank branches in New York.

A number of financial service companies already combine banking and insurance (e.g., Sears, American Express). Banks see the ability to act as an insurance agent as a natural addition to their services – and to their profitability, with a minimum of risk. Branch banks are viewed as obvious places to sell insurance.[87]

Insurance companies who oppose banks' entry into the insurance business have not hesitated to get into banking. According to the BNA Report quoted

85   See 43 *BNA Wash. Fin. Rep.*, No. 20, pp. 805–15, Special Report on 'Long running feud between banking and insurance industries . . .', for a summary of the situation and further references.
86   See 45 *BNA Wash. Fin. Rep.* 197, 8/5/85, reporting the Fed decision of 1 August 1985.
87   See the study conducted in 1983 by Arthur Young on bank expansion into new services, for the American Bankers Association.

above about ten insurance companies own nonbank banks that typically offer consumer banking services (Prudential, Travellers and New England Life). Another group of insurance companies own S&Ls. (As noted, Sears owns a large California S&L.) Insurance companies also offer products like Metropolitan's fully guaranteed money market instruments – which banks regard as competitive with their MMAs. (It is really the insurance *agents* and their associations that are most affected.)

Returning to the Citicorp–Dakota situation: the South Dakota statute allows state banks a broad range of out-of-state insurance activities, but they are limited in competing for local (South Dakota) business. (How far states may legally limit in-state activities which they permit their banks to conduct interstate is unclear.)

The issue is whether Bank Holding Company Act restrictions on insurance activities apply to *state*-chartered subsidiaries of bank holding companies. In the *Citicorp* case, the Fed answers in the affirmative. The Fed previously indicated that state bank subsidiaries of bank holding companies could engage in whatever activities the states permit to their own banks.[88]

Initially, the Fed tabled applications by Citicorp and other bank holding companies to acquire South Dakota banks as a means for entry into all aspects of the insurance business. In February 1985, Citicorp had asked the Fed to reactivate its May 1983 application to acquire a South Dakota bank so that it could engage in the insurance business nationwide. Citicorp sought to underwrite life, accident and health insurance and annuities and sell all lines of insurance through its South Dakota state bank.

On 1 August 1985 the Fed in a major ruling denied Citicorp's application to acquire American State Bank of Rapid City in South Dakota. The Fed rejected the application, explaining that Citicorp's primary, if not its sole, purpose in the proposed acquisition was to allow the bank holding company to engage in insurance activity which it ruled not an activity 'closely related to banking' as required under s.4(c) (8) of the Bank Holding Company Act.[89] The South Dakota statute, the Fed pointed out, severely limits the in-state banking activities in which out-of-state bank holding companies may engage, yet leaves entirely open the insurance activities bank holding companies may conduct outside South Dakota. The effect of the South Dakota statute, the Fed ruled, was to help Citicorp evade nonbanking insurance provisions of the Bank Holding Company Act.[90]

Citicorp's response to the Fed's decision included the argument that many states other than South Dakota had statutes authorizing insurance brokerage by state-chartered banks, and that these activities benefit consumers. As of

---

88 See BNA discussion of Title VI of Depository Institutions Act of 1982, ibid. at 808–9, for various views of whether state bank subsidiaries of bank holding companies are barred from insurance activities.
89 See *BNA Wash. Fin. Rep.*, vol. 45, 8/15/85, at 197–8.
90 Ibid.

August 1985, Citicorp had not yet filed for review of the Fed's decision. South Dakota has not responded to the loophole controversy by proposing new legislation; the position of South Dakota's director of banking was to emphasize the economic opportunities South Dakota would forego if the loophole was closed. South Dakota wants to maintain the loophole, but whether it will liberalize its restrictions on local activity is unclear. Even if it does so, the Fed is unlikely to change its view at this point.

Citicorp's ambition to extend its insurance activities faced another denial of an application by the Fed in connection with an application on behalf of its Australian investment subsidiary (which is incorporated in Delaware) to engage in underwriting property and casualty insurance in Australia. The Fed denied the application because for 'safety and soundness' reasons a majority of the members voting said the activities should not be conducted through a bank subsidiary. The application came through Citibank, rather than Citicorp because Australian policy required that insurance activities be conducted *through a bank subsidiary, rather than through a bank holding company.* The Fed's decision seemed to indicate that had Citicorp applied for the overseas subsidiary, the application may have been approved.[91]

The Fed has, however, expanded the insurance role of at least 16 'grandfathered' banks, who may sell insurance without limitation, in six states.[92] Generally, the Fed has urged Congress to amend legal restrictions prohibiting bank holding companies from engaging in insurance activities. In the meantime, the Fed, as the Citicorp rejection indicates, will not hesitate to enforce BHCA bars when it believes the applications go too far. The Fed's major ruling in the Citicorp matter is that insurance activities are not within those permitted under the Act. This ruling largely cuts off, for now at least, efforts by banks to engage in insurance activities directly or through their holding companies.

The FDIC and Insurance Activities for State Non-member Banks

The FDIC, on the other hand, has been considering a wide range of nonbanking activities for the nonbank subsidiaries of non-member banks, such as data processing and insurance. The expansionary position of the FDIC in this area has pleased some, and has concerned others. If a state bank has an insurance subsidiary, is it then subject to FDIC authority?

The FDIC's latest proposals would add to the already common 'stake-out' arrangements, where banks acquire non-voting equity interests in insurance companies, which could be converted to voting if the law changes. These passive arrangements are subject to Fed guidelines.[93]

91　See *American Banker*, 26 August 1985.
92　See *First Wisconsin*, following the *Norwest* 1984 ruling, discussed in *American Banker*, 11 January 1985.
93　See Bradfield letter, 5 November 1984, on stake-outs, 43 *BNA Wash. Fin. Rep.* 779.

The most recent FDIC proposal offered for comment on 3 June 1985 included provisions that would allow life insurance underwriting, real estate and insurance brokerage and electronic data processing within federally-insured commercial and savings banks. Direct real estate investment would be limited to 50 per cent of capital, with no more than 10 per cent of primary capital invested in any one project. The proposal for comment displays the FDIC's continuing concern regarding 'product deregulation'.

Bankers have objected to the proposal as being too restrictive, while insurance industry members have argued that the FDIC does not have the authority to decide what activities are permissible for national banks. FDIC officials have argued that the proposal would be in line with the powers already granted to banks by some states.[94]

The agency's June version of the proposal would allow banks to invest more than 50 per cent of their capital in real estate, but only through subsidiaries. Thus, under the FDIC's proposal, the banks could invest less than 50 per cent of their capital directly or invest more than 50 per cent through a subsidiary in real estate activities. Either way, recent problems with real estate investments by banks cast real doubt on these proposals. The Federal Reserve proposed more conservative rules on bank real estate investments, but some still believe that the 'safety and soundness' protections in these proposals are inadequate. The Fed has proposed rules requiring banks to invest in real estate only through a subsidiary and to limit investments to 5 per cent of their capital.[95]

Concern over expanded authority for banks to engage in real estate activities has been aggravated by the problems associated with the failure of several Maryland savings and loan institutions. Most recently, problems with the quality, rather than with the spread, of real estate investments have attracted attention in Maryland's EPIC (Equity Property, Investment Corp.) failure. Maryland, after its initial thrift crisis, needed federal insurance (FSLIC) for some of its less solvent state-chartered institutions. The Community Savings and Loan Association was associated with the EPIC group of real estate companies. The EPIC group had been engaged in mortgage insurance and tax shelter offerings of interests in real estate securities. Specifically, EPIC invested in model homes. Model homes were purchased in advance from capital-needy builders who, in turn, leased the homes from EPIC until they could be sold.

When the FSLIC reviewed Community Savings' application for federal insurance, the financial institution was ordered to 'spin-off' the mortgage and other real estate investments before it could be certified for federal insurance. Word of the low quality of the investments held by EPIC caused a depositor run at its bank subsidiary.[96]

The problems with the EPIC mortgages and other troubled real estate

94 See 70 *BNA Wash. Fin. Rep.*, vol. 45, 7/22/85, at 135.
95 See *American Banker*, 15 April 1985.
96 See *American Banker*, 26 August 1985.

investments held by or affiliated with banking institutions, present significant problems for those who argue for further 'deregulation' of depository institutions. Safety and soundness concerns have predominated the financial services scene this year. If banks are to expand the level of risk to which they are exposed by engaging in more insurance and real estate activity, increased supervision of the portfolios and management decisions of these institutions may be necessary, at least as long as FSLIC or FDIC insurance is available on deposits at these institutions. No one now seriously argues that the system could survive with only private or state insurance. So long as federal insurance is involved, federal oversight, standards and examinations will continue. As in the Maryland EPIC case, troubled or insolvent institutions who have invested in low-quality real estate products may need an institution the size of Chase Manhattan to bail them out through acquisition. The number of bail-outs that larger banks can afford is limited by their own loan losses and related problems. Accordingly, continued reliance on federal insurance indicates that more re-regulation, rather than deregulation, is in the offing. Expansion by banks into other fields such as insurance is still possible, the Fed notwithstanding. These pressures will continue and the future remains unclear. Congressional action still remains unlikely in the immediate future.

Banks and Mutual Funds

Thus far, banks have been acting as advisers, sub-advisers, administrators, record keepers, transfer agents and custodians, but have been blocked from 'sponsoring' or underwriting (distributing) mutual funds. The Fed has issued regulations designed to prevent the use of names, logos, banks facilities and personnel in the sale of fund shares. None the less, new arrangements are blossoming and are being carried as close to the Glass–Steagall line as possible – that is, with banks doing everything but distribution.

Thus, the *Wall Street Journal*, in a 22 January 1985 round-up of activity, reported that US Trust and Marine Midland planned to start stock mutual funds; distribution would presumably be done through brokers. Fidelity Investors (FMR) planned a stock fund to be managed by a bank. Shearson/American Express, Dreyfus and Federated were also either planning to sell or are selling stock mutual funds through major banks.

Even though the Fed prohibits use of similar names, Security Pacific uses 'Pacific Horizons Funds'; Marine Midland uses 'Mariner Funds'; US Trust uses 'UST Master Fund'; and Morgan Stanley uses the 'Pierpont Funds' managed by Morgan Guaranty Trust. Chase Manhattan advises 'Park Avenue Funds', distributed by Dreyfus. The *Wall Street Journal* (1/22/85) commented:

> To date, the results haven't been impressive. A mailing to 2.3 million Security Pacific Corp. customers last year netted only about $3 million in stock fund sales for individual retirement accounts. And Wells Fargo & Co. also raised only $3 million, far less than expected. 'Stocks aren't of real interest at the

moment,' says Howard Stein, chairman of Dreyfus, which distributed the Security Pacific funds.

But other industry executives predict a resurgence of financial assets as disinflation reduces the allure of real assets. 'In the long run, I believe the public is going to come back into the stock market through mutual funds,' says Barton Biggs, managing director of Morgan Stanley.

The potential for a bank-sponsored, fully underwritten, bank-distributed fund must await a change in Glass–Steagall, but the tide seems to be lapping at the sea wall.

On the commingled IRA front, where Citibank sought to market commingled IRA accounts to customers, a DC federal court rejected the ICI's challenge. Citibank's plan had been approved by the Comptroller as not violating the Glass–Steagall Act. Previously, a California federal court struck down a similar arrangement. The controversy will in all likelihood soon be heard by the Supreme Court.

In *ICI* v. *Conover*,[97] the US District Court for the Northern District of California considered a challenge to the legality of two OCC rulings approving proposals by two national banks to establish collective investment funds for individual retirement accounts, exempt from taxation under the Employee Retirement Income Security Act (ERISA). The ICI claimed that the rulings authorizing defendants Wells Fargo Bank and Bank of California to create mutual funds were in violation of the Glass–Steagall prohibitions against the marketing of securities by commercial banks. Wells Fargo and Bank of California responded that the approved programmes would not establish mutual funds, but common trust funds, which do not violate the Glass–Steagall Act and are expressly authorized by ERISA.

The District Court first considered whether the ICI had standing to sue, and then took up the merits of the claim. The court held that the ICI had standing because, although the Glass–Steagall Act's purpose was not to protect bank competitors, the plaintiffs fell within the 'zone of protected interests' test. The court further found that the Comptroller's rulings had to be set aside because the approved funds were investments prohibited under the Glass–Steagall Act.

The court came to its decision by applying the text outlined in *ICI* v. *Camp*, 401 US 617 (1971). Thus, the court examined whether the assets to be commingled in the defendant banks would be received for a 'true fiduciary purpose rather than for investment'. Here, the court found that the banks would not be retaining exclusive fiduciary responsibility for the common trusts; instead, the funds would be highly liquid and open to management by the potential IRA purchaser.

In the other ICI suit,[98] the District Court for the District of Columbia

97 *Investment Company Institute* v. *Conover*, 593 F. Supp 846 (Dist. Ct, N.D. California, 1984).

98 *ICI* v. *Conover*, 596 F. Supp. 1496 (D.D.C., 1984).

heard the challenge to the OCC ruling approving Citibank's plan to establish an IRA programme similar to those challenged in California. The District Court upheld the OCC ruling, noting that the Comptroller's interpretation of Glass–Steagall is entitled to great weight.

The court found that the Comptroller's ruling showed a reasonable interpretation of the Glass–Steagall Act. Glass–Steagall does not expressly prohibit national banks from establishing collective investment trusts for IRA trust assets, the court found, and the Citibank plan presents none of the hazards which Glass–Steagall was designed to prevent. The court saw no major risk to the safety and soundness of the institution from the IRA programme. The court also found minimal danger to the bank's reputation and minimal hazards to the bank from its promotional interests in the IRA programme. Hence, the court ruled that the hazards the Glass–Steagall Act intended to prevent were not raised by banks offering IRA programmes.

The Supreme Court may eventually hear and resolve the controversy. Presently, many banks offer IRAs. These accounts are popular for their tax advantages. Indeed, mutual fund distributors, insurance companies, banks and S&Ls all participate heavily in the IRA market. Few legislators would want to eliminate the tax incentives for opening retirement accounts. Whether the banks are performing a traditional trust function or using the IRA programme as a foot in the door of securities distribution may depend on the view of the observer. The view of the Supreme Court will be crucial and could have a broader effect than on just IRAs, if the court undertakes to draw specific Glass–Steagall lines.

NEW PRODUCTS

The following brief references indicate some of the new product developments which have an impact in the financial services area.

Flexible Premium Variable Life Insurance

For a description of products combining mutual fund features with variable life insurance, see 16 *BNA SRLR*, pp. 1787–8. SEC Exemptive Rule 6e–3(T) exempts the new product from the 9 per cent load limitations of the 1940 Act. See also SEC proposals for safe-harbour from registration for certain annuities (guaranteed investment contracts and single payment deferred annuities) meeting specific tests (16 *BNA SRLR*, at p. 1826).

Videotex – Home Banking and Securities

AT&T introduced a 5lb, low-cost videotex terminal to provide electronic information services to consumers. The new videotex product is part of an AT&T new joint venture with Chemical Bank, Bank of America and Time

Inc. The terminal is designed for the individual who is averse to buying or using a microcomputer. AT&T announced that the terminal would be priced 'substantially below' the cheapest microcomputers on the market (e.g., Atari, Commodore).[99] Chemical's Pronto home banking service is to be a major component of the new service.[100] Schwab & Co. recently announced a home trading and information system labelled SMARTS, also using home-based IBM and Apple computers.

Point-of-Sale (POS)

There have been various supermarket experiments with POS.[101] The use of POS terminals for direct deductions from cheque or banking accounts is aimed at replacing paper cheques. The use of debit cards has met resistance from consumers who do not want to lose the float on their cheques or credit cards. Supermarket transactions are usually cash, however, and thus offer a possible attraction. On the other hand, oil companies have instituted a system of discounts for cash. Use of a debit card would be the functional equivalent of cash and would apparently qualify for a discount. Supermarkets that normally do not accept credit cards for groceries would not be expected to adopt a two-tier pricing system.

Market studies of the popular response to the supermarket POS systems appear favourable. Studies have found that US households are sending fewer members out to the supermarket. These persons have less time to shop and are increasingly employed and educated. The studies suggest that POS systems will be received favourably by most consumers.[102]

Some smaller banks, however, are resisting the introduction of supermarket ATMs. Canadaigua National Bank and Trust is appealing to the Supreme Court against a decision by the Second Circuit,[103] which ruled that an ATM is not necessarily a branch of a national bank, even if the bank's customers use the machine. In the Canadaigua case, the supermarket owned the ATM, as distinguished from the bank in earlier cases.[104]

Mutual Funds that Invest in Mutual Funds
(Son of 'Fund of Funds')

Bank advised 'fund of funds' have been formed, aimed at smaller regional banks as vehicles for fund trust departments and retirement accounts. (For

---

99   *American Banker*, 25 June 1985.
100   *New York Times*, 5 February 1985.
101   See discussion in *American Banker*, 1 November and 2 November 1984.
102   *American Banker*, 1 March 1985.
103   *IBAA, Canadaigua Bank & Trust Co.* v. *Marine Midland Bank*, 757 F. 2d 453 (2nd Cir., 1985), pet. for cert. filed.
104   *American Banker*, 17 July 1985.

example, Fund-Trust advised by Republic National Bank (NY) and distributed by Furman, Selz et al.) The bank tie-in makes this product particularly interesting in this context.

Also, Vanguard's Special Tax-Advantaged Retirement Fund (STAR), which invests in four existing Vanguard-sponsored funds, was approved by the SEC on a no-load, no-management fee basis. The fund is aimed at the retirement plan market. (The SEC authorized the Vanguard application by a 3–2 vote, reflecting some of the SEC's historic antipathy to fund layering. In this situation, the risk seems fairly minimal and the advantage to the investor real enough to support a public interest argument).

Mutual Fund–Bank Card Brokerage Packages

CMA-type accounts (central asset accounts), including Merrill's offering of insurance on money market account instruments, are expanding. Next is the linking of CMAs to ATM networks. Merrill has well over one million CMAs. American Express, which has been slow to link its vast card base to Shearson's financial services offerings, is expected to announce some measured moves in this direction, although there is reported to be some reluctance by American Express executives to mix the two. There is some fear that bad investment results would reflect on Amexco's card.

Sears introduced its new Discover card this August. The Discover card is Sears' version of a VISA card; the card will carry an interest rate of 19.8 per cent. Other card-issuing companies had feared that Sears would try to undercut banks on its card's interest rate, but the Discover card was introduced within the rate range of its competitors. The Discover card package includes no annual fee; a rebate of up to 1 per cent of the customer's total annual purchases; a tiered savings account with access by cheque; and merchant discounts.[105]

J. C. Penney appears to be slowly expanding its activities in the financial services field. In April, Penney announced the opening of its financial services centres in four San Jose, California stores. The centres will begin accepting applications for unsecured loans of $1,000 to $10,000 offered by Security Pacific Finance Corp., and applications for auto loans and leasing from Security Pacific Credit Corp.[106]

CONCLUSIONS

This brief overview has attempted to highlight some of the current complex jurisdictional and industry problems receiving attention in the United States. The following conclusions can be drawn.

105 *American Banker*, 21 August 1985.
106 *American Banker*, 12 April 1985.

(1) The role and powers of banks will remain a major subject of legislative attention, but definitive legislation is not likely in the 1985–6 (99th) Congress. The attempt to deal with the regulatory structure through the Bush Task Group proposals, which are now undergoing review by Treasury and OMB, will also remain a focus of attention. Eventually, the Administration's review of its financial regulatory posture should yield a package of legislative proposals. The failure to produce such a package until now has obviously delayed Congressional action in this area. At present, there is no specific Administration programme on restructuring, the support for the Bush programme among the regulators having evaporated shortly after its publication. A new group of regulators is now in office or about to come into office. This includes a new Treasury Secretary, Mr Baker; a new Comptroller, Mr Clarke; a new FDIC chairman, Mr Seidman; and a new team at the Treasury. Some of these people may have modifications or changes of their own to propose. The longer legislative action is delayed, the less likely a Congressional rollback of new bank powers or interstate initiatives becomes. Litigation, however, has been used effectively to stop the proliferation of nonbank banks, reducing the pressure on Congress to act. Without some further Congressional action, the nonbank bank dispute seems resolved on the federal level, at least insofar as the Fed and the Comptroller are concerned, unless the Supreme Court acts on the US Trust petition and/or uses the opportunity in *Dimension Financial* to indicate its position on nonbank banks. The FDIC may decide to permit state nonbank banks to operate on the theory that they are not constrained by the federal court decisions thus far. State action remains a way in which interstate banking can be pursued and the developments in the states could be dramatic. (See, for example, discussion of regional compacts below.)

(2) Deregulation suffers as crises occur with disturbing regularity. The Ohio–Maryland S&L failures seem to have killed any prospects for much deregulation of thrifts, or for bank deregulation, which was severely impacted by Continental Illinois. It appears that tighter scrutiny of bank loan practices, investment risks and diversification is in the offing. The review of the depository insurance system is well under way and proposals are unlikely to give states or private insurance any significant role. Indeed, state insured banks and thrifts are likely to be phased out (as in Maryland and Ohio). These events could hurt the loosening of controls over bank powers and territorial requirements. The increased number of projected bank and thrift failures makes strengthening of the deposit insurance system a top priority – even more than in 1984.

(3) Meanwhile, bank efforts to penetrate new markets and offer new products continue. Efforts by banks to enter the securities underwriting market will continue, but face obvious Glass–Steagall issues. The FDIC proposals would substantially open the door to non-member banks' nonbanking activities, including underwriting and real estate. Glass–Steagall is an issue here as well. The 'South Dakota insurance loophole' seems to have been closed by recent Fed action, denying a Citicorp request to sell insurance through a South

Dakota state bank. Insurance companies and agents continue to resist bank efforts to offer insurance products, but insurance companies acquire bank capabilities of their own. Real estate is another active area. Real estate agents, like the insurance agents, seek protection from bank competition. Recent thrift failures related to real estate speculation and other activities may slow down any movement on this front.

(4) Interstate banking gains through the spread of ATM networks LPOs, interstate compacts and other devices, but there is continued resistance on every front – in the courts, the legislatures, the Congress and before the regulators. The Supreme Court's ruling on interstate compacts (*Northeast*) is the major recent development, triggering a spate of regional bank mergers and realignments. As noted above, the use of nonbank banks as an interstate banking mechanism has been stopped on the federal level in the courts, at least for the present. The power disputes remain unresolved.

(5) Mutual funds remain strong competitors for banks, who are now themselves entering the fund arena as investment advisers, sub-advisers, servicing agents or in other related roles, avoiding distribution – barely, in some cases – in order to come within the Glass–Steagall constraints.

(6) Banks enter the brokerage business, at least the discount brokerage business, and state banks may go even further. The expansion of state bank powers could gain momentum and importance (see discussion of underwriting above). Meanwhile, the SEC proposes to register bank personnel who act as brokers. Banks object vehemently. Functional regulation may work as a theory; we shall soon see how it works in practice.

(7) The role of the retailers may turn out to be crucial. Sears is fully into the financial services area with financial centres in major stores and a full-blown campaign for its new Discover card. American Express is slower in adopting financial service strategies, but the potential is there, and recent advertisements indicate some movement. J. C. Penney is studying its options, including its large credit card base, although it withdrew from a recent videotex test joint venture. Supermarkets' POS/ATM links may be the next arena for expansion of banking/investment services through retail networks. Banks are carefully watching the supermarkets, and retail chains move to own the terminals and set the terms for their use. This could portend a significant struggle over who runs the linked POS/ATM systems and constitute a major challenge to the position of the banks in the payments system.

(8) Fidelity, Merrill Lynch, Prudential Bache and other financial 'retailers' are moving ahead with technology, state nonbank banks and other marketing strategies. Fund managers have adopted new 12b–1 strategies, aimed at keeping distributors of funds shares interested in the product. Meanwhile, the SEC is reviewing the use and abuse of s.28(e), 'paying up' for research by institutions.

(9) The role of credit unions, with $100 billion in deposits and 48 million members, is yet to be assessed.

The financial services world is expanding and changing, with velocity and in all directions. The ability of Congress to affect these developments diminishes as time passes; new developments take root. Some regulatory agencies encourage expansion, while others demur. Courts issue opinions and regulatory agencies promulgate rules and pass on applications. New products and strategies are devised. The failure of Congress to act shifts the controversies to the courts for *ad hoc* determinations and to the agencies for policy development. The Supreme Court rules in favour of interstate banking compacts and other federal court rulings stop, at least for the present, the Comptroller's attempt to achieve interstate branching through nonbank banks (but watch the FDIC...). The next session of Congress is unlikely to resolve the critical issues of bank powers and territorial expansion. Nor does Congress seem ready to act on the Bush regulatory reform proposals. The Administration itself is still reviewing its policies, although prospects remain good for at least a general reaffirmation by Secretary Baker of White House Chief of Staff Donald Regan's policies favouring the interstate banking and additional bank powers which he initiated as Secretary of the Treasury.[107] None the less, the changes in major agencies and the new team at the Treasury may cast some doubt on such an outcome. Events could overtake policy positions; it is difficult to predict any particular outcome with certainty. This remains a time of fluidity and uncertainty in financial services policies, with conflicting pressures and policies still contending for one outcome or another.

It is not really a question of deregulation, but of what policy should be adopted in the allocation of powers and the rearrangement of existing regulatory structures. On that important matter, there is no Congressional consensus, no agreement among the industries involved and only partial agreement among the regulators. Clearly, neither the Bush proposals nor any others dealing with the reallocation or rationalization of regulatory powers have any chance without the resolution of substantive issues like those relating to powers and interstate banking. The prospect for the delineation of a rational, comprehensive and reasonable financial services policy does not yet appear very bright. The need for such a policy and its implementation is compelling; indeed, it is urgent – particularly in the depository insurance areas. Congressional hearings on the Bush Report were begun in September 1985 before the House Government Operations Subcommittee. The Committee rounded up the 'usual suspects' as witnesses. Nothing much happened. No one expects quick action. Unfortunately the question is, will there be *any* action? And if not now, when?

---

107 See, for example, *Legal Times*, 9 November 1984, 'Marinaccio, Glass–Steagall erosion raises key policy choices', for a critical view of developments.

AUTHOR'S NOTE

The opinions expressed herein are those of the author and do not necessarily reflect the official views of the Center on Financial Services or the University of California, Berkeley.

4

On the Empirical Detection
of Financial Innovation

DONALD D. HESTER

INTRODUCTION

Innovations in financial intermediation have strikingly altered the ways in which borrowers and lenders are served during the past decade. New assets and liabilities have appeared, and the speed and quality of services associated with existing assets and liabilities have improved markedly. Innovations occur for reasons that have been described by many authors (e.g., Hester, 1985). Financial market deregulation, which is itself partly a consequence of innovation, has further changed and expanded the channels through which borrowers and lenders transact. The continuing high rate of technical progress in information processing and retrieval and secondary consequences of deregulation and legislation strongly suggest that relations between borrowers and lenders will change further in unpredictable ways in the coming years.

Regulatory agencies and designers of monetary policy must keep abreast of current practices and modify their procedures as change is recognized. The present report proposes procedures for detecting commercial bank innovations in data that the Federal Reserve collects. The Federal Reserve and other bank regulatory agencies have access to substantially larger quantities of data than are considered here and receive additional information from examiners and the public that is invaluable in assessing changing practices. Indeed, there is so much information that identifying what is important and what requires a policy response is the major activity of agency research staffs. Data-based procedures that flag changes at an early stage should improve their performances and result in a quicker response. Nothing in what follows should be taken as an argument for reducing the need for additional data collection and analysis.

Bank portfolios and procedures are affected by many variables in market economies. Business cycles cause the demand for credit to rise and fall. Monetary policy induces changes in bank reserves and interest rates. Wars and other international shocks affect a country's financial institutions. None of these represent technical change or necessarily lead to a change in technology. When the cycle, policy move or international shock subsides, portfolios and procedures may revert to their previous state. A distinguishing characteristic of technical progress is that changes are *irreversible*.

A textbook example conveniently illustrates the statistical implications of irreversible change. Consider:

$$Q_d = a - bP + u \tag{1}$$
$$Q_s = c + dP + et + v \tag{2}$$
$$Q_d = Q_s \tag{3}$$

where Q, P and t respectively denote quantity per period, price and technology and u and v are random variables with expectation zero and finite variances. The supply function slips southwesterly as technical progress occurs. Because the demand function is assumed to be time-invariant, the probability of observing a high value of P or a low value of Q declines as innovations occur. If there is no technical progress, the probability of observing arbitrary values of P and Q has no trend. A test for an innovation follows immediately from these facts.

Financial intermediaries provide services whose values are not accurately determined by accountants. Bank balance sheets are measured frequently and accurately, if one accepts arbitrary accounting conventions. To design a test for the presence of technical progress, it would be necessary to assume a relation between assets or liabilities and the value of banking services. Suppose that the value of banking services is proportional to the levels of different assets and liabilities on a bank's balance sheet, with unique factors of proportionality for each. Then a hypothesis that technical progress exists could be tested by whether or not value added by banks rises relative to total bank assets, once allowance is made for variations in portfolio composition. The test might be very misleading because no adjustment has been made for the rising demand for banking services and deposits. Controlling for fluctuations in demand would require heroic assumptions about portfolio preferences.

Fortunately, for the purpose of understanding how monetary policy has been qualified by innovations, this traditional notion of technical progress as enhancing factor productivity is not required. Instead one is concerned with measuring the impact and predictability of the effect of a change in the monetary base on GNP. So long as changes in the monetary base are transformed into changes in bank liabilities in approximately fixed proportions and the relations between these monetary aggregates and GNP (income velocities) are constant, it is possible to argue that traditional measures of technical progress in intermediation are irrelevant.

It is, of course, true that income velocities of monetary aggregates are quite unstable. Indeed, year-to-year variability in income velocities of money is larger than year-to-year variability in corresponding monetary aggregates (Hester, 1981, pp. 178–9). As well as being the largest component of the monetary base, currency in the hands of the public is essentially uncontrollable, unless monetary authorities choose to promote artificial and ineffective coin shortages or queues at banks.

The remaining linkage that may be vulnerable to the possibility of financial innovation is the relation between reserves and bank liabilities. The question studied in the present paper is: has the mixture of demand deposits and other reservable time and savings deposits in bank portfolios irreversibly shifted when interest rates are high or rising with the effect of weakening the thrust of monetary policy? The study uses techniques suggested by the foregoing textbook example, but without formally controlling for interest rates.

In the next section an extended discussion of technical change and its evidential tracks is presented. The third section views the problem of inferring the presence of innovation from macroeconomic series, and the fourth describes the gains from studying the same problem with panel data. The fifth section concludes and indicates how innovations appear to have been translated into bank portfolios.

TECHNICAL CHANGE AND ITS OBSERVABILITY

Technology is unobservable. Changes in the application of technology are uninteresting if they leave no empirical trail; only changes that have empirical consequences are the concern of this paper. Because change is ill-defined, an optimal experimental design for its detection cannot be specified in general. However, changes that are important for implementing monetary policy can be catalogued. A non-exhaustive list of changes that have expansionary effects is:

1   A change that increases the volume of transactions that can be effected with a given stock of outside money.
2   A change that increases the speed with which new savings and amortization flows are converted into physical capital.
3   A change that increases the amount of capital that individuals are willing to hold either directly or through agents.
4   A change that increases the willingness of individuals or institutions to acquire risky assets or generally to assume risks.
5   A change that reduces the amount of risks that individuals and institutions perceive to fall upon themselves.
6   A change that increases the number of individuals or projects that can be financed by savers.

Innovations that fall into one or more of these categories are typically associated with the introduction of a new asset or organization or the introduction of some new expediting procedure. I also interpret entry by existing firms in a non-financial industry or by foreign enterprises as a financial market innovation.

Accounting practices are rarely capable of depicting new products or assets clearly enough to place them on balance sheets or income statements as they emerge. Similarly, new firms that differ from existing industry elements are not likely to be incorporated in sample designs. For anti-competitive and anti-regulatory reasons, details about new operating procedures are not likely to be clearly revealed in public documents; many will always be kept hidden by creating subsidiaries and through other creative accounting methods.

Interest rates that clear financial markets reflect the combined effects of monetary and fiscal policies, real shocks to private sector supplies of and demands for funds, changes in regulations, and innovations. The activities of speculators and arbitrageurs cause interest rates on different assets to move conformingly and, as Shiller (1979) has reported, with surprisingly similar amplitudes at different maturities. However, as noted respectively by Hester (1981) and Artis and associates (1978, p. 46), institutional arrangements involving US repurchase agreements and British reserve requirements do cause distortions to appear when monetary policy is restrictive. In both cases Treasury bill rates failed to keep pace with rising interest rates on other assets. The appearance of such gaps in the structure of interest rates indicates stress in financial markets that may lead to innovations. Arbitrageurs and speculators profit from closing such gaps; innovators also reinforce the law of one price. If anything, the *disappearance* of an interest rate gap indicates that an innovation has occurred or that some binding regulation has been eliminated.

Changes in the ratios of assets and liabilities on bank balance sheets may indicate ongoing financial innovation, particularly if the changes do not disappear when interest rates take on typical historical values. The innovation may have been an improvement in services offered by banks or other firms. Changes in ratios may also have been caused by changes in portfolio preferences by private investors. The source of changes is important for regulatory agencies, since safeguards and rules must constantly be revised to maintain the integrity of the payments mechanism. However, for monetary policy, the source of change is important only insofar as it affects one or more of the elements in the foregoing list. For example, a decline in the proportion of bank liabilities that are chequeable and subject to high reserve requirements implies that bank assets are rising more than proportionately with bank reserves. To the extent that bank liabilities are viewed as being a low risk and convenient form to hold physical capital indirectly, an expansionary impulse is transmitted to the economy. It matters little whether the source of this change is greater willingness to hold assets indirectly or a new breakthrough in cheque clearing. A more restrictive monetary policy stance must be adopted, if aggregate demand is not to increase.

In this paper, weekly balance sheets reporting 54 constituent assets and liabilities for the approximately 320 largest US commercial banks are studied over the years 1965–76. Both aggregate and individual bank data are analysed. Data are taken at the close of a reserve accounting week. While the balance sheets disclose portfolios in considerable detail, long-term assets are not necessarily valued at current market prices. For this reason it is desirable to emphasize bank liabilities and short-term assets when doing empirical research. For the most part attention is restricted to liabilities of individuals, partnerships and corporations (IPC).

What other criteria should be used to select variables for study? Three seem promising. First, because bank liabilities are subject to substantially differing reserve requirements, it is desirable to choose liabilities according to the reserve requirements that are applicable. Specifically, IPC demand, savings, and other time deposits and large denomination negotiable certificates of deposit are examined.

A second criterion is the extent to which portfolio measures serve as transactions media or indicate transactions activity. Candidate variables include federal funds purchased and funds acquired through repurchase agreements, IPC demand deposits and cash items in the process of collection.

Third is the extent to which liabilities are subject to binding interest rate ceilings and other regulatory controls. When market interest rates rise, these ceilings become increasingly onerous and are likely to spawn innovations as argued above. Variables include all types of IPC deposits, other liabilities, and federal funds purchased and funds acquired through repurchase agreements.

The strategy followed in the remainder of this paper is to analyse patterns of movements in these variables in an attempt to recognize the occurrence of innovations early on. It is implemented by posing some rather naive null hypotheses and then testing each week to see whether they are rejected. If a null hypothesis is rejected, it is inferred that one or more innovations have occurred. The nature of the innovation and its policy consequences must be determined by other methods; the goal here is only detection. The power of the tests depends on the properties of the process that generates changes in the variables being studied and on the likelihood that an innovation would affect them. The method is similar to testing the null hypothesis that the quality of output from a production process has not deteriorated, except that both tails of the distribution are relevant in the present instance.

The naive hypotheses are stated in terms of weekly changes in different assets and liabilities or in the ratio of them to total assets.[1] The simplest

1 The ratio form of the hypotheses is considered because it is a simple device for correcting for conspicuous trends in bank assets. However, it is troublesome because double-entry bookkeeping implies that shocks to some asset (or liability) appear in some other asset (or liability) or in the total. In the latter case both the numerator and the denominator are affected; tests are weakened because the distribution of changes tends to be skewed and kurtotic. One cannot correct for this distortion without *a priori* information about the extent to which different assets and liabilities serve as absorbing buffers.

hypothesis involves weekly changes in some variable over spans of time ranging from one to thirteen weeks. In a trendless 'pure white noise' process, the probability that a series would increase (or decrease) in a week is 0.5, in two consecutive weeks, 0.25, etc. Long strings of isosign changes indicate with a high probability that some innovation has occurred. For reasons suggested above (see n.1), changes in different series are not likely to be independent. The plan is to examine the number of consecutive isosign changes over periods of one to thirteen weeks following each week.

The test is weak when conspicuous trends are evident in a series or when a series has a large seasonal component. In principle, the procedure could be applied to a de-trended or de-seasonalized series. Such 'prewhitening', of course, consumes observations and raises embarrassing questions about the source of the trend or seasonal; removing either is not a trivial or innocent undertaking. In an attempt to maintain a purely historically data-based procedure, a variation of the basic procedure is attempted and reported. It is a 'forgiving' procedure that tabulates sequences with no more than one sign reversal. This nullifies arbitrary window dressing events and roughly allows for seasonal events that have an effect which does not last more than one week.

The sequence of signs method is illustrated in table 4.1. It is assumed in the table that the null hypothesis is true and that experiments are performed on up to four banks for up to seven periods. In each period each bank is shocked with a random number drawn from an i.i.d. process. The upper triangles in the first column show the probability under the null hypothesis that one would observe a sequence of positive (or negative) changes of the length given by a row index for a single bank. The upper triangle in the second column shows corresponding probabilities for two banks, etc. The lower triangles show analogous probabilities when the forgiving procedure is employed – i.e., when each bank is allowed to have at most one sign reversal. The forgiving procedure substantially reduces the power of tests of whether the null hypothesis can be rejected, but also is likely to eliminate distortionary noise that occurs in banking data.

If the method is applied to aggregative banking data and the foregoing assumptions are satisfied, a sequence of more than four isosigned changes (or seven with the forgiving procedure) would indicate that the null hypothesis should be rejected at the 0.05 level of significance. Indeed, changes of four and seven are probably critical if the ratio form of the model is tested. When the test is applied repeatedly in successive weeks, as occurs below, one should anticipate obtaining some false 'significant' occurrences. About one out of 20 independent trials should reject the null hypothesis at the 5 per cent level when it is, in fact, true.

For panel data, the interpretation is somewhat messier. Table 4.1 reports probabilities that each of the number of banks shown along the top has consecutive isosign changes over a period whose length is given by a row index. However, in a sample of, say, 320 banks perhaps four will have eight consecutive positive changes, ten will have seven, etc. Also it is likely that others

TABLE 4.1 Probability of observing positive changes or mostly positive changes when null hypothesis of no change is valid

		Number of banks observed			
		1	2	3	4
Number of periods observed	1	.500 / 1.000	.250 / 1.000	.125 / 1.000	.063 / 1.000
	2	.250 / .750	.063 / .563	.016 / .422	.004 / .316
	3	.125 / .500	.016 / .250	.002 / .125	~ / .063
	4	.063 / .313	.004 / .098	~ / .031	~ / .010
	5	.031 / .188	.001 / .035	~ / .007	~ / .001
	6	.016 / .109	~ / .012	~ / .001	~ / ~
	7	.008 / .063	~ / .004	~ / ~	~ / ~

Upper triangle indicates probability when all banks observed have positive changes. Lower triangle indicates probability when at most one negative change is observed.

will simultaneously have consecutive negative changes. The problem can be simplified by assuming that the distribution of changes is symmetrical; then attention can be focused on net changes.

The null hypothesis that the cross-sectional distribution of some variable or ratio is unchanging can be tested in a variety of ways. For example, the probability that in a single period, say, 215 banks experience increases and 105 decreases with an unchanging distribution is low. Using the normal approximation to the binomial distribution and assuming that the probability of the variable increasing is 0.5, such an outcome is 6.15 standard deviations from the expected null hypothesis value of 160. Additional tests, which are clearly not independent of this first one, can be performed by looking at the number of net two-consecutive changes etc., with or without forgiving. By monitoring a battery of such tests over a few weeks, an investigator should soon amass overwhelming evidence of the occurrence or non-occurrence of an innovation. With knowledge of the diffusion process, more powerful tests that combine tests of changes over different time horizons should be possible. In the present paper attention is restricted to testing simple hypotheses.

In addition, the sign of the cumulative change in the variable or ratio is recorded over the same spans. This second measure weighs large single-week changes heavily. Innovations that have a large impact in a single week would not be detected by the preceding tests, but are potentially as important for interpreting monetary events. This second criterion detects innovations that are picked up by the sequence of signs statistical test, and is useful for identifying reversibility. It is especially vulnerable to the presence of trends, and thus can only serve as a secondary confirmatory measure when searching for innovations.

Before turning to applications, one should briefly consider why resorting to such mechanistic procedures is necessary for detecting innovations. Are there are no other easy macroeconomic criteria that automatically flag the occurrence of an innovation? Three candidates come to mind. First, since innovations are in part a consequence of the struggle for profits by financial intermediaries and others, stock market prices may reveal their occurrence. In efficient markets investors are rewarded for ferreting out news about substantial changes in a firm's profits. The difficulty with this approach is that an innovation that is important for monetary control may have relatively little effect on a firm's or industry's profits. Also, stock prices are bombarded by many other shocks than innovations. The signal-to-noise ratio of stock prices as an indicator of an innovation is likely to be too low for their movements to be very discriminating.

Second, a sudden shift in asset market shares among intermediaries must surely indicate that some change has occurred. Possibly so, but market shares are reported with considerable delay and markets are notoriously difficult to define analytically. Further, an innovation may have occurred precisely to deter entry by a potential rival. An innovation that successfully deters entrance may be very important for conducting monetary policy, but leaves no market share trace.

Third, Goldfeld (1976), and subsequently other researchers, have looked at changes in the accuracy of predictions made using macroeconometric structural equations, especially the demand function for money. Goldfeld's analysis is a model of excellent econometric technique, but it is forensic post-mortem pathology rather than preventive detection. Goldfeld was not concerned so much with identifying emergent structural shifts as with explaining what had actually happened. He and Quandt (1973) have studied switching regime models, which are more in the spirit of the present exercise. Such methods require several observations on both regimes. Analysis of aggregative structural equation residuals or prediction errors may suggest that an innovation has occurred, but usually several quarters of data would be required. Here the emphasis is on exploiting high frequency data so that an early diagnosis can be made.

SIGNAL EXTRACTION FROM AGGREGATIVE WEEKLY SERIES

In this section aggregative data for the population of weekly reporting banks are studied using the techniques just described. Data are for the period January 1965 to December 1975 or for the shorter intervals in which some variables were actually measured. Because 14 observations are required to examine long sequences of changes, the maximum span reported is 560 weeks.

In addition to the unavailability of some series for part of the period, definitions on reporting forms were occasionally revised over this 11 year span. However, no revisions occurred between June 1969 and March 1976. Attention is largely confined to this period.

Table 4.2 reports summary statistics for ten variables that were explicitly or implicitly discussed above. The second column reports the time span for which the series is available and used in subsequent columns of the table. The third column shows the net balance of the signs of 13-week differences, i.e. the number of times that an item's value 13 weeks in the future exceeded its value in week t. The fourth and fifth columns respectively report the number of times that a series showed four consecutive positive and negative signs. The next two columns report the number of times a sequence of six changes was detected in which at most one was either negative or positive; the eighth and ninth columns report the same information for a series of seven consecutive changes. The first ten rows of the table concern weekly changes in the ratio of a series to total weekly reporting bank assets. The final three rows are first differences in the dollar levels of the indicated series.

The levels version of the series is dominated by trends that have little to do with innovation. The patterns differ considerably from their ratio counterparts, and are not considered further in this paper.

The third column in the top part of the table broadly repeats what is known about trends in individual series. Cash items in the process of collection, reserves, and demand and savings deposits fell over the period relative to total assets. For the first five series the number of reported consecutive changes that were all or nearly all positive (or negative) seems quite small in comparison to what one should expect from an examination of table 4.1. Under the assumption that signs of changes are i.i.d., one should expect a series of four consecutive plus (or minus) signs to occur once in 16 draws, even when no structural shifts had occurred. One should expect to observe approximately 18 sequences each of four positive and negative changes in a series of 560 draws.[2]

---

2   To see this, decompose the 560 weekly changes into 112 non-overlapping draws of five observations. Restricting attention to these sequences, the expected number of either positive or negative change series is $0.0625 \times 112 = 7$. However, there are an additional 448 sequences that are constructed by combining adjacent elements of these 112 draws. These 448 also include several isosign sequences of length 4. A labour-intensive enumeration of the possible sequences across one of the 111 divisions yields an expectation of an additional 10.84 isosign length four sequences, for both positive and negative changes.

TABLE 4.2 Summary measures for macro data on weekly reporting banks

Item	Span (wk)	Net sign changes over 13 wk	4-wk consecutive		Forgiving method Six wk		Seven wk	
			+	−	+	−	+	−
1 Cash items in the process of collection	560	−32	1	3	4	16	0	4
2 Reserves on deposit at Federal Reserve	560	−46	4	9	11	29	4	10
3 Federal funds sold and reverse repos	327	59	4	3	9	10	3	3
4 Federal funds purchased and repos	327	61	3	1	14	16	6	5
5 Net funds acquired through federal funds market and repos (4–3)	327	63	5	4	13	20	2	7
6 IPC demand deposits	560	−170	8	18	15	28	5	11
7 IPC savings deposits	560	−238	9	14	21	21	5	9
8 IPC certificates of deposit	483	75	41	34	55	42	36	35
9 IPC time deposits	560	176	18	10	51	17	24	9
10 Other liabilities	547	43	17	20	28	45	14	29
11 Net funds acquired through federal funds market and repos	327	115	5	1	13	15	4	3
12 IPC demand deposits	560	176	16	20	22	27	12	12
13 IPC savings deposits	560	154	171	76	79	56	72	47

Items 1–10 expressed as ratios to total assets; items 11–13 expressed as dollar levels.

Several reasons can be suggested for why isosign sequences are so sparse in these series. All, of course, constitute interpretations for why series may not be outputs from a white noise process. First, for much of the period bank reserve requirements were settled on a lagged basis with one- or two-week settlement intervals, and it was possible to carry forward a limited surplus or deficit position for one week. This may have caused a first-order negative autoregressive process to be induced on the first five variables in the table. Second, as the systems approach of Forrester seemed to demonstrate in the Club of Rome simulations (Meadows, 1972), economic models that ignore the feedback from prices are seriously mis-specified. In the present context interest rate and aggregate changes should be studied simultaneously. Third, seasonal factors and especially end-of-month payment cycles dominate weekly fluctuations and also serve to induce a negative autoregressive process on interbank transactions media. Finally, the Federal Reserve was in a position to monitor and neutralize any trends in these series; its interventions may have obscured ongoing innovations.

A very similar picture emerges from the forgiving procedure's seven-period sequences, although a few more patterns emerge. In short, the proposed methods seem ill-suited to detect innovations in the volatile reserve settlement process, at least at this aggregative level.

The last five series have numbers of both positive and negative four-period isosign sequences that are more in accordance with *a priori* expectations. This patterning is echoed in the seven-period sequences of the forgiving method. The dating and interpretation of movements in these series are considered in the remainder of this section.

IPC Demand Deposits

Demand deposits do not show an especially large number of four-week isosign changes; the observed number is consistent with a hypothesis that the data came from a stationary stochastic process. However, demand deposits are volatile and also are vulnerable to monthly payment cycles which induce a negative autoregressive process on changes. If so, the timing of changes may indicate when innovations were occurring.

There were no changes in definition or reporting for demand deposits held by individuals, partnerships and corporations, apart from a trivial redefinition on 31 December 1973 that was repealed on 15 October 1974. It involved certain deposits of postmasters. The top half of table A.1 in the Appendix reports beginning dates of isosign sequences of length four – positive and negative – and of sequences of length seven as defined by the forgiving method.[3] While

3 On several occasions sequences of length four (or seven) were detected in successive weeks, and were actually longer than four (or seven) weeks. I have used two reporting conventions in the Appendix tables. First, so long as lapses in successive weeks are at most one week, only the starting data of the first length four (or seven) sequence is shown. Second, isosign sequences that are at least six consecutive weeks (or ten weeks with the forgiving procedure) are marked with an asterisk. The probabilities of observing such long chains when the null hypothesis of no change is true are, of course, quite small.

starting dates are affected by random shocks, in the isosign columns there appears to be strong evidence of a seasonal pattern in 1965 associated with a build-up of funds before corporate tax dates, and of seasonal declines that began at year-end until 1972.

Seasonality by definition is a repeatable sequence. A decline in the amplitude and especially a reduction in the length of up- and downswings can, however, reflect adaptive behaviour or innovations. When market interest rates began to rise in 1966, in 1968 and 1969, and in 1973 and 1974, there was an incentive to reduce hoards of inventories, and to allocate funds accruing for the payment of taxes to short-term, interest-bearing forms. The latter adjustment is easier to make than the former, and might be expected to occur first. Better data processing and monitoring techniques and the incentives provided by rising interest rates seem to explain what appears to be an irreversible decline in seasonality in demand deposits. An alternative explanation is associated with the Federal Reserve's shifting towards placing greater emphasis on controlling monetary aggregates during those years. That too was an innovation of sorts. Apart from the pronounced decline in seasonality after mid-1972, no pattern is evident in the top of table A.1.

Savings Deposits

Before November 1975, partnerships, corporations and other 'for profit' organizations were not allowed to have savings deposit accounts. The only change in definition or coverage during the period of observation occurred in November 1974, when agencies of federal, state and local governments were first allowed to acquire savings deposit accounts; probably very few took advantage of this option during the sample period. In the bottom half of table A.1, again a rather pronounced seasonal pattern is evident with inflows tending to begin shortly after the Christmas spending season and occasionally at mid-year. Seasonal outflows tend to occur in late November, just as Christmas spending commences. There is little support for a hypothesis that this seasonality has changed. Apparently, innovations that smoothed seasonal fluctuations were confined to corporate depositors. Sustained declines in the ratio of savings deposits to total bank assets occurred in March 1966 and November 1972 – just as interest rates were about to rise – and a sustained inflow began at the end of 1971 when phase II of President Nixon's price control programme went into effect. They and other periods of isosign change have no immediate interpretation in terms of known innovations. Money market mutual funds and NOW accounts were introduced in 1972; they may have been picked up in the November 1972 outflows. Individuals were steadily shifting away from savings deposits, but apparently not specifically in response to some shock or innovation. A technical conclusion is that the longer-spanned forgiving method seems less vulnerable to seasonal fluctuations than the four-week isosign method.

IPC Time Deposits

Starting dates for sequences of positive or negative changes in time deposits for individuals, partnerships and corporations are reported in the upper half of table A.2. The definition and reporting basis of time deposits is constant over time, except for the trivial change in the treatment of postmaster deposits noted above. Until mid-1967 pronounced seasonal patterns are again evident in IPC time deposit sequences. This pattern disappeared in 1968 as interest rates paid on time deposits approached Regulation Q ceilings. Time deposits fell absolutely from January 1969 until February 1970. In mid-1970 interest rate ceilings on short-maturity, large-denomination time deposits were suspended in response to the Penn Central collapse and a series of sustained increases in IPC time deposits commenced with deregulation. A seasonal pattern briefly appeared to return at the end of 1970 and mid-1971. It did not persist, however, and a long sequence of outflows commenced in November 1972 that was followed by a similarly long sequence of inflows which culminated with the elimination of large denomination interest rate ceilings in May 1973. Subsequent strings of inflows and outflows seem to correspond with fluctuations in interest rates; no evidence of irreversible technical change is apparent.

If allowance is made for the removal of interest rate ceilings, the pattern of time deposit changes is similar to that of demand deposits. The only sustained change is that seasonality diminished sharply. The forgiving method was less contaminated by seasonal effects and rather sharply depicts the sensitivity of time deposits to nominal interest rate fluctuations. When interest rates declined in the second half of 1973, a series of deposit outflows began in September and October. When interest rates again rose in 1974, the ratio of time deposits to bank assets again rose.

Bank Liabilities for Other Borrowed Money

This series was substantially revised on 25 June 1969, when federal funds purchased and funds acquired through repurchase agreements were defined as an independent entry on bank reporting forms. Statistics in table 4.2 have been adjusted to remove the effects of this revision, and no trace of it appears in the dates for other liabilities for borrowed money that are reported in the lower half of table A.2. It is important to remember that the series changed substantially in June 1969; there was about an 80 per cent reduction in the dollar value of the series with the revision.[4]

4   The successor series includes 'the total amount borrowed by a reporting bank on its own promissory notes, on notes and bills rediscounted (including commodity drafts rediscounted) or on any other instruments given for the purpose of borrowing money not specifically required to be reported elsewhere' (Federal Reserve Board, *Micro Data Reference Manual*, Item Dictionary, p. 444). It also includes loans sold under agreements to repurchase and sales of participation in pools of loans, but it does *not* include discount window borrowings from Federal Reserve banks.

The early definition of the series showed sustained increases beginning in mid-1966 and in early 1969, as banks sought to raise funds through miscellaneous other channels in response to rises in interest rates and to binding interest rate ceilings. A seasonal decline in other borrowings is evident in 1967 and 1968 and in the separately reported net purchased funds that is shown at the top of table A.3. The innovation in corporate cash management evidently was to shift seasonally fluctuating cash requirements from demand and time deposit accounts to repurchase agreements and this seems to have occurred largely between June 1968 and the end of 1970.

The successor form of the series, while small in dollar magnitude, has movements that suggest attempts by banks to avoid credit restraint. Sustained increases began at the end of the period of monetary restraint in 1969 and throughout 1972 when the Federal Reserve chairman was occupied both with conducting monetary policy and implementing President Nixon's credit control programme. Further increases began in mid-1973 and in 1975; their interpretation is unclear, but this increase is likely to have included loans to real estate investment trusts. A strong seasonal pattern that begins at year-end is apparent in negative isosign changes.

However, the striking feature of the bottom of table A.2 is the presence of five sequences of negative isosign changes in 1970, that coincided with easing monetary policy. The pattern suggests that other liabilities served as a major safety valve which banks used to maintain customer relationships. A bank's capacity to provide loans to valued customers was maintained by laying off loans and other paper in unorthodox ways. Equally striking is the fact that banks did not need this mechanism in the subsequent crunches of 1973 and 1974. Other innovations and perhaps the Eurodollar market replaced it. Something changed!

IPC Negotiable Certificates of Deposit

Information on IPC certificates of deposit was first collected in July 1966; the definition and coverage have not changed over time. Interest rates paid on all maturities of certificates of deposit (CDs) were subject to Regulation Q ceilings until 24 June 1970, when ceilings were removed from issues having an original maturity of less than 90 days. Ceilings were completely removed from large denomination (more than $100,000) CDs in May 1973.

In table A.4 the presence or absence of binding ceilings can be seen to be the primary determinant of positive and negative sequences of changes. Between 1966 and 1969 sequences of positive deposit changes were reasonably frequent except when the interest rates on competing commercial paper exceeded the Regulation Q ceiling. When ceilings were binding in 1968 and 1969, prolonged sequences of declines in the ratio of CDs to bank assets are evident. In 1970, prolonged sequences of increases in the ratio were almost continually occurring for about 30 weeks. In 1973 and 1974 long sequences of inflows or outflows occurred when interest rates were respectively high or low. The only innovation of consequence appears to have been the regulatory decision to suspend ceilings.

SIGNAL EXTRACTION FROM A PANEL
OF WEEKLY REPORTING BANKS

Weekly data on individual banks are not ordinarily available to the public, but are to monetary authorities who enforce reserve requirements. This section examines the informational content of such series. As in the previous section, the ratios of short-term assets and liabilities to bank total assets are studied. There is no necessary relation between the ratio of, say, summed IPC demand deposits to summed total assets and ratios of individual bank IPC demand deposits to total assets. Because innovations are undertaken by individual banks, there is reason to believe that innovations will be relatively conspicuous in individual bank data.

The distribution of changes in the ratios of individual bank assets or liabilities to total assets is unknown, although clearly the sums of ratios of all assets (or liabilities and net worth) to total assets is unity. As in the preceding section, if assets and liabilities are independently distributed, then the distribution of either to total assets is likely to be kurtotic and skewed because both the numerator and denominator include the same shock. Without *a priori* information about the magnitudes of shocks and the extent to which different assets or liabilities serve as buffers, little can be said about the theoretical distribution.[5]

Table 4.3 reports summary statistics for calculations for the panel of 320 weekly reporting banks. Under the null hypothesis of no change and i.i.d. shocks, the probability of any bank showing four consecutive positive (or negative) changes is 0.0625. In a population of 320 banks, the expected number showing four consecutive either positive or negative shocks is 20. The first two columns in table 4.3 show the number of weeks out of 270 in the panel in which more than 20 banks had isosign changes over five-week spans.[6] The next two columns show comparable statistics for the forgiving method over an eight-week span. The fifth and sixth columns report statistics about 13-week changes in the ratio of some variable to a bank's total assets. If the null hypothesis were true, the expected number of banks with an increase (or decrease) in some ratio is 160. Using the normal approximation to the binomial, the standard deviation is 8.94. The fifth and sixth columns report the number

---

5 If one asset were highly liquid, divisible, reversible and bore a risk-free market rate of return, and if a bank used it to peg the level of total assets, then independence would be preserved. These conditions may be roughly satisfied by federal funds.
6 The time span runs from 2 July 1969 to 28 August 1974. Panel information is available to the end of 1974, but 13 forward weeks were required for calculated measures.

TABLE 4.3 Summary statistics from panel data: number of weeks large deviations detected

	Isosign–4 > 20 banks		Forgiving–7 > 20 banks		Cumulative up > 179	Cumulative down > 179
	+ve	–ve	+ve	–ve		
Currency, coin and reserves	0	0	0	0	6	0
Net federal funds purchased	0	0	0	0	3	4
IPC demand deposits	0	0	0	0	5	7
Other liabilities for borrowed money[a]	0	0	0	0	0	0
IPC certificates of deposit[a]	18	23	14	20	0	0
Cash items in the process of collection	0	0	0	0	3	15
Savings deposits	170	66	151	55	134	28
IPC time deposits	156	19	122	12	23	3

[a] Between 90 and 150 banks reported having no liabilities for borrowed money in different weeks. Approximately 70 had no IPC certificates of deposit in any week. Therefore, relative to other balance sheet measures, certificates of deposit and liabilities for other borrowed money statistics are biased downwards.

of weeks out of 270 in which the number of banks with positive and negative changes respectively exceed 179 – i.e., are slightly in excess of two standard deviations from the expected values.

Because very large banks are expected to be especially active innovators, analogous summary statistics were calculated for the 56 banks having total assets greater than $1 billion on 2 July 1969. The results are shown in table 4.4. The expected number of these large banks having isosign changes (positive or negative) over five weeks is 3.5. The first two columns of table 4.4 report the number of weeks out of 270 in which this expectation was exceeded. The third and fourth columns report analogous information for the forgiving method over a span of eight weeks. Under the null hypothesis, the expected number of positive (or negative) 13-week changes is 28, and its standard deviation is 3.5. The fifth and sixth columns indicate the number of weeks in which the number of banks showing positive or negative 13-week differences exceeded 36 – i.e., again slightly more than two standard deviations above the expected level.

Reserve and Cash Management Assets

Tables 4.3 and 4.4 do not differ greatly in the profiles they provide for currency, coin and reserves; net federal funds purchased; IPC demand deposits; and cash items in the process of collection. The conclusion from tabulating the number of times that four consecutive positively or negatively signed changes (and seven consecutive changes using the forgiving method) were observed is that there is no evidence of innovation. As in the preceding section, there appear to be fewer instances of long strings of changes in these four series, which are associated with management of cash balances and reserves, than one should expect if the series had been generated by white noise processes. Monthly payment cycles and carry-forwards across reserve settlement weeks are likely causes of the negative autoregressive processes that would tend to yield this pattern. Summed changes over 13 weeks are not vulnerable to payment and reserves cycles; with one exception they also provide no evidence of a sharply defined period of innovation.

Cash items did have a relatively large number of weeks in which many panel banks had negative 13-week changes – nearly four standard deviations above the expected level. Inspection of the changes indicated that most corresponded with post-Christmas and mid-summer slack seasons. However, three occurred in late 1970 when the US economy was slipping into a recession and three more occurred in late 1972 when the Federal Reserve reduced the period that deposited cheques had to be held as cash items – i.e. an innovation. Over the entire period, the ratio of cash items to bank assets was falling because both demand deposits were falling as a percentage of bank assets and an increasing fraction of transactions were being completed with wire transfers. This change in practice was continuing and not confined to a few well-defined periods.

TABLE 4.4 Summary statistics from panel data for the 56 largest banks

	Isosign−4 > 3 banks		Forgiving−7 > 3 banks		Cumulative up > 36 banks	Cumulative down > 36 banks
	+ve	−ve	+ve	−ve		
Currency, coin and reserves	0	0	0	0	3	4
Net federal funds purchased	2	0	0	0	2	6
IPC demand deposits	0	1	1	0	2	5
Other liabilities for borrowed money[a]	3	23	3	14	0	0
IPC certificates of deposit[a]	4	20	6	18	0	0
Cash items in the process of collection	0	1	0	0	2	3
Savings deposits	103	69	97	65	4	7
IPC time deposits	9	1	9	0	3	4

[a] Between 7 and 28 banks reported having no liabilities for borrowed money in different weeks. As many as two banks reported having no IPC certificates of deposit in some weeks.

IPC Negotiable Certificates of Deposit

The dominant pattern in the weekly statistics summarized in tables 4.3 and 4.4 is the extraordinary run-off that occurred in 1969, before interest rate ceilings on large denomination certificates were raised slightly in January 1970 and then suspended for short maturities in June 1970. Funds surged back into banks, especially smaller banks, beginning in late March 1970 as market rates began to fall. The flow began far in advance of the removal of ceilings at a time when CDs were paying about 150 basis points less than prime commercial paper, but about the same as Treasury bills. The pattern was quite erratic in April and May when unusually large numbers of large banks had increases *and* decreases in the ratio of CDs to assets.

Before the emergence of money market mutual funds, Treasury bills and CDs were much closer substitutes than CDs and commercial paper. It is very doubtful that such gaps between yields on prime commercial paper and CDs could occur with money market funds present. When interest rate ceilings on CDs were removed, yields on CDs immediately jumped to the levels paid on commercial paper and there was a large increase in the number of panel banks reporting consecutive increases in the ratio of CDs to assets. However, there was only a small increase in the number of large banks reporting consecutive increases in CDs.

Both at the beginning and end of 1971, relatively large numbers of large banks reported consecutive declines in the ratio of CDs to assets. It seems probable that some change in practice was occurring then, but its nature cannot be inferred from the data. The Eurobanking market was growing rapidly during that period and, perhaps not surprisingly, the real federal funds rate turned negative. The entire panel of banks differed considerably from the large banks in that panel banks had large numbers of banks reporting consecutive positive changes in CDs frequently during the first nine months of 1970. Only occasionally did large banks report sequences of positive changes in 1970. When remaining interest rate ceilings on large denomination CDs were removed in 1973, panel banks but not large banks showed sizeable increases in the frequency of four consecutive positive changes in the ratio.

In the pristine banking world of the early 1970s, approximately 20 per cent of the weekly reporting banks chose not to offer certificates of deposit. These banks tended to be small and apparently calculated that it would be more profitable to duck rather than compete. Therefore, it never happened that the panel of banks had 179 banks showing either 13-week increases or decreases in table 4.3. Only two of the 56 largest banks declined to offer CDs. However, even for this competitive group, it never happened that as many as 36 banks reported cumulative 13-week increases in the ratio of CDs to assets.

Other Liabilities for Borrowed Money

This item consists of a variety of components and is only reported in positive amounts by between 50 and 80 per cent of panel banks. It is suggestive that the number of banks reporting any such other liabilities tended to be high when nominal interest rates were high in 1969, 1973 and 1974 both for all banks in the panel and for large banks. The latter account for most of the intertemporal variation in reporting numbers in the panel. In part because of the small number of banks reporting any other liabilities for borrowed money is associated with few banks reporting four consecutive weeks of positive or negative changes and fewer than 160 panel banks reported 13-week positive or negative changes on any date.[7]

In table 4.4 there are numerous instances in which a relatively large number of banks report sequences of consecutive declines in the ratio of other liabilities for borrowed money to assets. Declines were concentrated in the early part of the period. Using the isosign-4 measure, out of 23 negative change weeks there were seven weeks in the high interest rate period of 1969, six in 1970 and six in the first eight months of 1971 when more than three large banks reported having four successive negative changes in this ratio. It is hard to guess what was going on, but three 'events' might have led to such patterns.

First, there was rapid expansion in Eurobanking by large US banks. It is probable that domestically booked liabilities were being shifted to the books of Eurobranches. Second, there was widespread speculation against the dollar, and banks may have been victimized by corporate customers who sought to limit their dollar exposures. The negative sequences ceased when President Nixon made his speech on 15 August 1971. Third, the Penn Central defaulted in June 1970 and the subsequent rapid growth in domestic reserves reduced the desire on the part of banks to resort to such unconventional mechanisms for acquiring funds. (All of the dates in 1970 coincided with or were subsequent to the Penn Central failure.)

Judging from the interest rate sensitivity of the number of banks reporting having other liabilities for borrowed money, it is reasonably clear that other liabilities are partly a safety valve (loophole?) through which large banks raise funds when conventional sources dry up or become dear. In addition, while the amounts involved are small in relation to a representative bank's total assets, movements in this item seem to indicate structural change occurring until about September 1971.

Savings Deposits

The ratio of savings deposits to bank assets at all panel banks and at very large banks exhibits very pronounced weekly patterns. In a majority of the

7   In tables 4.5 and 4.6 below, information is reported for single-week changes that is adjusted for the number of reporting banks.

270 panel weeks, the number of banks reporting either four consecutive positive or four consecutive negative changes exceeded the expected value by more than two standard deviations. Savings deposits were always subject to Regulation Q interest rate ceilings. Part of the sequences of deposit change pattern can be explained by the presence of ceilings, because the largest numbers of banks reporting outflows tended to occur when the ceiling was binding. While the ratio of aggregate weekly reporting bank savings deposits to aggregate total assets was declining over the 270-week period, both all the panel banks and the 56 largest banks sustained many more positive than negative isosign-4 changes. For reasons that are unclear (but surely partly seasonal), different banks on different dates experienced sequences of increases in the ratio of savings deposits to total assets. Except for periods of high interest rates these inflows were spread approximately uniformly over time.

Obviously, some very large banks had large declines in their ratios and it is likely that most weekly reporting banks experienced declines in the ratio over the period. Apart from the 56 large banks, panel banks also had significant numbers of positive 13-week cumulative changes in the ratio of savings deposits to assets in half of the weeks of the panel period. They were concentrated in the low nominal interest rate years of 1970–2. The introduction of money market mutual funds and NOW accounts in Massachusetts and New Hampshire may have caused savings deposit growth to attenuate in 1973 and 1974, but the pattern seems equally plausibly explained by conventional nominal interest rate movements. The fact that the largest 56 banks had no discernible cumulative increases in the ratio may mean either that their other deposits and liabilities were growing more rapidly or that their depositors had become more sophisticated and/or interest rate sensitive. It appears that there are potentially serious aggregation errors made when savings deposits of large and small weekly reporting banks are pooled. Large bank patterns may even be a precursor for smaller banks in the panel, but additional evidence is required before this hypothesis can be accepted.

IPC Time Deposits

IPC time deposits appear somewhat similar to savings deposits in the entire panel in terms of isosign changes over five (or eight) consecutive weeks. Relative to savings deposits, there are smaller numbers of negative isosign changes, which is partly explained by the presence of penalties for early withdrawal. At large banks, on the other hand, there is very little evidence of sustained sequences of time deposit inflows or outflows. All nine dates on which the number of large banks reporting four consecutive positive changes exceeded the expected value under the null hypothesis occurred in the first half of 1970, when interest rate ceilings were being either relaxed or eliminated. This can be interpreted as restoring balances to an equilibrium that would have existed in the absence of binding ceilings. After mid-1970 it appears that the 56 largest banks and their customers were using time deposits to manage cash balances – i.e. some sort of negative autoregressive process was operating. The absence of sequences of sustained increases or decreases in the ratio of time deposits to total assets suggests that no innovation was occurring. The difference in the isosign patterns for all panel banks and the large banks is difficult to explain; depositors at smaller weekly reporting banks view time deposits as if they are savings deposits and depositors at larger banks do not.

On relatively few dates did the number of banks reporting 13-week cumulative changes in the ratio of time deposits to total assets exceed the expected value under the null hypothesis by as much as two standard deviations. Out of 270 weeks one expects to detect about 14 'significant' outcomes when the null hypothesis is true. Seven were detected for large banks and 26 for the entire panel. The latter consisted of 23 positive and three negative cumulative changes. Fifteen of the positive changes occurred in 1970 and are probably best interpreted again as a response to the removal of interest rate ceilings and falling market interest rates.

CONCLUSIONS

Conclusions are to be drawn about the strengths and weaknesses of the techniques employed in this paper and about the timing of innovations during the years 1965–75. Before turning to these tasks, however, one final set of calculations should be considered. In both the third and fourth section of this paper it was noted that currency, coin and reserves, net federal funds purchased, cash items in the process of collection, and, perhaps, IPC demand deposits, had very small numbers of isosign change sequences. It was suggested that intra-month payment cycles were responsible for this result. Such cycles can crudely be eliminated by constructing monthly averages of weekly data.

A second obstacle that confounded interpretation of series for IPC CDs and other liabilities for borrowed money in the fourth section was that substantial numbers of banks held neither liability.

Some Final Calculations

Table 4.5 reports monthly averages of the number of banks reporting one-week increases in the ratio of an item to a bank's total assets, taken as a deviation from one-half of the number of panel banks that had non-zero amounts of that item. Table 4.6 reports analogous measures for the 56 largest banks. These tables thus are not contaminated by intra-monthly cycles or the presence of non-holders.

Table 4.5 indicates that a slight plurality of banks were steadily experiencing a decrease in ratios of currency, coin and reserves, IPC demand deposits and other liabilities for borrowed money. The ratio of cash items in the process of collection to total assets was essentially trendless. A plurality of panel banks had increases in the net federal funds purchased ratio, but the size of the plurality declined over time. By 1974 this ratio had become trendless. By the end of 1970, panel banks' holdings of IPC CDs had become essentially trendless. A majority of panel banks was increasing the ratio of IPC time deposits to total assets; the size of the majority was constant after 1970. The number of banks reporting increases in the ratio of savings deposits to total assets was very volatile from month to month. It seems to reflect quarterly interest payments on these accounts and to vary with a variable lag in response to fluctuations in other nominal market rates.

A different pattern is evident in table 4.6. Deviations in changes in IPC demand and time deposit and currency, coin and reserve ratios from the expected levels were small and trendless after 1970. The ratio of net federal funds purchased to assets was trendless until the end of 1972, when it began to decline. The ratios of other liabilities for borrowed money and savings deposits to assets were showing a downward trend, but that for cash items in the process of collection was showing an upward trend.

In other words, borrowing in the federal funds market and through repurchase agreements was a growing activity of smaller banks and cheque clearing and cash management were being increasingly handled by the largest banks. All banks were reducing their reliance on other liabilities for borrowed money after June 1969.

The Method

The conjecture that financial innovations would leave tracks in balance sheet ratios at panel banks is adventurous for several reasons. First, balance sheets of banks provide an incomplete picture. Much was going on in the books of other subsidiaries of a bank holding company and in offshore branches that will be unobserved. Second, in a general equilibrium framework it is likely that innovations in the demand for liabilities are partly offset by changing supplies by the public or by interest rate movements. It has not been possible to control for such eventualities in the present study, but it is a topic for future research. Third, innovations by nonbank intermediaries and corporate cash managers are hard to represent in studies of bank portfolio structure. Finally, different innovations were occurring at the same time; examination of paths and runs can only reveal their net effects.

Nevertheless, a great deal is known about institutional changes during this period. If the method has promise, those changes should have left obvious indications. In brief, US banks were subjected to a series of financial 'crunches', as Albert Wojnilower (1980) has forcefully argued. Nominal interest rates reached successively higher post-war peaks in 1966, 1969, 1973 and 1974. In each of these years banks and their clients were induced to improvise and devise mechanisms to protect valued relationships. Banks responded successfully to these shocks by acquiring an arsenal of defences that blunted the thrust of restrictive policy, as measured by the levels of real

TABLE 4.5   Monthly summaries of net deviations from expectations – panel banks

Month	CCR	NPF	IPC DD	IPC CD	OLB	CI	SD	IPC TD
7/69	-2	12	-3	-22	-15	2	-53	-1
8/69	1	13	-2	-29	-15	-4	-44	2
9/69	0	13	11	-24	-17	7	-7	-4
10/69	5	4	2	-24	-13	0	-13	-7
11/69	4	6	-4	-20	-11	-2	11	-4
12/69	3	12	3	-29	-13	4	-3	-1
1/70	0	0	-1	-1	-8	-1	-56	19
2/70	2	15	-3	4	-14	-2	17	31
3/70	-3	12	-4	16	-13	-3	66	44
4/70	3	0	5	18	-6	2	-4	31
5/70	-1	4	-5	6	-10	1	32	33
6/70	-2	6	2	12	-12	2	30	38
7/70	-2	7	1	26	-5	6	-5	55
8/70	-2	8	-12	18	-8	-3	-11	47
9/70	1	7	5	14	-2	3	36	44
10/70	3	4	-4	15	-5	-6	51	27
11/70	5	9	7	11	-9	2	61	32
12/70	-2	5	-2	0	-14	4	45	30
1/71	-11	4	-10	0	-6	5	51	40
2/71	6	4	0	-11	-6	-3	89	33
3/71	5	1	1	-24	-8	-3	82	8
4/71	-3	5	-1	-18	-7	-2	54	1
5/71	-4	7	4	-3	-7	5	73	21
6/71	2	6	0	-4	-9	2	19	5
7/71	0	1	-9	2	-5	3	-10	22
8/71	7	6	-3	17	-7	5	-23	36
9/71	-3	3	2	9	-6	-1	40	26
10/71	0	4	6	13	-8	-9	28	32
11/71	-2	-3	1	5	-10	2	43	21
12/71	-1	1	2	-6	-14	-1	33	9
1/72	-7	2	-5	-9	1	-2	26	25
2/72	-1	0	1	-6	-7	11	72	10
3/72	-1	7	-4	-15	-5	4	77	-3
4/72	8	1	-2	0	-9	-3	-17	12
5/72	5	-2	-1	3	-3	6	36	23
6/72	-4	5	-9	-11	-5	-2	27	18
7/72	-1	10	-6	-6	-4	1	-12	26
8/72	1	6	7	7	-11	14	-6	24
9/72	2	-2	-9	5	-7	2	37	15

TABLE 4.5 (cont.)

Month	CCR	NPF	IPC DD	IPC CD	OLB	CI	SD	IPC TD
10/72	2	4	0	−3	−10	−3	3	18
11/72	−5	9	−2	5	−10	−2	33	15
12/72	1	−3	0	−3	−15	9	28	2
1/73	−2	2	2	12	−8	6	−8	29
2/73	−3	−1	4	12	−10	0	43	29
3/73	1	8	−5	14	−12	11	46	13
4/73	1	2	−6	−1	−13	3	−28	16
5/73	3	4	1	2	−14	5	39	14
6/73	−1	3	−10	4	−17	−1	7	12
7/73	−7	12	−2	7	−8	4	−71	15
8/73	2	5	2	8	−11	3	−57	24
9/73	2	−2	−4	3	−10	−1	−7	16
10/73	−1	2	2	8	−5	4	8	20
11/73	0	1	−1	2	−6	−2	15	13
12/73	5	1	3	4	−12	2	18	7
1/74	−2	4	2	5	−6	7	−11	22
2/74	0	−4	1	−2	−12	−4	69	11
3/74	−5	−3	−3	−8	−17	2	66	12
4/74	0	−3	0	−11	−9	−1	−41	0
5/74	6	4	6	1	−4	10	9	12
6/74	6	1	−1	2	−10	2	−6	10
7/74	3	1	1	9	−11	−2	−43	9
8/74	3	2	−1	3	−13	3	−63	13

CCR, Currency, coin reserves; NPF, net purchased funds; IPC DD, IPC demand deposits; IPC CDs, IPC certificates of deposit; OLB, other liabilities for borrowed money; CI, cash items; SD, savings deposits; IPC TD, IPC time deposits.
These series have been adjusted to eliminate contamination from banks that have no IPC CDs and other liabilities for borrowed money.

TABLE 4.6   Monthly summaries of net deviations from expectations – 56 largest banks

Month	CCR	NPF	IPC DD	IPC CD	OLB	CI	SD	IPC TD
7/69	1	1	1	-4	-4	1	-11	3
8/69	3	-2	3	-8	-5	0	-8	0
9/69	1	-1	2	-4	-6	2	-1	-1
10/69	2	-1	1	-7	-4	2	-4	1
11/69	0	1	0	-4	-5	2	-2	-1
12/69	-2	1	0	-6	-4	0	0	-2
1/70	-2	-2	0	-2	-2	-2	-10	3
2/70	0	-1	-1	-1	-4	0	-2	2
3/70	1	2	3	0	-4	-1	9	8
4/70	-1	-1	0	2	0	-1	-3	1
5/70	-1	-2	-1	-2	-2	2	7	1
6/70	1	0	-2	0	-4	0	1	6
7/70	-1	-1	0	3	0	1	-6	3
8/70	-2	-1	-1	0	-4	1	-5	3
9/70	1	1	-1	2	1	3	4	3
10/70	-1	2	0	3	-2	0	6	0
11/70	2	0	0	1	-2	-1	9	0
12/70	2	0	0	1	-6	2	6	3
1/71	-2	-1	0	-3	-1	0	7	1
2/71	1	0	1	-2	-1	-1	9	-1
3/71	0	-1	0	-3	-3	-2	8	-2
4/71	-2	1	1	-2	-3	2	6	-1
5/71	-2	0	1	-2	-1	-3	7	-1
6/71	-2	3	-2	3	-3	0	-3	1
7/71	2	0	-1	1	-2	0	-4	-1
8/71	1	-1	1	0	-5	1	-5	2
9/71	-2	-2	0	1	-2	1	2	-1
10/71	-1	2	1	3	-1	-2	0	1
11/71	1	0	-1	0	-3	0	8	3
12/71	1	1	2	-3	-4	-2	3	-1
1/72	-1	0	-2	-2	-2	2	4	0
2/72	4	-1	2	-3	-2	2	10	2
3/72	-1	0	-3	-3	-3	1	7	-2
4/72	2	4	0	-1	-4	-1	-2	-1
5/72	4	-2	2	-3	-1	2	2	-1
6/72	-3	1	-1	1	-3	0	5	4
7/72	1	1	0	-2	-2	1	-4	1
8/72	1	2	0	1	-3	2	-3	2
9/72	1	0	0	1	-5	-2	3	0

TABLE 4.6 (cont.)

Month	CCR	NPF	IPC DD	IPC CD	OLB	CI	SD	IPC TD
10/72	0	-2	3	-3	-6	1	-5	2
11/72	1	2	2	1	-3	-1	3	-1
12/72	-1	-1	0	-2	-4	3	3	-1
1/73	-1	-3	1	-2	-2	3	-3	-2
2/73	0	-1	3	1	-3	1	4	1
3/73	3	0	0	1	-2	4	5	2
4/73	-1	-1	0	-1	-3	-1	-4	1
5/73	0	0	-1	0	-4	0	2	-1
6/73	-1	1	-1	1	-2	0	0	-3
7/73	-3	0	-1	-1	-2	1	-11	0
8/73	-1	-1	-1	0	0	0	-7	1
9/73	3	-1	-1	1	-1	0	0	1
10/73	1	-2	1	-1	-1	3	1	1
11/73	2	0	0	-1	0	0	0	3
12/73	0	-2	-1	1	1	-3	0	-2
1/74	1	1	3	0	-2	0	-3	1
2/74	-2	-1	1	-3	-4	-3	8	-1
3/74	-1	-1	-1	0	-5	1	6	3
4/74	1	2	-2	-3	-2	-1	-6	0
5/74	0	-3	1	-1	0	3	1	0
6/74	0	-1	0	1	0	0	-1	0
7/74	2	-2	0	0	-1	-1	-8	1
8/74	3	0	2	1	-2	1	-9	-1

Abbreviations as for table 4.5.

interest rates. The 'real' federal funds interest rate at year-end was 3.03 per cent in 1966, 2.96 in 1969, 0.52 in 1973 and -1.17 per cent in 1974.[8]

Applied to aggregative data the method appears to have identified the following changes, where variables are expressed as a ratio to total weekly reporting bank assets:

1   A decline in seasonality of IPC deposits, first demand and then time, and an increase in the seasonality of first other liabilities for borrowed money and then net purchases of federal funds.

8   The real federal funds rate is measured as the difference between the year-end nominal federal funds rate and the annualized end-of-year quarterly change in the GNP price deflator.

2   Increased borrowing through other liabilities for borrowed money and
    through net purchases of federal funds in 1966 and 1969, but not in 1973
    and 1974. Other liabilities for borrowed money fell sharply in 1970 after
    the crunch of 1969, and then increased again in the post-crunch months
    of 1973 and 1975.
3   Substantial run-offs of CDs in 1966 and especially in 1969 when interest
    rate ceilings were binding, but not subsequently.

The convention of looking at successive changes over five-week spans (or
eight in the case of the forgiving method) seemed to be reasonably successful
as a screen at the aggregative level. Longer or shorter spans (with different
significance levels) could have been applied. In future work-efforts will be
made to compare simultaneously several different patterns in order to achieve
sharper discrimination.

When applied to both aggregative and individual bank data, the method
suffered from the presence of high-frequency intra-monthly fluctuations, that
are associated with administration of reserve requirements and payments cycles.
This problem had been anticipated, but the forgiving method which had been
intended to cure it was only partially effective. In future work a more formal
filter will be designed to eliminate this noise. Important undetected patterns
may exist in several series considered in this paper.

Panel data for 320 weekly reporting banks were studied for 270 weeks,
2 July 1969 to 28 August 1974. When applied to the panel, the method revealed
several interesting movements that reflect regulatory change. For example,
negative isosign changes in cash items in the process of collection in 1972
were a result of reforms that were designed to speed the processing of cheques
and modernize the clearing mechanism. Extraordinary movements in IPC CDs
were associated with binding Regulation Q ceilings in 1969, and to a lesser
extent with their removal in June 1970.

Of greater interest in terms of innovation are seemingly unreversed declines
in the ratios of IPC CDs (after 1970) and other liabilities for borrowed money
to total assets at the largest 56 banks. Differences in the patterns of liabilities
at large and small weekly reporting banks suggest structural change and innovation that can never be detected analysing monetary aggregates. Aggregation
always entails some loss of information. The loss is likely to be substantial if
only a small number of banks are actively innovating. Aggregation losses tend
to be serious when behavioural relations vary across decision-making units.

The evidence of heterogeneous behaviour by banks presented above is
rudimentary and does little more than raise questions. What distinguishes banks
that seem to be reducing their dependence upon IPC CDs from others? Scale
seems to be involved, but having a foreign branch or being located in a highly
competitive market may be better discriminants. Innovating banks are in disequilibrium and probably operating under different sets of constraints than other
banks. Even if they could be identified *a priori*, theoretical analysis of their
desired portfolios and econometric testing of hypotheses are a long way off.

The method was not successful at the micro or macro level in finding periods where sharply defined movements in portfolio ratios signalled the occurrence and diffusion of an innovation, unless one broadly interprets innovation to include deregulation. Deregulation was detected. An explanation for this difference in the success of the method in these two cases can now be proposed. Deregulation is a universal phenomenon that induces all banks to move their portfolios in some direction at about the same time. Therefore, it will be readily detected by procedures that monitor runs or unreversed changes.

Innovations, on the other hand, often assist some banks to profit at the expense of other banks, or to specialize in a way that indirectly benefits all banks. Innovations realign profit opportunities and may, for example, induce some banks to increase cheque clearing services and induce other banks to reduce cheque processing. Diffusion and realignment are likely to be time consuming and will not result in the monotonic and irreversible portfolio changes for individual banks that the method of this paper is designed to detect.

In other words, the analogy of technical change occurring for a representative firm that motivated the approach at the outset may not be very illuminating when one moves away from the world of well-defined perfectly competitive industries. In imperfectly competitive markets, a movement out of some market or service by an innovating bank is likely to create a void that will be filled by other banks. Detecting innovations in an imperfectly competitive world is immensely more difficult than in the world of the representative firm. The extent to which the representative firm paradigm was a good approximation was and is an empirical question.

Innovations in the Years 1965-75

Innovations are a rational profit-maximizing response to opportunities in financial markets that are created by high or rising nominal interest rates. In 1966 the first major crunch resulted in widely recognized innovations such as congeneric transformations of banks into one-bank holding companies, the establishment of Eurobranches, the issuance of bank-related commercial paper and a reported but undocumented expansion of net purchases of funds in the federal funds market and through repurchase agreements.

The results from analysing aggregate series in the present paper support and amplify this theme. First, substantial withdrawals from savings accounts, but not demand or time accounts, began in March 1966. Disintermediation was a small saver phenomenon in 1966. Second, a significant decline in the seasonality of demand and time deposits began in 1966; this almost surely reflects changed behaviour by large depositors. Rising interest rates made the traditional seasonal accumulations of idle cash intolerably expensive. Corporate treasurers moved to reduce their amplitudes. Data used in this study do not disclose how this was accomplished, but changes in billing and collecting practices, well-timed commercial paper, CD and government securities purchases and repurchase agreements were probably the principal tools. Certificates of deposit exhibit considerable seasonality in table A.2 between the crunches of 1966 and 1969. Third, other liabilities for borrowed money, which are primarily net purchased funds at large banks, expanded considerably; beginning in May 1966, they fluctuated at seasonal frequencies thereafter until the series was revised in June 1969. Innovations that modify seasonality surely impair the short-run controllability of a monetary aggregate.

In the crunch of 1969, as is well known, US banks experienced large amortization of CDs when their interest rates fell below those on commercial paper and Treasury bills. A substantial recovery in the ratio of aggregate IPC CDs to weekly reporting bank assets began in June 1970 when ceilings were removed, as is shown in table A.3. The use of IPC CDs to manage seasonal cash fluctuations was largely suspended between June 1968 and June 1970. Seemingly unnoticed was the fact that the largest banks increasingly experienced declines in the ratio of CDs to bank assets after 1970, and that the ratio of CDs to assets became increasingly cyclical.

An interpretation is that corporate treasurers increasingly were using repurchase agreements to manage seasonal fluctuations after 1970. The ratio of net purchased funds to total assets was largely trendless at the 56 largest banks – i.e., there were about as many banks reporting net increases in the ratio of federal funds purchased and funds acquired through repurchase agreements to total assets as banks reporting net decreases. However, a plurality of all panel banks had increases in this ratio between July 1969 and about December 1973. This pattern is shown in tables 4.5 and 4.6 and is easily interpreted as the last stage of the diffusion process of the repurchase agreement innovation from large banks to smaller weekly reporting banks. The change in the ratio is more or less matched by a plurality of panel banks having a decline in the ratio of IPC demand deposits to total assets. While correlations prove nothing, the pattern is at least consistent with a hypothesis that repurchase agreements are short-term interest bearing repositories for transactions balances. If corporate treasurers maintained contingency balances for a few quarters during the conversion to repurchase-agreement funded transactions balances and proceeded at a cautious pace, the implied shift in money demand roughly corresponds with the dating of the money demand function shift that Goldfeld (1976) reported.

After the 1969 revision of reporting forms in which federal funds and funds acquired through repurchase agreements were separated from other liabilities for borrowed money, a plurality of all panel banks and the 56 largest banks reported declines in the ratio of other liabilities for borrowed money to total assets. The reasons for this decline are unclear, but it is not implausible that banks were shifting such irregular liabilities to the books of their holding company subsidiaries or to offshore branches where less complete disclosure was the norm. Both subsidiaries and offshore branches were growing considerably more rapidly than the conventional weekly reporting bank. After adjusting for the number of banks included in tables 4.5 and 4.6, it is apparent that the largest banks were most frequently experiencing declines in this ratio; they were also most likely to have subsidiaries and Eurobranches.

In the 1973 and 1974 crunches a remarkable feature of the tables is the infrequency of isosign strings and strong and unreversed movements in all ratios, with the single exception of savings deposits. It appears that earlier innovations had provided banks with enough infrastructure to protect their valued customer relationships. As it turned out, savings depositors would eventually be protected by the 1978–80 explosion in money market mutual funds and subsequent deregulation. After that episode, high real interest rates and consequent borrower bankruptcies would deliver the medicine in monetary crunches.

Finally, the large majority of panel banks reporting increases in the ratio of IPC time deposits to assets after mid-1970 almost exclusively consisted of smaller banks. Large banks had made this adjustment earlier, as is suggested in table A.2. Diffusion or 'trickle down' occurs with a considerable lag. Slow adjustment was probably an optimal policy for small banks in those years. There is little incentive for small banks to rush to pay market interest rates on time deposits, unless pressed by competitors. A topic for future research is whether the lagged adjustment evident in tables 4.5 and 4.6 was a consequence of differences in interest rates that they and large banks paid on time deposits and CDs.

With nationwide money market mutual funds and equivalent structures elsewhere, diffusion and speed of adjustment are likely to be much faster in the future. This will obviously make control of monetary aggregates much more difficult in the face of continuing innovation in the United States, and perhaps elsewhere.

AUTHOR'S NOTE

Financial support from the University of Wisconsin Graduate Research Committee for conducting this research is gratefully acknowledged. Mark Kennet provided valuable research assistance. I am also much indebted to Al Schubert, Paul Spindt, Gerhart Fries and Monica Friar for assistance in making panel data on the Federal Reserve's weekly reporting banks accessible on Wisconsin's Univac 1100 computer. The excellent typing was by Alice Wilcox.

REFERENCES

Artis, M. J. and associates 1978: Competition and credit control: submission to the committee to review the functions of financial institutions, mimeo. University of Manchester, August.

Feller, William 1957: *An Introduction to Probability Theory and its Applications*, vol. 1. New York: Wiley.

Goldfeld, Stephen M. 1976: The case of the missing money. *Brookings Papers on Economic Activity* 3, 683–730.

Goldfeld, Stephen M. and Richard E. Quandt 1973: A Markov model for switching regressions. *Journal of Econometrics*, March, 3–15.

Hester, Donald D. 1981: Innovations and monetary control. *Brookings Papers on Economic Activity* 1, 141–89.

Hester, Donald D. 1985: Monetary policy in an evolutionary disequilibrium. SSRI Workshop Series Paper No. 8506. In *Financial Innovation and Monetary Policy: Asia and the West*, ed. Y. Suzuki. Tokyo: Tokyo University Press.

Meadows, Donella H. et al. 1972: *The Limits to Growth*. New York: Universe Books.

Shiller, R. J. 1979: The volatility of long-term interest rates and expectations models of the term structure. *Journal of Political Economy* 87, 1190–219.

Wojnilower, Albert M. 1980: The central role of credit crunches in recent financial history. *Brookings Papers on Economic Activity* 2, 277–339.

APPENDIX

TABLE A.1 Beginning dates for sequences of positive and negative IPC deposit changes

	Isosign–4		Forgiving–7	
	+ve	−ve	+ve	−ve
Demand				
	2/17/65[a]	1/13/65	2/17/65	12/14/66
	5/19/65	1/12/66	11/5/69	12/31/69
	8/18/65	1/4/67	11/11/70	12/23/70
	9/29/65	4/12/67		6/30/71
	12/31/69	7/12/67		7/12/72
	5/5/71	1/14/70		
	12/6/72	12/30/70[b]		
	1/22/75	7/14/71[b]		
		12/29/71		
		3/15/72		
		7/12/72		
Savings				
	6/30/65	3/23/66[b]	12/15/71	3/9/66
	12/31/69	12/7/66	2/19/75	11/29/67
	12/30/70	11/29/67		7/30/69
	7/7/71	5/22/68		11/8/72
	12/29/71[b]	11/22/72[b]		8/22/73
	3/5/75	11/21/73		

[a] All dates are given by US convention, where the month precedes the day.
[b] Indicates chains of at least six isosign or ten forgiving.

TABLE A.2 Beginning dates for sequences of positive and negative time deposit and other liability changes

	Isosign–4		Forgiving–7	
	+ve	–ve	+ve	–ve
Time deposits				
	6/30/65[a]	11/29/67	6/30/65	7/23/69
	3/16/66	8/13/69	2/16/66	11/15/72
	6/29/66	11/22/72[b]	6/29/66	9/19/73
	12/28/66	10/17/73	6/21/67	10/17/73
	7/5/67	11/21/73	7/1/70[b]	
	12/31/69	3/19/75	6/30/71	
	7/1/70		1/13/73	
	8/5/70		6/26/74	
	9/30/70		7/24/74	
	12/30/70		8/6/75	
	6/30/71			
	2/14/73[b]			
	7/24/74			
	11/20/74			
Other liabilities for borrowed money				
	5/18/66[b]	1/4/67	4/27/66	1/4/67
	3/12/69	1/3/68	2/19/69	1/10/68
	12/17/69	6/26/68	1/26/72	6/5/68
	2/16/72	2/25/70	7/4/73	2/11/70[b]
	5/31/72	6/10/70	8/1/73	5/20/70[b]
	9/27/72	7/22/70	6/11/75[b]	9/2/70[b]
	12/27/72	9/2/70	11/5/75	10/7/70
	8/1/73	10/7/70		12/23/70[b]
	2/12/75	1/6/71[b]		11/13/74
	6/18/75[b]	12/5/73		
	11/5/75	7/31/74		
		11/27/74		
		1/22/75		

Before 25 June 1969 other liabilities for borrowed money included federal funds purchased and funds acquired through repurchase agreements.
[a] All dates are given by US convention, where the month precedes the day.
[b] Indicates chains of at least six isosign or ten forgiving.

TABLE A.3 Beginning dates for sequences of positive and negative changes for net purchased funds, cash items and reserves

	Isosign–4		*Forgiving–7*	
	+*ve*	−*ve*	+*ve*	−*ve*
Net purchased funds				
	8/20/69[a]	12/2/70	9/18/74	12/2/70
	3/15/72	8/9/72	4/2/75	8/9/72
	10/24/73	7/4/73		7/4/73
	12/26/73	7/16/75		7/3/74
	4/23/75			
Cash items in the process of collection				
	1/16/74	6/30/71	—	6/30/71
		3/6/74		2/20/74
Reserves on deposit at Federal Reserve				
	12/6/67	3/3/65	5/29/74	3/3/65
	5/22/68	1/26/66		1/5/66
	6/12/74	7/20/66		6/22/66
		4/26/67		4/5/67
		1/22/69		4/26/67
		5/21/69		4/30/69
		10/14/70		2/18/70
		11/14/73		9/2/70
				10/24/73

[a] All dates are given by US convention, where the month precedes the day.

TABLE A.4 Beginning dates for sequences of positive and negative CD changes

	Isosign–4		Forgiving–7	
	+ve	−ve	+ve	−ve
		8/24/66[b]		
	6/21/66[a]	11/29/67	6/29/66	8/17/66
	7/5/67	5/22/68	12/14/66	11/29/67
	6/19/68	8/21/68	6/21/67	2/28/68
	9/18/68	1/8/69[b]	10/18/67	1/1/69[b]
	6/17/70[b]	5/7/69[b]	6/19/68	2/26/69
	9/16/70[b]	7/23/69[b]	6/3/70[b]	4/23/69[b]
	12/16/70[b]	10/8/69	8/5/70[b]	6/11/69[b]
	9/15/71	11/19/69	12/2/70	8/27/69[b]
	1/17/73[b]	12/17/69	6/30/71	11/26/69
	11/6/74[b]	3/24/71	9/1/71	8/29/73[b]
		9/19/73[b]	4/5/72	10/10/73[b]
			7/5/72	
			1/3/73[b]	
			2/21/73	
			1/4/74	
			6/26/74	
			8/6/75	

[a] All dates are given by US convention, where the month precedes the day.
[b] Indicates chains of at least six isosign or ten forgiving.

5

Measuring the Opportunity
for Product Innovation

MEGHNAD DESAI and WILLIAM LOW

INTRODUCTION

There has been extensive writing on financial innovation in recent years at the academic and the policy-maker levels (Silber, 1975, 1983; Federal Reserve Board, New York, 1981-2; Bank of England, 1983). There are clearly a number of interesting aspects about the microeconomic, macroeconomic, policy and political economy aspects of financial innovations which need to be explored. If we take Silber's 1983 paper in the *American Economic Review* as a convenient starting point, we see that as far as the causes of financial innovations are concerned the main ones are:

1 Policy: existing regulations or legislative initiatives to relax regulations.
2 Inflation and uncertainty: the level and volatility of nominal and real interest rates.
3 Technological change: the introduction of new electronic and telecommunication facilities.
4 Internationalization: increasing integration of money markets.

But while these causes are important, they are still only proximate ones. Even now we have only begun to scratch the surface of the question of the origins, diffusion and implications of financial innovations.

The focus in this paper is on the microeconomics of financial innovations. The precise question to ask is: *what are the reasons that motivate the suppliers of financial services to innovate?* While this is not a surprising question, it has, as far as we know, not been asked before. An early beginning was made by Greenbaum and Heywood (1973). They look at assets as combinations of characteristics, but having defined the problem, they do not use the characteristics approach subsequently in their paper.

This approach is, however, a fruitful starting point, as we shall see below. The focus then here is on the microeconomics of financial innovation. There are other aspects, such as the effects of financial innovations on the design of a monetary policy, which we do not deal with. But even within the microeconomic framework, of the many possible strands that could be pursued, we concentrate on the retail deposit market, i.e. those financial assets in which households are interested in putting their money. Topics that refer to banks' liability management or the developments in wholesale markets such as the Eurodollar markets are not our concern. Of course, for financial institutions, access to wholesale markets directly increases their ability to provide a greater variety of retail assets and we take this as given.

The financial innovations in which we are interested take the form of:

1 The introduction of new financial instruments in which individuals could put their money.
2 The emergence of new financial institutions which supply instruments/ services not provided by existing financial institutions.

Examples of both are easy to provide. There are indexed bonds, NOW deposits, cheque-save accounts, money market accounts etc. as far as new assets are concerned. As far as new institutions are concerned, the United States has seen much more by way of entry of non-banking even non-financial sector firms into the market for providing financial services – travel agencies/ credit card companies such as American Express, stockbrokers such as Merrill Lynch etc. The peculiarities of the Glass–Steagall Act and other regulations on the banking industry provide much greater scope for innovations under point 2 above in the United States than in Britain. But even in Britain the emergence of money market funds, an import from the United States, has been remarkable in recent years.

At the outset it should be said that the very existence of the two forms of innovations tells us something about the nature of the financial services industry. Ideally there should only be the first type (point 1 above). It should be possible for existing firms to provide new instruments to meet consumer needs if they are dynamic and competitive enough. (By competitive one need not mean perfectly competitive but a situation where there is competition for market shares even among a small number of firms.) If existing firms are not providing services for which a latent demand exists, then this can be either due to regulations preventing them from doing so or because they may be in a 'cosy oligopoly' situation where they do not perceive the need to meet latent demand. In such a case new firms may move into the market and fill the gap that exists.

This process of a latent demand existing and new products/new firms responding to fill the gap in the existing product spread is what we shall attempt to formulate and measure. Although it is a commonplace occurrence, it turns out to be quite difficult to analyse. Let us illustrate some of the problems.

The first problem concerns the identifying of innovation. In oligopolistic markets with product differentiation, it is a standard selling strategy to describe products as 'new, improved'. A handful of firms each providing a similar if not identical range of products may continuously announce new, improved, super versions of their products which may only be new in trivial aspects of product design. It is difficult for an outside observer to judge whether a 'new' toothpaste is new or just has a polkadot stripe added to the old ingredients. The US automobile industry in the 1950s and 1960s is a good example of this phenomenon. A small number of automobile manufacturing firms competed in producing new models of a similar product range year after year but these improvements were merely in style. It was only when European car makers such as Volkswagen appeared on the US scene that it became obvious that in terms of fuel efficiency there had been no improvement over the years in the US cars. The same could be said about safety aspects of cars. What we need then is some distinction between 'important' innovations and 'trivial' innovations. A bank providing its customers with cheque books in different colours may claim to be innovative, but it is when a rival bank/ nonbank offers higher interest rates for the same withdrawal facility that one would say that we have an important innovation. This implies, of course, *a priori* ordering of characteristics by their importance. Such ordering may be revealed by consumer preference but this is not guaranteed. For our purpose, we shall select two characteristics which we consider important.

In terms of this analysis, we would define an important innovation as one that locates and fills a gap in the range of available products. Such a gap should be definable in terms of the most important product characteristics. An innovation will also sometimes activate a characteristic that may hitherto have been latent, e.g. fuel efficiency in cars.

The problem then is to measure gaps in the product range. Innovations are trivial in the sense that if you can locate a gap in the product range, the gap will persist despite these trivial innovations occurring. The key here is the existence and identifiability of the gap as a proxy for latent demand.

To identify such gaps is not easy of course. If one believes in consumer sovereignty and perfect markets, such gaps, *by definition*, cannot exist. Firms that indulge in trivial innovations can point to consumer satisfaction in the sense that their new products are bought and they are profitable. They may also point to the intense competition they face from rivals who are also producing similar trivial innovations. If one of them did not produce new style car models each year, it would definitely lose its market share. Demand for fuel-efficient, safe, durable cars was very latent in the 1950s and emerged into view only when VW began to penetrate the US market successfully. Even then, it was only after the oil price rise that the European and Japanese car makers began to penetrate the US market seriously.

A third problem, apart from the two of separating trivial from important innovations and identifying latent demand, is the lack of an adequate theoretical framework in which to pose the problem. Even the theory of industrial innovations is in its infancy. There is a small but growing body of work on research and development strategies and the decisions of firms whether to innovate or not, but there are significant differences between industrial and financial products which need to be borne in mind in choosing a framework.

1 A most important difference is that there are no production function type considerations in introducing new financial instruments but these are crucial in industrial product innovation. At its basic level, the financial instrument is a contract written on paper and potentially all possible financial contracts can be written without any technological barrier. In this sense, financial innovations are not *new* goods. They are implicitly always there, but in zero supply (see also Greenbaum and Heywood, 1973).

2 Financial instruments are difficult if not impossible to patent. Like other services/goods whose main content is information, once a financial instrument has been launched it is open to quick and almost costless imitation.

3 Although there are no technological considerations, there are tremendous economies of size. Once a financial intermediary launches a new financial instrument, its profitability will depend crucially on how many people buy that instrument. This is for two reasons. First is the fact that the intermediary's return depends on the yield he pays to the customers and the yield earned by lending that money out. In wholesale markets, the larger the sum and the longer it can be lent out, the higher the earned yield. Second is the fact that the greater the number of customers the greater the pool of money for lending, since the risk of sudden withdrawal of a substantial portion of the pool will be less the larger the number of customers. (This risk pooling is of course not always effective as runs on banks do occur when everyone wishes to withdraw simultaneously.) (For evidence in economies of scale, see Greenbaum and Heywood, 1973.)

4 Given the absence of technological considerations, the only factor costs of launching a new financial instrument are the costs of product development, advertising etc. Since most financial intermediaries are multiproduct firms in this respect, the production costs of a new product launched or the current operating costs of particular assets can be neglected.

With this background in mind we proceed in the next section to pose the question of how product innovation and opportunities for product innovation can be measured in the financial markets.

A THEORETICAL FRAMEWORK

We need therefore to do two things. First, find ways of identifying and measuring gaps in the range of available products in the financial market which will indicate the potential opportunity for creating and launching new products: this is an *ex ante* measure. Second, find measures *ex post* of whether a financial innovation, of an important rather than trivial sort, has occurred.

There is an extensive discussion in location theory which seems to be a fruitful starting point for our purposes (Rosen, 1974; Lancaster, 1982 and the papers contained in that issue of *Journal of Industrial Economics*). The location of firms existing at any point of time could be described in terms of nearness to each other or in terms of nearness to the consumer. Then it would be easy to visualize a gap in the market if existing shops are too far apart in some sense. A potential entrant could locate his shop in the gap if he could calculate *ex ante* that such a location would be profitable.

It is obviously helpful if instead of physical space, we take the characteristics space as our starting point. The idea of goods as being combinations of characteristics is now a familiar one as a result of the work of Gorman, Lancaster, Makower and others. Let us begin with the immensely simpler case of a two characteristics space. As we shall see later, the higher dimensional case creates many problems.

Let there be two characteristics, R and A. For financial instruments we shall think of return (yield) (R) and access (liquidity) (A) as the two main characteristics. In figure 5.1, yield (R) is measured along the y axis and liquidity is measured as ease of access (A): assets being most liquid at zero and becoming more illiquid the farther away one goes from this point. One measure would be the number of days' notice required before one could liquidate the instrument. As normal, the more illiquid the instrument, the higher the return. If there were no other constraints, one should observe a continuous spectrum of assets from zero yield zero illiquidity (ready cash) to the highest yield on the most illiquid instrument. If we then had consumers with diverse tastes, they could choose their most preferred instruments along such a frontier depending on their MRS between the two characteristics, etc.

As we shall see later, we have no data on consumer holdings of different financial instruments, even in the aggregate let alone by individual consumers. What we do observe is the range of products available. In as much as they are

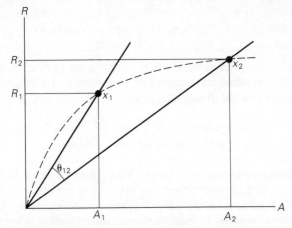

FIGURE 5.1 Two instruments – x_1 and x_2

available, i.e. being actively offered, we shall assume that they satisfy some consumers' preferences. In the absence of consumer holding data, we have to concentrate on product descriptions to locate the gap.

In figure 5.1 then we have two assets available x_1 and x_2: x_1 offers low yield and high liquidity and x_2 offers high yield and low liquidity. These are points in the characteristics space. We join them to the origin but we must be careful to avoid thinking that any combination along ox_1 (or ox_2) is also available. What is offered is the combination x_1 with coordinates OR_1 and OA_1; similarly for x_2.

The point of joining them to the origin is that now we can define nearness of assets and the gap between assets. Think first of a cosy oligopoly case where every firm offered two instruments, e.g. demand deposits, with implicit return OR_1 and ease of access OA_1 and time deposits with yield OR_2 and ease of access OA_2. If all firms offered the same or similar terms then all the available product points would be closely clustered around x_1 and x_2. There could be $2n$ instruments offered by n firms but in fact these would represent two instruments. Very close but slightly differentiated products could be offered – e.g., interest rates calculated daily rather than on balance at the end of the week. But most other differentiation might involve adding unimportant characteristics – multicoloured cheque books etc.

The distance between the two instruments can then be measured by the angle between them. This is to measure it from the origin. If we knew where the frontier was, we could measure the arc length between the two instruments at the frontier. Thus we take θ_{12} the angle between x_1 and x_2 as the measure of distance rather than the arc length x_1x_2 which is drawn as a dotted line to indicate our doubts about its shape and location. (The closer x_1 is to x_2, the less would the two measures diverge.)

We can now illustrate what we mean by trivial and important innovations. In figure 5.2, x_3 is a very close substitute of x_1 and the distance between them, θ_{13}, is very small. If we only had x_1, x_2 and x_3, the *maximum* distance *after* the introduction of the new asset x_3 between neighbouring assets max $(\theta_{13}, \theta_{23})$ would not be very different from the maximum distance *before* its introduction, which was θ_{12}. On the other hand, if x_4 was introduced to a world of x_1, x_2 the maximum distance between neighbouring assets would be given by max $(\theta_{14}, \theta_{24})$ and this distance would be much reduced as a result of the introduction of the new asset. Thus x_4 *fills the gap* in the product range but x_3 does not.

We can thus define θ_{ij} as the angle between two assets x_i, x_j. We take the distance between adjacent assets x_1, x_{i+1} as $\theta_{i,i+1}$. The distance between adjacent assets indicates existing gaps in the market at a point of time. Indeed given I assets the distribution of the $(I-1)$ adjacent distances $\theta_{i,i+1}$ at a point of time is a useful indicator of market structure. Thus in a cosy oligopoly we may find many small distances (close substitutes due to trivial product differentiation) and a few large distances (gaps uncatered for by existing firms). This would mean a larger variance or even kurtosis around the mean compared to a more competitive market.

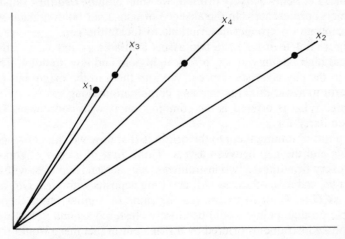

FIGURE 5.2 A trivial innovation (x_3) and an important innovation (x_4).

Over time, the number of assets will change. Let us assume they will increase. Thus I_t will be the total number of instruments at t and I_t will change with t. Now let the maximum distance between adjacent assets at t be θ_t^*, i.e. $\theta_t^* = $ max $(\theta_{i,i+1;t}$; all $i \ \epsilon \ I_t)$. A measure of how innovative a financial market is would be the change in θ_t^*. Over time one would expect innovations to fill in all the gaps so that the spectrum of assets will be a continuum. This would mean that θ_t^* will decline to zero over time – the gap would vanish. (Of course, it is always possible that while assets are getting 'crowded' in the two characteristic space, there will be a great incentive to innovate by opening up a new characteristic.) This, of course, is a limiting case. But as long as we can confine ourselves to the two characteristic space, these two measures are sufficient for our purposes – (*a*) the distribution of $\theta_{i,i+1}$ at a point of time and (*b*) the trend in θ_t^* over time.

DATA AND MEASUREMENT

In this section we proceed to measure the distances between assets over time using British monthly data on financial instruments available to British households. In order to collect data that were not only accessible to us but also, in principle, available to ordinary households, we gathered the information from the family finance page of the Saturday edition of *The Times*. This is an easily accessible source. There is obviously some sample selection bias since only the more 'successful' of the instruments would be included. We found, however, that new instruments were added to the list almost constantly. Where necessary, we filled in additional details on characteristics etc. from a specialist source such as *Investors' Chronicle*.

The financial assets we had information on can be grouped under the principal suppliers: banks, money market funds, National Savings, building societies. For each of these groups, one could proliferate information by using assets which were near substitutes. Thus all the banks provide a similar menu of deposit accounts – 7 day, 30 day, 90 day, 180 day, annual. We noted a specific bank's asset only if it was listed in the source as different. The same goes for building societies. Rather than note each separate society we looked at the types of accounts available: ordinary share, term share, regular saving etc. On money market funds we found that there was some difference in the yield being offered and so each fund was noted separately. It has been pointed out to us by members of some seminars that National Savings investments cater to a different type of clientele (older and with lump sums to invest) than do the other three. But having decided to go to one source, we did not think it right to start excluding assets on such grounds. These are thought to be assets of interest to retail depositors and so they are kept in.

The data were gathered on a monthly basis as of the last Saturday of each month. Since we saw our research in the nature of an exploratory study, monthly data were gathered from January 1982 to December 1984, giving us 36 time periods. For each month, we took all the financial instruments listed in *The Times* and noted all the characteristics that were given. These were: rate of interest (return), whether gross or net; frequency of interest payment; number of days of notice required; minimum and maximum amounts that could be invested; the term of the instrument; minimum amount for withdrawal; any penalties that would be incurred by premature withdrawal etc. There are thus clearly a lot of relevant characteristics besides return and access. We could however make a case that many of the other characteristics could be subsumed under one or the other. Thus by describing yield not as a single number but as a function we could incorporate aspects such as frequency of payment, penalties, term etc. Similarly, the conditions on amount to be deposited, limits on withdrawal etc. are elements of the access variable if taken as a function rather than as a scalar. We will not, however, enter into any elaborate rationalization since ideally we should like to deal with the n characteristics case. For the time being we deal with a subset of characteristics, regarding the others as nuisance.

In table 5.1 we give the information for January 1984 as an illustration. There are more than 30 entries. For all of them we have data on the rate of interest and also whether it was gross or net of taxation. (Since different depositors would pay different marginal tax rates, we could only adjust for taxation at the base rate for the present.) We then have fairly full data on period of notice (access), minimum and maximum deposit and the term of the asset. It is clear from the table that data on these other characteristics get patchy. We could not use all the information at our disposal if even basic information on the two characteristics was not available. This slimmed down the number of assets we could analyse. (Given the exploratory nature of the study, we did not pursue the gathering of missing information further by

TABLE 5.1 Financial assets available to households in January 1984

Asset	Return to 30% tax payer	Days' notice	Minimum	Maximum	Term
Banks					
7D	3.85	7	—	—	
30D	5.69	30	10 000	25 000	30d
90D	5.78	90	10 000	25 000	90d
180D	5.95	180	10 000	25 000	180d
365D	5.95	365	10 000	25 000	365d
Monthly Y	6.39				
Lloyds X	6.30				
NWX					
Money market funds					
Simco 7D	6.08	7	10 000	—	
UDT	6.04	7	5 000	—	
Tyndall 7D	6.13	7	2 500	—	
Simco $					
Western Trust	6.06	0	2 000		
Millanhall	6.20	0	5 000	—	
Save & Prosper	6.01	0	2 500	—	
Money Market Trust	6.26	7	2 500	—	
Tullet & Riley Call	6.08	0	10 000	—	
Tullet & Riley 7D	6.16	7	2 500	—	
Schroeder 7D	6.04	7			
Aitken-Hume	6.06	0	2 500		
Britannia	6.21	0	2 500		
Schroeder-Wagg					
Tyndall Call	6.15	0	2 500		
Bank of Scotland	6.22	0	2 500		
Charterhouse	6.30	0	2 500		
Choularton		1	1 000	—	
M&G Klein		0	2 500		
Midland HKA					
Henderson		0	2 500		
HFC		7	2 500		
National Savings					
Ordinary account	3/6	0	1	10 000	
Investment account	7.7	31	1	200 000	
Index-linked bond	4.8	38	10	10 000	5 yr
Certificate	8.26	8	25	5 000	5 yr
Income bond	8.05	90	1000	200 000	
Deposit bond	8.05	90	500	50 000	
Yearly plan		20		200/mth	5 yr
Building societies					
Ordinary share	7.25	7	0	30 000	
Term share	7.75–9.25	90	1000	30 000	1–5 yr
Regular savings	8.50				
Extra-interest	8.25				
7D share		7	500	30 000	
28D share		28	500	30 000	
90D share		90	500	30 000	

interviewing the suppliers or looking into other sources. If the present analysis is found to be promising, we may explore a questionnaire survey of financial firms.)

In table 5.2 we give therefore the data on the total number of assets used in the analysis. This variable is labelled I_t: the number of assets for month t. We can see that there was a rapid growth in I_t over the three years from 10 in January 1982 to 28 in December 1984. In no month was the number lower than the month before, i.e. $I_{t+1} \geqslant I_t$ for all t (figure 5.3). There are big jumps in March 1983 and May 1984, when the number goes from 14 in the previous month to 19 (1983) and 23 to 27 (1984). The growth in March 1983 was the launching of four new money market funds: Money Market Trust, Tullet and Riley Call, Tullet and Riley 7 Day, and Schroeder. In May 1984 it was the building societies which launched new types of accounts. This set of innovations meant changing the characteristic of an old asset – the ordinary share account – and launching three new types of shares – 7 day, 28 day and 90 day. The statutory notice (not actually very rigidly insisted on) before withdrawal from the ordinary share account was formally abolished. The details on all the 28 assets in December 1984 are given in table 5.3. This shows the data of introduction of the new assets and the assets already existing in January 1982.

To begin with we look at our assets in the two characteristics space. The idea is to see whether we can locate and measure the gap in the asset structure and whether new innovations appear to fill the gap. Figure 5.3 corresponds to figure 5.2, but now we have actual data. On the y axis we have yield net of tax and on the x axis we have days' notice as a measure of access. In order to avoid a bunching of many assets at zero days or seven days we also took into account the minimum amount that could be accepted as deposit. We saw

TABLE 5.2 Number of assets over time (I_t)

	1982	1983	1984
January	10	14	23
February	10	14	23
March	10	18	23
April	11	18	23
May	11	20	27
June	11	21	27
July	11	22	28
August	12	22	28
September	12	22	28
October	13	23	28
November	13	23	28
December	13	23	28

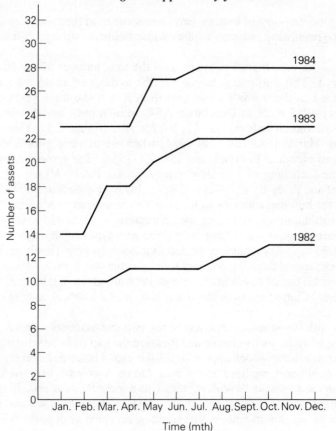

FIGURE 5.3

minimum amount as an additional illiquidity characteristic and added (admittedly arbitrarily) one day for each £100. Thus a seven day account with £1,000 minimum was taken to be 17 days. This is quite an arbitrary adjustment but it seemed adequate to clarify the diagram and served our present purpose.

With these adjustments, let us look at the data for April 1982. The data are given in table 5.4 and figure 5.4 illustrates them. As we see from table 5.2, the first new asset arrives in April 1982 and we also know which one it is – Western Trust (WT in figure 5.4), a new money market fund with a yield of 9.14 per cent, no notice but a minimum deposit of £2,000. The various assets appear as points in the two characteristic space. At the left, we have the building society ordinary share which had a yield of 8.75 per cent and 7 day notice and no minimum. Next to it is National Savings certificate with a yield of 8.92 per cent, 8 day notice and a minimum of £25. There is alongside but below it, the 7 day bank account which only gives

TABLE 5.3   Assets and dates of their introduction

Asset	Date of introduction or change[a]
Banks	
7D	
30D	
Money market funds	
Simco 7D	(October 1983)
UDT	
Tyndall 7D	
Western Trust	April 1982
Millanhall	August 1982 (April 1984)
Save and Prosper	January 1983
Money Market Trust	March 1983
Tullet and Riley Call	March 1983
Tullet and Riley 7D	March 1983
Schroeder	March 1983
Aitken and Hume	May 1983
Britannia	May 1983
Tyndall Call	July 1983
Bank of Scotland	June 1983
Henderson	May 1984
HFC	July 1984
National Savings	
Ordinary account	
Investment account	
Index-linked bond	
Certificate	
Income bond	October 1982 (April 1983)
Deposit bond	October 1983
Building societies	
Ordinary share	(May 1984)
7D share	May 1984
28D share	May 1984
90D share	May 1984

Number of assets: January 1982 = 10; December 1982 = 28.
[a] No date given implies the asset existed in January 1982. Dates in parentheses signify major changes in characteristics other than yield.

TABLE 5.4   Financial assets available to households in April 1982 (see also figure 5.4)

Key[a]	Asset	Return to 30% tax payer	Days' notice	Minimum	Maximum	Term
	Banks					
A	7D	7.18	7	—	—	
B	30D	8.75	30	10 000		30d
C	90D	8.40	90	10 000		90d
	180D		180	10 000		180d
	365D		365	10 000		365d
	Monthly Y					
	Lloyds X					
	NWX					
	Money market funds					
D	Simco 7D	8.64	7	1 000		
E	UDT	9.37	7	5 000		
F	Tyndall 7D	8.75	7	2 500		
	Simco $	9.74				
G	Western Trust	9.14	0	2 000		
	Millanhall					
	Save & Prosper					
	Money Market Trust					
	Tullet & Riley Call					
	Tullet & Riley 7D					
	Schroeder 7D					
	Aitken-Hume					
	Britannia					
	Schroeder-Wagg					
	Tyndall Call					
	Bank of Scotland					
	Charterhouse					
	Choularton					
	M&G Klein					
	Midland HKA					
	Henderson					
	HFC					
	National Savings					
H	Ordinary account	5.0	0	1		
I	Investment account	9.45	30	1	200 000	
	Index-linked bond		8	10	5 000	5yr
J	Certificate	8.92	8	25	5 000	5yr
	Income bond					
	Deposit bond					
	Yearly plan					
	Building Societies					
K	Ordinary share	8.75	7	0	30 000	
L	Term share	9.25–10.75	90	500	30 000	1–5yr
	Regular savings	10.0				
	Extra-interest					
	7D share					
	28D share					
	90D share					

[a] See figure 5.4.

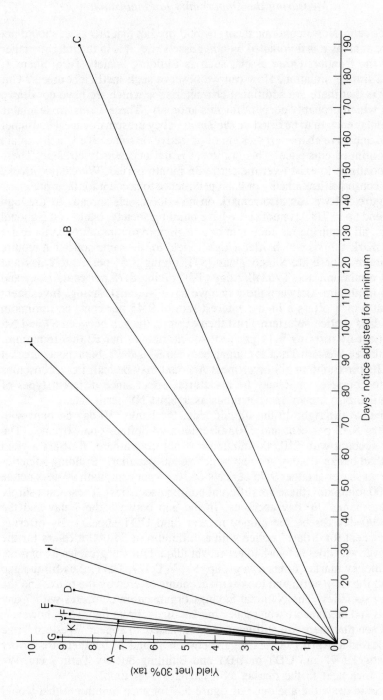

FIGURE 5.4 Financial assets available to households in April 1982 (for key see table 5.4)

7.18 per cent. Now economic theory would predict that this asset should not be there at all as it is dominated by other assets, i.e. it is in the interior rather than at the frontier. Other assets, such as Building Society Term Share 1, are in a similar situation. How can we observe such inefficient assets? Our answer is that there are additional characteristics which we have not drawn in here which probably account for this anomaly. These assets are available and popular enough to be listed in *The Times*. They presumably meet consumer demand and have characteristics either objective or subjective which explain their continued existence. This argument is not necessarily circular. These assets continue to exist over the entire 36 month period. We cannot invoke merely consumer irrationality or habit persistence to account for their presence.

In figure 5.4 we can also remark on how the assets spread. At the high access end up to 7/8 days notice we have building society, banks and National Savings, all requiring no minimum or a negligible minimum. Next there are money market funds which offer a higher yield for the same notice but require a minimum. These are Simco 7 day (S7), giving 8.64 per cent, 7 day and £1,000 minimum, and Tyndall 7 day (T7), giving 8.75 per cent, 7 day and £2,500 minimum. Between these two we have National Savings Investment Account which offers a higher interest rate of 9.45 per cent, no minimum but 30 days' notice. Western Trust then exploits the gap between S7 and NS Investment by offering 9.14 per cent for no notice, but £2,000 minimum. We could see Western Trust as coming between S7 and T7, both money market funds. Its proximity to NS Investment Account may be real, i.e. a conscious effort to compete, or it may be a pictorial effect since different types of households buy money market funds as against NS certificates.

Further to the right on the illiquid side, the banks' 30 day account with a yield of 8.75 per cent and £10,000 minimum defines one extreme. (The 90 day account with £10,000 minimum is not drawn here. It offers a yield lower than banks' 30 day account which seems peculiar.) Building societies offer term shares at either 9.75 per cent or 10.75 per cent, with 90 days notice and £500 minimum (these are different building societies). These must surely dominate banks' 90 day accounts. In the gap between the 7 day and the 30 day/90 day assets, the money market fund UDT appears. By offering 9.37 per cent for 7 days' notice with a minimum of £5,000 it caters for the large saver who does not wish to get caught illiquid for any great length of time.

The money market funds as a group, S7, WT, T7, UDT, thus fill the gap between the short-term and long-term accounts offered by the banks and the building societies. The National Savings organization competes with 7 day accounts and presumably with money market funds. From figure 5.4, however, we can see that there are still gaps for new assets to appear. Western Trust has appeared in April 1982 in the gap between S7 and T7 but there are further gaps between T7 and UDT or UDT and Building Society Term 2 etc. We need to turn next to the market as it changes over time.

We could draw the analogue of figure 5.4 for each month but that would give too much detail. We give two more figures, one for May 1983, where the total number of assets is 20 (figure 5.5 and table 5.5), and one for May 1984, where the total is 27 (figure 5.6 and table 5.6). The definitions in the axes are the same as before and the assets which continue on from the old date are labelled in the same way.

We notice immediately that figures 5.5 and 5.6 are much more 'crowded' than figure 5.4. In figure 5.5 there are many more assets in the middle range previously occupied by the money market funds apart from NS Investment Account. Between S7 and UDT, there were three assets in April 1982 – WT, T7 and NS Investment; now there are ten assets in that gap. The rate of introduction of new assets is slow at first: one in August 1982 (Millanhall MM Fund), one in October 1982 (NS Income Bond), one in January 1983 (Save and Prosper MM Fund). Then there is an explosion in March 1983 with four new money market funds (Tullet and Riley Call and 7 Day, Schroeder and Money Market Trust). This is followed by two more in May 1983 (Aitken and Hume, and Britannia). Except for NS Income bond, all the others are money market funds filling in the small gaps in the S7–UDT range. The left-hand side, short-term accounts, is relatively undisturbed: B7 has gone down in yield and NS ordinary has come up. Generally yields are lower in May 1983 than in April 1982 but the spread is similar. At the long end, NS Income bond (NSY) and Tullet and Riley Call with £10,000 minimum seem to fill in the gap between Building Society Term 1 and Term 2.

We see then that as between April 1982 and May 1983 the major innovations come from 'follower' money market funds which see the gap left by the leaders S7, T7, WT, UDT. Only Tullet and Riley Call fund with £10,000 minimum is analogous to a Building Society Term Account. It is here that the National Savings Income bond offering 7.7 per cent, 90 day and £2,000 minimum comes in to compete with the building societies' 6.75–7.25 per cent, 90 day, £500 minimum term shares.

It is the gap on the long end that gets filled by May 1984. Between May 1983 and May 1984, there is again a slow growth to begin with. Money market funds continue to appear: one in June 1983 (Bank of Scotland), one in July 1983 (Tyndall Call), but after that there is no further action in money market funds until May 1984, when Henderson appears. The big explosion is in the long end. National Savings improved their income bond in April 1983 and launched the deposit bond in October 1983. But it was the building societies which fought back by improving the yield and conditions on their term shares. They introduced 7 day, 28 day and 90 day shares and formally abolished the 7 day notice on their ordinary share account. The minimum on their term shares was still £500 but the reduction in notice and the spread of 7 day, 28 day and 90 day were the real innovations.

These innovations get the building societies competing across the spectrum. Thus the 28 day competes with money market funds (drawn in figure 5.5 as B Soc 30D), the 90 day competes at the long end with National Savings Deposit (NSD) and Income (NSY) accounts as well as with the high minimum, low notice money market funds.

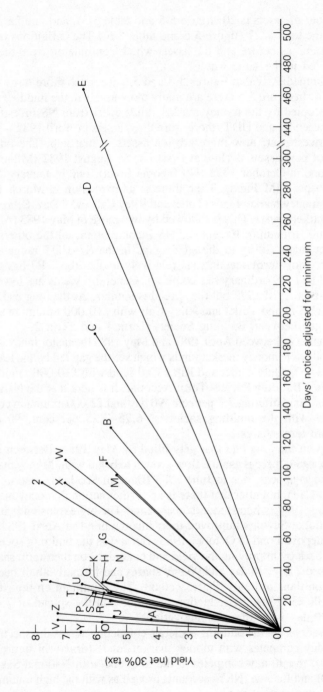

FIGURE 5.5 Financial assets available to households in May 1983 (for key see table 5.5)

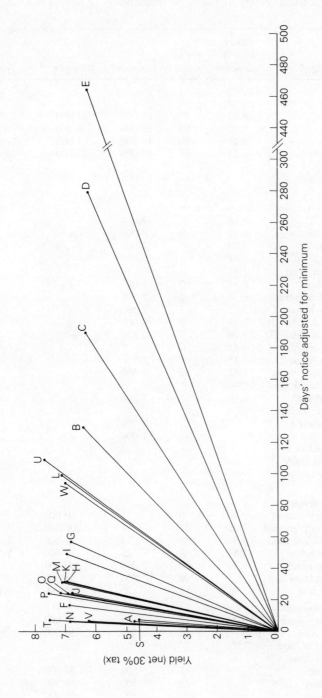

FIGURE 5.6 Financial assets available to households in May 1984 (for key see table 5.6)

TABLE 5.5 Financial assets available to households in May 1983 (see also figure 5.5)

Key[a]	Asset	Return to 30% tax payer	Days' notice	Minimum	Maximum	Term
	Banks					
A	7D	4.73	7	—	—	
B	30D	6.48	30	10 000	25 000	30d
C	90D	6.30	90	10 000	25 000	90d
D	180D	6.21	180	10 000	25 000	180d
E	365D	6.21	365	10 000	25 000	365d
	Monthly Y					
	Lloyds X					
	NWX					
	Money market funds					
F	Simco 7D	6.88	7	1 000	—	
G	UDT	6.83	7	5 000	—	
H	Tyndall 7D	7.00	7	2 500	—	
	Simco $	5.38				
	Western Trust	6.87				
I	Millanhall	6.97	0	5 000	—	
J	Save & Prosper	6.78	0	2 500	—	
K	Money Market Trust	7.01	7	2 500	—	
L	Tullet & Riley Call	7.14	0	10 000	—	
M	Tullet & Riley 7D	7.08	7	2 500	—	
N	Schroeder 7D	6.85	7			
O	Aitken-Hume	7.18	0	2 500		
P	Britannia	7.52	0	2 500		
	Schroeder-Wagg					
Q	Tyndall Call	6.96	0	2 500		
	Bank of Scotland					
	Charterhouse			2 500		
	Choularton		1	1 000	—	
	M&G Klein					
	Midland HKA					
	Henderson					
	HFC		7			
	National Savings					
	Ordinary account	3/6	0	1	10 000	
R	Investment account	7.35	31	1	200 000	
S	Index-linked bond	4.60	8	10	10 000	5yr
T	Certificate	7.51	8	25	5 000	5yr
U	Income bond	7.70	90	2 000	200 000	
	Deposit bond		90	500	50 000	
	Yearly plan		20	200/mth		5yr
	Building Societies					
V	Ordinary share	6.25	7	0	30 000	
W	Term share	6.75–7.25	90	500	30 000	1–5yr
	Regular savings	7.50				
	Extra-interest					
	7D share		7	500	30 000	
	28D share		28	500	30 000	
	90D share		90	500	30 000	

[a] See figure 5.5.

TABLE 5.6 Financial assets available to households in May 1984 (see also figure 5.6)

Key[a]	Asset	Return to 30% tax payer	Days' notice	Minimum	Maximum	Term
	Banks					
A	7D	4.20	7	—	—	
B	30D	5.51	30	10 000	25 000	30d
C	90D	6.13	90	10 000	25 000	90d
D	180D	6.21	180	10 000	25 000	180d
E	365D	6.48	365	10 000	25 000	365d
	Monthly Y	6.39				
	Lloyds X	5.78				
	NWX					
	Money market funds					
F	Simco 7D	5.66	7	10 000	—	
G	UDT	5.69	7	5 000	—	
H	Tyndall 7D	+5.78	7	2 500	—	
	Simco $					
I	Western Trust	5.56	0	2 000		
J	Millanhall	5.43	1	1 000	—	
K	Save & Prosper	5.53	0	2 500	—	
L	Money Market Trust	5.74	7	2 500	—	
M	Tullet & Riley Call	5.33	0	10 000	—	
N	Tullet & Riley 7D	5.74	7	2 500	—	
O	Schroeder 7D	5.81	7			
P	Aitken-Hume	6.13	0	2 500		
Q	Britannia	5.60	0	2 500		
	Schroeder-Wagg		1	2 500		
R	Tyndall Call	5.74	0	2 500		
S	Bank of Scotland	6.06	0	2 500		
	Charterhouse		0	2 500		
	Choularton		1	1 000	—	
	M&G Klein		0	2 500		
	Midland HKA					
T	Henderson	6.65	0	2 500		
	HFC		7	2 500		
	National Savings					
	Ordinary account	3/6	0	1	10 000	
U	Investment account	6.48	31	1	200 000	
	Index-linked bond		8	10	10 000	5yr
V	Certificate	+7.25	8	25	5 000	5yr
W	Income bond	7.00	90	2 000	50 000	
X	Deposit bond	7.00	90	500	50 000	
	Yearly plan		20		200/mth	5yr
	Building Societies					
Y	Ordinary share	6.25	0	0	30 000	
	Term share		90	1 000	30 000	1–5yr
	Regular savings	7.5				
	Extra-interest	7.25				
Z	7D share	7.25	7	500	30 000	
1	28D share	7.5	28	500	30 000	
2	90D share	7.75	90	500	30 000	

[a] See figure 5.6.

This last bunch of innovations by the building societies is thus retaliatory. They ape the existing assets – money market funds, NS bonds – to restore their market shares. If we had data on market shares, we could make this retaliatory nature of the innovations more precise, but even at the descriptive level, our figures make the point obvious.

The course of financial innovations in Britain over the three years 1982–4 is thus clear. There is a growth in the total number of assets available to the retail depositor from 10 to 28. This growth is monotonic but not smooth. There are periods of slow growth interrupted by sudden bursts but no decline in the number of assets. It would seem that initially banks and building societies provided similar products at the short and the long end. Competition came first from National Savings and then more seriously from the money market funds. The money market funds moved into the gap between the 7 day and 30 day assets by offering more attractive – higher yield – assets at the 7 day end. The proliferation of assets in this middle range then was from 'follower' funds moving in where 'leader' funds had found the gap. The gap was certainly filled by May 1983. The next bunch of innovations came from the building societies. They were responding to National Savings' attempt to cut into their long end accounts by introducing Income and Deposit bonds. Their response took the form of offering a wider spread of assets. This put them in a competitive position in the short, middle and long ends. The only non-innovative agents in all this seem to be the banks. Their hold on the current cheque-book account was threatened only during 1985 when building societies again introduced cheque–save accounts as well as offering electronic cash withdrawals. That, however, takes us outside our chosen period.

AN ANALYTICAL VIEW OF INNOVATION

In the previous section, we took a descriptive approach to our data. We listed assets by date, isolated new entrants and projected them on a two (or in effect three) characteristics space. The figures for the three time periods, April 1982, May 1983 and May 1984, seemed to tally with our expectation that gaps will be filled by innovation. But we can go further than that. We can use our θ measures to give slightly greater precision to our understanding of the process.

Recall our definition of θ above. At any point of time t, we measure $\theta_{i,i+1}$ (call it $\hat{\theta}_i$) as the angle between the neighbouring assets. The notion of a neighbouring asset raises no problem in two dimensions. We can look upon the distribution of $\hat{\theta}_i$ for each time period as a measure of the thinness of the market. In a deep market, with many assets closely competing with each other, the $\hat{\theta}_i$ will all be small. If there are gaps, some $\hat{\theta}_i$ will be large, others small.

In table 5.7 we present the size distribution of $\hat{\theta}_i$ for each month for the entire period. We have divided the full length into 12 size classes. The usual interval is 0.05, starting from 0.00 and ending at 0.55, but over time the

TABLE 5.7 Size distribution of $\hat{\theta}_i$ January 1982–December 1984

$\hat{\theta}_i$	1.82	2.82	3.82	4.82	5.82	6.82	7.82	8.82	9.82	10.82	11.82	12.82	1.83	2.83	3.83	4.83	5.83	6.83	7.83	8.83	9.83	10.83	11.83	12.83	1.84	2.84	3.84	4.84	5.84	6.84	7.84	8.84	9.84	10.84	11.84	12.84
	*										*	*	*			**	**	*		**	**	**	*			*	*		**	**	**	*		*	*	*	*
0.00(1)	1	1	1	1	3	3	1	3	2	5	7	4	5	6	8	6	9	14	14	10	11	16	16	16	17	17	18	12	11	12	17	18	18	18	18	18
0.05(2)	3	3	5	6	3	5	4	4	6	5	2	5	5	3	4	6	7	3	4	4	3	4	4	4	3	3	2	6	5	5	5	5	3	3	4	4
0.10(3)	4	4		1	2	2	3	2	1	1	1	1	2	3	2	2	2	2		4	3	1			1	1	1	2	3	2	1	1	2	2	2	2
0.15(4)			2	2	2	2	1	1	1			1	2	1	1		1		1	1	3				1		1	1		1						
0.20(5)										1	1	1								1																
0.25(6)	1	1	1		1					1	1	1	1	1	1	1	1	1	1	1			1		1	1		1	1							
0.30(7)									1						1							1														
0.35(8)						1	1	1	1		1	1	1	1		1	1	1	1	1	1	1	1													
0.40(9)												1																								
0.45(10)			1																		1															
0.50(11)						1				1			1										1	1												
0.55(12)	1																																			
Mean	0.139	0.139	0.125																																	
Median	0.098	0.098																																		
S.d.	0.160	0.150	etc.																																	

* For explanation, see text.
**

maximum length narrows. In some cases, while keeping to 12 size classes, we have narrowed the interval to 0.04, ranging from 0.00 to 0.44 (indicated by * in the table) and also to 0.02, ranging from 0.00 to 0.22 (indicated by ** in the table).

The table should be seen as a series of histograms, one for each month, but written numerically rather than drawn in. To begin with, we see in January 1982 that the mode occurs at 0.10, the bulk of the distribution is below that (8 out 10) but there are some extreme values, e.g. 0.55. There are two gaps. Over time, the distances diminish on average, i.e. the mean value of $\hat{\theta}_i$ for each t goes down over time. This is presented in figure 5.7. We can see that there is a mild but definite downward trend in the mean $\hat{\theta}_i$: it goes down from 0.139 to 0.027. The movement is not monotonic, i.e. the curve is bumpy and there is a rise in the value sometimes. This may be due to macroeconomic factors such as changes in nominal interest rates 'opening out' some gaps when they rise while squashing them when the rates fall. Over time, however, the average $\hat{\theta}_i$ falls.

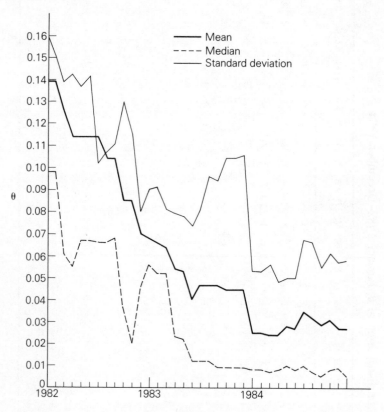

FIGURE 5.7

More important than the average, however, the distribution is squashed nearer to the zero value, i.e. there are an increasing number of closely competing assets. The first size class (0.00) has the largest number, i.e. becomes the mode most emphatically by February 1983 and stays the modal value. The first size class is also the median consistently after June 1983. (There are earlier instances when 0.00 is the mode or the median but we ignore these.) Thus the median follows the mean, falling from 0.098 in January 1982 to 0.005 in December 1984.

There is thus a decline in the mean over time, and the mode as well as the median occur in the first size class quite early on. This is a sure indicator of assets increasingly being close substitutes of each other. There is also evidence of increasing homogeneity, i.e. increasing degree of substitution in the market since the standard deviation of $\hat{\theta}_i$ also shows a downward trend. As table 5.7 shows, the standard deviation goes from 0.160 in January 1982 to 0.058 in December 1984. Again, while there are fluctuations in this figure, the trend is definitely downwards.

Thus we have found evidence of the increasing presence of assets that are close substitutes. We still need to look further, however. Recall that in the discussion of the theoretical framework above we made a distinction between trivial and important innovations. An explosion in trivial innovations will reduce $\hat{\theta}_i$ over time in mean, median and mode. This could happen while the gaps stay wide open. We need therefore an additional measure. This is the measure of θ_t^*, the maximum of the $\hat{\theta}_i$. If there are important innovations, θ_t^* should go down over time.

The course of the maximum angle θ_t^* can be seen in table 5.8. To begin with we have $\hat{\theta}_i$ as large as 0.55 in January 1982. This corresponds to the highest range in which an observation occurs in table 5.7. As the highest range in which an observation occurs moves down, we see that θ_t^* goes down. The course of θ_t^* is not, however, monotonically downwards. It goes up and down. Over the period as a whole, it goes down from 0.55 in January 1982 to 0.28 in December 1984. The lowest it gets is 0.22 in mid-1984. There is thus a closing of the gap over time and although there are 'copy cat' new products, as we saw above for May 1983, there are sufficient new products to lower the maximum gap (see also figure 5.8).

Although the largest gap is going down over time, our data enable us to ask one further question. Do new products always appear where the gap is the largest? Do we, in other words, see potential producers of new products as scanning the market, finding the largest gap and then tailoring their new product to fit the gap? If this were so, it would mean that our method of locating the gap simultaneously locates the most profitable opportunity for a new entrant. This is, of course, not necessarily so. Higher profits may be made by locating closer to existing products than going in a larger gap. This is what happens in April 1982. As of March 1982, the distribution of $\hat{\theta}_i$ shows a clustering of six out of ten assets into the first two intervals (0.00 and 0.05). This was followed by a gap of one interval

TABLE 5.8 θ_t^*: the maximum gap

	θ_t^*
1.82	0.55
2.82	0.50
3.82	0.45
4.82	0.50
5.82	0.50
6.82	0.50
7.82	0.35
8.82	0.35
9.82	0.35
10.82	0.50
11.82	0.40
12.82	0.28
1.83	0.40
2.83	0.40
3.83	0.30
4.83	0.28
5.83	0.28
6.83	0.28
7.83	0.30
8.83	0.22
9.83	0.20
10.83	0.24
11.83	0.45
12.83	0.45
1.84	0.24
2.84	0.24
3.84	0.28
4.84	0.22
5.84	0.22
6.84	0.22
7.84	0.30
8.84	0.30
9.84	0.24
10.84	0.28
11.84	0.28
12.84	0.28

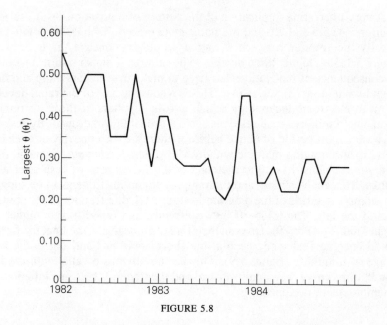

FIGURE 5.8

and two more assets were in the fourth interval (0.15), again followed by one gap to one more asset at 0.25. The maximum gap was between 0.25 and 0.55, where the last asset appeared. In April 1982, the new asset appeared not in the gap between 0.25 and 0.55 but between 0.05 and 0.15. We saw this in figure 5.3. The biggest gap is between UDT and the Building Society Term Shares. Leaving NS Investment Account out of consideration for the time being, it would seem that the gap between S7 and T7 is the second largest one, and this is where the new product WT appears. Thus from the potential entrant's point of view, we have to translate the size of the *ex ante* gaps into *ex ante* profitability. This requires data on market shares of existing assets which we do not have at present. It is interesting, however, that the new product appears in the second largest if not the largest gap.

To translate the gap into *ex ante* profitability we need some further information on the volume transacted in these assets. Thus think of a producer of financial assets thinking *ex ante* of entering the market. He locates various gaps. Corresponding to a large gap $\hat{\theta}_i$ there will be two 'neighbouring' assets x_i and x_{i+1} with which he will compete. His expected profits will depend upon the volumes transacted in x_i and x_{i+1} and the share of these volumes that the potential entrant can entice away from these two neighbouring assets, minus the cost of the interest/access combination he offers to his depositors. This could be formally set out very easily, but we see no point in such empty theorizing in the absence of data. (See, however, Deshmukh et al., 1983, for a similar problem and its formulation.)

A very interesting implication of the pattern of innovations as revealed by figures 5.4, 5.5 and 5.6 and the statistics in table 5.7 should be pointed out. Ideally the frontier between R and A would be concave, as is drawn in figure 5.1, i.e., higher illiquidity has to be suffered if higher return is required. A consequence of innovations has been to make instruments more and more liquid without sacrificing return. This is a consequence of the rapid development in electronic technology which allows suppliers of these instruments to maintain minimal cash reserves against probable withdrawal. By insisting on a very short period of notice before withdrawal, say one day or even less, and by discouraging multiple withdrawals of small amounts, financial firms can guard against having to maintain costly inventories of cash at clearing banks. This enables more and more highly liquid instruments to be supplied profitably. In terms of the diagram in figure 5.1, the frontier shifts upwards and to the left. The trade-off between return and liquidity gets higher and higher ($\delta(dR/dA)/\delta t > 0$). One can therefore imagine that in the limit the frontier could become Γ shaped, steep at the short liquid end and flat in the large range of illiquidity (figure 5.9). This has an obvious parallel with the long run Phillips curve, becoming vertical and the trade-off between inflation and unemployment disappearing.[1]

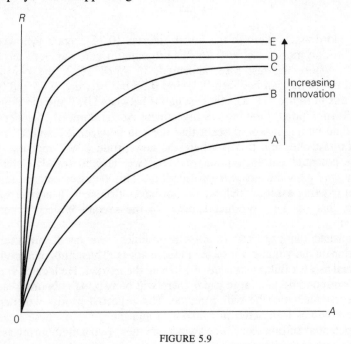

FIGURE 5.9

1   We are grateful to Christian de Boissieu for providing this insight during discussions on the paper at the Conference.

If such a process occurs, the effect is to render the financial market highly liquid, very short-term and hence subject to volatile changes in the volume of transactions as depositors quickly and, nearly costlessly, move funds from one asset to another. In this sense, the fragility of the financial system increases as innovations occur. This is a concern shared by other contributors to this volume.[2]

CONCLUSIONS

We would claim that the measures $\hat{\theta}_i$, average $\hat{\theta}_i$ and θ_t^* are useful and interesting indicators of the process of innovation. They tell us about the state of the market at a point of time, as well as its evolution over the course of time. The attempt to define gaps in terms of angles seems to give an intuitively plausible way of looking at the problem.

Several problems remain. First, we should try to extend our data set by getting information on individual banks and building societies as well as money market funds. It would be most helpful if we could have information on the amount invested in these different assets and hence on market shares.

We also need to look at the multiple characteristic case. This is not at all straightforward as we move from two to many characteristics (see Lancaster, 1982, for a discussion). The notions of 'nearness' and of 'gap' are not easily amenable to intuitive interpretation in many dimensions. We have made some beginnings in this direction by looking at the Euclidean distance as a measure, but our results are as yet too preliminary to be discussed. We hope to report on them in the near future.

AUTHORS' NOTE

Financial support from ESRC to the LSE Econometrics DEMEIC Programme is gratefully acknowledged. We are grateful to Christian de Boissieu, Mahmud Pradhan, Steve Pudney, Peter Robinson and Peter Swan for comments. We also thank Mrs Alison Aspden of the LSE Drawing Office, who helped with the diagrams.

The views expressed herein are those of the authors and do not necessarily reflect any official views of the LSE or the University of Essex.

2   See in particular the contribution by A. Wojnilower.

REFERENCES

Bank of England 1983: The nature and implications of financial innovations. *Quarterly Bulletin*, September, 358–76.

Deshmukh, S. D., Greenbaum, S. I. and Kanatas, G. 1983: Interest rate uncertainty and the financial intermediary's choice of exposure. *Journal of Finance* 38, 141–7.

Federal Reserve Board, New York 1981–2: Innovations in the financial markets. *Quarterly Review*, Winter, 1–41.

Greenbaum, S. I. and Heywood, C. V. 1973: Secular change in the financial services industry. *Journal of Money Credit and Banking*, May, 571–603.

Lancaster, K. 1982: Innovative entry: profit hidden beneath the zero. *Journal of Industrial Economics* 31, 41–56.

Rosen, S. 1974: Hedonic process and implicit markets: product differentiation in pure competition. *Journal of Political Economy*, Jan/Feb.

Silber, S. 1975: Towards a theory of financial innovation. In *Financial Innovation*. Lexington, Mass.: D. C. Heath.

Silber, S. 1983: The process of financial innovation. *American Economic Review*, May, 89–95.

6

Financial Innovation in Britain

JOHN H. FORSYTH

THE PROCESS OF INNOVATION

Financial innovation is the process by which the financial system adapts itself to new conditions. For this reason, most financial change reflects a reaction to broader economic and political developments. However, the process of causation is complex and at times broader developments can be traced back to financial causes. Few can doubt that the history of Europe in the sixteenth century, both economic and political, was profoundly affected by the presence of large gold and silver deposits in the New World. In the present century, the German hyperinflation can hardly be seen as the inevitable consequence of broader political and economic changes but its importance for subsequent development in these areas cannot be contested.

If change in the political and economic system is typically the ultimate cause of most financial innovation, it is evident that two factors are usually more proximately involved in the process: regulation and technology. Financial systems rarely go unregulated for long, so that regulations in some form or other limit the range of possible innovation. In many cases this is a result of deliberate policy, but the unintended effects of regulations are often as important as their original objective. The introduction of the Office of Foreign Direct Investment (OFDI) regulations in the United States, which was intended to strengthen the capital account of the US balance of payments, in practice reduced the willingness of US corporations to repatriate capital and encouraged them to build up financial reserves offshore: thus regulations aimed at strengthening the capital account of the US balance of payments were of dubious benefit in that respect, but had major consequences in terms of the development of offshore dollar business.

Regulation is often seen as a brake on financial innovation, but this view is too simplistic, for there are two mechanisms by which regulation can stimulate innovation. The first is the familiar process by which the financial system develops new techniques in order to circumvent regulatory obstacles which can then be applied in other contexts. It is not often realized that the techniques of currency and interest rate swaps, which are now regarded as one of the leading edges of banking innovation, were originally developed by British banks in the form of back to back loans, which were set up in order to deal with the problems posed by British exchange control. Exchange control can be regarded as a source of massive market imperfection, but the techniques used to exploit such imperfection can, it has now been shown, be applied to a very wide range of minor market imperfections. The second and less common process is where regulatory policy is deliberately used to impose change on an unwilling financial system. A current example of this must be the changes taking place in the London stock exchange, which could hardly be described as the reluctant response of government to pressure from an innovative financial system. While it was perhaps natural that the stock exchange has shown great reluctance to see changed institutional arrangements that provided an extremely satisfactory income level for its members, it is worth noting that other institutions within Britain, although unwilling to defend the stock exchange structure, were in no way vigorous proponents of change.

Technological progress can influence the financial system in two ways. The first is to lower the costs of particular operations, so both encouraging substitution of new techniques as they become more competitive and stimulating increased use of such techniques as costs fall. A good example of this is the way in which the falling cost of electronic communications relative to postal services is leading to the replacement of cheque payment methods by the use of credit cards and electronic payment systems. The interesting question is what new financial institutions will develop as a result of the exploitation of this technology for, certainly in Britain, the emergence of large national deposit banks in the early part of this century depended on the replacement of the inland bill by cheques as a method of payment.

The second and more fundamental influence occurs when technology makes entirely new types of operation possible. Such developments are infrequent and it may be worth observing that the sterling–dollar exchange rate is still colloquially referred to as the 'cable' by London dealers, a useful daily reminder of the way in which the laying of transatlantic cables changed the financial world.

BRITAIN AS A SPECIAL CASE

The process of financial innovation is thus a complex one in which simple models can be misleading. This is nowhere more true than in the case of Britain, where the City of London's dual role as the centre of Britain's financial system and as an international financial entrepôt market has produced a system of great complexity, in which innovation can only be understood by reference both to developments in the domestic economy and change in the international system.

In this sense London is unique, for, of the three financial centres that are now developing a dominant role in the international financial system – Tokyo, New York and London – the other two are the financial centres of the two major open economies and in both centres domestic business plays the dominant role. This is not the case in London, where by a number of criteria, international business plays the preponderant role. In the United States non-residents' deposits payable in foreign currency account for less than 0.5 per cent of bank deposit liabilities, and their dollar deposits just over 10 per cent of total deposits. In Japan non-residents' deposits in yen and all foreign currency deposits amount to less than 8 per cent of bank deposits. The comparable figures for Britain are 78 per cent of deposits owned by non-residents and 75 per cent of deposits in foreign currency. In the capital market area, the proportion of Eurobond turnover accounted for by London, which is usually taken to be of the order of 60 per cent, would indicate that the volume of transactions in which British institutions participate in the Eurobond market alone amounts to twice the turnover of the London stock market.

The uniqueness of London may, in one sense, make the British experience of less relevance to an analysis of the process of innovation in other countries. However, in another sense, it is of particular relevance, for in all open economies the international system is, to a greater or lesser degree, an influence on domestic developments, and Britain, through London, has in recent years exerted a quite disproportionate influence on the way in which the international financial system has developed.

This is not to argue that the growth of international financial flows is the result of London's innovative skills and commercial dynamism. Such a fundamental development as the revival of international financial flows stems from basic changes within the international system. The growing penetration of the international financial system into national financial systems, with the concomitant integration of financial markets, can be seen as a necessary consequence of the integration of the world trading system which preceded it. For the growth of trade was accompanied by a growth in current account imbalances and a consequent need for growth in capital flows. At the same time, the growth of firms organized on an international basis led to a greater complexity in the pattern of capital flows, with gross flows showing significantly faster growth than net flows. Such an expansion in the volume of international capital flows could have led to a very broadly based growth of international business in the various national financial centres. However, such a rapid development of financial flows, with the concomitant need for the evolution of institutional techniques and mechanisms, requires a high degree of concentration of skills and services. In these circumstances, the entrepôt market that can develop a sufficiently critical mass of participants will have a crucial advantage over the competing centres. By the same token, as the new technologies become established, they will be more widely diffused throughout the system and the entrepôt centre's absolute preponderance will be reduced. The early 1970's saw London with an absolute domination of the

Eurocurrency banking markets, which in recent years has lessened as other centres have emerged. In the same way, at the present time, London has an extraordinary domination of the emerging international long-term capital markets, readily illustrated by the fact that two-thirds of all Eurobond market making firms are based in London, but this dominance can be expected to decline, even though London's business continues to grow, as the techniques become diffused to other centres.

If the revival of international capital flows was set off by forces external to Britain and over which British influence was minimal, the form which the growth has taken has been greatly influenced by London and thus by the British system. At the same time, the presence of a booming entrepôt market in London has had a profound influence on the development of the domestic financial system. For, while it is possible to talk of a domestic and an international financial system, within the City of London the interpenetration of the two has had profound institutional effects. The range of institutions within the City of London, which operate in both the domestic and international markets, is huge, and skills and resources are readily transferred from one to the other.

The process by which financial innovation has transformed the financial system in Britain over the past 25 years has been, at every stage, connected with the parallel development of entrepôt financial business in the City of London. Institutions and capital, which were attracted to London because of its entrepôt role, have exploited opportunities within the domestic market, introducing new techniques and competitive forces. The evidence to the Wilson Committee, which inquired into the working of the British financial system, showed that the US banks, who had come to London to participate in the Eurodollar market, not only gained a significant share of term industrial lending business but also introduced new techniques and processes which the domestic British clearing banks had been forced to adopt as a result of competitive pressure. At the same time British institutions, whose role was severely circumscribed within the domestic system, have been able to grow in financial strength and technical resources as a result of international business and utilize that strength to effect change within the domestic market.

LONDON ON THE VERGE OF CHANGE

The interesting questions concern why London as a financial centre has been so successful at exploiting the opportunities provided by the revival of international capital flows and the way in which this process has accelerated the process of financial innovation within Britain. Twenty-five years ago the British financial system was a highly specialized one in which competition was strictly contained within specialist groups and even within those groups was on a very restricted basis.

It may be worth observing that for many years the British clearing banks all retained the same advertising agency and among British merchant banks it was regarded as unusual if not unacceptable behaviour to approach the clients of another bank. A small number of large clearing banks dominated the banking system, operating on a national basis and charging agreed interest rates for both deposits and loans. These cartel rates were customarily adjusted in line with the Bank of England's Bank Rate and enabled the clearing banks to make a very satisfactory return from their wholesale business. Retail business was growing slowly, reflecting rising incomes and demand for money transfer services, but the principal importance of the retail business was as a source of balances on current accounts on which no interest was paid. The importance of these current account balances to bank profits was such that, as a group, they made no attempt to promote their savings function as it was thought that by doing so they might encourage retail customers to expect interest, with a consequent reduction in their willingness to maintain large interest free current account balances.

The other main participants in the retail market were the government, which through National Savings and the Trustee Savings Bank, absorbed a high proportion of the personal sector's discretionary savings, and the building societies. National Savings had, during the war and early post-war period, played a major role in the finance of the government. Its role expanded very rapidly at a time of general consumer rationing and was maintained in the 1950s as rationing was removed by the use of competitive interest rates and tax concessions. However, in time, the government came to regard National Savings as a cheap source of finance and consequently allowed the rates paid to become less competitive.

The other significant element in the retail savings market was the building societies. These peculiarly British institutions are best described as cooperative savings banks, whose activities are limited to the financing of mortgages and investment in public sector debt. Building societies are mutual institutions in which both borrowers and lenders are regarded as members. Typically, the rates which they offered to investors were significantly above those offered by either banks or National Savings so that their share of the retail savings market tended to grow in the absence of serious competition from either the banks or the public sector. The banks' share of the personal sector's liquid assets is at present 33 per cent, the same level as in 1963. Over the same period, the building societies' share has risen from 20 per cent to 50 per cent.

Within the City of London, the discount houses maintained a precarious, privileged position as the intermediaries between the banking system and discount facilities at the Bank of England. Their stock in trade were bills provided either by the government through its Treasury bill issue or by the banking system, where the merchant banks maintained bill acceptance as a vestige of their nineteenth-century banking business. The acceptance credit business was highly lucrative but the scope for growth was minimal and for this reason the accepting houses, deprived of their traditional entrepôt role, began to expand their business into two major areas. The first was the finance of the British corporate sector, where they were able to exploit the financial weakness of stock exchange firms to achieve a role in the primary underwriting of company securities and then to utilize that role to develop an advisory function and to evolve a major business in mergers and acquisitions which exploited the preponderance of publicly quoted companies in the British private sector. The other major area of growth was in fund management, where they identified at an early stage the scope for growth in occupational pension schemes, a tax-privileged form of saving within Britain.

An important new element in the financial system was provided by the finance houses, which had grown by specializing in businesses such as hire purchase and financed themselves from wholesale deposits. Many of these finance houses were owned by the clearing banks and referred to commonly as the clearers' 'back doors'. This enabled the clearers to compete in wholesale lending and deposit markets without disturbing their cartel deposit and loan arrangements, which they maintained throughout their branch banking networks, which operated under their own name.

At that stage there were, of course, British overseas banks and foreign banks based in the City of London, but their role was largely limited to the conduct of international businesses and to a limited domestic banking business with subsidiaries of companies to whom they acted as bankers in their own countries.

The presence of foreign banks in London reflected the historic importance of London as a financial entrepôt and its continuing position as the centre of the sterling area, but both the entrepôt business and the sterling area were spent forces. The system of exchange control imposed at the beginning of the Second World War had been maintained intact during the post-war period and by 1960 was commonly regarded as a permanent feature of the British financial system. It severely restricted the use of sterling as an international currency with a consequent impact on London's business. International loans had continued to be made in sterling but, with the contraction of the sterling area and an official commitment to reducing sterling's reserve currency role, the business was a declining one. It is worth noting that, by 1960, London's role as an international financial centre had come to depend on its role as an international market for commodities and for financial services such as insurance and shipbroking. However, of the true business of the financial entrepôt, the market in money and in capital, only a vestige remained.

THE REVIVAL OF THE ENTREPÔT ROLE

The subsequent growth in the international markets has been dominated by London as a financial centre. More than 75 per cent of bank deposits in Britain belong to overseas residents at the present time, as compared to a figure of 10.4 per cent in the United States and less than 7 per cent in Japan. On the face of it, this is a surprising development, as the revival of London as an international capital market was until very recently combined with a continuing decline in the role of sterling as an international currency. Many reasons are adduced for London's success in establishing a major role in international business, but two factors are often mentioned. The first is US regulatory restrictions, which encouraged the US financial system to move its international business offshore. The restrictions concerned related both to banking regulations, in particular Regulation Q, which limited the payment of interest on deposits, and measures such as those implemented through the Office of Foreign Direct Investment and the Interest Equalization Tax. The second factor is that London's location in the European time zone made it a highly attractive place for banks to do business.

Neither of these two factors provide an entirely convincing explanation as to why London should have been the principal beneficiary of the growth of international dollar business. The former explains why the business did not occur onshore in the United States, while the latter provides an explanation for a European centre emerging, rather than a specific reason for London's emergence.

One simple explanation is that Britain is an English-speaking country and English was emerging as the international business language: the advantages conferred on London by its English-speaking labour force were significant but not, in my view, decisive, as the other side of the coin was that the linguistic skills of the English have tended to be significantly less than those of other Europeans, precisely because of the ease with which they can use English in other countries.

A much more decisive factor is that there existed within the London market historic mechanisms which could be applied to developing international business in an efficient manner. To take one specific example, the great international bill market in London had, in the nineteenth century, evolved the technique of forming syndicates for the provision of acceptance of bill facilities. These facilities were set up to deal with the requirements of firms of substantial size in countries throughout the world, so that the credit risks involved in the facilities were large relative to the size of the merchants in London who were providing the bill facilities. For this reason, they sought to spread their risk by syndicating it among firms in a similar line of business who would in turn syndicate their risks, so that most merchant houses in the City of London were both participants in the syndicates of other houses and the leaders of syndicates in which others participated. Similar techniques were used in the insurance market of Lloyds and in the shipping market, where it was common for the ownership of ships to be split down to fractions as low as 1/64. This technique of spreading the risk between institutions, rather than managing risk by creating institutions large enough to contain any likely risk within the structure of their portfolio, was a very old one but, in the early part of the twentieth century, the emergence, through merger, of very large clearing banks and of large insurance companies had meant that risk had begun to be taken within institutions rather than shared between those institutions.

When the Eurocurrency market first began to emerge, the London merchant banks were quick to apply the syndication techniques, which they used in their acceptance credit business, to bank lending, for in this way they were able to mobilize large amounts of capital out of the small amounts of dollar surplus funds which international banks operating in London acquired in the course of their business. These had previously been redeposited in the New York banking market at a relatively marginal gain to the banks concerned, achieved by aggregating individual balances to secure higher rates of interest than were available in New York to their individual clients. However, once the merchant banks began to organize loans on a syndicated basis, it became possible for these banks to participate in loans at rates competitive with lending rates in the New York market. As these lending rates reflected significant reserve costs within the US banking system, the scope for profit was considerable and they began to bid much more aggressively for dollar deposits, thus drawing international dollar deposits out of New York and into London.

It is interesting to note that once the large commercial banks around the world began to recognize the potential of the emerging Eurodollar market based in London, their initial reaction was to approach it as sole lenders or, where the volume of their business did not appear to justify such an approach, to join with commercial banks from other countries to form consortium banks in the City of London. The concept of such a consortium bank was that it would provide a permanent syndicate for international lending so that a member of the consortium would direct his domestic customers to the consortium for their international banking requirements and the consortium bank would have a sufficiently large business to be able to operate as a sole lender. It was always envisaged that the consortium bank might fall back on direct syndication to its member banks. It should be stressed that the consortium bank was the innovation adopted by most of the major commercial banks in the industrialized countries to handle international banking business. It was an innovation that failed because the alternative syndication techniques developed in the London market at a much earlier period proved able to offer a superior degree of flexibility and efficiency. The 1960s saw the creation of a large number of consortium banks within the City, but the 1970s began to see their disbanding, typically by one consortium member buying out the others. It is now a general expectation that by the end of this decade there will be few consortium banks left within the international system.

It was London's institutional knowledge and techniques which enabled it to play such a major role in the development of the international capital market. Those techniques have proved to be highly adaptable to modern conditions and exceptionally well suited to the operations of an entrepôt market, which is hardly surprising as they were developed during a period when London was a dynamic entrepôt centre. However, as noted earlier in this paper, it was not only the techniques developed in the nineteenth century which proved to be readily adaptable in the new environment, but also techniques developed during the period of British exchange control, such as back to back loans, which have subsequently provided such a remarkable tool for exploiting institutional imperfections in the international capital markets through swap transactions.

The techniques possessed by the London banking community were not the only important factor, for London had two invaluable advantages. The first was that the Bank of England, for historic reasons, considered it a part of its function to encourage the international business of the City of London. The result was that it pursued an open door policy, enabling foreign owned firms to conduct business in London and regulating those international firms in a way that encouraged them to conduct business in London. A very important feature of the Bank's regulatory attitude was that it would not provide protection for domestic firms, *vis-à-vis* foreign firms, although in most cases the policy was not reciprocated. Such a policy made London immensely attractive to foreign firms as an entrepôt centre. It benefited British firms by bringing business to their doorstep, but the corollary to it was that as foreign firms, which had been coming to London to conduct domestic business, began to exploit business opportunities in the domestic market, the Bank did not discourage the competitive pressures which were thus engendered.

The second factor was that London's regulatory system was largely discretionary, with the Bank of England able to exert very broad powers not only over the banking system but also over the insurance and long-term capital market. The result was that regulatory policy adjusted much more smoothly to change than could be the case in a less discretionary and more legally precise system. Examples of this range from the Bank's sponsorship of the Takeover Panel to regulate the conduct of mergers to its intervention in the affairs of Lloyds. This is not to say that the British regulatory system has been without its failures, for these have been well publicized. It has, however, shown a considerable capacity to manage change and if elements of the system smack of enlightened despotism, that has not prevented financial intermediaries from throughout the world crowding into London.

THE IMPACT ON THE DOMESTIC MARKET

In this way, the Bank of England's commitment to a competitive and open door policy in the City's international business implied a willingness not to restrict the growth of competition within the domestic market, a market which had, during the dormancy of the City's international business, become specialized and uncompetitive.

Developments in the domestic market also contributed to this growth of competition. In the wholesale markets, accepting houses, overseas banks and finance houses, including the clearers' back doors, began to compete more aggressively for deposits and large companies became progressively less willing to leave deposits with clearing banks at uncompetitive rates. In the retail sector, as already mentioned, the building societies began a sustained expansion: in

1960 they accounted for less than 20 per cent of the liquid assets of the personal sector, a figure which rose to nearly 50 per cent by the late seventies. They offered consumers a straightforward savings service with few service frills but a rate of interest that was typically highly competitive relative to other investments that were readily accessible to the personal sector. Moreover, they began to market themselves as savings institutions, a step which the clearing banks were loath to follow because of the potential impact on their interest free balances.

The result of the defensive attitudes of the clearers as compared to the building societies was that the retreat of the public sector from the retail market in Britain was marked, not by an expansion of the market share of the large commercial banks, but by an increase in the market share of the building societies. Building societies were then, and to a lesser extent still are, very much less concentrated than the clearing banks and, although the major societies organized on a national basis dominate the business, there remained a large number of smaller societies, which have frequently been a source of innovation and change as they attempted to gain competitive advantage by the invention of new products for the saver.

The result of these parallel movements in the wholesale and retail markets has been to lessen the dominance of the clearing banks within the British system, and that has had profound implications for the way in which the system worked. From the 1930s the British financial system had worked on a low interest rate basis where credit was allocated by the major clearing banks at the direction of the authorities, who would indicate which should be the approved sectors for lending and at what rate lending portfolios should increase. In a similar way, the building societies' mortgage rates were typically held below market clearing rates and mortgage queues were accepted as a feature of the system.

With the growth of competition, it became less possible to administer the system in that way and policy shifted towards accepting a high interest rate policy in which credit would be allocated largely by price. The major change in policy within Britain is usually regarded as the introduction of competition and credit control in 1971 which had the declared intention of shifting from a fixed price to a market clearing system. In practice, however, the process which made such a development inevitable began long before the introduction of competition and credit control. The conversion of the authorities to a market clearing system was in any case less than complete. As recently as the early 1980s the authorities have used quantitative controls on the banking system and are still prepared to issue directives as to the allocation of credit.

The importance of competition and credit control can be exaggerated, for the critical factor was the emergence of vigorous intermediaries who were prepared to exploit the opportunities which had been created by the cartel operations of the clearing banks. During the 1960s, this pressure remained marginal but by the 1970s, the capital resources and scale of activities of non-clearing banks in the wholesale market and of the building societies in the retail market had reduced the dominance of the clearing banks within the financial system to a point at which it would be difficult to see a cartel being re-established even if they and the government wished to do so.

CHANGE IN THE CAPITAL MARKETS

Within the capital market the pace of change has been very much slower. The principal reason for this has been that the stock exchange has been able to maintain a ban on external membership up to the present time. This, together with the maintenance of a dual capacity system which prevented the public from having direct access to market makers, has meant that the organization of the securities industry has not been able to adjust so as to exploit opportunities in either the domestic or the international market.

The importance of these restrictions became apparent in the late 1970s with the development of international institutional portfolio management. The experience of floating exchange rates and the realization that investment returns showed significant international divergence led institutions throughout the world to take a more international view of investment management. The result was a sharp rise in the demand for international fund management services, which London institutions were quick to respond to and, it should be said, played a significant role in stimulating. The very rapid growth of international investment management in London stimulated a demand for financial services and attracted a high proportion of the major securities houses in larger industrial countries to establish operations in London. This growth was further stimulated by the removal of British exchange control, which released pent-up demand for international securities from British institutions who had remained very internationally orientated, not least because of the high proportion of companies with international quoted stocks in the London market.

The consequence of these two developments has been the creation of a critical mass of demand for international capital market services which has served to revive London's entrepôt role in the long-term capital market.

A LOST OPPORTUNITY

The result of the rigidity in the domestic market has been the growth of a parallel international market based in the City of London but dominated by foreign firms dealing in international capital market instruments, particularly debt, in which British participants have tended to lose market share in recent years owing to their lack of domestic product. Efficient international securities distributors need to have a broad product range so as to reduce their costs and provide the basis for constant communication with their customers. Within their product range they need to have products in which they have a natural competitive advantage, for in these areas customers will feel that they must deal with the intermediary concerned. Once that relationship is established, it becomes substantially easier to expand the business to cover other products where their competitive position is more marginal. For most financial intermediaries in the international market, the major area of comparative advantage relates to international demand for their domestic securities rather than to international securities. For this reason, intermediaries who are confined to the latter are at a severe competitive disadvantage.

The closure of the stock exchange to corporate members has, of course, prevented international securities firms in London from penetrating the British securities market to any significant degree, for, although they have been able to exploit loopholes in the British regulatory and tax structure by trading British equities in US depository form in New York without access to the stock exchange, their ability to act as efficient intermediaries in this business is very limited. The changes that are now under way in the stock exchange, the so-called 'Big Bang', which will allow corporate membership and dual capacity trading by the end of 1986, will produce a period of revolutionary change in the British capital markets. Foreign firms established in London will be able to enter the British domestic market, which is by international standards a very substantial one, while those British firms who can organize themselves so as to exploit the new opportunities should have a greatly enhanced competitive position in the international capital markets: whether they can do so with sufficient speed to protect their position against internationally based competitors remains to be seen, but the history of the London market would suggest that at least some of the major firms will show the necessary ability to adapt swiftly to new circumstances.

THE IMPLICATIONS OF THE BIG BANG

The present separation between primary underwriters, brokers and market makers seems likely to disappear as a result of the planned changes in the stock exchange. The market makers have, without exception, taken steps to gain distribution through links with brokers and to acquire capital by linking with banks. The major primary accepting houses have also, with few exceptions, taken steps to gain market making and distribution capacity. In the broking field, some firms have opted for a pure agency role but there is some room for doubt whether any major firms will be able to exist for long without market making capacity. The changes will create a much more immediate connection between the various elements of the business, which should make the market considerably more receptive to changes in the requirements both of the providers and the users of capital. This seems likely to produce a more innovative system, for the experience of the Eurobond markets would suggest that innovation flourishes where there are few institutional barriers between providers and users of funds.

The other, and potentially more far reaching, consequence is that, with the end of fixed commissions, institutional business is likely to become very much less profitable relative to retail business. Commissions for private client business in the British stock market have been exceptionally low so that few firms have been willing to develop the private client side of their business. It is often argued that the British stock exchange offers an extremely cheap and high quality service to private clients, but it must be observed that the availability of this service is highly restricted and the vast majority of the British public has no access to stockbroking services. Britain has no security dealing firms on the US or Japanese model but it must be observed that, under the low cartel rates set for British personal sector business, it would have been very surprising if such firms had emerged in recent years. The decline of direct personal shareholding in the stock exchange and the rise of institutional investment through pension funds and insurance companies is often adduced as the reason for the decline of retail broking in Britain but it is at least possible to argue that the relative lack of profitability in retail stockbroking inhibited direct personal investment in the stock exchange by ensuring that there was no dynamic securities retailing sector at a time of rapid social and economic change. If the move from fixed commissions encourages brokers to devote more attention to developing their retailing capacity, it could allow them to exploit the redistribution of wealth within Britain which has occurred over the past 15 years as a result of rising home ownership and inflation.

CHANGING PATTERNS OF WEALTH HOLDING

The British personal sector now has very substantial personal wealth in the housing market. Inflation has benefited all those who have substantial mortgage debt in respect of their houses and it is worth noting that while British building societies had been prepared to advance mortgages for 80-90 per cent of the value of a property, the average mortgage outstanding is at around 30 per cent of the property value, the balance being accounted for by the owner's equity. Two factors have encouraged this fall in the level of gearing within the housing market. The first is that institutional factors have prevented the development of second mortgage lending within Britain and the second is that there is a limit on the size of mortgage loan on which interest can be deducted against income tax. This limit has fallen in real terms so that British householders have been less inclined to gear up on their inflationary gains than those in the United States. Nevertheless, the existence of very substantial equity in the housing market has encouraged many householders to use mortgage-related loans to finance other activities so that financial behaviour is now being significantly affected by the increase in wealth.

It must now be a possibility that the British personal sector will wish to diversify their asset portfolios in coming years as, although housing outperformed most other investments during the 1970s, during the 1980s financial assets have offered positive real interest rates and, in the case of equities and gilts, substantial capital gains. For these reasons, the British personal sector has a very heavy concentration of its direct asset holding in the housing market, which has become relatively less attractive and has a lower proportion of this wealth in financial assets than for many years past. In such circumstances, a portfolio shift away from housing and towards financial assets would seem very likely. If this is the case, it should provide very substantial scope for financial innovation, which if successful will tend to accelerate the process.

CHANGE IN PUBLIC FINANCIAL POLICY

A critical factor in determining the future growth of Britain's personal sector asset portfolios will be the evolution of government financial policy. During the 1970s, the government was prepared to expand the public sector share of the economy and to finance the expansion principally by the issue of long-term government debt. At a time of large public sector deficits the government's share of the retail savings market fell continuously while government debt issues came to account for around 90 per cent of capital market issues. In these circumstances the private sector's financing, not unnaturally, shifted to the shorter-term markets and the personal sector's direct and indirect holdings of gilts rose substantially. Since the change of government in the autumn of 1979, public sector policy has shifted radically. The Conservative government adopted a far more aggressive stance in the retail savings market, which has once again become a major source of finance for the government. Within the government debt market there have been two major changes of policy. First, the volume of long-term funding has been reduced significantly so that the structure of government debt is shortening, a development reflected in a reversal of the yield curve. Second, a new type of government security, the index linked bond, was introduced after prolonged debate as to whether the introduction of such bonds would perpetuate or curtail inflationary pressures within the economy. The initial yields on index linked gilts were very low, with the original tender being struck at 2 per cent and a large number of marginal applicants whose aggression in bidding was fuelled by the experience of a decade in which real returns on government securities had been negative. Subsequently, the volume of government issuing and the emergence of real returns in other markets have moved yields up to a more realistic level.

It is worth noting that this innovation by the government has been less successful than might have been anticipated in that index linked yields have risen substantially, in part because the insurance companies have not, as yet, developed any new products based on these securities. For this reason index linked gilts rely on general investment portfolio demand and do not yet command the specialist following which conventional fixed interest rate stocks have, linked to specific insurance products.

The major innovation that the government has introduced is privatization, which has involved very substantial sales of equity to the private sector with two consequences. First, the proceeds of these asset sales have met a substantial portion of the public sector's financial requirements, reducing its claims on the debt market. Second, the reduction in the size of the public sector and of its capital investment programme, which in Britain has been made through the issue of central government debt, has reduced the government's natural demands on the capital market. Although decisions on the correct level of government borrowing in Britain have typically been based on broad macroeconomic considerations, the economic activities of the public sector should influence their policy on external financing. While the public sector contains industries with major investment programmes, it would be natural for government to tap the capital market. Equally, the removal of major investment programmes from the public sector should reduce the total public sector claim on the capital markets, for to argue otherwise is to suggest that demands on the capital market should automatically increase when the owner-ship of an industry moves from the public to the private sector. This point is widely misunderstood in Britain owing to the practice of financing all nationalized industries through Treasury borrowing which creates a significant dislocation in the capital market.

The other major effect of privatization has been to increase the supply of equities to the private sector on a dramatic scale, a development which has encouraged the financial intermediaries to market securities directly to the public in a way that has not occurred in the past. Such direct marketing was aided by statutory concessions in the case of the largest flotation so far, that of British Telecom, which attracted an exceptionally large number of personal investors, most of whom had previously never held equities. There are those who argue with some cogency that the massive new supply of equity consequent on the privatization programme has led to a significant broadening in the asset preferences of the British personal sector. This will certainly be improved if the government presses ahead with its plans to encourage transferable pensions, which, if accomplished, will certainly diffuse power away from the large occupational pension schemes.

It must be evident that in Britain at least in recent years, one of the major impulses to financial innovation and change has come from government, through the mechanisms of changes of regulatory policy and, possibly more important, changes in government financial policy.

THE DIRECTION OF CHANGE

The ability of the private sector to innovate so as to exploit these opportunities has been much greater in the banking area than in capital market business, for in the former case the breakdown in the dominance of the clearing banks and the ability of borrowers in the international markets to enter the domestic market has led to rapid response to the opportunities which have been created. In the case of the capital market the barriers between the domestic and international market created by the restrictions on entry into the stock exchange have led to a much slower pace of institutional development. The changes now taking place in the stock exchange seem likely to be analogous to those involved in the introduction of competition and credit control in the banking system. In each case, the roots of change can be traced back over a number of years and the consequences are fraught with uncertainty.

It is possible to argue that, just as the introduction of competition and credit control preceded secondary banking crises in the 1970s, the changes in the stock exchange will lead to comparable problems in the capital markets in the next few years. That, however, is too limited a view of the process of change, for the consequences of the changes of which competition and credit control were a part were much more far reaching than the secondary banking crisis. For those changes included the movement to a much more widely diffused power structure within the banking system, a more competitive retail sector and a banking structure that was capable of playing a major entrepôt role within the international economy. It also shifted the balance of power within the financial system decisively in favour of savers rather than borrowers and did much to sustain the personal sector's savings in Britain at a level that has now created a substantial redistribution of wealth within the economy.

SUCCESSFUL ADAPTATION

The changes now taking place within the capital market would seem to be laying the groundwork for a significant shift in the asset portfolio of the British personal sector with major implications for the development of the British economy. At the same time, these changes should be conducive to British firms' playing a more active role in the international long-term capital market and thus sustaining London's entrepôt position in this market. At the beginning of this paper I argued that financial innovation was the process by which the financial system adapts itself to new conditions. On this basis the success of financial innovation can be judged in terms of how well the system adjusts itself to new conditions, with success, as in most processes of adaptation, being judged by the smoothness of the process of adjustment and the continued ability of the financial system to contribute to the workings of the broader body politic.

When financial systems change there are inevitably exposures to risk and over-rapid or ill-judged innovation can bring swift and unpleasant consequences, which may well flow beyond the financial intermediaries to the broader economy. For this reason, financial conservatism is always an attractive option because conservative finance and an absence of innovation reduces the chances of sharp and painful shocks to the system. However, the price of such conservatism is that the financial system will gradually become less and less well adjusted to the economy which it serves. In the longer term the effect of such conservatism can be just as painful as the results of the financial shocks which must from time to time accompany rapid financial innovation.

The growth of international trading and the impact of technology have created a period of very rapid economic change and in such circumstances the financial system is bound to adjust so as to reflect those changes. In these circumstances, regulatory policy comes to be of great importance in that a narrowly based and legalistic policy will inevitably fail to control major areas of growth. In this sense Britain is fortunate in that it has a financial regulatory authority in the Bank of England whose powers are highly imprecisely defined but which is able to operate with considerable authority throughout the financial system. Many of the problems that are now apparent in the United States stem from a multiplicity of regulatory agencies with competing and overlapping jurisdictions which nevertheless manage to leave substantial parts of the financial system wholly unregulated and dangerously exposed. The more informal regulatory powers of the British authorities ensure that the Bank of England is able to intervene with vigour and efficiency in areas where its legal rights are not immediately apparent. Two recent instances of this have been those concerning the problems in the insurance market centred around Lloyds and the changes in the stock exchange. In each case the Bank has played a major regulatory role and its authority in doing so has not been seriously questioned. The broader financial regulatory role of the Bank of England has been recognized in its most immediate reorganization, which has again reasserted the importance of this function.

One conclusion from British experience is that if the process of financial change is to be well managed it requires adaptable and innovative financial regulation. For this, regulatory authorities must have a very broad degree of discretion or they will not be able to react with sufficient speed to the adaptations within the system and legislation will arrive too late to prevent the development of unsound structures. The British interest in successful and adaptable regulation is twofold, in that the financial system for Britain is not only a service to the other sectors of the British economy but also a service to the world economy, and as such a major source of wealth and income to the British economy.

7

Financial Innovation in Germany

HERMANN-JOSEF DUDLER

FINANCIAL INNOVATION OUTSIDE GERMANY

The contemporary lively international discussion on financial innovation is dominated by observations, analyses and concerns emanating from rapid changes in financial instruments, practices, rules and institutions in North American and British money and capital markets since about the late 1970s. In this context, the term financial innovation has acquired specific meanings and connotations which may not be fully applicable to other countries and earlier periods of financial change. The growth of the Euromarket, its innovative practices and its important macroeconomic repercussions were, for example, recognized by academics, policy-makers and the general public at an early stage. But the resulting international debate was, at least for a long time, couched largely in terms of familiar analytical approaches, such as the money multiplier or portfolio theory of money and credit creation, the concept of financial integration, the demand for international reserves and the determination of interest and exchange rates.

The present discussion on financial innovation appears to owe its specific flavour to a large extent to the pervasive reasoning with which the leading economists of the English-speaking world have been able to translate their countries' national financial experiences into an intellectually fascinating topic for general academic debate, and it is, of course, also inspired by the demonstration effects and exchange and interest rate surprises which new developments in the world's largest money centres transmit to smaller financial markets. Stripped of stylish accidentals, the newly emerging concept of financial innovation nevertheless contains a number of paradigmatic elements which seem to render it useful as a shorthand description of lasting changes within the financial sector of larger industrial economies in which such developments seem to carry unique historical features.

Starting from the recent common use of the term, financial innovation may be said to comprise a combination of all or most of the following phenomena.

(1) In an analytically rigorous, 'Schumpeterian' sense, financial innovation involves the profit-generating application of new payment, communication or computing technologies in the financial sector. In the wake of this process, new financial products and services come into existence, or cheaper ways of providing traditional ones are implemented. Speedier payment and bank clearing methods, which reduce financial transaction costs, more sophisticated forms of cash and portfolio management and the provision of home banking services represent examples of this type of innovation.

(2) In a wider sense, financial innovation includes the introduction or more general use of sophisticated financial instruments (e.g. certificates of deposit, CDs, financial futures, variable rate or indexed debt), the dissemination of advanced operating practices (such as active liability management or debt securization) and the emergence of new financial institutions or the transformation of existing ones (e.g. the setting-up of money market funds and the breakdown of borderlines between specialized financial intermediaries). As a rule, such innovations, which are not necessarily associated with shifts in technology, meet new corporate and consumer demands arising from changing economic conditions. But in some cases financial institutions may even have succeeded in launching new, tempting luxury type services or 'pet' products (such as CATS or TIGRS[1]) which primarily satisfy newly generated demands for betting and gambling in financial markets.

(3) Financial innovation was facilitated by rapid and comprehensive financial deregulation measures. In many cases decontrol was more or less forced upon the authorities, because changes in market practices tended to erode the existing regulatory framework.

(4) The term typically designates clustered new phenomena in financial markets, which emerge in rapid succession and are therefore capable of giving rise to serious policy problems at the macroeconomic level. These include, in particular, transitory or more lasting difficulties for monetary management, exchange rate policies or bank supervision.

(5) Financial innovation was to some extent promoted or provoked by accelerating and variable rates of inflation, unusual economic and political shock events, rigorous implementation of short-run monetary targets and massive government borrowing. These factors caused unanticipated shifts and oscillations in interest rates and thus served to reinforce speculative and hedging activities in money, capital and exchange markets.

(6) Last, but not least, the successful popularization of financial *dernier-cri* creations may owe something to the unique imaginative productivity of the financial service industry in Anglo-American countries and the particular appeal which financial luxury and 'pet' products can acquire in formerly puritan

---

1 CATS, Certificates of Accrual on Treasury Securities; TIGRS, Treasury Investment Gross Receipts.

societies, where the public has become accustomed to indulging in unabashed financial greed and seems to be more and more inclined to play bingo-hall and casino games in money and capital markets by putting its financial wealth at stake.

In the specific sense described above, financial innovation has hardly been in evidence in Germany in recent years. Important changes occurred in the German financial sector between the mid-1960s and mid-1970s. These exhibited at least some of the features characterizing financial innovation elsewhere during the past seven to ten years. However, until now general economic conditions, institutional arrangements and public attitudes seem to have prevented new waves of innovation from reaching the financial markets in Germany.

It is, of course, not impossible that the present wind of financial change may touch Germany at a later stage. In order to provide some insight into the German situation, the importance which some of the international driving forces of financial innovation have had for Germany is discussed in the subsequent section. This discussion is followed by a brief description of minor changes in the German financial system since the mid-1970s, including a tentative evaluation of prospects for accelerating financial evolution in the near future.

FACTORS PROMOTING AND RETARDING FINANCIAL INNOVATION IN GERMANY

Technology

The introduction or wider application of computer technology by the banking system transformed banks' bookkeeping and accounting systems in the 1960s and increased their willingness to offer new streamlined services to the general public. Among other things, the processing of cashless wage and salary payments was made more attractive to both employers and consumers. Within a relatively short time, many bank clients opted for the new system. As a result, the nonbank private sector's demand for cash fell markedly between the mid-1960s and the early 1970s, while consumers' preference for sight deposit holdings rose (figure 7.1). The changeover to cashless wage and salary payments was completed well before the transition to monetary targeting in 1975. The marked shift in the demand for cash therefore did not create insurmountable difficulties for the Bundesbank, although it did complicate econometric investigations undertaken to identify the statistical properties of the Bundesbank's preferred target variable central bank money stock (CBM) (i.e. cash in the hands of the public and banks' compulsory reserves against deposits held by residents at constant, January 1974 reserve ratios).

During the past ten years, the percentage share of currency in the broad money stock stabilized (at about 11.5 per cent of M3 – which, apart from

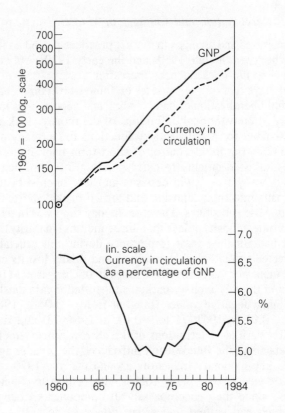

FIGURE 7.1 Currency in circulation (excluding banks' cash holdings) and
gross national product (GNP).
Source: Deutsche Bundesbank.

currency, includes sight and time deposits of less than four years' maturity
and savings deposits at three months' 'statutory' notice). During the same
period, the ratio of currency to GNP, which had declined sharply before,
rose again (from 5 to 5.5 per cent). This development came somewhat as
a surprise, since the successful launching of the Eurocheque system (in 1969),
the introduction of 'Eurocard' and the more recent wider use of other forms
of 'plastic money' should have served to further reduce the demand for coin
and banknotes. Non-residents' and the domestic 'black' economy's demand
for deutschmark notes in large denominations presumably contributed to the
comparatively fast rise in currency in circulation. Moreover, since German
banks began to levy relatively heavy, cost-related charges for cashless payment
transactions and, as a rule, to pay virtually no interest on ordinary sight
deposits, consumers retained and regained a certain preference for using
banknotes to effect day-to-day payments.

Deregulation and Changes in Market Practices

Decontrol measures and changes in market practices played an important role in Germany between the late 1960s and the early 1970s, but ceased to have significant economic consequences thereafter.

The initial decontrol of interest rates on longer-term time deposits and the subsequent full liberalization of bank lending and deposit rates in 1967 eroded the reliability of conventional definitions of the money stock and served to destabilize demand for narrow-money functions in Germany until well into the 1970s. Following the decontrol of short-term bank interest rates, time deposit rates adjusted quickly to corresponding interbank loan rates. This induced shifts away from sight deposits and low interest bearing standard savings deposits into time deposits, and turned banks' shorter-term deposit liabilities into close substitutes. The basic money supply M1a (currency, sight deposits and time deposits at less than three months' maturity), to which the Bundesbank had attached some importance during this crucial period, was severely affected by statistical instabilities and finally lost its meaning as an intermediate monetary indicator. The elasticitity of changes in M1a with respect to variations in the key money market rate shifted continuously. It showed at first declining negative values (ranging from -0.04 in 1961–7, -0.03 in 1961–9, -0.02 in 1961–71 to -0.01 in 1961–73) and finally became positive. After various redefinitions of the narrow money stock had proved to be unsatisfactory, the Bundesbank introduced the broader aggregates M3 and CBM as key monetary indicators around the mid-1970s. These broad money stock concepts were more robust with respect to changes in money market rates, since they encompassed all components of monetary bank liabilities which had shifted under the impact of decontrol, and demand functions for these aggregates have until now remained fairly stable.[2]

Close arbitrage links between the domestic money market and the rapidly expanding Euromarket, international demonstration effects and the growing influence of younger bank managers unfamiliar with the banking crisis of the 1930s prompted German commercial banks to abandon their traditional practices of cautious asset management in the early 1970s. Prior to this period, German banks had kept sizeable voluntary holdings of low interest bearing secondary reserves, under-utilized their rediscount quotas and reduced their security investments and new loan commitments, whenever the Bundesbank squeezed their 'free liquid reserves' through contractionary policy measures. This mechanism, on which monetary management had relied for many years, had broken down completely by around 1973/4. The erosion of its familiar policy base forced the Bundesbank to re-establish its control over commercial banks' supply behaviour in credit and security markets by strictly rationing its own supply of primary reserves to the banking system. The new rigorous

2 See 'The longer-term trend and control of the money stock', *Monthly Report of the Deutsche Bundesbank* 37, No. 1 (1985), pp. 13–26.

operating procedures caused unusual disturbances in the money market and large, erratic swings in interbank loan rates during 1973/4, comparable to the volatility which the federal funds rate exhibited in the United States after October 1979 (table 7.1). Following a fairly long period of experimentation, the Bundesbank was able to return to smoother operating procedures when it adopted monetary targeting in the mid-1970s.

Decontrol of interest rates, the gradual phasing-out of tax privileges granted to savings banks and credit cooperatives and the curtailment of government savings promotion schemes have contributed to changes in bank liability management and tighter competition among banks in many fields of 'universal' banking during the past 10–15 years (see discussion of recent financial changes below). Those banks that lost their tax advantages began to expand the scale and scope of their traditional banking activities, and savers, who no longer profited from government premium payments, were offered more attractive, new types of deposits and bank securities by the banking system. In the event, all important banking groups were ultimately ready to make the full range of financial services available to their customers and expanded their local branch office system to the point of market saturation.

Economic and Monetary/Fiscal Policy Shocks

Germany shared the experience of accelerating inflation which plagued the industrial world from the second half of the 1960s (table 7.2); market interest rates and exchange rates fluctuated more heavily after the early 1970s and 'structural' budget deficits widened until the early 1980s. However, the repercussions of these disturbances on the financial system were limited (see below). This can, no doubt, partly be attributed to the fact that economic instabilities and policy shocks tended to be milder in Germany than elsewhere.

The ratcheting-up of inflation was less pronounced and relatively short-lived in Germany; market interest rates moved more or less in unison with the general price level (limiting savers' inflation losses) and the Bundesbank tended to avoid erratic and abrupt shifts in money market conditions after it had taken up monetary targeting in 1975. The German government temporarily switched to large-scale monetary financing when budget deficits first assumed unusual proportions in the second half of the 1960s, but it has more or less abandoned such borrowing practices during the past ten years. Moreover, the public sector deficit, which had peaked at 5.5 per cent of GNP (in 1975) and 4 per cent of GNP (in 1981), has been sharply reduced in recent years and is expected to have come down to 1.5 per cent of GNP in 1985.

It is true that German bond prices have become more volatile in the wake of international interest rate and exchange rate disturbances. Short-term speculation in security markets has increased and domestic bond investors seem to have become more averse to risk. However, there is little evidence that this is giving rise to fundamental changes in security trading practices or to the creation of entirely new financial instruments. Similarly, foreign

TABLE 7.1 Money market rates (per cent p.a.) in Frankfurt am Main by month

Month		Day-to-day money		One mth loans		Three mth loans	
		Monthly averages	*Highest and lowest rates*	*Monthly averages*	*Highest and lowest rates*	*Monthly averages*	*Highest and lowest rates*
1972	July	2.24	⅛–4¼	3.95	3½–4⅝	4.65	4⅜–5⅛
	Aug.	4.48	4–6	4.33	4–4⅝	4.80	4½–5
	Sep.	4.83	4–5¾	5.04	4¾–5¼	5.32	5–5½
	Oct.	6.07	4–7⅜	5.95	4¾–6⅞	6.88	6¼–7⅜
	Nov.	5.71	1–8	7.11	6⅝–7½E	8.07	7⅛–8⅜
	Dec.	6.69	5⅝–8[a]	8.59	8¼–8⅞	8.60	8⅜–8⅞
1973	Jan.	5.58	1¾–7	6.96	6½–7½E	7.89	7⅝–8¼
	Feb.	2.18	⅛–7¼	6.50	5¾–7	7.96	7¾–8¼
	March	11.37	6¾–20	8.67	7–9½E	8.77	8–9⅜E
	April	14.84	2–30	11.51	10–13E	10.62	9½–12E
	May	7.40	½–14	11.69	10–13E	12.42	11–13E
	June	10.90	2–17½	12.43	10½–14E	13.62	13–14
	July	15.78	2–30	13.29	12½–14E	14.30	14–15E
	Aug.	10.63	6¾–40	12.14	10–15½	14.57	13¾–16E
	Sept.	9.76	½–18	13.30	12¼–14	14.25	13¾–15E
	Oct.	10.57	0–15½	13.18	12–14	14.49	13¾–14⅞
	Nov.	11.30	5¾–22	12.08	10½–13½	13.62	13–14⅝
	Dec.	11.89	8–13½[b]	13.33	13–13¾	13.20	13–13½

1974						
Jan.	10.40	3–13¼	11.68	10½–13	12.09	11–13
Feb.	9.13	6–12½	10.05	9–11⅛	10.67	10–11⅞
March	11.63	7–13	11.21	10⅝–11¾	11.20	10⅝–11⅞
April	5.33	1–11¾	9.28	8–11⅜	10.07	9⅛–11½
May	8.36	4¼–16	8.16	7¼–9½E	9.10	8½–9¾E
June	8.79	6.8–12	9.01	8.5–9.8	9.46	9–9.9
July	9.40	8.8–11.5	9.23	8.5–9.8	9.48	9.2–9.9E
Aug.	9.30	9.0–9.7	9.41	9.2–9.6	9.65	9.4–9.9
Sep.	9.22	9.0–9.6	9.41	9.2–9.6	9.69	9.5–9.8
Oct.	9.10	8.5–9.5	9.29	8.9–9.5	9.78	9.5–10E
Nov.	7.38	4.7–8.7	8.21	7.5–9.2	9.04	8.5–9.8
Dec.	8.35	7.5–8.7ᶜ	8.63	8.3–8.8	8.60	8.2–8.8

Money market rates are not fixed or quoted officially. Unless stated otherwise, the rates shown are based on daily quotations reported by Frankfurt banks; monthly averages computed from these rates are unweighted. E, estimated.

ᵃ At end of December, 6 per cent.
ᵇ At end of December, 11½–12½ per cent.
ᶜ At end of December, 8.2–8.4 per cent.

Source: Deutsche Bundesbank.

TABLE 7.2 Inflation, bond yield and 'real' bond yield (per cent p.a.)

	Inflation[a]			Bond yield[b]		'Real' yield[c]	
	OECD	USA	FRG	USA	FRG	USA	FRG
1960–8	3.2	2.4	3.1				
1968–73	6.1	5.1	6.3				
1973–9	8.8	7.6	4.7				
1979–83	8.2	7.5	4.1				
1975	10.5	9.2	6.1	8.8	8.7	–0.3	2.6
1976	7.7	5.9	3.4	8.4	8.0	2.5	3.6
1977	7.5	5.7	3.7	8.0	6.4	1.4	2.6
1978	7.6	7.4	4.2	8.7	6.1	0.9	3.3
1979	8.2	8.5	4.0	9.6	7.6	–1.5	3.4
1980	9.9	9.6	4.5	10.9	8.6	–2.3	3.1
1981	9.0	8.9	4.2	14.2	10.6	3.4	4.0
1982	7.2	6.0	4.6	13.8	9.1	7.3	3.6
1983	5.2	3.8	3.2	12.1	8.0	8.6	4.5
1984	4.7	3.8	1.9	12.7	7.8	8.1	5.3

[a] Change in GNP price deflator.
[b] Yield on Aaa bonds (USA), yield on domestic bonds outstanding (FRG).
[c] Change in consumer price index used for adjustment.
Source: OECD, Deutsche Bundesbank.

traders and bankers seem to be relatively unimpressed by the wider fluctuations in exchange rates, although it is not known to what extent new forms of exchange rate hedging and speculation (such as option trading) are being practised in Germany today.

Factors Retarding Financial Innovation

The surprisingly high degree of financial and monetary stability in Germany during the period of rapid international financial innovation can to some extent be attributed to specific institutional arrangements and public attitudes. As already mentioned, monetary decontrol and the move towards 'universal' banking took place at an early date, so that such factors have not played a major role in Germany during recent years. Moreover, the fairly smooth functioning of the broadly based 'universal' branch banking system appears to leave only limited room for dramatic shifts in the working of money and capital markets.

In a positive sense, this conclusion may be drawn from the fact that German 'universal' banks efficiently 'package' and diversify financial risks and provide the full range of virtually all financial services economically and conveniently 'under one roof'. Apart from insurance companies, almost all nonbank financial intermediaries have been squeezed out of the system, and independent money or security dealers, investment banks or portfolio managers play only a very minor role as competitors of the 'universal' banks.

Looking in more detail at the services that banks supply, the scope for financial innovation would, at first sight, appear to be quite restricted.

(1) Cashless payments can be effected conveniently through the banks' own nationwide 'giro' systems and the Bundesbank's central clearing facilities. Bank clients can make payments through universally accepted bank guaranteed cheques, money transfer orders, standing transfer instructions for regular fixed payment obligations and standing bank debiting authorizations for meeting regular variable payment commitments. They can draw cash against a personal cheque from any bank anywhere in Germany and from correspondent banks in European countries; execute security transactions; effect loan amortization payments and foreign currency dealings; honour credit cards and utilize generously granted corporate and consumer overdraft facilities; and have all these transactions; handled through a single current bank account.

(2) Banks are legally authorized and ready to offer their clients, as a comprehensive service package, practically any form of financing for domestic trade, business investment, housing, private consumption and foreign trade; to meet public sector borrowing needs; to execute customers' security dealings; to manage their financial portfolios and organize public or private share and bond replacements; and to provide all these services in customer-tailored forms, amounts and maturities. Hence little scope is left for financial disintermediation and competition from specialized financial institutions.

(3) Along with fixed interest rate contracts, German banks have always made available variable rate bank loans and deposits, and they likewise provide short-term 'bridging finance' to business firms, homeowners and public sector borrowers during high interest rate periods. They also 'securitize' a substantial part of their lending by issuing collateralized bank bonds to refund home mortgage loans, loans to the government and shorter- and longer-term credits to industry.

Satisfying their customers' needs 'from the cradle to the grave', commercial banks thus dominate the German financial scene in almost every respect. They 'pool' a wide range of financial and economic risks, possess intimate insights into their customers' financial affairs and can advise them on business, personal and tax issues (they even cast proxy votes at company meetings for clients who deposit industrial shares with them). On the other hand, the banks' powerful financial position, their capital and organizational links with big industry and the public sector, and their cartelized pricing practices and defensive, oligopolistic market strategies may prevent useful financial changes, to the disadvantage of the economy as a whole. Moreover, public attitudes seem to render the German system less susceptible to all types of innovation which appeal to financial greed and involve tough competition from nonbank financial institutions.

Bank customers tend to stick – for better or for worse – to their traditional local banking connection or 'house-banks'. The historic German submissiveness to authority and bureaucracy, the public's quest for protection against the vagaries of life, and a certain degree of caution in financial dealings caused by the almost total destruction of personal financial wealth after two lost wars, to some extent still govern the relationship between many ordinary bank clients and their bankers. Customers hesitate to break off established business links with their banks for purely pecuniary reasons and often regard financial speculation as indecent or suspect. Banks in turn maintain a close relationship of mutual trust (*Vertrauensverhältnis*) with the Deutsche Bundesbank and are reluctant to introduce new instruments or practices into German financial markets if this is likely to provoke raised eyebrows at the central bank.

RECENT FINANCIAL CHANGES AND THE FUTURE
OUTLOOK FOR FINANCIAL INNOVATION

Since the mid-1970s there have been few financial changes that might have complicated the Bundesbank's task of efficiently controlling the money stock. Similarly, given the wide range of financial activities covered by German banking legislation and legally binding prudential rules, bank supervision has up till now not been seriously affected by financial innovation. To take banks' foreign exposure into account, special regulations were introduced after the 1974 Herstatt crisis, limiting banks' uncovered foreign exchange position, and more recently banks have been forced to submit their foreign operations to domestic capital requirements by consolidating the balance sheets of domestic parents and their subsidiaries abroad. New types of transactions which create 'off-balance-sheet' risks (e.g. banks' open positions in financial futures or NIFs and RUFs are difficult to subject to prudential rules, but so far carry little weight in German banks' operations.

Money Substitutes

During the last two periods of high market interest rates (1973/4 and 1980/1) banks rapidly expanded their placements of very short-dated bonds with maturities of one year or less. This type of bank liability could be regarded as a potential substitute for the shorter-term time and savings deposits included in the broadly defined money stock (M3 or CBM). Banks' issuing activity in this field is therefore carefully watched by the Bundesbank. However, the circulation of short-dated bank securities, which certain banks issued mainly to refund increasing demand from industry for shorter-term bank 'bridging loans', quickly decreased when interest rates returned to more normal levels. Various econometric tests, in which the stability of money–demand functions was compared for broad aggregates including and excluding short-dated bank bonds, did not suggest that basic monetary relationships were disturbed by the fluctuating circulation of short-term bank refinancing paper. This instrument can therefore at the most be regarded as an innovation of minor importance.

The expatriation of domestic banking business to the Euromarket is also closely watched by the Bundesbank, especially with respect to its monetary policy implications. German nonbanks hold their liquid assets partly in the form of Eurocurrency deposits, which they may count as relatively close substitutes for domestic sight and short-term time deposits. However, such Eurodeposit holdings are quite small in relation to the domestic money stock and fluctuate only moderately, so that they pose no serious problem for monetary management.

Growing International Financial Integration

Monetary management in Germany has to some extent been complicated by increasingly tighter links between the German money and capital markets and international financial markets. This process was facilitated by the early and almost complete abolition of exchange and capital controls in Germany, and later on by the growing importance of the deutschmark as an international reserve, intervention and investment currency. For a while, the Bundesbank attempted to restrain the international use of the deutschmark so as to limit Germany's exposure to international interest rate and exchange rate shocks. The Bundesbank therefore blocked with some success the introduction of attractive deutschmark-denominated financial instruments such as CDs, 'floaters', zero-coupon bonds and currency swaps. This may have delayed the dissemination of some international financial innovations in the domestic market, but it hardly weakened the deutschmark's international role substantially. In the meantime, most of the Bundesbank's earlier reservations have been dropped, so that financial changes originating elsewhere can more easily be disseminated in the home market.

Changes in Nonbanks' Asset Preferences

For a number of reasons, private financial wealth holders in Germany seem to have become more interest-sensitive and risk-averse or risk-conscious during the past 10–15 years. This has encouraged some inconspicuous innovations in the financial market, which – hardly surprisingly – have largely been carried out by the domestic banking system.

In particular the maturity of bank bond issues shortened, since private households and institutional investors were reluctant to commit funds on a very long-term basis during periods of high and volatile interest rates. Moreover, starting in the mid-1970s, corporate buyers developed, for the first time, a growing appetite for bond investments and often preferred shorter maturities. The average remaining maturity of total bonds outstanding thus fell from nearly seven years in 1975 to below four years ten years later. As borrowers showed a preference for shorter maturities too during the same period, banks had little difficulty in matching the requirements of borrowers and lenders in the capital market.

Private households have invested more heavily in short-term time deposits (up to one year's maturity) during the past seven to ten years, shifting liquid funds out of sight deposits and low interest bearing standard savings deposits. At the same time, banks have offered consumers a variety of new attractive medium- and longer-term savings instruments (table 7.3). These have included, in particular, savings certificates, contractual savings schemes on a 'zero-coupon', 'premium' or rising accrued interest rate basis and savings accounts carrying bond yield related variable interest rates. This development probably reflects a combination of influences, i.e active liability management by the banks, tougher competition for deposit-type funds following the decontrol of interest rates and the abolition of the tax privileges granted to certain institutions and groups of private savers, growing familiarity of private wealth holders with financial investment opportunities and consumers' desire to maximize their interest income during the past period of higher inflation.

TABLE 7.3   Composition of German banks' liabilities to domestic nonbanks (percentage of total liabilities)

	Sight deposits	Time deposits	Savings deposits	Savings certificates	Bearer bonds
1975	8.0	14.5	25.4	2.0	9.4
1976	8.0	13.4	26.0	2.4	9.6
1977	7.7	13.2	25.2	3.0	9.5
1978	7.9	13.1	24.1	3.3	9.2
1979	7.6	13.6	23.0	3.4	9.4
1980	7.1	14.6	21.0	4.1	10.3
1981	6.6	15.8	19.3	4.3	11.4
1982	6.4	15.9	18.7	4.5	11.8
1983	6.6	15.2	19.0	4.7	11.7
1984	6.4	15.5	18.6	5.0	12.2

Source: Deutsche Bundesbank.

The average cost of bank funds has tended to increase as a result of these changes, and savings deposit rates have, on the whole, become somewhat less variable. This has affected the local savings banks most. These institutions used to administer very large blocks of savings accounts at 'statutory' notice, which traditionally carry rather low, variable rates of interest. Savings banks have therefore begun to compete actively with other banks for market shares in the field of high yielding fixed interest rate loans.

Future Prospects

The pace of financial innovation may accelerate in the near future, but the outlook is far from clear. Banks have begun to offer deposit facilities to prime customers, enabling the latter to earn market interest rates on day-to-day funds; they have started issuing deutschmark floating rate notes on the basis of a newly created three- and six-month daily 'FIBOR' ('Frankfurt interbank offered rate') quotation, and they may soon be permitted to launch deutschmark denominated CDs. Liquid funds could therefore be shifted from non-interest-bearing sight deposit accounts into new monetary instruments. The wider distribution of 'plastic money', the installation of automated teller machines (ATMs) and the introduction of point-of-sale (POS) terminals or home banking services are still at an experimental or planning stage. But such developments have recently gained new momentum under the impact of competition among various domestic banking groups and they could cause the demand for currency to decline again in the medium run. Future financial innovation could thus tend to destabilize familiar demand for money relationships and provide new challenges to monetary management.

The diffusion of new financial products and practices originating in the world's leading financial centres could give an additional stimulus to innovation in Germany, since virtually all the remaining administrative obstacles to international financial integration have been abolished in Germany in recent years. However, only a few of the confusingly wide variety of new international products and financing techniques surfacing during the past few years are likely to survive in the longer run and find acceptance in more conservative financial markets. Moreover, as shown above, a wide range of customer-tailored services is already supplied by German 'universal' banks in their home territory, and institutional and attitudinal obstacles seem to militate against revolutionary financial change in Germany. The German financial system may therefore continue to show a certain degree of resistance to 'imported innovation' and undergo a gradual process of financial evolution rather than experience shock waves of changes in monetary instruments, techniques and institutions.

AUTHOR'S NOTE

The content of this paper reflects the personal views of the author.

8

Financial Innovation in Italy: a Lop-sided Process

CESARE CARANZA and CARLO COTTARELLI

INTRODUCTION

Financial innovation is not a continuous process, but comes in waves that transform the financial structure of a country. It is not a new phenomenon: the latest wave may be currently sweeping the domestic monetary and financial markets of a number of countries, but if we look back, we see that a major success story in financial innovation already occurred during the sixties with the formation of the Euromarket, which is still the cradle of the most innovative financial techniques and products. Financial innovation was also relevant during the sixties in some domestic markets, as we shall argue below for Italy. It is none the less true that the inflationary climate of the seventies, resulting in increased uncertainty and regulation, together with profound changes in income shares among sectors and categories, provided a strong impetus for 'product innovation' and a general change in the financial structure of almost every country. Another important agent of innovation has undoubtedly been the spread of new information technology which allowed 'process innovation' in the financial industry, as well as in non-financial enterprises and even household sectors.

This paper surveys the main features and causes of financial innovation in Italy during the past decade. It is argued that, to date, financial innovation has only been a partial process, involving relevant changes in important areas (particularly the birth of a Treasury bill market and the diffusion of indexed bonds issued by the government and special credit institutions (SCIs), but it has left areas that have shown high innovative drive abroad, namely enterprise and banking sectors' fund-raising techniques and bank lending almost unaffected. In some of these areas the Italian economy is still lacking in certain structures that represent the main pivots of the financial system in most western countries.

The plan of this paper is as follows. The next section reviews the main trends in the evolution of the Italian financial structure during the sixties and the main forces that moulded the Italian economy in the seventies and eighties. The third section contains a rather detailed description of the innovations introduced during the past decade in the financial system, together with an analysis of their causes. The reader who is already acquainted with these developments may skip this section and move to the next, where the main causes of innovation are singled out and commented upon. It is concluded that, together with inflation and the development of the public deficit, regulation has been the main cause of innovation, but it is argued that regulation has been important in Italy not only because it stimulated circumventing innovation. Indeed, the introduction of a regulatory framework can encourage – and has encouraged in Italy – the development of financial markets because it reduces the risk implicit in financial transactions.

The fifth and sixth sections are devoted to the analysis of the factors that have prevented innovation in large sectors of the Italian financial structure. These factors are classified as influencing the demand for or the supply of new financial products and it is concluded that the importance of the supply factors has been somehow underestimated. Yet, they are relevant to explain the resilience of the banking system in innovating and the stunted development of markets channelling funds directly from savers to the enterprise sector. However, some of these factors have recently been removed and the rapid development of 'new' intermediaries, like the investment funds, as well as the growing interest of large- and medium-sized companies to raise money in the capital market, are encouraging signs of change.

MAIN REAL AND FINANCIAL TRENDS DURING THE SIXTIES AND SEVENTIES

The Italian financial structure has inherited some peculiar features from the past that are worth mentioning to put the present discussion of recent developments and transformations into the right perspective.

One important characteristic is the wide gap (in comparison with other OECD countries) between sectoral financial balances. Looking at the net financial saving (or indebtedness) of different sectors of the economy as ratios to GDP, it appears quite clearly that during the past 20 years, apart from cyclical fluctuations which have spectacularly influenced the behaviour of the business and foreign sectors, the most important development has been represented by the diverging trend of the financial balances of households and of the public sector (figure 8.1).

Such a system requires a high degree of financial intermediation. The limited development of the Italian capital market has created a situation in which credit institutions perform a predominant role in financial intermediation. This situation was strengthened by institutional and regulatory changes during the

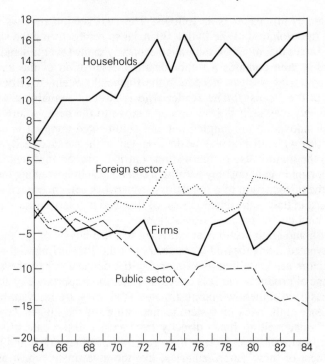

FIGURE 8.1   Sectoral financial balances as a percentage of GNP.

sixties and reached its climax in the mid-seventies when high and variable inflation rates and the collapse of the bond market led to a hyperintermediation by the banking system that was reflected in the melting of the economy's financial assets into bank deposits. As we shall describe later, it was only in the second half of the seventies that the Treasury increasingly developed direct links with private savers, by floating short-term and indexed securities that found their way into households' portfolios.

It is interesting to note that these features of the Italian financial system emerged during the sixties as a consequence of important phenomena in financial innovation. Between 1958 and 1962, the years of the Italian economic 'miracle', the stock market expanded rapidly. The market value of traded shares grew from 7,000 billion lire in 1958 to 19,000 billion in 1962. The ratio between outstanding fixed interest securities and shares decreased from 0.81 to 0.53 per cent. It seemed possible to develop a capital market alongside the existing financial intermediaries, i.e. banks issuing deposits and credit institutions specialized in medium- and long-term financing, issuing fixed rate bonds.

After 1962 the changing economic climate, the nationalization of the electricity industry and a less favourable fiscal treatment of dividends led to a collapse of the stock market. An alternative was found in the development of a broad bond market from which public enterprises and special credit institutions could take the funds necessary to finance investments. Private enterprises made little use of this market, partly because of the less favourable fiscal treatment of their issues *vis à vis* those floated by public bodies and financial intermediaries, and partly because they had the possibility of borrowing at soft rates from special credit institutions. On the supply side, the growth of the bond market was sustained by the policy followed by the central bank up to 1969 of pegging the long-term rate, thus granting to bond holders a positive return in real terms. The reduced risk of capital losses increased the share of long-term bonds in households' portfolios to the detriment of bank deposits and shares. The above-mentioned ratio between outstanding fixed interest securities and shares rose to 1 in 1966 and to 1.52 in 1970.

The 'creation' of the bond market in Italy during the sixties is an interesting example of financial innovation mainly induced by changes in the institutional and regulatory framework. This market collapsed in the early seventies, when inflation and exchange rate problems imposed a rise in interest rates and a change in the rules of the game of monetary policy. To cut a long and complex story short, this left – on the eve of the first oil shock – the Italian financial system on a weak basis, with (a) enterprises heavily indebted to banks, both directly and via special credit institutions, whose bonds at that time were to a large extent bought by banks themselves; (b) the public sector compelled to resort to the central bank and to commercial banks to finance its deficits; and (c) a strong preference of households for liquid assets, namely – as a consequence of the absence of a money market – bank deposits, on which banks were allowed to pay high and variable rates.

On the whole, in the early seventies, the traditional 'imperfections' of the Italian financial structure had become more marked, constituting a weak starting point at the beginning of a decade during which domestic and external shocks exposed the financial system to new and harsher strains.

The more difficult economic climate of the seventies and eighties is summarized by a few economic indicators (table 8.1).

TABLE 8.1   Select indicators for the Italian economy

	1960–9	*1970–9*	*1980–4*
Percentage growth rates			
GNP	5.3	3.3	1.1
Consumer prices	3.7	12.3	16.1
PSBR as ratio to GNP	2.8	9.8	14.3

The rises in inflation and in public sector deficits have imposed very severe constraints on the conduct of monetary policy during the past ten years. Balance of payments considerations and the necessity to cool down inflationary pressures induced monetary authorities to moderate the effects of mounting public sector borrowing requirements on aggregate demand through higher and more flexible interest rates, thus allowing a rising proportion of the deficit to be financed by means of Treasury debt instruments placed directly with private savers.

At the same time, new and heavier administrative controls on bank intermediation were introduced. Ceilings on bank loans were first imposed in 1973 and, with the exception of a short interval between 1975 and 1976, were maintained until June 1983. The system of reserve requirements on bank deposits was reformed in 1975 and gradually made more biting (the reserve coefficient increased from 13 per cent in 1975 to nearly 18 in 1984). The constraints on the banking system were completed by a portfolio requirement to invest a percentage of deposits in long-term bonds issued by the special credit institutions (SCIs), a measure aiming at channelling funds towards fixed investment and housing.[1]

The forces that we have so far mentioned – inflation, public deficits and stricter monetary policy through interest rates and direct controls – moulded the evolution of the Italian financial structure during the past ten years. It is to discussion of this that we now turn.

FINANCIAL INNOVATION IN THE PAST DECADE: A DETAILED DESCRIPTION

In the description of innovative processes it is essential to avoid partial interpretations that lay excessive emphasis on the changes that have occurred, while disregarding an analysis of the reasons limiting the spreading of the process.

This requirement is particularly strict in the case of Italy. While, on the one hand, financial innovation has instigated some major changes of manifest importance in key sectors of the financial structure, it has, on the other hand, also left other areas untouched, despite the fact that some of these have shown a high propensity to innovate in other western countries. In this respect, this section attempts to give an exhaustive description of what has – and has not – changed in the Italian financial system over the past ten years. The material is assembled under two headings: first, the evolution of the credit instruments that are exchanged in organized markets; and second, the activity of financial intermediaries. Summary tables of financial assets and liabilities of the private sector will then be commented upon to provide both a detailed analysis and an overall view.

---

1 For a more detailed discussion of the evolution of methods and instruments of monetary policy in Italy during the past decade see Caranza and Fazio (1983).

Innovation in Monetary and Financial Markets

At the beginning of the seventies Italy was endowed with a well-developed and broad bond market, but was lacking in any form of money market in which borrowers and lenders could exchange short-term assets at rates closely reflecting the liquidity conditions of the economy. The only money market instrument was the Treasury bill, but it was available only in limited amounts and was held almost completely by the banking system. As we have already noticed, the inflationary outburst of 1973–4 put the bond market under a severe strain and caused high capital losses to savers. It represented, however, the turning point for the strongly innovative phase that followed. Table 8.2 summarized the radical changes that accompanied this phase.

BOT and CCT

The most outstanding feature emerging from the table is the growth of the Treasury bills (BOT, *Buoni Ordinari del Tesoro*) and indexed Treasury certificates (CCT, *Certificati di Credito del Tesoro*) markets. Their share of the total instruments circulating in the monetary and financial markets (excluding shares) equalled 62 per cent at the end of 1984 as against 20 per cent in 1975 (table 8.2).[2]

The process was fostered by the explosion in the PSBR (see above), by the outburst of inflation – which made recourse to the bond market to finance the deficit unavailable – and by the commitment of the monetary authorities to stricter monetary control aimed at curbing this inflation.

Moreover, from a more structural point of view, the Bank of Italy supported the growth of the BOT market because the existence of an efficient money market was seen as a prerequisite for more effective monetary control. In April 1975 the BOT auction system was reformed: the Bank of Italy, which up to then had, as a practice, bought all the unsold bills but was excluded from auction, was admitted on the same footing as the other participants and was therefore able to affect the interest rate. The number of operators taking part in the auction and the degree of competition among them also increased.

The increasing supply of Treasury bills was at first met by the availability, in bank portfolios, of funds that could not be invested in loans due to the ceiling on bank credit. The banking system also felt the need for an efficient instrument of liquidity management: this laid the foundations for the expansion of a fairly efficient secondary market. Since 1977, purchases of BOT by households and firms have become more substantial: they have been favoured by the lack of other short-term assets yielding positive real interest rates in a period of high inflation, by the tax exemption and by the availability of a market (physically constituted by the whole network of bank branches) on which the bills could be easily purchased.

2 It should be noted that more than 60 per cent of BOT in circulation at the end of 1975 were held by the central bank.

TABLE 8.2 Monetary and financial markets[a]

Instruments	Central and local government	Non-financial firms	Financial intermediaries			Total
			Banks	SCI	Others	
Short- and medium-term bills						
BOT	28.9 (19.9)	—	—	—	—	28.9 (19.9)
Bankers' acceptance	—	0.1	—	—	—	0.1
CDs	—	—	1.4	4.2 (4.2)	—	5.6 (4.2)
Fixed rate bonds	10.6 (30.5)	1.5 (9.9)	—	11.1 (34.6)	—	23.3 (75.0)
Bonds with financial indexation						
CCT	33.0	—	—	—	—	33.0
Others	—	2.7 (0.9)	—	4.7	—	7.4 (0.9)
Bonds with new features						
Drop lock and deep discount bonds	—	—	—	0.1	—	0.1
In ECU	0.7	—	—	:	—	0.7
Real indexation	0.2	:	—	:	—	0.2
With warrant[b]	—	—	—	0.1	—	0.1
Others[c]	—	:	—	0.2	—	0.2
Unregulated debentures and investment funds	—	—	—	—	0.4	0.4
Total	73.4 (50.3)	4.3 (10.9)	1.4	20.5 (38.8)	0.4	100.0 (100.0)

[a] Data refer to percentage shares over total debentures in circulation at the end of 1984; data relative to 1975 are reported in brackets.
[b] Warrant for the purchase of a fixed rate bond.
[c] Drop lock, cash-back, mixed fixed and variable coupon, with advanced repayment clause etc.

The rise of the market for indexed CCTs followed a similar pattern. Indexed CCTs are debentures whose yield is linked to the BOT rate. They were first issued in July 1977 with a rather short maturity (of two years) to encourage the development of the market. Again, they were initially purchased by commercial banks and it was only after the 1981 reform, which linked their yield to the six month Treasury bill rate (instead of the previous average rate on three, six and twelve month bills), introduced a spread with respect to this rate and shortened the indexation lag, that the CCT also boomed as an instrument of private saving. As this instrument became more and more successful, maturities were lengthened (up to ten years) and the spread was reduced.

The BOT and CCT markets also provided a field for innovative techniques and experiments in market organization and intervention by the monetary authorities. In 1978 a centralized clearing system for the exchange of BOTs, CCTs and other bonds among banks was organized with the sponsorship of the central bank. A mid-month BOT auction was introduced in September 1981 and, from May 1982, the issue of CCTs became monthly too. A major change in the intervention techniques occurred in 1979 when the central bank started to trade BOTs and CCTs with the banking system on a temporary basis (repurchase agreements): this provided an additional and more flexible tool with which to finance the banks and absorb temporary liquidity surpluses. Since July 1981 these transactions have been settled through a system of 'competitive' auctions in which the price is determined on the basis of the rates offered or required by different banks.[3] In the same month the Bank of Italy also suspended the commitment to purchase residually the BOT unsold at the auction (the so-called 'divorce' between the Bank and the Treasury), thus increasing the possibility of regulating the monetary base. The CCTs were also the object of two important forms of innovation: in February 1982 the first Treasury Certificates in ECU were issued, and by August 1985 they represented 2.6 per cent of outstanding CCTs. In August 1983 an issue of certificates with real indexation took place: the amount issued was, however, modest (1,000 billion lire) and their success limited (Monti and Onado, 1984, p. 171).

Other Bonds

The second major feature emerging from table 8.2 is the increase in indexed bonds. The main cause of the adoption of indexation was the high and volatile interest rates that accompanied the inflationary outbursts of 1973–4, of 1976 and of 1979–80. This also caused the tendency towards maturity shortening which was clearly apparent in the case of public debt.

---

3   In May 1983 the competitive method was extended to the primary market for three and six month BOTs.

Although the diffusion of indexation was initially slow,[4] its success since the end of the seventies is undisputed. It has, however, been restricted to financial indexation: there have only been two cases of real indexation. The diffusion of other innovative techniques in the bond market has been limited too: bonds with warrants, i.e. with the right to purchase stocks or bonds at fixed conditions at some predetermined time, have been in circulation since 1981 but still have a restricted market. Deep discount, zero coupon, drop lock bonds and private bonds in ECU are also still at an experimental level.[5]

A final remark must be made concerning the role played by bonds in financing non-financial firms. This has remained modest throughout the period. Indeed, most innovation in the bond market has come from SCIs.

Certificates of Deposit (CDs)

Two types of asset can be classified under this heading: SCI and bank CDs. The CDs issued by SCIs are certificates with maturities ranging from 18 to 60 months, sometimes with indexed coupons, sometimes with payment of capital and interest on a unique date (i.e. like zero coupon bonds). Their growth, which was limited until 1981, speeded up after a law was passed allowing all SCIs to issue them. However, there is no secondary market yet on which CDs are traded and quoted daily.

The case of bank CDs is rather interesting: while this instrument has been introduced in other countries, mainly to circumvent regulation, in Italy bank CDs were promoted by the monetary authorities themselves at the end of 1982 when they granted an interest rate on the compulsory reserves against CDs which was higher than that paid on reserves against ordinary deposits. The aim was to promote a greater stability of bank liabilities and to provide the banks with an instrument to face the competition of other new financial instruments (BOT, CCT and SCI CDs); moreover, insofar as the CDs would compete directly with other money market instruments, monetary impulses would be transmitted to bank interest rates more quickly. The growth of bank CDs, which are issued with maturities of six, twelve and eighteen months, has recently accelerated. In June 1985 they represented 3.2 per cent of total bank deposits. However, the instrument has so far been void of money market features: the after-tax yield on CDs has been considerably lower than the BOT yield for corresponding maturities (table 8.3) and the CDs have attracted funds from other deposits rather than from Treasury bills. Again in this case a secondary market is virtually absent.

4 The first indexed bonds were issued in 1974 by ENEL, the public corporation that manages the nationalized electricity sector. The adoption of indexation by SCIs, which are the main issuers of bonds besides the Treasury, was not initially felt to be compelling owing to the portfolio constraint that obliged commercial banks to invest a rather higher proportion of their deposits in SCI bonds.
5 Convertible bonds are worth a separate comment: in spite of the more favourable tax treatment introduced in 1974, this instrument still plays a minor role in the financial market: it indeed shares with the stock market serious problems in attracting private saving.

TABLE 8.3   After-tax interest rates[a]

	1979	1980	1981	1982	1983	1984
Bank deposits						
Current accounts (average)	8.0	9.5	11.1	11.5	10.3	9.5
Current accounts (top rate)	10.5	13.1	15.1	14.6	2.9	12.0
Savings accounts	8.6	10.2	12.1	12.3	11.0	10.1
CD (6 mth)	–	–	–	–	–	11.6
Treasury bills (6 mth)	15.7	17.0	21.4	19.11	17.0	14.7
CCT	14.0	17.3	22.3	21.3	18.8	16.0
SCI CDs	..	..	..	..	14.6	13.0
Long-term bonds[b]	14.3	16.3	21.0	19.9	17.3	13.8

[a] End of period values.
[b] Yield of bonds issued by SCI.

Bankers' Acceptances

The market for bankers' acceptances has been subject to a phase of great expansion followed by a rapid contraction (figure 8.2). This evolution has mainly been due to changes in regulation: in 1978 the stamp tax on bankers' acceptances was reduced from 1 to 0.01 per cent. Bankers' acceptances, however, took off only in 1980, when the ceiling on bank lending became

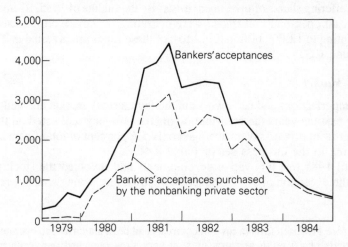

FIGURE 8.2   Bankers' acceptances (billions of lire).

more stringent; the unregulated tax status of the interest on acceptances, which was virtually equivalent to a tax exemption, also prompted the development of the market. The decline began with a series of measures first limiting the issue of acceptances quantitatively, and then regulating the tax treatment of interest payments. The removal of the ceiling on bank loans in June 1983 took away the last remaining incentive to issue bankers' acceptances.

Titoli Atipici

The relevance of *titoli atipici* (atypical debentures) lies in the fact that they represented virtually the only attempt by new intermediaries to issue unregulated instruments of credit. The term refers to a set of instruments of credit issued by nonbank financial firms and bearing a claim on the return of an investment. The range of investments financed in this way has been wide but has mainly concerned real estate or leasing activities. The development of *titoli atipici* was stimulated by high inflation: they also offered the possibility of an (indirect) investment in real assets to small savers.

The legality of *titoli atipici* was largely debated before the 1983 law subjected their issue to the supervision of the Commissione di Controllo sulle Società quotate in Borsa (CONSOB) and of the Bank of Italy. In 1984, due to the crisis in the real estate market, one of the major issuers of *titoli atipici* failed, and the entire sector began to subside.

Investment Funds

The troubled case of *titoli atipici* can be easily contrasted with the smooth and rapid expansion of the new investment funds that began operating in Italy in 1984.[6] As for bank CDs, the turning point was a law that regulated the activity in this area and allowed traditional intermediaries to set up financial firms offering shares of investment trusts. By the middle of 1985, 37 investment funds, all open-end unit trusts, were operating in Italy, having raised funds amounting to 12,000 billion lire. Most of these funds are invested in Treasury bills and CCTs.

Stock Market

The imperfections and narrowness of the Italian stock market are well known: in the past ten years the contribution of 'fresh money' collected on the stock market from private savers averaged only 5.6 per cent of total financial flows accruing to the business sector (table 8.4).

Until 1985 few innovative developments had involved the stock market, with the exception of the introduction of so-called 'saving shares', regulated

---

6 Before 1984, ten foreign investment trusts had been authorized to operate in Italy. The funds raised by these trusts grew at very slow rates and they even presented negative growth in several years.

TABLE 8.4 Composition of total funds raised by the private sector

Year	Bank loans (lire)	Bank loans (foreign currency)	SCI loans	Private debentures[a]	Foreign loans and trade credit	Shares	Total
1974	51.0	3.0	25.6	2.0	15.4	3.0	100.0
1975	49.4	-2.9	35.5	9.1	4.0	4.9	100.0
1976	47.0	10.8	22.4	5.2	10.6	4.0	100.0
1977	43.3	20.3	26.7	5.1	-1.5	6.1	100.0
1978	46.4	-3.2	30.5	5.1	13.1	8.1	100.0
1979	58.5	5.4	18.0	2.8	12.8	2.5	100.0
1980	41.2	14.6	21.9	4.2	13.6	4.5	100.0
1981	35.8	-3.8	28.9	4.7	29.1	5.3	100.0
1982	40.3	-2.6	35.6	13.3	6.6	6.8	100.0
1983	53.2	8.2	23.3	5.2	3.6	6.5	100.0
1984	47.1	15.0	21.2	2.1	5.1	9.5	100.0
period average	46.7	5.9	26.3	5.4	10.1	5.6	100.0

[a] This item includes bonds, bankers' acceptances and other instruments of credit issued by the private sector.

in 1974 and favoured by a lighter tax treatment.[7] In 1985, however, the stock exchange experienced a surge of activity. The introduction of the new investment funds into the market led to a boom in stock prices with an increase of 43 per cent of the stock index in the first semester of 1985. Given the still limited number of purchases by investment funds, these increases may be interpreted as a proof of lack of market depth, but it is conceivable that the presence of a more stable component of demand will stimulate new issues; indeed in the first six months of 1985 issuing activity increased by 20 per cent compared to that of the same period in 1984.

International Capital Movements

The trends shown during the past ten years in private foreign assets and liabilities have been heavily influenced by administrative controls on capital movements introduced in Italy from the beginning of the seventies. Portfolio investments abroad by residents have been virtually prevented by the non-interest-bearing deposits required on these assets, which have been only recently reduced. On the other hand, foreign liabilities have shown a remarkable growth especially during the eighties, rising from 5.1 to 11.2 per cent of private liabilities (from 1979 to 1984) and representing the third most important source of funds after bank loans in lire and SCI long-term loans (see table 8.9). This increase was clearly influenced by the restrictive monetary policy of the past decade and specifically by the credit ceiling on bank credit which became more stringent between 1980 and 1982, the years when foreign liabilities rose most rapidly.

The Innovative Action of Financial Intermediaries

We shall consider here the innovation activity of financial intermediaries other than investment funds, focusing our attention on the developments which have occurred in the credit markets.

Commercial Banks

Tables 8.5 and 8.6 show the composition of the commercial banks' balance sheet from 1975 to 1984. If compared with the large changes which have occurred in the financial markets, the stability of this composition is striking. Moreover, the major changes can hardly be attributed to forms of innovative behaviour. We observe:

---

7   Saving shares do not give the holder voting rights, but they guarantee a minimum yield of 5 per cent of face value and a total dividend at least two points higher than ordinary shares. There have been only 40 issues of saving shares; in terms of flow of funds, they were only substantial in 1981, in connection with the boom of stock market prices.

TABLE 8.5 Bank assets (percentage composition)

	1975	1976	1977	1978	1979	1980	1981	1982	1983	1984
Liquidity	2.5	1.5	1.6	2.1	1.3	1.3	1.3	0.8	0.7	0.8
Compulsory reserves	8.9	10.1	10.0	10.2	10.5	9.8	9.5	10.0	10.2	10.5
Bank loans (lire)										
Short-term	37.3	36.8	30.3	27.2	27.5	25.8	26.1	24.5	23.6	24.9
Long-term	5.7	5.7	5.5	5.6	6.2	6.7	6.6	6.1	5.9	6.2
Bank loans (foreign currency)	0.6	1.9	3.2	2.3	2.5	4.2	4.1	3.6	4.1	5.1
Bad loans	0.8	0.8	1.0	1.1	1.4	1.7	1.8	2.0	2.2	2.4
BOT	5.0	3.9	8.4	9.1	8.2	9.7	9.6	11.2	9.0	7.1
CCT	1.2	1.0	1.9	3.4	4.9	3.6	3.7	5.6	10.2	11.2
Other bonds	22.8	22.4	22.9	22.4	21.1	19.2	17.7	16.7	14.6	13.1
Shares	0.8	0.8	0.8	0.8	0.8	0.9	0.9	1.1	1.2	1.4
Interbank assets	14.5	15.1	14.5	15.7	15.6	17.1	18.7	18.3	18.3	17.2
Total	100.0	100.0	100.0	100.0	100.0	100.0	100.0	100.0	100.0	100.0

TABLE 8.6 Bank liabilities (percentage composition)

	1975	1976	1977	1978	1979	1980	1981	1982	1983	1984
CDs	0.0	0.0	0.0	0.0	0.0	0.0	0.0	0.0	0.6	1.3
Saving deposits	20.8	23.5	25.9	26.2	26.2	25.1	25.3	25.5	24.6	23.4
Current accounts	41.0	39.9	40.1	41.9	43.7	42.4	41.0	40.6	39.6	39.6
Time deposits	17.8	14.6	12.3	10.8	9.9	8.7	8.1	8.0	7.9	8.0
Repos	0.0	0.0	0.0	0.0	0.0	0.0	0.0	0.9	0.2	0.1
Interbank liabilities	16.5	16.6	14.9	15.4	14.4	15.8	17.0	17.0	17.3	16.3
Net foreign debt	0.7	2.1	3.3	2.4	2.4	4.2	4.1	3.1	4.0	4.8
Bank capital	3.2	3.3	3.4	3.3	3.5	3.7	4.5	4.8	5.8	6.4
Total	100.0	100.0	100.0	100.0	100.0	100.0	100.0	100.0	100.0	100.0

1 A fall in the share of loans over total assets, brought about by the credit ceiling imposed from 1973 to 1983 and by the reduced dynamic of the demand for credit by firms during the past ten years (see discussion of innovative failures below).

2 A recomposition of bank loans towards the foreign currency component; the steady growth of the foreign currency share has been sustained by the exemption of these loans from the ceiling[8] and by the compulsory component that firms were required to take up by way of foreign trade credits. Foreign currency loans to residents, which had already represented 8.5 per cent of total bank loans by 1967 but had fallen to 1.5 per cent by the end of 1975, reached 14 per cent of total bank loans in June 1985.

3 A rise of the net foreign debt among liabilities that, due to regulation, approximately matched the increase in foreign currency loans. The increase in gross foreign assets and liabilities has been, however, much faster. Italian banks have entered the new international financial markets deeply, although they do not participate actively in the most innovative sectors of the Euromarkets.[9]

4 A rise in own capital, stimulated by increasing risks and made possible by high profits.

5 A fall in time deposits due both to the general drive of savers towards more liquid assets and, more recently, to the competition of BOTs.

The new techniques developed by US banks to raise funds have found limited scope (CDs have already been mentioned above). The ups and downs of repurchase agreements (repos) reveal the interrelationship between innovation and regulation; commercial banks developed this fund-raising technique only after the Bank of Italy adopted repos as a short-term liquidity management tool, making them familiar to the financial community. Within a short period of time, repos reached an estimated level of 15,000 billion lire (Monti and Onado, 1984), but their relevance was destroyed when, in December 1982, they were made subject to the reserve payment. Changes in the technical forms under which banks loans are granted (table 8.7) have also been rare, with the exception of foreign currency loans, which partially represent a return to the past, and of syndicated loans, which, at the end of 1982, amounted to 3.2 per cent of total loans (Rettaroli, 1984).

Again, innovation has been more the exception than the rule in interbank markets. Several studies (for example, Pepe, 1982) have been produced to document the prevalence in these markets of bilateral agreements and of privileged financial channels that limit the mobility of funds. It is indeed

8 Foreign currency loans were subject to a distinct ceiling in 1981 and 1982.
9 This subject is dealt with in a forthcoming paper prepared by a group of experts at the BIS. The study considers four recent innovations on the Euromarkets (NIF, swaps, foreign currency options and forward rate agreements); in none of these areas do Italian banks appear to be very active. On the other hand, Italian non-financial firms are deeply involved in these operations.

TABLE 8.7 Bank loans in lire (percentage composition)

Bank loans	1978	1979	1980	1981	1982	1983	1984
Short-term							
Overdrafts	61.0	60.5	60.1	59.3	60.4	60.6	62.8
Bill portfolio	12.1	11.1	11.3	10.8	10.2	9.7	8.1
Fixed term loans	9.4	9.4	7.4	9.0	9.0	9.4	9.0
Other	0.8	0.6	0.9	0.9	0.8	0.7	0.6
Long-term							
Mortgage loans	4.6	5.1	5.7	5.9	5.8	6.0	6.2
Other	12.1	13.3	14.6	14.1	13.8	13.6	13.3
Total	100.0	100.0	100.0	100.0	100.0	100.0	100.0

significant that an overnight market has operated only in the past three years and has represented almost the only innovation in interbank business. The size of this market is, however, modest and not comparable to foreign examples.[10]

Finally, with respect to the payment services offered by banks, innovation has so far been rather limited, the state of the Italian payment system being well described by the following quotation from the BIS (Bank for International Settlements) (1984):

> Overall the Italian payment system continues to be characterized by the extensive use of cash, not only to settle small everyday transactions but sometimes also for high-value transactions. . . Credit cards and electronic payment systems have a rather limited market share.

In the past ten years, high interest rates on cheque accounts and a general tendency towards more sophisticated financial behaviour have, however, led to a fall in the use of cash (see table 8.10). The installation of ATMs started in 1983 when a national interbank network (Bancomat) came into operation to provide depositors with the possibility of cash withdrawal from any ATM in the network. Although this system implies relevant efficiency gains, it can hardly be considered as a radical change in the payment system: indeed, it stimulates the use of cash although it reduces its average holdings. A foreseeable development may, however, be the use of the same network to allow customers to make payments. So far, as the above-mentioned survey reports: 'the development of home banking and other forms of payment in a telematic context is still at a very early stage in Italy.'

Special Credit Institutions (SCIs)

SCIs are financial institutions that, according to the 1936 Banking Law, are specialized at the long-term end of the credit and financial markets. Not surprisingly, inflation deeply affected the structure of their balance sheets. Both the asset and liability sides underwent a process of maturity shortening and indexation, which also benefited from the relaxation of the legal constraint on the issue of CDs. The evolution of the liability side (table 8.8) has already been discussed above; the activity of SCIs in the financial market has been deeply innovative and has produced important results. The capacity of SCIs to attract private funds has recovered after the crisis of the mid-seventies and for the first time after the introduction of the compulsory purchases of SCI bonds, private funds now exceed bank funds among SCI liabilities (Pontolillo et al., 1985). On the asset side, the main change is related to the growth of short-term credit and to the adoption of variable interest rates.

10 See Banca d'Italia. Relazione annuale sul 1984 (p. 187). There have only been two issues of interbank CDs – one in 1982 and one in 1985.

TABLE 8.8 Special credit institutions (SCIs) (percentage composition)

	1975	1976	1977	1978	1979	1980	1981	1982	1983	1984
ASSETS										
Cash and demand deposits	18.2	17.7	14.3	13.3	8.4	8.1	5.5	5.3	4.4	3.7
Loans										
Short-term	2.3	2.5	2.9	3.8	5.0	6.3	8.0	8.4	7.9	9.2
Long-term	79.0	79.2	82.2	82.3	85.5	84.5	85.2	84.8	86.1	85.4
Securities	0.5	0.6	0.6	0.6	1.1	1.1	1.3	1.5	1.6	1.7
Total	100.0	100.0	100.0	100.0	100.0	100.0	100.0	100.0	100.0	100.0
LIABILITIES										
CDs	9.4	8.4	9.0	10.1	9.6	9.4	10.3	15.8	14.7	16.1
Indexed bonds	—	—	—	—	0.5	2.4	5.9	10.2	15.2	19.0
Non-indexed bonds	75.7	75.4	76.1	76.1	78.1	74.8	68.7	57.2	50.0	42.4
Net foreign debt	9.6	10.5	8.9	7.3	4.1	4.8	6.0	8.0	10.4	12.0
Capital	5.5	5.7	6.0	6.5	7.7	8.6	9.1	8.8	9.7	10.5
Total	100.0	100.0	100.0	100.0	100.0	100.0	100.0	100.0	100.0	100.0

TABLE 8.9 Outstanding total financial liabilities of the private sector (percentage composition)

	1975	1976	1977	1978	1979	1980	1981	1982	1983	1984
Bank loans[a]										
Lire[a]	52.5	53.3	50.9	52.1	53.9	51.7	48.6	46.8	48.7	48.8
Foreign currency	0.9	2.7	5.0	3.8	4.2	6.8	6.1	5.6	6.2	7.6
Bankers' acceptances	/	/	/	/	0.4	1.2	1.4	0.9	0.5	0.2
SCI loans[b]										
Short-term	1.2	1.2	1.3	1.7	2.0	2.3	2.7	2.9	2.8	3.3
Long-term	31.8	30.6	29.4	28.6	26.0	24.1	23.8	24.2	22.1	21.0
Factoring[c]	/	0.4	0.8	0.9	1.0	0.9	1.0	1.1	1.1	1.4
Leasing[c]	/	/	0.1	0.1	0.2	0.2	0.3	0.6	0.7	0.9
Indexed bonds	1.0	1.5	2.2	2.7	2.6	2.3	2.3	3.5	3.5	3.7
Other bonds	8.4	7.5	6.1	5.4	4.6	3.7	3.1	2.7	2.5	1.9
Foreign liabilities	4.2	2.8	4.2	4.7	5.1	6.8	10.7	11.7	11.9	11.2
Total	100.0	100.0	100.0	100.0	100.0	100.0	100.0	100.0	100.0	100.0

[a] Including bad loans and excluding loans to leasing and factoring firms; the data are corrected for an estimate of the effect of the make-up procedures used by the banks during the periods when the ceiling on bank loans was binding.
[b] Excluding loans to leasing and factoring firms.
[c] The data on loans through leasing and factoring have been estimated; the figures for leasing refer to the outstanding value of leasing contracts not of the repaid instalments.

Leasing and Factoring

A unified treatment of leasing and factoring is convenient because of the several common features presented by the evolution of these new channels of finance. In Italy, recourse to leasing and factoring remained somewhat restricted until the end of the seventies.[11] The ceiling on bank loans as well as certain tax benefits that may be connected to leasing stimulated their development (Mieli, 1985). Despite the removal of the ceiling, the activity of leasing and factoring firms has maintained a high growth rate, although at the end of 1984 the total credit granted through leasing and factoring amounted to only 2.3 per cent of total private liabilities (table 8.9). Strong property links exist between traditional intermediaries (banks and SCIs) and leasing and factoring firms: moreover, most of the funds raised by these firms come from capital contribution or loans by traditional intermediaries.

The Overall Picture

The above description has presented areas of intense financial innovation together with areas resisting the introduction of change. An overall summary on what has been quantitatively relevant can be based on the changes that have occurred in the balance sheet of the private sector (tables 8.9 and 8.10). The following features stand out clearly:

1 The major change that has affected the Italian financial structure has been the birth of the markets for new government debt instruments (BOTs and CCTs), whose share represented, at the end of 1984, more than a quarter of total financial assets, excluding shares (figure 8.3). While the creation of an efficient money market for Treasury bills has simply filled a gap, the new Treasury certificates have represented a more innovative development, allowing for several experiments in maturity, form of indexation, interest payments, currency of denomination and procedures of issue.

2 The spreading of indexation and of maturity shortening to most financial assets and liabilities, of which BOT and CCT represent special cases, is the second major innovative aspect. It should be recalled that this process has not implied relevant changes in the forms in which banks raise and lend funds. On the other hand, a pioneering activity in this field has been performed by SCIs, which have applied new techniques, developed in parallel with other countries, to the issue of bonds.

3 The composition of private sector liabilities has remained relatively stable, the main change being the higher recourse to the international market; the leasing and factoring contributions are still low, the recourse to the capital market (shares and bonds) has not so far shown appreciable improvements, a commercial paper market is absent. The process of securitization

11 The first firms in this area, however, began their operations in 1963.

TABLE 8.10 Outstanding total financial assets of the private sector (percentage composition)

Financial assets	1975	1976	1977	1978	1979	1980	1981	1982	1983	1984
Notes and coins	8.7	8.2	7.7	7.3	6.8	6.8	6.7	6.2	5.8	5.3
Bank deposits	66.5	67.7	69.0	67.5	66.1	64.6	61.0	60.1	55.8	51.6
Bank CDs	–	–	–	–	–	–	–	–	0.5	1.0
Postal savings	9.4	9.3	9.3	9.4	9.9	9.1	8.2	7.5	7.0	6.6
BOT	0.1	1.5	3.0	3.9	5.8	9.3	13.5	13.5	13.7	14.3
Bankers' acceptances	–	–	–	–	–	0.3	0.4	0.3	0.2	0.1
SCI CDs	2.6	2.2	1.9	2.0	1.7	1.6	1.7	2.7	2.5	2.6
CCT	–	–	0.6	1.5	2.2	2.3	2.7	4.2	8.3	11.5
Other bonds	12.3	10.4	8.1	8.0	6.8	5.3	5.2	4.9	5.6	6.0
Titoli atipici and investment funds	–	–	–	–	0.1	0.1	0.2	0.2	0.2	0.4
Foreign assets	0.4	0.7	0.4	0.4	0.6	0.6	0.4	0.4	0.4	0.6
Total	100.0	100.0	100.0	100.0	100.0	100.0	100.0	100.0	100.0	100.0

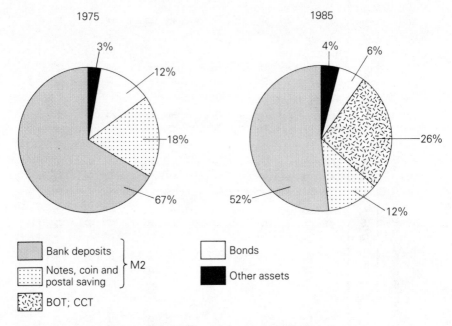

FIGURE 8.3   Private financial assets, excluding shares
(percentage composition of stocks at year-end)

of private debt, which has been occurring in many other financial structures, is still virtually unknown in Italy. As a matter of fact, even after ten years of credit ceilings, the share of commercial bank loans over total credit has shown a surprising stability.

4 In their first year of existence, investment funds have shown a relevant capability for growth: the conditions exist for this new intermediary to become in the future one of the protagonists of the Italian financial scene.

MAIN CAUSES OF FINANCIAL INNOVATION

Like the synoptic tables presented by Silber (1983) or Van Horne (1985) relating to the United States, table 8.11 provides a compact picture of the main innovations that have occurred in the Italian financial system during the past decade. On the base of the analysis in the previous section, eight exogenous causes of innovation have been identified together with the five sectors that introduced the new financial instruments.

It emerges from the table that inflation and the high variability of interest rates are by far the most frequently quoted causes of innovation. Indeed, they are, to a very large extent, directly responsible for the spreading of floating rate debt and for the maturity shortening of the instruments exchanged in the markets and offered by intermediaries. The relationship between innovation and uncertainty on prices and interest rates is well known (see, for example, Akhtar, 1983), and in this respect Italy shares the experience of many other industrialized countries.

The surge of the PSBR is the obvious cause of the rise of the BOT and CCT markets, the most important innovations of the past ten years. This is because inflation and interest rate variability, together with the policy decision of limiting the monetary financing of the deficit, forced the adoption of new forms of financing the growing PSBR. Incentives, in terms of tax exemption and measures adopted by the central bank to favour the birth of the new market, are also listed as relevant causes. It must be stressed that the development of the BOT and CCT markets can be seen as an indirect cause for other innovations because it determined a general improvement in the efficiency of financial transactions which encouraged the introduction of new instruments and procedures. This is one example of the chain reaction that often characterizes financial innovation phases, as experienced by various countries.[12] Finally, policy action, in one of its three possible aspects (harsher regulation, removal of regulation and incentives) affected almost all listed forms of innovation.

Policy action is only partially recognized as a cause of financial innovation: indeed, most studies consider harsher regulation to be among the main determinants of innovative developments in the financial structure (for example, Johnson, 1985) and some authors even view it as basically their only cause (Greenbaum and Heywood, 1971). The development of new financial channels as a reaction to regulation has been observed in Italy too, especially in response to the ceiling on bank lending and to the increasing reserve requirement on deposits. The ceiling on bank lending in lire stimulated the growth of bank loans in foreign currency, short-term SCI loans, bankers' acceptances, and, to a lesser extent, leasing and factoring. It was also partially responsible for the increase in the share of foreign debt out of total private liabilities from 5.1 per cent in 1979 to 11.2 per cent in 1984 (see table 8.9). The rising reserve requirement on bank deposits prompted the surge of repos and generally contributed to the disintermediation of the banking sector in favour of the assets offered by other sectors.

Faced with these developments, the monetary authorities intervened by extending regulation to the new instruments whenever they represented a serious threat to the achievement of policy targets. This was notably the case of bank loans in foreign currency, of bankers' acceptances and of repos. As far as *titoli atipici* were concerned, the intervention aimed mainly at safeguarding savers, although the central bank was also given the power to ration new issues. The surge of these alternative channels of finance was, however, a relevant cause of the abandonment of the ceiling on bank loans, thus confirming the difficulty of imposing regulatory constraints for prolonged periods of time.

12 See, for example, the case of Sweden, where the introduction of bank CDs primed the development of the money market (Wissen, 1985).

TABLE 8.11 Determinants of financial innovation in Italy, 1975–84

Type	Exogenous causes[a]					PY			Sector[b]				
	IF	V	IB	T	IZ	A	B	C	P	F	B	SCI	NI
BOTs	x	x	x					x	x				
CCTs (lire)	x	x	x					x	x				
Other financially indexed bonds	x	x								x		x	
CCTs (ECU)	x	x	x						x				
Bonds with real indexation	x	x							x			x	
Other bonds[c]	x	x										x	
Bank CDs								x			x		
SCI CDs	x	x					x					x	
Bankers' acceptances	x					x		x		x		x	
Unregulated debentures	x					x							x

	IF	V	IB	T	IZ	PY	A	B	C	P	F	B	SCI	NI
Investment funds saving shares				x										
Repos	x	x				x							x	x
Syndicated loans				x					x			x		
Long-term SCI indexed loans	x			x										x
Leasing		x	x		x		x							x
Factoring		x	x		x		x							x
Convertible bonds	x	x		x		x								
Short-term SCI loans	x			x									x	
ATM		x		x		x								
Home banking		x		x		x								

---

[a] IF, inflation; V, volatility of interest rates; IB, increasing borrowing requirement; T, technology; IZ, internationalization; PY, policy action; A, more binding regulation; B, lifting of regulation; C, incentives.

[b] Sector that issued the new instrument. P, public sector including public agencies; F, firms; B, banking system; SCI, special credit institutions; NI, new intermediaries.

[c] This item includes zero coupon bonds, bonds with warrant, drop lock bonds or other bonds offering innovative conditions in interest payment or in principal reimbursement.

The link between innovation and policy action is not, however, limited to the rise of new financial channels aimed at circumventing regulation, as is also evidenced by table 8.11; the Italian experience is a good example of the existence of other aspects which have sometimes been disregarded in the recent literature on the subject. Clearly, policy action can influence innovation through incentives and the removal of previously binding constraints. For example, in Italy this has influenced the development of BOTs and CCTs, saving shares and of bank and SCI CDs. What is even more important, however, is the fact that regulation itself may generally encourage the development of financial instruments even when it is not accompanied by incentives.

There are at least three ways in which regulation can protect the birth of a financial market:

1 It can reduce the riskiness of trade: in fact, in financial markets, where the quality of the goods exchanged is often not immediately perceivable by all the agents involved in the transaction, the introduction of a regulatory framework, specifying common standards and guaranteeing minimum levels of trustworthiness, may reduce the riskiness of trade (Gorton, 1981; Goodhart, 1985). Indeed, this has been the main contribution to the development of markets given by public agencies such as the Securities and Exchange Commission (SEC) in the United States, the French Commission des Operations de Bourse or the Italian CONSOB, which was established in 1974 to supervise the stock market.[13]

2 The organization of the market for certain financial assets can be carried out equally well by public authorities; as a matter of fact, in some European countries (such as Italy) even the stock exchange is a public institution.

3 Finally, regulation can reduce an undesirably excessive competition that can potentially undermine the rise of a new market; this link explains why some innovative sectors (for example factoring and leasing in Italy) have frequently required the introduction of a regulatory framework.

This aspect of regulation (which we may label 'protective regulation') has been clearly relevant in the Italian experience: in particular, most new financial instruments have been introduced in Italy by legislation specifying common standards as discussed in the first point above. The most recent example is provided by the new investment funds, whose capability of growth may easily be contrasted with the stunted development of new but unregulated financial instruments such as *titoli atipici*.[14]

13 It is, of course, questionable whether the need for a law fixing common standards of financial instruments is felt more in Italy than in other countries, especially the Anglo-American countries where a sort of mistrust *vis-à-vis* the public sector is coupled with a higher trust in private agents. We do not rule out this possibility; however, public regulation designed to guarantee small savers and reduce the risk of financial investment is a common feature of both European and Anglo-American countries.
14 The favourable attitude maintained towards innovation by the Italian monetary

INNOVATIVE FAILURES IN THE PRIVATE AND BANKING SECTORS

A necessary complement to an analysis of the causes of financial innovation is a review of the reasons why some sectors have shown such a low propensity for innovation. Indeed, table 8.11 and the evidence presented in the third section above point out that financial innovation in Italy has so far left large areas of the financial markets untouched. Among final users of financial saving, the public sector has been highly innovative, as witnessed by the abundance of the new instruments (BOT, CCT in lire and in ECU, real indexed CCT) and techniques (innovations in the auction systems, repos) introduced. On the other hand, the innovative activity of the private sector has been limited to a few issues of indexed bonds and to so-called 'unregulated securities'.

Among financial intermediaries SCIs have played by far the leading role, with the banking system merely walking on to the stage of financial innovation. Clearly, SCI assets and liabilities were put under a more severe strain due to their long-term nature. However, the banking system also had to face dramatic changes in the financial environment in which it was operating, in particular in terms of increased regulation and of competition from new financial assets. Yet, the innovative capacity of Italian banks to offer new products appears at first glance to have been moderate, especially when compared with the capacity of other banking systems to react to similar pressures.[15]

In this section the innovative failures of the private and banking sectors are explained in terms of contingent reasons (notably the 'innovative crowding out' of the private sector due to the high PSBR of the past ten years) and of specific characteristics of the Italian financial and industrial structure (technological gap, a low propensity to issue shares, the typology of bank accounts).

---

authorities in the past ten years has been explicitly inspired by the attempt to increase the efficiency of the system and the level of competitiveness by multiplying the instruments of credit and the number of operators. This is also confirmed by the central bank's policy of authorizing the opening of new bank branches, which led to an increase in the number of bank branches per million residents of from 201 in 1969, to 253 in 1984.
15 The obvious term of comparison is the US banking system, which faced the competition from money market mutual funds by offering new deposit instruments (NOW, Super-NOW and money market deposit accounts being in the forefront). It is true that US banks were able to react with a full-scale effort only after the 1982 Garn-St Germain Depository Institutions Act deregulated interest payments on a large share of deposits. But Italian banks have never been limited by interest rate regulation; yet, no relevant change has occurred in their fund raising or lending techniques in the past ten years.

In this section we shall discuss a more general explanation in terms of the connection between the legal system of a country and the propensity of its financial markets to innovate.

Innovative Crowding Out

The need to finance an increasing deficit, without losing control of aggregate demand, forced the monetary authorities to offer high interest rates on public debt. In the past few years, the yield on tax-exempt government securities has always been higher than that on any other financial asset, especially with respect to bank liabilities, even if compared with the top rate on deposits (table 8.3). The high level of interest rates contributed to slack private demand – the usual crowding out effect – but was also probably responsible for the lack of private sector financial innovation. In other words, while some competition stimulates innovation, too much competition makes innovation useless. This is particularly true for the banking system, penalized by both a high tax on deposits (25 per cent from 1983) and an increasing reserve requirement.

Technological Gap

In industrial economics, this is among the main reasons usually given for the lack of innovation. In the financial case, it may explain the lags with which Italian banks have followed the US experience in the area of payment systems. The gap is, however, wider in the use of the new techniques than in their availability. Indeed, high bank profits have allowed investment in new equipment (including hardware and software) in the past years[16] and, in this respect, the gap now seems to have been filled.[17]

Supply Factors

The limited development of some sectors of the Italian financial system has often been explained in terms of demand factors. For example, the failure to develop of the stock market and, more generally, of a long-term private securities market, has again been interpreted in terms of a high liquidity preference on the part of Italian households (Cotula, 1984). Demand factors are certainly important, but too little relevance has so far been given to supply factors, i.e. to what reduced the incentive or the need for the banking and firm sectors to innovate.

Let us consider the banking sector first. It would appear that the external changes (inflation and the competition of new public debt instruments) should have resulted in a swift reaction and at least a serious attempt to innovate. Two facts should, however, be considered. The first consideration is that,

16   See Convenzione Interbancaria per i Problemi dell'Automazione (1983).
17   Nevertheless a gap persists in the degree of financial sophistication in some Italian areas where even BOTs and CCTs represent new instruments. The disintermediation of the banking sector, for example, has been much more pronounced in the northern than in the southern regions.

in Italy, most bank accounts bear variable interest rates. On the asset side, 63 per cent of bank loans in lire are represented by overdrafts on which interest rates can be renegotiated at any time. On the liability side, variable interest rates have always been paid on both current and savings accounts; indeed the function of these two instruments has been most identical given that most savings accounts have no withdrawal limit.[18] On the other hand, the imperfections existing in the deposit market (especially the lack of information) allowed the banking system to differentiate deposit rates without having recourse to new technical forms (Cottarelli et al., 1985), higher rates being paid on larger accounts and to more sophisticated customers. In this respect it has been argued (Vaciago, 1982) that the real innovation in the banks' fund-raising techniques came in 1969 when the cartel on deposit rates was broken and the banks offered an asset with an optimal combination of liquidity, risk and yield, which did indeed turn out to be 'unbeatable in the first half of the seventies'.

The second factor that explains the lack of innovative pressure on the banking system emerges by looking at its profit and loss accounts in the past decade. Table 8.12 shows an increase of gross income and profit during the years of higher disintermediation, a remarkable performance for an industry that lost such a large market share in favour of BOTs and CCTs. To explain this performance it is convenient to take a closer look at the composition of revenues. From the table we observe the increasing share of revenues from services, especially from security transactions. Indeed, Italian banks act as virtually the only intermediaries for the purchase of BOTs and CCTs – or of any other financial asset – by households and firms. In this respect, they maintain a sort of 'natural' monopoly due to the fact that no other financial institution has at its disposal a framework of branches comparable with that of the banking system.[19] Until this monopoly is broken down, for example by a door-to-door sale of financial assets, the banking system will be partially protected from the appearance of new financial instruments, although it may be forced to shift towards a more service-oriented activity.

Let us turn now to the firms sector. The lack of direct channels of finance from savers to firms has been explained in two ways; the truth probably lies somewhere in the middle. There are demand factors: the tax disincentives on commercial bills and on shares; the lack of any real protection against inflation provided by investment in shares during the first half of the seventies

18 Significantly, the payment of flexible interest rates on deposits has spread to nearly every financial system during the eighties. Some authors (for example Revell, 1985) have argued that the outcome of this process will be the so-called 'Swedish account', namely a unique account that will serve both as a payment instrument and as a store of value, which seems a fair description of the main features of Italian bank deposit accounts.

19 The situation is quite different in Great Britain, for example, since the branches of building societies are as widespread as those of banks.

TABLE 8.12 Profit and loss accounts of the banks: formation of profit[a]

	1974	1975	1976	1977	1978	1979	1980	1981	1982	1983	1984
As a percentage of total resources[b]											
Net interest income	3.29	3.70	3.42	3.21	2.92	2.75	3.45	3.54	3.30	3.37	3.36
Non-interest income	0.56	0.77	0.89	0.94	0.98	0.95	1.00	1.23	1.27	1.19	1.28
of which: securities transactions	0.05	0.27	0.25	0.34	0.46	0.45	0.44	0.56	0.66	0.56	0.66
Gross income	3.85	4.47	4.31	4.15	3.90	3.70	4.45	4.77	4.57	4.56	4.64
Operating expenses	2.69	2.98	3.04	2.91	2.78	2.72	3.01	2.95	2.97	3.15	3.15
of which: staff costs	0.22	2.33	2.42	2.21	2.08	1.99	2.20	2.14	2.06	2.31	2.27
Net income	1.16	1.49	1.27	1.24	1.12	0.98	1.44	1.82	1.60	1.41	1.49
Provisions (net)	0.84	1.10	0.95	0.87	0.76	0.69	0.99	1.30	0.99	0.72	0.71
of which: for loan losses	0.26	0.38	0.29	0.37	0.37	0.33	0.44	0.44	0.46	0.42	0.39
Extraordinary income and withdrawals from loan loss funds	−0.06	−0.02	0.01	0.01	—	0.04	0.01	0.03	0.08	0.03	0.02
Profit before tax	0.26	0.37	0.33	0.38	0.36	0.33	0.46	0.55	0.69	0.72	0.80
Tax	0.13	0.24	0.18	0.21	0.18	0.14	0.24	0.27	0.40	0.43	0.44
Net profit	0.13	0.13	0.15	0.17	0.18	0.19	0.22	0.28	0.29	0.29	0.36

Other data

Number of employees	203,505	216,346	227,338	239.901	249.999	261,505	274,889	287,420	293,002	299,282	302.755
Total resources per employee (billions of lire)	589	639	745	868	1,002	1,177	1,355	1,536	1,755	2,001	2,216
Cost per employee (millions of lire)	13.1	15.2	18.0	19.2	20.8	23.4	29.9	32.8	36.1	46.2	50.2

Percentage rates of increase

Cost per employee	8.4	16.0	11.8	6.7	8.3	12.5	27.8	9.7	13.2	28.0	8.7
Total resources per employee in nominal terms	...	8.5	16.6	16.5	15.4	17.5	15.1	13.4	14.3	14.0	10.7
at constant prices[c]	...	-7.4	0.1	1.4	2.7	1.5	-5.0	-4.5	-1.8	-1.0	0.1

[a] Excluding central credit institutions and, except for the item 'Number of employees', credit institutions which at the dates in question submitted profit and loss returns at times other than the end of the year. The figures for net interest income and non-interest income, in particular income on securities transactions, are not comparable to those for previous years. They differ from the date published earlier in the definitions of some items.

[b] Net of costs and operating and extraordinary losses.

[c] Deflated using the cost-of-living index.

Source: Banca d'Italia, *Abridged Report* on 1984.

(figure 8.4); and the consequent high liquidity preference of Italian households. According to this view, innovative developments could be attained, for example, by means of tax measures and by favouring the birth of new inter-mediaries (merchant banks and investment and pension funds) that would channel savings into the stock market.

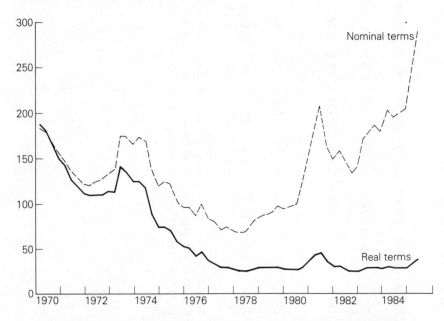

FIGURE 8.4   Stock market index. The index in real terms is obtained by deflating the nominal term index with the GNP deflator (1970=100).

The opposite view, which stresses the importance of supply factors, is described by Onado (1985):

> Indeed, our stock market has never taken off, not because of savers' preferences, but because of firms' preferences, who have traditionally enjoyed privileged self-financing and, among external sources, bank and SCI loans, possibly granted at subsidized rates. Historically, firms refused forms of finance that were at the same time 'external' and through shares. In other words, the stock market was seen more as a menace to the control of the firm than as a channel to attract permanent financial resources...[20]

To the reasons adduced by Onado (fear of takeovers), should be added that the model of industrial development followed by Italian firms during the seventies certainly did not favour, or indeed exclude recourse to capital markets. The model, which has been nicknamed 'industrialization from below',

20   On this point, see also Della Torre (1980).

hinged on decentralization and on the rise of small-scale industries, of 'the millions of small retail traders who have sprung up everywhere and the millions of "self-employed professionals" who have flourished to assist the small entrepreneur and the small trader' (de Cecco, 1983).

The prevalence of this form of industrial evolution also contributed to the steady fall in the demand for credit from the private sector observed during the seventies, given the higher relevance of self-financing for small firms. The fall in the credit-to-output ratios was, however, also due to the prolonged restrictive monetary policies of the last decade. Figure 8.5 documents the fall in the ratios between three definitions of credit aggregates and the value-added of the private sector. Clearly, Italian firms undertook a process of credit saving which is manifested in the fall in credit aggregates relative to output during the periods when monetary policy became more stringent and ceilings on bank credit were imposed. After each fall, the ratios stabilized around the lower level previously reached. This process of credit saving, which found a counterpart in the fall of stockbuilding and improved liquidity management, helps to explain why Italian firms were not very innovative in their fund-raising techniques, while the rise in the PSBR explains the innovativeness of the public sector.

If these are the reasons for the limited growth of the stock market, what are the prospects for the future? In the article quoted above, Onado stresses that the attitude of Italian firms towards the stock market may have changed recently, especially as a result of the high cost of credit during the eighties. This may be a prelude to a change in the attitude of the firms sector towards financing through market instruments.

Signs of these new developments in the stock market are already visible; as mentioned above, investment funds have begun to play a role as institutional investors in this market. A law on merchant banking is being discussed in parliament, as well as a bill regulating venture capital activities. The number of firms 'traded' on the stock exchange is still small but it has increased noticeably during 1985, under the supervision of CONSOB. Although it is still premature to predict a full development of the stock market[21] – there have been other periods of boom in stock prices and issues – there are clear signs that this structural gap may soon be filled, as both the demand and supply factors that prevented innovation are removed.

THE LEGAL SYSTEM AND FINANCIAL INNOVATION[22]

There are few fields in which the legal and economic aspects interact more than in financial innovation.

21 See, for example, the relevant opinion expressed by the former president of the CONSOB, Rossi (1984).
22 The authors wish to thank F. Carbonetti and M. Eisenberg for their helpful comments on this section.

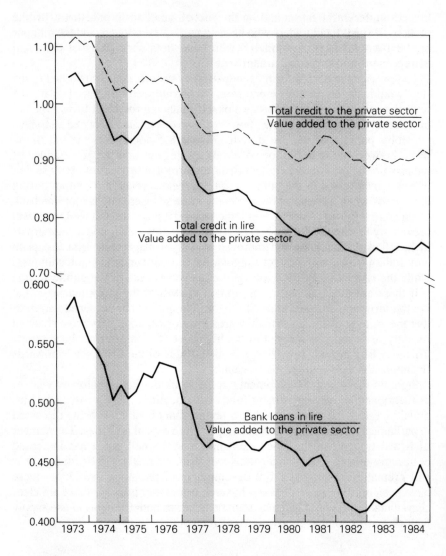

FIGURE 8.5   Total credit and output. The credit aggregates are defined as:
(a) banks loans in lire, including bankers' acceptances held by the banking
sector and bad loans, corrected for an estimate of the effect of the make-up
procedures used by the banks during the periods when the ceiling was binding;
(b) total credit in lire, including those listed at (a), SCI loans, bonds, bankers'
acceptances and other private instruments of credit; (c) total credit to the private
sector, including those listed at (b), bank loans in foreign currency, external
trade credit and foreign loans. Shaded areas mark the periods in which credit
ceilings are believed to have been binding.
Source: Cottarelli et al. (1985).

The effect on innovation of specific regulations, whether entailing a constraint or an incentive, is obvious, and, in this respect, Italy is a good example. The arguments used above to explain how regulation encouraged innovation can in fact be applied equally well here to explain the lack of innovation. In particular, the delays with which some sectors of financial activity have been regulated are certainly among the causes of the missing innovation. The most topical example is given by the law that introduced investment funds into Italy 22 years after the first bill was discussed in parliament. Similar difficulties are being experienced with bills on merchant banking and on venture capital, which are yet to be approved. Moreover, the impending approval of a law introducing some innovation tends to impede other forms of innovation that may eventually be cut off when the law is finally passed. Tax disincentives also operated towards the firms sector to discourage the issue of shares and other financial instruments, especially commercial paper. Together with the rising reserve requirements, they were also responsible for the loss of competitiveness of bank deposits.

Besides the above-mentioned specific links, it has been suggested that from a more general viewpoint a country's legal system, i.e., the sum of its legal principles, procedures and provisions, can influence the capability of the financial system to evolve. In particular, comparison of the far-reaching innovative changes in the financial systems of the United States and Britain,[23] both of which are common law countries, with the relatively static performance of civil law European countries,[24] including Italy, may suggest that the common law grants businessmen greater freedom by facilitating the use of new forms of contractual arrangements in financial transactions, as well as the emergence of new intermediaries:

> All this was possible because of the Common Law approach, according to which 'all that is not expressly forbidden, is permissible, while the Roman Law tradition is, as it is known, rather the opposite, that is to say, that what is permissible is expressly identified by the written law. In the case of the US, the Common Law and Roman Law traditions have coalesced and this allows the cognoscenti to play a 'hide and seek' game with the law keepers which is very profitable, as the sanction can apply to new realities only *ex-nunc*, and by that time the able are somewhere else trying a new trick. Most of what has lately gone under the name of 'financial innovation' originates from this juridical peculiarity.[25]

A thorough analysis of this hypothesis is beyond the scope of this present paper and, accordingly, we shall confine ourselves to a few comments:

---

23 The changes under way in the London Stock Exchange, one of the most traditional English institutions, are very substantial; see Terry (1985).
24 France and Germany are important examples; see BIS (1984).
25 See M. de Cecco (1983), p. 14.

(1) Several important legal principles that are typical of common law systems undoubtedly lend themselves to innovation in the economic and especially in the financial field. First and foremost there is the trust principle, i.e. the management of other people's money. This is not foreseen in Roman Law, but has none the less become extremely important in the activity of securities markets. On the other hand, however, some common law constraints limit parties' freedom to do business to a greater extent than civil law systems. For instance, corporations' freedom of action is strictly determined by their charters; the disadvantages of charter restrictions and their effect on trading have generally been attenuated in common law systems only by *general provisions* expanding the scope of actions permitted to commercial companies.[26]

(2) While the absence of regulations specifying what is permitted is almost inherent in common law, the derogations to this principle in the economic field are, *of necessity*,[27] very common. The regulation of economic transactions by law is the rule rather than the exception.

(3) In even more general terms, while in common law the absence of regulation is an implicit recognition of the parties' contractual freedom, in civil law this freedom is explicitly provided – in Italy by Article 1322 of the Civil Code. Thus, whenever doubts have been raised about the legitimacy of a new financial instrument, they have always concerned a conflict with the *existing legislation*[28] and not the abstract possibility of creating new financial instruments. A good example is provided by the discussion on *titoli atipici*, which actually circulated freely in Italy for nearly six years before being regulated.

Thus, the fact that the common law is generally accepted as allowing more innovative behaviour than the civil law does not necessarily have practical consequences. What, then, is the explanation for the stronger innovative propensity of Anglo-American financial systems? Here, we suggest a tentative answer, in terms of the attitude of Anglo-American countries, and especially the United States, to limit government intervention in economic and, more generally, private affairs. This attitude is clearly reflected in many aspects of the political and legal systems in the United States. In financial matters, the

26 A second example concerns the principle of consideration, whereby contracts are not binding unless they foresee the performance of an act by both parties. Theoretically, this implies, for example, that it is impossible to have binding offers or deferred payment conditions without the counterpart bearing a charge.

27 *Of necessity* because a sentence under Common Law creates a precedent with retroactive effect since it does not create a law but 'enounces' it. In more practical terms, the principle of retroactivity would undermine economic relationships. Hence the need for government regulation to prevent judges from making innovative interventions.

28 The law regulating *titoli atipici* gave rise to further discussion as to its regulatory effects in the light of the possibility of conflict between existing regulations and new forms of securities. Cf. the bibliographical notes in Capriglione and Mezzacapo (1985).

desire to restrict government interference in private affairs has not, however, implied a lack of regulatory powers, but it has influenced the form and the extent of these powers, with respect to European examples. Thus, the supervisory activities of the SEC or of the Comptroller of the Currency are far from being ineffective; they both have a significant degree of administrative and rule-making power, but their powers are limited by the law.

By contrast, the distinguishing feature of the European and, notably, of the Italian case are the *discretionary powers* conferred on the monetary authorities. In the 1936 Banking Law, which in Italy is still the principal act regulating the relationships between the monetary authorities and the financial system, 'in addition to provisions with a well-defined and limited legal scope there are others that confer responsibility in certain matters, with regard to which the authorized body from time to time specifies the scope of a directive, order or provision' (Vitale, 1972).

Thus, just to provide an example, the definition of the financial institutions subject to the Banking Law not only lays down a list of bank categories, but also goes on to an all-embracing finale covering: '. . . banks and credit firms in general, however they may be established, that take sight, short-term, savings or current account deposits from the public or any other such deposits of whatever form or name'.[29]

Under these conditions, forms of financial innovation aimed at circumventing some binding constraint come up against the ability of the monetary authorities to react swiftly with new and wider regulations: the story of bankers' acceptances and repos is a good example. The 'hide and seek' game between innovator and monetary authority recalled by de Cecco (1983) becomes much more difficult for the former when the latter is able to remove not one hiding place at a time, but all (or most of them) at one stroke.

AUTHORS' NOTE

The opinions expressed in this paper are those of the authors and do not necessarily represent those of the Banca d'Italia.

REFERENCES

Akhtar, M. A. 1983: *Financial Innovations and their Implications for Monetary Policy: an International Perspective*, BIS Economic Papers, No. 9, December.
Banca d'Italia: *Relazione Annuale* and *Abridged Report*, various years.
Bank for International Settlements (1984): *Financial Innovation and Monetary Policy*, Basle, BIS.
Capriglione, F. and Mezzacapo, V. 1985: Evoluzione del sistema finanziario italiano e attività di merchant banking. *Bancaria*, March.

29 RDL n. 375, 1936 (legge bancaria), art. 5.

Caranza, C. and Fazio, A. 1983: Methods of monetary control in Italy: 1974–1983. In *The Political Economy of Monetary Policy: National and International Aspects*. Federal Reserve of Boston, Conference Series No.

Convenzione Interbancaria per i Problemi dell'Automazione 1983: *Rilevazione dello stato dell'automazione del sistema creditizio*. Centro Stampa della Banca d'Italia.

Cottarelli, C., Cotula, F. and Pittaluga, G. 1985: Deposit rate discrimination: effects on bank management and monetary policy in Italy. Paper presented at the 1985 SUERF meeting on Shifting Frontiers in Financial Markets, Cambridge, 28–30 March.

Cottarelli, C., Galli, G., Marullo, P. and Pittaluga, G. 1985: Monetary policy through ceiling on bank lending. Paper presented at the Economic Policy Panel meeting held in London, 11–12 November.

Cotula, F. 1984: Financial innovation and monetary control in Italy. *Banca Nazionale del Lavoro Quarterly Review*, September.

de Cecco, M. 1983: *Italian Monetary Policy in the 1980s*, European University Institute Working Papers, No. 64.

Della Torre, G. 1980: I legami tra l'evoluzione finanziaria e l'accumulazione reale del dopoguerra: alcuni spunti per una lettura come processo di innovazione finanziaria. *Note Economiche*, No. 6.

Goodhart, C. A. 1985: The implication of shifting frontiers in financial markets for monetary control. Paper presented at the 1985 SUERF meeting on Shifting Frontiers in Financial Markets, Cambridge, 28–30 March.

Gorton, G. 1981: A theory of banking panics. Mimeo University of Rochester, June.

Greenbaum, S. I. and Heywood, C. V. 1971: Secular change in the financial services industry. *Journal of Money, Credit and Banking*, May, 571–603.

Johnson, C. 1985: Shifting frontiers in financial markets: general report. Paper presented at the 1985 SUERF meeting on Shifting Frontiers in Financial markets, Cambridge, 28–30 March.

Mieli, S. 1985: Lo sviluppo del leasing in Italia. Mimeo, Banca d'Italia.

Monti, E. and Onado, M. 1984: *Il Mercato Monetario e Finanziario in Italia*. Il Mulino, Bologna.

Onado, M. 1985: Una voglia di capitalismo. *Il Sole 24 Ore*, 24 August.

Pepe, R. 1982: I Rapporti Interbancari in Italia (1975–80). *Bollettino della Banca d'Italia, Supplemento*, No. 64.

Pontolillo, V., Ugolini, F. and Battini, F. 1985: Gli interventi sulla struttura e sulla operatività del sistema creditizio: problemi e prospettive. Associazione per lo Sviluppo degli Studi di Banca e Borsa, Quaderno No. 68.

Rettaroli, R. 1983: Principali caratteristiche dell'innovazione finanziaria in Italia. *ABI, Quaderni di Ricerche e Documentazione*, No. 4.

Revell, J. 1985: Implications of information technology for financial institutions. Paper presented at the 1985 SUERF meeting on Shifting Frontiers in Financial Markets, Cambridge, 28–30 March.

Rossi, G. 1984: Il mercato finanziario dopo la legge 216. *Rivista delle Società*, January–April.

Silber, W. L. 1983: The process of financial innovation. *American Economic Review*, May, 89–95.

Terry, N. G. 1985: The 'Big Bang' at the stock exchange. *Lloyds Bank Review*, April.

Vaciago, G. 1982: *L'innovazione finanziaria in banca e fuori banca: considerazioni introduttive e valutazioni delle recenti tendenze*, Associazione per lo Sviluppo degli Studi di Banca e Borsa, Quaderno No. 37.

Van Horne, J. C. 1985: On financial innovations and excess. *Journal of Finance*, July.

Vitale, P. 1972: Il modello organizzativo dell'ordinamento del credito. *Rivista trimestrale di Diritto Pubblico*. No. 3.

Wissen, P. 1985: The birth of a new market: the case of the Swedish money market. Paper presented at the 1985 SUERF meeting on Shifting Frontiers in Financial Markets, Cambridge, 28–30 March.

9
Lessons from the French Experience as Compared with some other OECD Countries

CHRISTIAN DE BOISSIEU

INTRODUCTION

Most recent works consider financial innovation as a means of avoiding various banking and financial regulations; as instruments used by private agents (financial or non-financial) to circumvent discretionary measures taken by the monetary authorities. However, recent developments in OECD (Organization for Economic Cooperation and Development) countries highlight another, complementary side to this view: financial innovation may also be considered as an expression of economic policy. In many countries, the public decision-makers both exercise tight control over financial innovation and contribute to the process by offering new and attractive financial products, which are indispensable for the financing of growing budget deficits.

This paper will illustrate these two aspects of the financial innovation process, using the example of the French experience and comparing it with the experience of certain other OECD countries.

FINANCIAL INNOVATION: A CHALLENGE TO ECONOMIC POLICY

The Concept of Financial Innovation

Financial innovation includes new technology (electronic funds transfer, the use of computers in banking operations, etc.), as well as new financial products. Specialists in industrial economics generally make a distinction between process innovation and product innovation. To be sure, the borderline between the two is sometimes arbitrary and this is as true for financial innovation as it is for industrial innovation. Innovation, whatever its form, is associated with the production of information,[1] and information is both a product and a process. At the same time, new financial products often provide a vehicle for new financial technology.

Despite the sometimes arbitrary distinction between products and processes, this paper will concentrate on new financial products. While the financial systems of all the major OECD countries have shown more or less the same pace in developing similar types of process innovations (electronic funds transfer, development of cash management techniques etc.), they have differed considerably when it comes to the pace at which new financial products have been introduced. As this paper considers new financial products, rather than new financial processes, the emphasis will be on the differences between rather than the similarities of financial systems.

Innovations in financial products rarely represent a major break. As Dufey and Giddy (1981) point out, they generally involve piecemeal modifications of certain basic characteristics of financial assets or of the combination of such characteristics – the range of maturities offered, tax treatment, the system of indexation of capital and interest rates etc. One may study new financial products using various criteria – the clientele affected by the new products (a distinction often being made here between the 'wholesale market' and the 'retail market'); the balance sheet entries of financial institutions (liability management or asset management); the scope of application of the product innovations (with a distinction between innovations relating to 'indirect finance' and those relating to a 'direct finance' process).

Theories of Financial Innovation

There are two main interpretations of financial innovation – the theory of constraint and the theory of demand for characteristics. Whilst these may be said to converge rather than diverge, they leave certain questions unanswered.

The Theory of Constraint

This theory, discussed in the works of W. Silber (1975, 1983), seeks to analyse both the supply and demand for new financial products and is particularly well adapted to explain the supply of new products by financial institutions. It considers product innovation as a response of the organization (bank, firm etc.) to the constraints placed upon it. There are numerous constraints, stemming from regulation, competition etc., as well as those that the organiza-tion places upon itself. From this perspective, the incentive to innovate depends on the costs associated with quantity or price constraints.

For example, the dual variable corresponding to a quantity constraint is a shadow price and the bank will be induced to ease this constraint through

---

1 On this, see the article of K. Arrow (1962).

financial innovation if this shadow price goes beyond a certain threshold. Ben-Horim and Silber (1977) used this analysis to interpret significant financial innovations introduced by large New York banks during the period 1952–72. Certain innovations were preceded by a significant increase in the shadow prices associated with quantitative constraints, sometimes with a time lag between the incentive to innovate and the actual innovation.

The theory of constraint seems particularly well adapted to the US experience because both regulations (Regulation Q, reserve requirements and so on) and competition between financial institutions have played a dominant part in the process of financial innovation in the United States since 1961 and, in particular, since 1972. According to Silber (1983), nearly 60 per cent of the financial innovations in the United States between 1970 and 1982 can be explained by the constraint theory. This theory holds that financial institutions introduced products such as money market funds, or, more recently, money market deposit accounts (MMDAs), NOW accounts or super-NOWs etc. as a means of both avoiding Regulation Q and of increasing – or at least maintaining – their market share. Even if it is generally used to explain the supply of new financial instruments, the theory also explains the demand for financial innovation by savers. In the United States, the acceleration of inflation and the associated rise in nominal interest rates induced a demand for new financial products on the part of non-financial agents. In short, financial innovation arises when it is in the interest of all parties concerned (pareto-optimality of the financial innovation process).

The correlation between regulation and financial innovation is not invariably positive and this will be discussed in detail below. Up to a certain threshold (which varies in space and across time), the level of product innovation grows with the degree of regulation, as suggested by the theory of constraint. Above this threshold, regulation becomes so effective that it controls and blocks all financial innovation. Thus, although fewer new financial products have been offered in France than in the United States, everyone would agree that the French financial system is more regulated than that in the United States.

The Theory of the Demand for Characteristics

This theory explains the demand for new financial products from the point of view of investors, in the light of changes in the environment, in particular the increase and diversification of risk. The demand for new financial instruments is a demand for new characteristics, or for new combinations of traditional characteristics. Therefore, it seems legitimate to analyse it in the light of new theories of consumption,[2] and it is surprising that up until now so few models of financial innovation have been developed from this perspective.

The demand for new characteristics has two main causes:

(1) The acceleration of inflation and the rise in nominal interest rates which, by raising the opportunity cost of holding non-interest bearing cash balances

2   In particular, the analysis of K. Lancaster

made the traditional trade-off between liquidity and return on investments more and more unbearable. The new financial products which have appeared over the past ten years have reduced, if not eliminated, this trade-off because they combine liquidity with a return which is often close to market rates.

(2) The increase and the diversification of risk. The increase in the volatility of interest rates and exchange rates created a demand for financial innovation, i.e. shortening of maturities in financial operations, increase of variable interest rate transactions, creation of financial futures markets etc. It must be pointed out that, to a certain degree, the shortening of maturities is a substitute for variable interest rates. The first phenomenon exists in most OECD countries, but, in certain cases, it has been encouraged by the absence of indexation of interest rates (in West Germany, for example).

The theory of financial innovation based on the demand for new characteristics is not a substitute for, but a complement to, the constraint theory. The increase and diversification of risk since the early 1970s created new constraints on highlighted existing constraints on firms, banks etc. However, the respective weight of the different arguments changes over time. A long-term study carried out in the United States by Sylla (1982) suggests that in the eighteenth and nineteenth centuries, financial innovation originated from the real sector of the economy and was largely the result of a demand for growth. According to the same study, financial innovation has been mainly a response to regulation since 1929.

Unresolved Questions

Among the numerous problems not yet solved by the emerging theories of financial innovation, three deserve special attention:

(1) Thresholds play an important part but they are difficult to quantify. There is no incentive to innovate unless the opportunity cost of holding traditional financial products or employing existing financial technology exceeds a certain threshold. Porter and Simpson (1980) discuss the idea of a threshold representing a 'ratchet effect' (maximum interest rates for the preceding periods etc.) in the equations for the demand for money.

(2) Financial innovation is irreversible to a certain extent. As noted above, the acceleration of inflation and the rise and increase in the volatility of interest rates have been catalysts in the development of new financial products. What will happen if disinflation continues in major OECD countries; if nominal interest rates keep falling; if they become less volatile? The new financial instruments and the new markets will not disappear. However, the attractiveness of these new products and the number of transactions in, for example, the financial futures markets, are likely to decrease.

Until now, theories of financial innovation have not succeeded in incorporating the partial irreversibility of the phenomenon and the asymmetry between the effects of the acceleration of inflation and an increase in risk, and the impact of disinflation and the reduction of risk.

(3) The macroeconomic consequences of financial innovation have been

analysed far better than its microeconomic impact. Today, it is essential to understand the influence of new financial instruments on banks' margins and lending rates. This is only possible by combining two areas of research which have developed separately: the theory of the banking firm and the analysis of financial innovation.

Financial Innovation: A Challenge to Monetary Policy

Financial innovation is a major source of difficulty for monetary policy in two respects. First, it is frequently used as a reaction against discretionary measures taken by monetary authorities. Secondly, it jeopardizes monetary control.

Financial Innovation as a Reaction against Discretionary Measures

In most OECD countries there is a dynamic sequence between regulation and financial innovation: regulation gives rise to the supply of and demand for financial instruments, and the advent of the latter, after a time lag corresponding to the recognition of the financial innovation by the monetary authorities,[3] leads to a modification of the regulation, and so on. Kane, (1981, 1982) suggests the existence of a regulatory 'dialectics', corresponding to this sequence. It involves a game, in the sense of a game of strategy, because each party concerned – the monetary authority on the one hand and the private agent on the other – modifies his behaviour depending on the present or expected actions of the other player.

Two examples may be given to illustrate this game of strategy:

1 In the United States, most new financial products which have been implemented since 1972 have been answers, sometimes temporary ones, to Regulation Q, to the system of reserve requirements, etc.
2 In Britain the phase-in and phase-out of the 'corset' caused significant 'disintermediation' and 're-intermediation' associated with modifications in the 'menu' of financial assets.

Financial Innovation and the Limits of Monetary Control

The process of financial innovation jeopardizes monetary policy in three closely related ways.

(1) Depending on the financial system, it raises questions to a greater or lesser extent concerning the validity of monetary aggregates. Central bankers have traditionally referred to the distinction between transaction and investment cash balances. With the new financial instruments which combine liquidity with return, this canonical distinction has become obsolete.

(2) The introduction and disappearance of financial instruments, by altering the range of substitution between financial assets, causes variations in the

---

3 Concerning this problem, see the study of D. Hester (1981).

monetary aggregates which reduce the controllability of the money stock. (NB: this problem has been extensively discussed in the United States since 1978 and, in particular, during the period 1982–4).

(3) Financial innovation not only reduces the controllability of the money stock, it also reduces the predictability of the effects of monetary policy by increasing the instability of the relations between the intermediate targets and the ultimate ones (employment, production, prices etc.). The empirical instability of the demand for money function can be explained, for the most part, by product innovation and new financial technology.[4] The impact of financial innovation on the level and the degree of stability of the credit supply function by financial intermediaries is often mentioned (Meigs, 1975; Lamfalussy, 1981). This impact remains more uncertain and less understood today than the impact of new financial products on the demand for money. This is due to the lack of microeconomic foundations for theories of financial innovation.

FINANCIAL INNOVATION AS A TOOL FOR ECONOMIC POLICY: THE FRENCH EXPERIENCE

The US financial system provides an example of how the product innovation process has challenged monetary policy.

In other financial systems product innovation is principally due to the monetary authorities, in particular the Treasury, being constrained to supply attractive instruments to finance growing public deficits.

Intervention of the Public Decision-makers in the Financial Innovation Process

The Distinction between Private and Public Financial Innovation

Financial systems can be grouped into two categories:

(1) Those in which product innovation comes essentially from non-governmental sectors (banks, firms). It arises spontaneously and in a decentralized way. *Ex ante* control by the monetary authorities over these new financial instruments is non-existent or extremely limited. Monetary authorities only intervene *ex post*, possibly to monitor the phenomenon, to take into account the new products in the definition of monetary aggregates, or to determine whether they should be included in reserve requirements ratios etc. Private financial innovation is predominant in Anglo-Saxon countries, particularly the United States and Canada. This is reinforced rather than rebutted by the Garn–St Germain Act. The passing of this law by Congress in October 1982 certainly endowed the creation of MMDAs and Super-NOW accounts with an official form, but it must be remembered that, by virtue of this law, banks were granted the means to compete with investment banks and brokers.

---

4   J. Judd and J. Scadding (1982) present a fairly complete picture of the US situation.

(2) Financial systems in which financial innovation comes mainly from the public sector. Public financial innovation represents the inverse of private innovation. First, it generally results from the initiative of the public decision-makers who either introduce the new product themselves or place restrictions on other parties, thereby inducing the creation of the new product. In this sense, public financial innovation is a centralized process. Secondly, such innovation must receive prior approval by the governmental authorities. Thus, financial institutions will not take the initiative in offering savers new products without having first received the express authorization of the monetary authorities.

The concept of public innovation highlights the situation in France and West Germany. In France, the centralization of the financial innovation process was accompanied by a significant expansion in public financial innovation and explains the limited part played by private financial innovation.

Even if Silber's analysis was developed specifically to analyse what is referred to in this paper as private financial innovation, it can also be used to analyse public innovation. Public authorities introduce new financial instruments in order to loosen certain constraints, such as budgetary constraints or external constraints (since the domestic banking sector, nationalized or not, is exposed to international competition).

The Control of Financial Innovation by the Monetary Authorities

Economic theory frequently justifies state intervention on the grounds that innovation is a public good, benefiting all from the moment it is introduced, unless the innovation is protected in some way, e.g. by a patent.

In practice, the public good argument counts for little and the state intervenes because the monetary authorities seek to control the working of the financial system. This is the case in France as well as in West Germany, where the Bundesbank traditionally has been hesitant to allow greater flexibility in interest rates.

The relationship between the degree to which a financial system is regulated and the level of product innovation can be represented by a 'humped' curve (figure 9.1). The curve representing the incentive to innovate (AA^1) begins from point (A) and not from the origin because product innovations arise even in the absence of regulations. It increases monotonously with the degree of regulation of the financial system, as suggested by the constraint theory. The costs for banks, firms etc., associated with the regulatory constraints, increase with the degree of regulation. The actual curve is the same as the notional curve up until the threshold (S). Above this threshold, the strict control of the innovation process by public authorities causes a gap between the amount of innovation desired by non-governmental agents and the actual volume. There are *latent* financial innovations that would develop if monetary authorities did not exercise such tight control. (Graphically, latent innovations are represented by the segment (BC).) Thus, in certain OECD countries the government authorities ration product innovations since the level of innovation does not continue to grow with the degree of regulation.

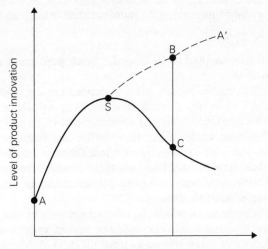

FIGURE 9.1 Regulation and product innovation in the financial system

The intervention of public authorities by means of law or regulation often relates to the tax component of the financial innovation which may take many forms: fiscal incentives introduced to encourage savings by households, to make government securities attractive and so on.

The Predominance of Public Financial Innovation in France

Main Characteristics

Several features in particular characterize the financial innovation process in France. First, this process developed relatively later than in other major OECD countries. Although it started in 1978 with the Monory law,[5] it did not really develop until the end of 1981. Secondly, the process is centralized because, as is discussed below, public financial innovation overrides private innovation. Thirdly, financial innovation is closely linked to credit policy. The credit ceilings policy in effect between 1973 and 1984, followed by the *régulation du crédit* which has been implemented since the beginning of 1985,[6] favoured

5 The Monory Law of 1978 introduced important fiscal advantages in connection with the purchase of shares. Some of these advantages were kept by the creation of share savings accounts (*comptes d'épargne en action*, CEA) in 1983.

6 Credit regulation, effective since January 1985, eliminated the credit ceilings imposed on banks but introduced a steeply progressive system of reserve requirements to such extent that it is still more restrictive than the former credit ceilings on system.

the growth of the financial market and new financial products which made it possible by encouraging banks to increase their equity and bond issues.

The Steps in the Process

The fiscal measures adopted in 1978 aside, three steps mark the process of financial innovation:

(1) 1981: Following the modification of deposit rates in September 1981,[7] short-term SICAV (*Sociétés d'investissement à capital variable*) and short-term mutual funds (*les fonds communs de placement*, FCP) developed. Certain regulatory differences aside, these two institutions both specialize in the purchase of short-term or variable interest rate financial instruments. Capital risks exist for short-term SICAV (the jolts of the financial market in November and December 1984 confirmed this) but *a priori* these are less intense than they are for traditional SICAVs.

Since 1981 these financial products, offered not only by banks but also by insurance companies and stockbrokers, have had an enormous success. As of 31 July, 1985 there were 108 short-term SICAVs (as compared to 25 as of 31 December 1982) holding close to 200 billion francs.

Short-term SICAVs and FCPs may appear to represent the prototype of private financial innovation because they were offered by financial institutions and demanded by savers (particularly since 1983 by firms) in order to circumvent the effects of the new deposit rate regulation. However, a more careful study reveals that, had it wanted to, the French Treasury was in a position to prevent the mushrooming of these new instruments. The monetary authorities let short-term SICAVs and FCPs develop because they deemed it in their interest to do so. This was partly because the progression of short-term SICAVs and FCPs, which are currently excluded from the monetary aggregates, facilitated the intermediate target policy, in particular by slowing down the growth of the monetary aggregate chosen as an intermediate target (M2 between 1977 and 1982, M2 residents (M2$_R$) since 1983). Furthermore, the growth of these new financial products allowed for the development of the bond market at a period when the Treasury was the principal beneficiary of this development because a significant part of budget deficits had to be financed by non-monetary means (government borrowings).

(2) 1983: During 1983 several financial innovations were introduced through the initiative of the monetary authorities. The Delors Act of January 1983 implemented some of the ideas set out in the Dautresme Report of 1982, and introduced two new categories of financial products:

(i) Instruments specifically tailored to nationalized firms (industrial enterprises and banks), i.e. the *titres participatifs* ('participating debt'). These receive the same fiscal treatment as bonds but, in exchange for the relinquishment of any control of the firm (in particular, voting rights), they carry a

---

7   Since September 1981, the threshold for unregulated deposit rates has been raised from 100,000 FF to 500,000 FF (and a minimum time-period of six months).

variable remuneration which likens them to shares. In fact, the return on these securities is composed of two parts: a fixed amount (for example, a guaranteed minimum interest rate) and a variable amount, pegged to an indicator of the firm's activity (depending on the case, the value added, the turnover, or the profit may be taken as references). The *titres participatifs* turned out to be very successful. French banks were encouraged to issue them since, from the point of view of credit policy, these instruments were proxies for equity funds.[8]

(ii) Financial instruments, principally directed towards private, small and medium-size firms, encouraging them to offer a part of their equity to the public without losing control of the enterprise. Included in this category are investment certificates (*certificats d'investissement*) and non-voting preferred shares (*actions à dividende prioritaire sans droit de vote*).

At the beginning of 1983, a *second marché boursier*, based on the organization and rules of the London Unlisted Security Market, was opened. The purpose of this *second marché boursier* is to induce small and medium-size enterprises to sell a part of their capital to the public (10 per cent minimum) without losing control of the enterprise and at the same time avoiding the formalities required by the official stock market.

A third innovation began in October 1983, when the monetary authorities allowed financial institutions to offer savers 'industrial development accounts' (*comptes pour le développement industriel*, CODEVI). These accounts, which are subject to a ceiling and are tax-exempt, serve partly, and in a fairly complicated way, to finance industry.[9] As a consequence of the ceiling, however, the amounts collected have been modest. By the end of 1984, CODEVI accounts opened with banks totalled 48.3 billion francs (as compared to 33.2 billion francs at the end of 1983), representing about 5 per cent of quasi-money (defined as the difference between $(M2_R)$ and $(M1_R)$).

(3) 1985: Since the second half of 1984, the Minister of Economy and Finance (Mr Beregovoy) has insisted on the 'liberalization' of the financial system, thereby accelerating reforms. Three innovations deserve mention.

First, since February 1985 banks have been authorized to issue negotiable certificates of deposit (*certificats de dépôts négociables*), whether in French francs, US dollars or ECUs. The regulations *de facto* eliminated individuals from subscribing directly (the minimum denomination is, as a matter of fact, 10 million francs), but individuals may purchase participations in short-term SICAVs or FCPs and, in turn, these organizations may hold CDs in their portfolios ('indirect participation'). Up till now, corporations have been wary of these instruments, undoubtedly holding the six month to two year maturity

---

8 The same multiplier (1.5) applies to the *titres participatifs* as to equity: when a bank issues *titres participatifs* for 100, it can grant additional credits for 150 free of the progressive reserve requirements.

9 The money is conveyed through the Industrial Modernization Fund (*Fonds industriel de modernisation*) and the Caisse des Dépôts et de Consignations.

certificates until maturity. Purchase and sales transactions occur essentially in the interbank market; the secondary market does not yet function. By July 1985 such certificates issued in French francs amounted to nearly 19 billion while the total amount in foreign currencies was significantly less than this.

The second innovation came in the middle of 1985, when a proposal was made to create a commercial paper market in Paris. This market, due to start functioning by 1986, will have the following features: it will institutionalize the practice of *face à face* between firms,[10] encouraged by the credit ceiling policy; it will not only be open to enterprises, but also to individuals; its establishment will be linked to the opening up of the money market to allow current account Treasury bills[11] to be available to non-financial agents; interest rates will not be regulated, although the Bank of France will retain the right to intervene in order to enforce the interest rate hierarchy.

Thirdly, it has been decided to create a financial futures market (MATIF) in Paris, commencing operations in 1986. In the first place it will allow medium-term contracts on financial instruments, to be followed by contracts on short-term instruments. Open to all agents, it will provide them with another means to circumvent the regulation imposed in September 1981 concerning interest rates on deposits and enable savers to invest funds for terms of less than six months, at close to money market rates.

This description of the financial innovation process in France underlines the part played by the monetary authorities. They took the major initiatives and even when they acted in response to the demand of banks and enterprises (as in the case of CDs, or the commercial paper and financial futures markets) they retained control over the substance and timing of these innovations. Given the control exercised by the Treasury over the banking system (almost entirely nationalized), the short-term SICAVs and FCPs are only seemingly private innovations (according to the definition used here). In fact, the Treasury accepted this 'circumvention' of deposit interest rates regulation, because, for reasons stated above, it found it to be in its interest to do so. The French financial system is 'overdetermined'[12] and this has implications for the process of financial innovation. In the context of the statement that financial innovation occurs because it is in the interest of all parties concerned (pareto-optimality), the term 'concerned parties' includes financial institutions, non-financial agents (household and firms) and, in the French experience, the public decision-makers.

10 *Face à face* involves a loan between non-financial agents (mainly firms). The transaction could involve bank endorsement. Since the early 1970s, French banks have no longer had the authorization to guarantee such operations. The *face à face* developed in France, particularly at the time when the credit ceiling policy was enforced and credit rationing severe.
11 Traditionally, in France, current account Treasury bills were limited to financial institutions while non-financial agents could only subscribe Treasury bills *sur formule*.
12 In an analytical sense, the 'overdetermination' derives from the fact that the French monetary authorities control both the volume of credit and the interest rates.

The Functions of the Financial Innovation Process

Since 1981, the rate of introduction of new financial instruments has accelerated for a number of reasons. Some of these reasons are common to all OECD countries while others pertain only to France. The following is a non-hierarchical list of the principal functions of financial innovation in France.

(1) To increase the efficiency of the French financial system by combining product innovations with process innovations, and to promote the role of Paris as a financial centre. France can hardly avoid the financial innovation process since the banking sector is 'exposed' to international competition (both in France or abroad, and between French and foreign banks).

(2) To reinforce the efficiency and scope of competition between financial agents. Up till now, the French financial system has hardly been competitive because of the high concentration of banking resources and the 'over-determination' exercised by the monetary authorities. The new savings products introduced in the past few years – in chronological order, the *Livret d'épargne populaire* (LEP) created in 1982,[13] the CODEVI discussed above and the *Livret d'épargne-enterprise* offered since July 1984,[14] are now 'banalized'. They are proposed by all financial intermediaries, which intensifies the competition between banks and nonbanking financial institutions.

(3) To encourage small- and medium-size enterprises to strengthen their equity by allowing for public participation (role of investment certificates, non-voting preferred shares, *second marché boursier*).

(4) To reduce public expenditure. One example of this is that the issuing of *titres participatifs* by nationalized firms or banks reduces accordingly the capital funds provided by the Treasury to these firms as a shareholder. It must be pointed out that the interests of the nationalized enterprises, which are required to separate voting rights from pecuniary interests, are similar to those of small- and medium-size enterprises wishing to augment their equity without sharing the control of the enterprise. Another example is that certain financial innovations introduced by the Treasury seek to carry forward some interest payments of the public debt. In France, at December 1982, 100 per cent of current account Treasury bills issued had pre-paid interest. Since that time, however, they have been replaced by Treasury bills with monthly interest payments or with interest refunded at maturity. The same carry-forward feature is true for the *obligations renouvelables du Trésor* (ORT) which have been issued since 1983 with a maturity of six years and interest refunded at maturity. These innovations in the interest payments of the public debt do not lower the total debt service but rather redistribute it over time, by reducing short-term maturity payments and by increasing longer ones.

13 The LEP, limited to households paying less than a certain amount of income tax, has the advantage of being indexed on inflation.
14 This account, which represents a form of contractual savings, serves to finance the creation and the transfer of ownership of firms.

(5) To facilitate the non-monetary financing of budget deficits. The Treasury has been the main (although not the only) beneficiary of the growth of the primary bond market in France since 1980.[15] Like other financial innovations, those introduced by the Treasury respond to a demand for new characteristics or for a new combination of traditional characteristics. To attract savers, the Treasury had to adapt itself to market conditions and offer new financial instruments or new issuing techniques – the development of variable rate government borrowings or, more recently, two-part borrowings, one at a fixed rate, the other at a variable one; the extension of the range of maturities offered; borrowings with 'fenêtres', with warrants and so on.

(6) To support the intermediate target policy. The growth of the financial market and the multiplication of new financial instruments resulted in a consolidation of private savings and a transfer of a part of these savings originally included in (M2) (time deposits held by banks...) to financial instruments not included in the monetary aggregates (not even in the largest aggregate, M3). By exerting strict control on the financial innovation process, the French authorities were in a position to use it as a tool of targeting policy with respect to (M2) or ($M2_R$). In this field, financial innovation was a necessary – though not sufficient – condition: the transfer was made possible by an active term structure policy. Any lasting inversion of the yield curve would question the achievements since 1980.

The Consequences of Financial Innovation in France

If, substantively, the financial innovation process appears different in France compared to the United States, Britain or Canada, due to the importance of public innovations, its consequences are similar to those in all these countries. Thus, today, France is experiencing later and less acutely problems that rose in the United States in the middle of the 1970s.

Influence of Financial Innovations on Private Saving

The process of financial innovation in France has not prevented a decline in the rate of household saving,[16] which dropped from 17.5 per cent in 1978 to 13.7 per cent in 1984. This trend, essentially due to the slowdown in the growth of real income and, since the end of 1983, to the decline in absolute terms of real income, would possibly have been more marked in the absence of financial innovation. It is, however, difficult to validate such an assumption empirically.

If the acceleration of the financial innovation process in France went hand in hand with a decline in the rate of household savings, it clearly accelerated

15 The growth of the primary bond market is evident from the fact that annual issues rose from 65 billion francs in 1979 to 242 billion francs in 1984 and 295 billion francs in 1985 (forecast).
16 Measured as the ratio between gross saving and disposable income.

a redistribution of such savings, from the housing sector to the financial market. The financial innovation process, concomitant with the crisis of the past few years in the housing market, explains to a large extent modifications in the structure of private saving (there is a close substitution between real assets, such as investments in the housing sector, and financial assets), if not the changes in the savings ratio.

In general terms, the introduction of a new financial instrument causes two types of effect. One is a 'contribution effect', consisting in a greater mobilization of private savings by financial institutions (a rise in the rate of private saving or, simply, an increase in the rate of financial saving despite the stabilization or reduction of the global saving ratio). The other is a 'substitution effect' between different financial assets, such as, for example, a consolidation of private saving (transfer from bank deposits to the financial market).

In France, the substitution effect seems to have been the most important, although there appears to have been a partial contribution effect to the extent that investments in the financial market replaced housing investment and the reduction in financial saving was less marked than that of the global saving ratio. 'While the global saving ratio fell 2 points between 1982–1984, the financial saving ratio only declined by one point.'[17]

Influence of Financial Innovations on Demand for Money,
Definition of Monetary Aggregates and
Choice of Intermediate Targets

Money demand functions in France, estimated according to traditional monetary aggregates (M1, M2, M3) generally indicate a 'break' in 1973–4, due, to a large extent, to the change in the rate of inflation and nominal interest rates. It is clear that since 1981 the profile of these aggregates has been upset by the financial innovation process. Surprisingly, the shift in the income-velocity of M2 has been limited until now. This velocity, after a downward trend during the period 1950–77, has increased at an average annual rate of 1 per cent since 1978. Compared to the US case, the present fluctuations in the velocity of money in France are small and do not constitute the main source of difficulty for the efficacy of monetary policy.

Concerning monetary aggregates, the 'crisis' is less severe in France than in countries where the financial innovation process is less recent and more intense (the United States, Canada, Britain), but the question of redefining the aggregates is topical.

For the time being, the monetary authorities have left major financial innovations (short-term SICAVs and FCPs) outside the monetary aggregates.

17 *Report of the National Credit Council for the year 1984*, p. 99. The household financial saving ratio measured as the ratio between financial saving and available income dropped (from 6.1 per cent in 1982 to 5.1 per cent in 1984).

It is necessary that a broad aggregate, denominated (L), that would add the short-term SICAVs, FCPs, CDs etc. to (M3), be created.[18]

It has been indicated repeatedly that, given the slowdown in the growth of (M2) and (M2$_R$), the financial innovation process has facilitated the implementation of monetary norms. For 1985, the Bank of France indicated that it would monitor the evolution not only of (M2$_R$) but also of the unofficial aggregate (M2$_R$ + CDs). On the other hand, combining the financial innovation process with a high volatility of the external counterpart of the money stock explains the attention paid, since 1983, to domestic credit expansion. Credit aggregates are more sheltered from the impact of financial innovation than monetary aggregates and thus, in the years to come, in France as in other OECD countries, they may play a more important role – officially or non-officially – as intermediate targets for monetary policy.

Influence of Financial Innovations on Banks' Profitability

In France, as in other OECD countries, the substitution effect of financial innovation on the liability side of banks' balance sheets caused an increase in the average cost of banks' resources. In France this trend was accelerated by monetary policy (strong incentives for banks to develop their long-term funds – equity or quasi-equity, bond issues).

For many French financial institutions, re-financing takes place today at the margin, through the bond market rather than through the money market, underlining the importance of interest rates in the bond market for determining the average and marginal cost of re-financing.

By increasing the average deposit rate, does the financial innovation process prevent nominal interest rates from falling to the extent that would be justified by disinflation? To answer this question accurately, it would be necessary to incorporate financial innovation in a model of the behaviour of the banking firm. Even in the absence of a general model, one can observe that since 1984 French banks have been led to reduce their operating costs (overheads, and wages in particular) and to increase productivity in order to offset – at least partially – the increase in the average cost of funds. In France, the rise in average deposit rates, due to the introduction of new financial instruments, accelerated the recent gains in labour productivity in the banking sector.

18 In November 1985 important steps were taken to change the French 'menu' of monetary aggregates. The new system will be effective as of January 1986. A broad aggregate (L) includes the commercial paper (in creation), and the different aggregates (M1, M2, M3, L) include the liquidities held by the SICAVs and FCPs according to their nature. CDs will be a part of (M3–M2). This new system has the advantage of phasing-out the 'institutional criteria' (i.e, the distinction between banks and nonbank financial intermediaries). It can be seen still as a 'second best', since the incorporation of the money invested in short-term SICAVs and FCPs remains partial.

Final Remarks

The French experience suggests several observations:

(1) Despite the tight control over the process of financial innovation by the monetary authorities and the predominance of public financial innovation, the challenges facing the French monetary authorities today are the same as those facing the authorities in other OECD countries: financial behaviour and equations that are becoming more and more unstable, and growing difficulty in defining the monetary aggregates, for example.

(2) Given that financial innovations have been introduced by the Treasury either to reduce the budget deficit or to facilitate its non-monetary financing, the phenomenon of financial innovation in France must be approached at the interface between monetary and fiscal policies.

(3) The French experience suggests a connection between the speed at which financial innovations are incorporated and the degree of fragility of the financial system. Since the beginning of the 1980s, France has partially caught up with the Anglo-Saxon countries with respect to financial innovation. This being the case, in certain instances new financial products were introduced too quickly and in a disorganized way. The difficulties of the bond market at the end of 1984, due to the announcement of the creation of CDs, illustrate this point.[19]

(4) It is difficult to determine the effect of disinflation on the substance and pace of financial innovation in France, as elsewhere. If inflation during the 1970s played an important role, directly or indirectly (particularly via the rise of nominal interest rates), in the multiplication of financial innovations, the phenomenon is not quite symmetrical in a period of disinflation. 'Ratchet effects' and a certain irreversibility will continue to make financial innovations a challenge for monetary policy, despite the slowdown in inflation.

BIBLIOGRAPHY

Arrow, K. 1962: Economic welfare and the allocation resources for investment. In *The Rate and Direction of Inventive Activity: Economic and Social Factors*. Princeton, NJ: Princeton University Press.
Ben-Horim, M. and Silber, W. 1977: Financial innovation: a linear programming approach. *Journal of Banking and Finance* 1.
de Boissieu, C. 1982: Innovations financières et contrôle monétaire. *Revue Banque*, January.

19 In December 1984 the announcement of the creation of CDs induced certain corporate financial managers to sell their shares of short-term SICAV and, thereby, obliged the Caisse des Dépôts et de Consignations and commercial banks to intervene in the bond market to limit the discount.

de Boissieu, C. 1983: Les innovations financières aux Etats-Unis. *Observations et Diagnostics Economiques, Revue de l'Observatoire Français des Conjonctures Economiques*, February.

de Boissieu, C. 1984: Innovations financières, politique monétaire et financement des déficits publics. In D. E. Fair and F. de Juvigny (eds), *Government Policies and the Working of Financial Systems in Industrialized Countries*. The Hague: Martinus Nijhoff.

Dautresme Report, 1982: *Le développement et la protection de l'épargne*. Paris: La Documentation Française.

Dufey, G. and Giddy, I. 1981: The evolution of instruments and techniques in international financial markets. *SUERF Series* 35 A.

Hester, D. 1981: Innovations and monetary control. *Brookings Papers on Economic Activity* 1.

Judd, J, and Scadding, J. 1982: The search for a stable money demand function: a survey of the post-1973 literature. *Journal of Economic Literature*, September.

Kane, E. 1981: Accelerating inflation, technological innovation and the decreasing effectiveness of banking regulation. *Journal of Finance*, May.

Kane, E. 1982: Micro-economic and macro-economic origins of financial innovation. Paper presented to a Conference organized by the Federal Reserve Bank of St Louis, September.

Lamfalussy, A. 1981: Observation de règles ou politique discrétionnaire? Essai sur la politique monétaire dans un milieu inflationniste. *Etudes économiques de la Banque des Réglements Internationaux*. Basel.

Meigs, A. J. 1975: Recent innovations: do they require a new framework for monetary analysis? In W. Silber (ed.), *Financial Innovation*. Lexington, Mass.: D. C. Heath.

Porter, R. and Simpson, T. 1980: Some issues involving the definition and interpretation of the monetary aggregates. In *Controlling Monetary Aggregates III*. Federal Reserve Bank of Boston Conference Series.

Silber, W. 1975: Towards a theory of financial innovation. In W. Silber (ed.), *Financial Innovation*. Lexington, Mass.: D. C. Heath.

Silber, W. 1983: The process of financial innovation. *American Economic Review*, May, 89–95.

Sylla, R. 1982: Monetary innovation and crises in American economic history. In P. Wachtel (ed.), *Crises in the Economic and Financial Structure*. Lexington, Mass.: D. C. Heath.

10
Financial Innovation in Japan: its Origins, Diffusion and Impacts

YOSHIO SUZUKI

ORIGINS OF FINANCIAL INNOVATION

Driving Forces

The establishment of floating exchange rates after the collapse of Bretton Woods and the decline in rapid economic growth following the first oil crisis ushered in a new phase in the history of the Japanese economy. Since 1973–4, both the real side and the financial side of the Japanese economy have undergone significant changes. The newly emerging economic conditions have given rise to a wide range of changes in the financial system, commonly known as financial innovations (Economic Planning Agency, 1984; Royama, 1983; Suzuki, 1983a,b, 1984a, 1986).

Generally speaking, financial innovations occur in the course of a given country's economic development when the regulations, practices and institutions of the existing statutory financial framework no longer conform to changed circumstances (Goto et al., 1983). In such a situation, the private sector initiates financial innovations to circumvent the old regulations, usually by introducing new financial instruments and services.[1] The pace of financial innovation accelerates when the financial authorities recognize the obsolescence of the old regulations and respond by relaxing or eliminating them. This paper will analyse the recent financial innovations in Japan in terms of this theoretical framework.

1 In some cases, financial innovations may occur independently of regulatory constraints – for instance, when technical progress makes it possible to reduce transaction costs or to diversify transaction risks under the existing regulations. Usually, however, it is necessary to circumvent current regulations for innovations to be implemented effectively.

Newly Emerging Economic Factors

Among the new economic conditions that have emerged in Japan in the past ten years, the following five have constituted the major influences in the process of financial innovation.

Large-scale Issue of Government Bonds and the Development of Open Financial Markets

After the first oil crisis, the Japanese economy entered an era of slow growth. The rate of real economic growth, which averaged 10 per cent p.a. before 1973, is currently 5 per cent p.a. This drop in growth has been accompanied by a slowdown in private investment, with the result that the excess of savings over investment (corresponding to the financial surplus of the private sector shown in the flow-of-funds figures, see table 10.3) has been rising. This private sector surplus has been balanced by the growing fiscal deficits of the public sector, and a large amount of government bonds has been issued to finance them (figure 10.1). Since government bonds are traded in large lots with low default risk, they are most suitable for trading in open securities markets. Therefore, the large-scale issue of government bonds has promoted the development of open capital and money markets, such as the secondary market for long-term government bonds, the issue market for medium-term government bonds and the *Gensaki* (repos) market, all of which are free from interest rate regulations and open to all investors (see tables 10.1 and 10.2).

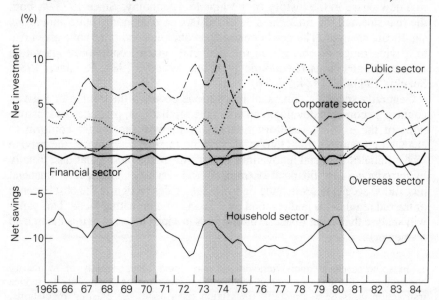

FIGURE 10.1 Sectoral net investment (deficit) and net savings (surplus) as a percentage of GNP

TABLE 10.1 Trends in money market transactions

Calendar year	Call money market ¥ bn	Share (%)	Commercial, bills discount market ¥ bn	Share (%)	Gensaki market ¥ bn	Share (%)	CDs market ¥ bn	Share (%)	Total ¥ bn	Share (%)
1965	809	100.0							809	100.0
1966	747	100.0							747	100.0
1967	1,012	86.9			152	13.1			1,164	100.0
1968	985	77.2			291	22.8			1,276	100.0
1969	1,546	79.1			408	20.9			1,954	100.0
1970	1,817	74.6			619	25.4			2,436	100.0
1971	1,472	54.1	369	13.5	882	32.4			2,723	100.0
1972	1,048	25.8	1,792	44.1	1,224	30.1			4,065	100.0
1973	1,227	17.4	4,089	58.0	1,738	24.6			7,053	100.0
1974	2,160	23.9	5,207	57.6	1,673	18.5			9,039	100.0
1975	2,332	27.2	4,403	51.4	1,835	21.4			8,570	100.0
1976	2,567	26.3	5,091	52.3	2,089	21.4			9,742	100.0
1977	2,616	22.7	6,084	51.4	3,136	26.5			11,837	100.0
1978	2,326	17.7	6,590	50.2	4,207	32.1			13,123	100.0
1979	3,473	22.3	6,327	40.6	3,960	25.4	1,820	11.7	15,580	100.0
1980	4,133	24.7	5,738	34.3	4,507	26.9	2,358	14.1	16,736	100.0
1981	4,699	28.5	4,016	24.3	4,481	27.2	3,291	20.0	16,486	100.0
1982	4,494	24.2	5,413	29.2	4,304	23.2	4,342	23.4	18,551	100.0
1983	4,456	21.0	6,763	31.9	4,288	20.3	5,665	26.8	21,172	100.0
1984	5,037	20.1	7,998	31.9	3,562	14.2	8,461	33.8	25,058	100.0

TABLE 10.2 Trends in secondary bond market transactions

Year	Government bonds		Local government bonds and guaranteed bonds		Interest bearing bank debentures		Corporate bonds		Total including other bonds		Outright transactions		Gensaki transactions	
	¥bn	Share (%)	¥bn	Share (%)	¥bn	Share (%)	¥bn	Share (%)	¥bn	Share (%)	¥bn	Share (%)	¥bn	Share (%)
1970	0.4	5	0.9	11	3.3	43	0.7	9	7.7	100	n.a.		n.a.	
1971	0.3	3	1.5	14	4.3	40	0.9	8	10.8	100	n.a.		n.a.	
1972	0.4	3	2.2	16	5.9	41	0.9	7	14.3	100	n.a.		n.a.	
1973	0.9	4	3.2	15	9.6	45	1.2	6	21.2	100	n.a.		n.a.	
1974	1.6	5	4.1	13	14.0	43	1.7	5	32.3	100	11.8	37	20.5	63
1975	1.1	2	11.5	23	20.4	40	2.9	6	50.9	100	22.3	44	28.6	56
1976	2.4	4	20.5	32	24.4	38	3.3	5	64.9	100	27.7	43	37.2	57
1977	13.6	12	34.9	31	39.0	34	6.2	5	113.2	100	52.4	46	60.8	54
1978	61.6	32	43.9	23	52.3	27	9.7	5	193.2	100	86.9	45	106.3	55
1979	91.3	45	39.4	19	43.2	21	6.6	3	204.2	100	87.4	43	116.8	57
1980	158.8	58	41.7	15	40.6	15	5.5	2	272.5	100	116.5	43	156.0	57
1981	181.6	63	37.3	13	39.2	14	7.1	2	288.4	100	146.9	51	141.5	49
1982	203.9	62	44.4	14	30.9	9	7.2	2	327.1	100	191.8	59	135.3	41
1983	247.2	64	51.5	13	29.5	8	7.5	2	385.1	100	247.9	64	137.2	36
1984	394.8	57	54.3	8	27.2	4	6.4	1	692.5	100	543.8	79	148.7	21

Total of volume of transactions through securities companies in Tokyo.

Inflation and Interest Rate Volatility

During the period from 1973 to 1975 the economy suffered from an abnormally high inflation rate, induced by excess liquidity and the first oil crisis. At this time, a contractionary monetary policy, enacted to curb inflation, pushed short-term and long-term interest rates to around 13 and 12 per cent, respectively. Later, as inflation calmed down, short-term and long-term interest rates dropped to the 4–5 per cent and 6–7 per cent ranges, respectively. When contractionary policy was again enacted in 1980 to prevent the second oil crisis from ushering in another inflationary period, interest rates rebounded to the previous high level. Since 1981 interest and inflation rates have been declining (figure 10.2).

Cumulating Financial Assets and Increasing Interest Rate Preference

The third newly developing economic factor is the increasing interest rate sensitivity among households and businesses, whose holdings of financial assets have increased dramatically (Suzuki, 1983b). Financial asset holdings of the private non-financial sector (that is, households and businesses) remained at a level equal to 1.5 times that of GNP throughout the era of rapid economic growth (except for a period of excessive liquidity around 1972). As economic growth slowed down, however, this ratio rose rapidly, and the ratio has recently reached 2 (figure 10.3). Also, as the population structure becomes older, the demand for non-deposit financial assets such as pension and insurance schemes has been increasing. The accumulation of financial assets and the slowdown of economic growth have led households and businesses to pay more attention to interest rate considerations in managing their portfolios efficiently.

Increasingly Active International Capital Flows
under the Floating Exchange Rate System

The fourth new factor to be considered is the increasingly active flow of international capital, coupled with the growing demand from abroad for liberalization of the Japanese money and capital markets. Since the transition to the floating exchange rate system in 1973, monetary authorities have no longer intervened in the foreign exchange market except to facilitate operations. As a result, arbitrage transactions that balance the demand for and supply of foreign exchange in the domestic and foreign markets, and uncovered speculative capital flows induced by expectations of exchange rate changes, have grown in volume. Internationally mobile funds are concentrated in the open markets domestically and have therefore contributed to the development of these markets.

Technological Innovations in Electronics and Telecommunications

A further factor is the significant reduction in the cost of financial transactions (such as those involved in the transmission of financial information and transaction instructions or in asset-liability management) and the wider

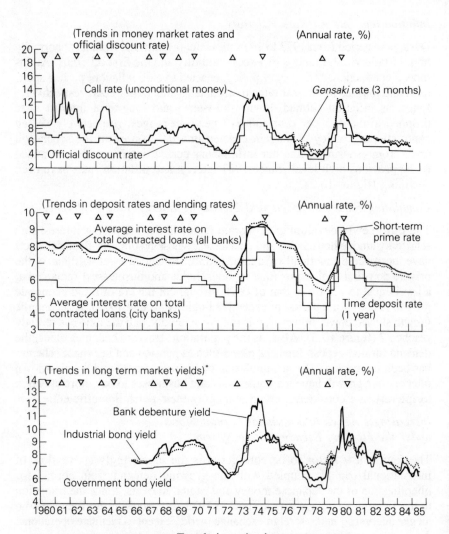

FIGURE 10.2 Trends in major interest rates.
$\triangle$ = beginning of tight money period; $\triangledown$ = beginning of easy money period.
* Average of end of month.

diversification of accompanying risks made possible by recent innovations in electronics and telecommunications. These innovations have promoted the development of new financial instruments and services (for example, cash economizing instruments and instruments that combine transaction and investment accounts) that facilitate transfer of funds from open market assets to a customer's regulated-yield demand deposit account at low cost. The development of these financial instruments has minimized the need to maintain

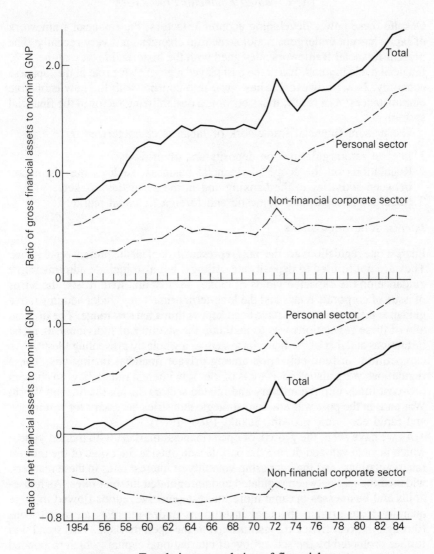

FIGURE 10.3 Trends in accumulation of financial assets.

transaction balances and has released funds for investment in the open markets. In sum, innovations in electronics and telecommunications have provided the technological prerequisite for the introduction of all sorts of financial instruments and services that make use of the open financial markets with market-determined interest rates.

The Outdated Financial Framework

Despite these newly developing economic factors, the financial framework of Japan has not undergone major structural changes until very recently. The present financial framework, designed with the historical legacy of the 1927 financial panic in mind, has in the past played a progressive role in the Japanese economy. Now, however, it has come into conflict with the new economic circumstances; as a result, it has become a destabilizing factor in the financial system.

The present financial framework of Japan is characterized by:

1 Interest rate regulations on deposits and other assets.
2 Regulations on the scope of financial business, such as the distinction between activities in the banking and in the securities markets.
3 Regulations separating domestic and foreign financial markets.

Interest Rate Regulations

Interest rate regulations are the most representative of all the present regulations. They are not limited to deposit rate ceilings, but also include administrative guidance on the expected yields of money in trust and loan trusts, the terms of issue of corporate bonds and the long-term prime rate. Under administrative guidance these asset yields have been kept within a narrow range. The original aim of these regulations was to maintain the stability of individual financial institutions and that of the financial system as a whole by preventing 'destructive competition' in fund-collection among private financial institutions. These regulations were also used as tools of the 'low interest rate policy' to channel low-cost funds into the military and related sectors during the Second World War and, in the post-war era, into strategic industries necessary for restoration and rapid economic growth (Suzuki 1980, 1986).

As we have seen, the growth of open financial markets with market yields, which have developed during the past decade outside the range of the interest rate regulations, and the increasing volatility of interest rates in these markets, widened the gap between regulated and unregulated interest rates. As households and businesses became more interest-sensitive, funds flowed in large quantity from private financial institutions under interest rate regulations (through indirect financing institutions) to the open markets. This trend was further promoted by the active flow of international capital (which responded sensitively to interest rates).

As a result, the share of total funding held by private financial institutions declined continuously until 1983. In particular, the share of deposit banks declined from more than 60 per cent before 1974 to nearly 40 per cent in 1983 (table 10.3). Changes in the size of the outflow of funds, reflecting changes in interest rate differentials, have become a disturbing factor in bank operations. Therefore, under recent economic conditions, the framework of

TABLE 10.3 The flow of funds channels from lenders to final borrowers in the domestic financial system (per cent)

| Calendar year | Private financial intermediaries | | | | Securities market | | | | | Total |
| | | Deposit banks | Trust sector, insurance companies | Public financial inter-mediaries | | Domestic | | | Overseas | |
						Bonds	Stocks	Investment trusts		
1965	78.6	63.2	11.3	15.5	5.9	3.5	5.1	3.0	0.3	100.0
1966	78.4	69.6	10.0	19.3	2.3	2.6	2.2	1.7	0.8	100.0
1967	77.4	66.1	12.0	16.2	6.4	3.1	1.0	1.1	3.4	100.0
1968	72.5	58.3	13.0	18.4	9.1	2.5	2.7	0.2	3.7	100.0
1969	73.3	60.3	11.7	16.9	9.8	2.3	2.9	1.1	3.5	100.0
1970	71.0	60.3	12.8	16.7	12.3	3.0	4.8	0.6	3.9	100.0
1971	70.2	57.8	11.7	16.2	13.6	3.4	2.8	1.0	6.4	100.0
1972	77.5	66.2	10.5	16.1	6.4	1.3	2.0	1.4	1.7	100.0
1973	74.6	64.1	10.9	18.6	6.8	3.1	3.6	0.6	0.5	100.0
1974	69.0	58.0	10.7	21.1	9.9	1.7	2.3	0.3	5.6	100.0
1975	69.8	58.8	10.4	23.3	6.9	3.5	2.0	1.6	0.2	100.0
1976	67.4	56.0	10.2	23.7	8.9	3.9	1.8	1.0	2.2	100.0
1977	60.5	49.6	9.5	29.2	10.3	6.6	2.4	0.9	0.4	100.0
1978	62.4	54.2	6.7	25.4	12.2	6.4	1.4	0.7	3.7	100.0
1979	59.3	48.0	9.6	28.6	12.1	6.3	2.2	0.4	3.2	100.0
1980	54.9	41.9	11.6	31.2	13.9	7.6	1.6	0.6	5.3	100.0
1981	61.4	49.8	9.9	25.5	13.1	7.3	2.4	1.9	1.5	100.0
1982	56.1	42.4	12.7	29.2	14.7	5.5	2.9	3.0	3.3	100.0
1983	54.5	41.6	10.0	26.6	18.9	8.5	1.2	5.8	3.4	100.0
1984	64.0	49.2	12.0	23.6	12.4	2.2	2.2	5.5	2.5	100.0

interest rate regulations has become a factor that impairs, rather than promotes the stability of bank operations and the maintenance of financial discipline. In this situation, private financial institutions have naturally begun to introduce innovative financial instruments and services to overcome the handicap imposed by interest rate regulations. The financial authorities have also recognized the obsolescence of these regulations and have begun relaxing or abolishing them (Kure and Shima, 1984).

Regulations on the Range of Financial Business

The second component of the existing financial framework that has lagged behind economic reality is the strict statutory division of intermediary functions among specialized financial institutions. There have been sharp distinctions between banking and the securities business, between banking and trust business and between institutions handling short-term and long-term financing. The risks involved in allowing simultaneous participation by one institution in both banking and the securities business were revealed in the 1927 financial panic. Article 65 of the Securities and Exchange Law (the counterpart of the Glass–Steagall Act of the United States) was enacted to prohibit the simultaneous handling of banking and securities business by one institution, both as a result of the 1927 panic and as an attempt to protect depositors by preventing 'conflicts of interest'. The separation of short-term financing from long-term financing was promoted to help secure funds for plant and equipment investment, to encourage division of labour among specialized financial sectors and to avoid liquidity risk caused by a maturity mismatch in the sources and uses of funds. The division of banking and trust operations was promoted for similar reasons.

It is doubtful that the above rationales for the compartmentalization of the financial system remain valid today. As these regulations have come into conflict with the newly emerging economic reality, the sharp distinctions between different types of financial business have been fading. For example, the reduction in transaction costs accompanying innovations in electronics has made it possible to introduce new financial instruments and services that facilitate the shift of funds among different financial sectors. The growing sensitivity of the household and business sectors to interest rate movements has boosted demand for financial services involving functions traditionally performed by different sectors of the financial system. As a result, regulations governing the scope of financial business and restricting entry have inhibited the introduction of more efficient financial services. In this sense, they obstruct progress in the financial system. Moreover, in fields where financial business opportunity is rapidly expanding, such as pension funds, investment trust management or consumer loans, these regulations promote an oligopolistic market structure and impede a more equitable arrangement of financial transactions.

The statutory distinction between long- and short-term financing has been eliminated for fund-using operations but is still strictly enforced for fund-raising operations. As a result, mismatching of maturity has become a permanent phenomenon in the balance sheets of the city banks and is a potentially destabilizing factor in the financial system. Risk-hedging in this market is generating innovations like floating rate loans, floating rate bonds and financial futures markets.

Regulations on International Transactions

These regulations were based on the experience of the Great Crash and sought to maintain financial stability by insulating the domestic financial system from foreign financial disturbances. Under the floating exchange rate system, however, such regulations have become inefficient, and in an economic situation in which there are active international flows of capital and innovations in telecommunications that have lowered the costs of international financial transactions, information transmission and asset-liability management, such regulations have become inefficient. They have deprived financial institutions and both domestic and foreign investors of many opportunities for profitable investment. The private sector has attempted to bypass these regulations by lending and borrowing in the Eurodollar market and International Banking Facilities. The growing demand from foreign governments to open the Japanese financial markets is also an important driving force behind the process of financial innovation.

DIFFUSION OF FINANCIAL INNOVATION

This section will identify stages in the process of financial innovation in Japan.

Increasing Deposits by Means of
Cash Economizing Innovations

In Japan the first form of financial innovation was the creation of cash economizing financial instruments and services by banks. In a financial system subject to interest rate regulations, the interest rate differentials between the assets and liabilities of various private intermediaries are more or less the same, and the difference in overall profit reflects the ability to collect funds. Banks therefore concentrated their efforts on attracting deposits by means other than interest rate competition (in other words, they offered shadow interest). Recent cash economizing innovations include free services such as the payment of salaries through bank remittances (since 1969); the payment of public utility charges and taxes by automatic transfer through bank accounts (since 1955); the installation of cash dispensers (since 1969) and automated teller machines (ATMs) (since 1979, see table 10.4); and the direct debiting of bank accounts for credit card usage (since 1969). These innovations are devices that pay shadow interest by making use of technical progress in computers and telecommunications and thus circumvent interest rate regulations on deposits.

TABLE 10.4 Number of cash dispensers and automated teller machines installed by financial institutions, March 1984

	Number of CDs and ATMs installed[a]		Number of offices with CDs or ATMs installed (A)	Total number of domestic offices (B)	Diffusion rate (A/B) (%)
All banks	22,466	(10,360)	9,072	9,659	93.9
City banks	11,264	(6,251)	2,943	2,952	99.7
Regional banks	10,713	(3,763)	5,779	6,298	91.8
Trust banks	489	(346)	350	350	100.0
Long-term credit banks	0	(0)	0	59	0.0
Sogo banks	5,155	(1,317)	3,663	4,227	86.7
Shinkin banks	6,486	(3,149)	5,276	6,509	81.1
Credit cooperatives	329	(77)	298	2,750	10.8
Agricultural cooperatives	1,588	(548)	1,552	15,658	9.9
Others	144	(42)	144	2,799	5.1
Total	36,168	(15,493)	20,005	41,602	48.1

[a] Figures in parentheses represent number of ATMs only.

Economizing on Transaction Account Balances and Strengthening of Investment Accounts

In the second stage, efforts to prevent the outflow of funds from deposits with low and regulated interest rates resulted in the introduction of deposit combined accounts (*Sogo-koza*) in 1972. A deposit combined account offers higher yields by combining a demand deposit with an overdraft facility, using an investment trust or time deposit as collateral. The combination of the investment and transaction accounts functions ushered in a new era in the banking business. This innovation also circumvents interest rate regulation by utilizing recent progress in computer technology.

Maturity Shortening and Risk Reduction of High-Yield, Risky, Long-term Financial Assets

The securities sector has also been an active source of innovation. In Japan, the maturities of corporate bonds have been uniformly regulated, and no instruments existed with a range of maturities appropriate to be traded in the money market. This situation hampered the development of open markets for short-term safe assets. The non-financial private sector sought more efficient use of short-term funds, and the demand for short-term funds by city banks and others increased as large-scale absorption of government bonds led to a deterioration in their liquidity positions.

As a result, securities companies helped shorten the bond maturities to reduce the risk of long-term risky assets. Among the innovations were the introduction of *Gensaki* transactions (sales with repurchase agreement) in 1976 and short-term investment trusts, such as medium-term government bond funds, in 1980. The *Gensaki* market has a relatively long history, but it has grown most rapidly during the past ten years (see table 10.1). Together with the other short-term open markets that developed after it, the *Gensaki* market has promoted the outflow of large-lot funds from the banks and has greatly influenced the process of financial innovation.

The medium-term government bond funds are short-term investment trusts invested mainly in medium-term government bonds. They carry higher interest rates than six-month time deposits and provide a high degree of liquidity by allowing depositors to withdraw funds from their accounts one month after depositing. They have therefore attracted funds – mainly small-sized lots – away from the banks. Medium- and long-term investment trusts with a range of maturities have also been introduced. These innovations have helped transform long-term risky assets into relatively short-term safe assets.

Raising the Yields of Low-yield Safe Assets

Banks have undertaken countermeasures to prevent the outflow of funds to the securities markets and the investment funds. First, certificates of deposits (CDs) were introduced in 1979. The introduction of CDs constituted an attempt to raise the yield and marketability of low-yield safe assets traditionally offered exclusively by banks (see table 10.1). At first there were strict regulations on the minimum denomination (¥500 million), maturity (over three months) and volume (10 per cent of bank net worth) of CDs; but these regulations have been gradually relaxed. In April 1985 the minimum denomination was reduced to ¥100 million, maturity to one month and the quantitative ceiling raised to 100 per cent of net worth.

Secondly, non-negotiable money market certificates (MMCs) with a minimum denomination of ¥50 million were introduced in March 1985. The interest rates of MMCs are based on those of CDs with a constant differential.

Thirdly, banks have sought to prevent the outflow of small-sized funds by introducing new financial instruments and services that make use of the open markets. These include the retail sale of newly issued government bonds and the introduction of *Kokusai-teiki-koza* (government bond time deposit accounts) and *Kokusai-shintaku-koza* (government bond trust accounts) in 1983. Such accounts keep the government bonds sold to customers and transfer the interest automatically to the customers' time deposit or money-in-trust accounts (which are subject to interest rate regulations). In June 1985 banks were allowed to offer *Kokusai-sogo-koza* (combined accounts), which allow overdrafts secured by government bonds sold to customers as collateral. In this way, banks are able to offer higher-yield instruments than the traditional deposit accounts.

The above innovations have been further facilitated by a relaxing of the old regulations by the authorities. One of the favourable results of these innovations for banks was a recovery by the deposit banks of their share in the flow of funds channels in 1984 (see table 10.3).

Cooperation between Banks and Securities Companies.

The relationship between banks and securities companies is no longer confined to conflict or competition. On some occasions they join together in their efforts to promote financial innovation. Cash management services (introduced in 1984) tie transaction accounts (demand deposit and ordinary deposit accounts) offered by banks to high-yield investment accounts (medium-term government bond funds and government bond funds) offered by securities companies and allow automatic and easy transfer of funds between these institutions. They thus provide services similar to the cash management accounts (introduced in 1977) and the sweep accounts (introduced in 1981) in the United States. Although they are still subject to some regulations, cash management services are suggestive of the future course of financial innovation.

FUTURE PROSPECTS OF FINANCIAL INNOVATION
AND DEREGULATION

The Financial Environment after 1985

Judging from the present state of financial innovation, it is most likely that its pace will accelerate. The financial system of Japan will undergo more significant changes in the second half of the 1980s, when some of the newly emerging economic factors are reinforced. Such new factors include the large-scale refinancing of government bonds; the large-scale application of an advanced telecommunications system; and the growing demand from abroad to open the Japanese financial markets in the interests of reciprocity.

Large-scale Refinancing of Government Bonds

A large-scale issue of government bonds is needed to refinance the maturing ten-year, long-term government bonds issued in large quantities in 1975. Annual government bond issues, which recently amounted to more than ¥10 trillion, are expected to increase sharply to more than ¥20 trillion when refinancing issues are included. The macrobalance between the supply of and the demand for funds is achieved by matching refinancing issues with the funds available from the repayment of maturing bonds, so that net annual government bond issues will remain at the previous level. On a more disaggregated level, however, there is no guarantee that the investors who are repaid will reinvest their funds in ten-year bonds. In particular, it is most likely that those who hold ten-year government bonds as near-maturity bonds may prefer to reinvest their funds in short-term bonds. As a result, the market may have difficulty in absorbing the additional long-term government bond issues if they do not offer rewarding terms. It is therefore essential to make government bonds more attractive to investors. This can be achieved in the following ways. First, the yield to subscribers offered to underwriting syndicates should closely follow interest rates in the secondary market. Secondly, there should be further diversification in the types of government bonds available to meet the differing needs of investors; for this purpose, it has been decided that short-term government bonds with maturities of less than one year will be issued this year. Thirdly, further reliance should be placed on public auctions when issuing government bonds. The present system of issuing medium-term government bonds through public auction should be extended to Treasury bills as well as to short-term and long-term government bonds. The resulting enhanced attractiveness of government securities will no doubt trigger further innovation by private financial instruments and further interest rate deregulation.

Developments in Advanced Telecommunication Networks

The methods of transaction between customers and financial institutions, and among financial institutions, will be thoroughly revised by innovations in electronics. A high-technology information and telecommunication system using fibre-optics, called the Information Network System (INS), started full-scale operations in 1985. In addition, many private companies are planning their own information networks. The spread of an electronic fund-transfer system will be promoted by a computer-linked information network and will lead to further fundamental changes in the financial system, particularly in the payment system.

Growing Demand from Abroad to Open the
Japanese Financial and Capital Markets

Parallel with the increase in direct investment abroad and the growth in the volume of international capital flows, Japanese financial institutions are expanding their business into overseas markets, where they usually enjoy national treatment with a considerably larger degree of freedom than at home. On the other hand, because of differences in the Japanese financial system, foreign financial institutions are more constrained in Japan than in their home countries, in spite of the fact that they also enjoy national treatment in Japan. The Japan–US Ad Hoc Group reached an agreement in May 1984 that contains far-reaching measures for financial liberalization and internationalization; it will provide further impetus to financial innovation after 1985.

Liberalization of Interest Rates on Deposits

It would be very difficult to make concrete predictions regarding the future course of financial innovation and deregulation. In view of the present financial environment, however, in the second half of the 1980s innovation and deregulation along the following lines is highly probable. As already mentioned, the minimum denomination of CDs, which had been reduced from ¥500 million to ¥300 million in January 1984, was further reduced to ¥100 million in April 1985. The ceiling on the volume of CD issue had been raised step by step from 75 per cent of broadly defined net worth of the issuing bank to 100 per cent by April 1985, and it will be raised further. For funds amounting to less than ¥100 million, MMCs with a minimum denomination of ¥50 million were introduced in March 1985.

Liberalization of the terms of issue of CDs and the introduction of MMCs lead naturally to growing demands to relax interest rate controls on ordinary large-lot deposits accounts. The deregulation of interest rates on time deposits (of maturities of three months to two years) with a minimum denomination of ¥1 billion was planned for October 1985. The minimum denomination will be gradually reduced to that of CDs within two years.

With the liberalization of interest rates on short-term large-lot deposits, the short-term prime rate will no longer be linked to the official discount rate but will be based on market yields. In fact, some top-ranking city banks have already started large-lot spot loans based on market interest rates, and loans of this sort are expected to expand further. Also, the growth of large-lot loans based on market interest rates will soon render the regulated long-term prime rate obsolete.

The liberalization of interest rates on small funds (such as time deposits below the ¥3 million ceiling on non-taxable savings) would, however, be difficult to achieve without first finding a unified way to determine the interest rates on these deposits in line with the market rates of both private financial institutions and postal savings offices. Problems regarding interest rates on postal savings must be viewed in relation to the public financial institutions as a whole, including the proper roles of the Trust Fund Bureau (in which funds of postal savings are deposited) and other government financial institutions that make use of Trust Fund Bureau resources. Since rival products with free interest rates are expected to increase as a result of the development of various types of investment trusts etc., pressure to liberalize interest rates on small deposits and savings accounts will inevitably increase.

Another problem that remains to be solved is the payment of interest rates comparable to open market interest rates on demand deposits such as current deposits, ordinary deposits and notice deposits (the attachment of transaction functions to investment accounts). Although there is still no plan to create counterparts of the United States' Super-NOW account (introduced in 1983) and money market deposit account (introduced in 1982) cash management services have already been introduced. In the meantime, these new services will make use of investment accounts, like investment trusts with unregulated interest rates, offered by the securities sector. It is only a matter of time, however, before banks themselves begin to offer cash management services that make use of their own investment accounts carrying market-related interest rates. A further step in this direction will probably come with the introduction of computer-managed demand deposit accounts that offer interest rates comparable to market rates, because this type of account will reduce the cost of fund transfer between demand deposits and investment accounts.

Prospects for the Statutory Distinction between Various Financial Sectors

In addition to the creation of new financial instruments and services, and their promotion by deregulation, future financial innovation will include the reduction or elimination of the statutory distinction between different financial sectors.

The Segregation of Banking and Securities Business

The traditional statutory separation of banking from securities business – the former specializing in low-yield safe assets and the latter in high-yield risky assets – has been fading as banks and securities companies extend their business into each other's domains. On the fund-raising side, banks are now engaging in the retail sale of newly issued government bonds, dealing in already issued government bonds and offering government bond time deposit accounts based on government bonds sold through the banks. On the other hand, securities companies supply highly liquid short-term investment trusts, such as medium-term government bond funds and interest management funds (Rikin funds). On the fund-using side, it has become more and more difficult to draw a strict line between syndicate loans offered by banks and newly issued bonds underwritten by securities companies. Furthermore, in June 1985, banks started to offer combined accounts that allow overdrafts secured by government bonds sold to customers as collateral, and securities companies may also now offer loans secured by government bonds sold to customers. As banks and securities companies continue to expand into other domains, the distinctions between them will gradually diminish.

Regulations prohibiting banks from underwriting and dealing in risky assets like stocks and business debentures will probably remain, however, for such operations may give rise to conflicts of interest and serve as destabilizing factors in the financial system.[2] Conflict of interest was the original consideration behind the enactment of the Glass-Steagall Act of the United States and Article 65 of the Securities and Exchange Law of Japan to separate banking from the securities business.

In contrast, universal banking is the basic principle in continental Europe. As pointed out in the Gessler Report from West Germany, the simultaneous handling of banking and securities business may help to stabilize the profit of financial institutions. (Profit in securities business and profit in banking business tend to move in opposite directions during tight money and easy money periods, thus compensating each other.) It is generally believed that the problem of conflicts of interest associated with universal banking can be avoided to a certain extent by making 'China Walls'.

Nevertheless, even in Europe some observers have recently attributed West Germany's lag in the field of high technology to the practice of universal banking. It is argued that under universal banking the conservative attitude of banks toward the holding of risky assets has impeded the development of venture capital business, and that in order to promote the development of markets for risky assets, the securities business should be separated from banking business.

The Distinction between Banking and Trust Business

The trend is also towards liberalization of the statutory distinction between banking and trust business. After the Second World War trust banks in Japan developed mainly by expanding the volume of special joint operation trusts – such as money in trust and loan trust – rather than by expanding the traditional trust business itself. The instruments offered by trust banks today are therefore essentially the same as time deposits, and it will become impossible to distinguish between the two when banks start offering market rates on long-term

---

2 For example, in order to call in risky loans to an unprofitable business, underwriting banks could urge a banking business customer to issue a new bond or stock and sell it to security business customers. This would constitute a conflict between the interests of bank customers and those of security customers.

time deposits. Moreover, both the rapid increase in company sponsored pension funds as the population ages and the growth of investment trusts indicate the need to expand the trust industry. Since existing regulations on new entry to trust business may harm the efficiency and fairness of the financial system as a whole, relaxation of these regulations is inevitable.

The Separation between Long- and Short-term Financing

The separation between long- and short-term financing has almost disappeared. The rationale for separating short-term from long-term financing was that, by investing short-term liabilities in long-term assets, financial institutions would run both a liquidity risk and an interest risk, which might act as destabilizing factors in the financial system. Financial institutions might not have enough reserves to meet short-term liabilities, or they might suffer a profit squeeze when short-term interest rates rose above long-term rates during tight money periods. Actually, the distinction between long-term and short-term financing has been fading, but only on the assets side. Banks are now engaging in long-term financing, either by offering short-term loans that can be renewed after maturity, or simply by offering direct medium- and long-term loans. If the artificial separation between short-term and long-term financing were allowed to persist on the liabilities side, mismatching of short-term liabilities and long-term assets would become a permanent phenomenon. The resulting liquidity and interest rate risks might render the financial system unstable. As financial innovation advances, the interest rates on both the assets and liabilities of financial institutions will become market-related, and customers will be able to hedge the risk of interest rate fluctuation through the financial futures markets. As a result, long-term variable rate lendings will prevail over long-term fixed rate lendings.

Internationalization of the Japanese Financial and Capital Markets

The Promotion of Financial Deregulation by the Joint Japan–US Agreement

The working group of the Japan–US Ad Hoc Group on Yen/Dollar Exchange Rate, Financial and Capital Market Issues reached a general agreement on the future course of financial liberalization in Japan in May 1984 (hereafter referred to as the joint Japan–US agreement). This agreement was followed up in May 1985 and has definitely accelerated the pace of financial innovation in Japan by promoting the liberalization of interest rates and the lowering of barriers between different financial sectors. Nevertheless, although foreign influence may have played a role in promoting the process, the basic impetus for financial liberalization in Japan can be found in factors endogenous to the domestic financial system. Indeed, the joint Japan–US agreement contained measures that had already been judged essential from the domestic point of view.

For example, the reduction in the minimum denomination and the increase in the quota of CD issues, the creation of MMCs and the liberalization of interest rates of large-lot deposits were inevitable steps in the process of interest rate deregulation. Permission for foreign banks to participate in the retail sale of, and to deal in, government bonds was needed to facilitate the large-scale issue of these bonds. The entry of nine foreign banks into the trust business, which was permitted in June 1985, was also inevitable, because the distinction between various financial sectors has lost much of its original meaning and the need to improve the efficiency of the financial system has become more urgent. Finally, it is necessary to expand the facilities of the short-term financial markets, including the Treasury bills market, in order to improve the efficiency of the short-term financial sector. This will enable the Bank of Japan to conduct monetary policy by means of open market operations in these markets.

Whereas the above measures of financial liberalization are directly related to Japan's money and capital markets, the joint Japan–US agreement also contains measures that promote the liberalization of transactions between domestic and foreign financial markets. The resulting increase in international transactions will undoubtedly provide further stimulus to financial innovation. Of particular importance are the abolition of the regulations on the conversion of foreign currencies into yen and the relaxation of the regulations on Euro-yen transactions. On conversion, three points are worth noting. First, arbitrage between the domestic and foreign interbank markets will become more active, and this may have a substantial impact on the interbank rates. Secondly, the expansion in domestic foreign currency deposits converted from yen will promote the liberalization of interest rates on yen-denominated deposits as a whole. Foreign exchange banks will also be able to bypass the regulations on the issue of bank debentures by accepting domestic long-term foreign currency deposits converted from yen. This will help to eliminate the distinction between short-term and long-term financing. Finally, the increase in inter-bank foreign currency deposits converted from yen will render regulations on the interbank deposit rates obsolete and, at the same time, reduce the role of the discount market and the call-money market.

The following effects are expected as a result of the liberalization of Euro-yen transactions. First, the issue of Euro-yen bonds by residents will enhance deregulation of interest rates on domestic bonds. Secondly, the liberalization of short-term as well as medium- and long-term Euro-yen borrowings for residents will introduce a new system of domestic lending rates based on Euro-yen rates; this will accelerate the decline of the traditional system of regulated interest rates that centres around the short-term and long-term prime rates.

Impact on the Collateral Principle

Internationalization of Japan's financial markets also gives rise to problems concerning the traditional practice of requiring collateral for loans and bonds (hereafter referred to as the 'collateral principle'). In Japan, the collateral principle is in widespread use. It is applicable to both long-term and short-term financing, including the issue of corporate bonds, bank loans and interbank money transactions. In contrast, the domestic financial markets of western countries and the Eurodollar market permit transacting parties to choose between secured and unsecured loans and bonds.

In Japan, the collateral principle was introduced as a precaution against repeating the experience of the 1927 financial panic. The principle worked well throughout the Second World War and the post-war period in maintaining the safety of financial transactions and in promoting rapid economic growth. Its success was made possible by the abundant supply of assets suitable for mortgage in the rapidly growing heavy and chemical industries. But the collateral principle has raised the cost of, and imposed a constraint on, fund-raising for venture capital businesses and enterprises in the tertiary sector, which usually do not possess suitable assets. Moreover, the collateral principle is not compatible with international financing practices like Euro transactions. The pressure to re-examine this principle has therefore become intense, and, actually, it has been relaxed step by step. For example, the restrictions on the issuance of uninsured private bonds in Japan have been considerably relaxed since 1984 in accordance with the liberalization of Euro-yen bonds issuance. In the domestic interbank market, call-money transactions without collateral have been permitted since July 1985.

As a matter of course, financial stability remains important, and safety devices other than the holding of mortgages should be firmly established before the collateral principle is further relaxed. Concrete steps are now being taken towards the establishment of safety devices such as the principle of self-responsibility concerning financial transactions, the principle of disclosure, the establishment of credit lines and authoritative credit rating institutions.

FUTURE EFFECTS OF FINANCIAL INNOVATION, DEREGULATION
AND REFORM ON BANK MANAGEMENT AND THE BANKING SYSTEM

Changes in Bank Assets, Liabilities and Profits

Current Changes

As shown in table 10.5, a marked change has recently occurred in the proportion of each major item of assets and liabilities to the total outstanding. In assets, three major changes are apparent. First, the proportion of negotiable securities has increased since 1975 (securitization). Second, the proportion of investment in money markets, such as call loans and bills purchased, has also increased (dependence on money market). Third, the proportion of long-term loans has increased – although this increase includes the significant growth of long-term loans with variable interest rates by commercial banks and, conversely, the decline of those with fixed interest rates by long-term credit banks (prevalence of variable rates).

TABLE 10.5 Changes in assets and liabilities among all banks in Japan (percentage of total outstanding assets)

	End of 1960 (%)	1965 (%)	1970 (%)	1975 (%)	1980 (%)	1984 (%)
LIABILITIES						
Deposits and bank debentures	84.7	83.9	86.0	85.8	83.7	76.8
of which: demand deposits	28.0	29.5	28.6	28.5	22.7	18.6
time deposits and bank debentures	56.7	54.4	57.4	57.3	61.0	58.2
Negotiable certificates of deposit (A)	–	–	–	–	1.0	2.6
Non-resident yen deposits and foreign currency deposits (B)	–	1.3	0.7	2.4	4.3	5.9
Borrowed money from other financial institutions	1.1	1.9	1.2	0.3	0.2	0.2
Borrowed money from the Bank of Japan	5.6	5.0	4.6	1.5	1.1	1.0
Call money and bills sold (C)	1.8	4.1	4.3	6.1	5.6	7.3
Total (A + B + C)	1.8	5.4	5.0	8.5	10.9	15.8
ASSETS						
Loans	81.4	80.2	81.8	80.3	74.2	76.3
Term:[a] less than 1 year		79.7	74.9	61.8	58.9	60.1
over 1 year		20.3	25.1	38.2	41.1	39.9
of which: long-term credit banks		10.8	11.2	11.4	10.4	8.9
Negotiable securities	15.3	16.0	14.5	15.5	21.0	17.7
Bonds	12.8	13.4	11.4	12.3	17.2	13.7
Stocks	2.3	2.6	3.1	3.1	3.6	4.0
Call loans and bills purchased	1.1	1.4	1.6	1.5	2.0	3.7
Cash and deposit	2.1	1.7	1.8	2.5	2.5	2.0

[a] Distribution percentage (end of fiscal year).
Source: Bank of Japan, 'Application table of flow of funds accounts', etc.

In liabilities, the proportion of demand deposits has declined significantly (economization on holdings of demand deposits). In contrast, the proportion of liabilities based on liberalized interest rates – such as CDs, foreign currency deposits, call money and bills sold – has increased (deregulation of interest rates). The ratio of current profits of all banks in Japan to total outstanding assets has remained steady at around 0.5 per cent since the fiscal year 1977 (see table 10.6). If one observes current revenues and current expenditures separately, however, it is obvious that significant changes have occurred, especially in current expenditures. The proportion of interest expenses – especially interests on deposits, CDs, call money and bills sold – has increased considerably since the fiscal year 1980. These increases in interest expenses have been covered by cutting other expenses, including both personnel- and non-personnel-related expenses. This may suggest that in the process of financial innovation, deregulation and reform, banks are reducing transaction costs to offer more competitive interest rates on their products.

Future Prospects

How will the conditions of bank assets, liabilities and profits change as a result of the progressive innovation, deregulation and reform of Japan's financial markets? There is no doubt that the tendency for the proportion of liabilities bearing deregulated interest rate to increase will become even greater. In addition to the introduction of MMCs in March 1985 and the lowering of the minimum unit for CDs in April 1985, restrictions on the large deposit rate were relaxed in October 1985. The minimum denomination of deposits with liberalized interest rates will be reduced gradually. When it reaches ¥10 million the proportion of market interest bearing liabilities for all banks will be around 50 per cent. For assets, there will be a further diversification of investment at home and abroad; and in order to avoid the interest rate risk caused by increases in the liabilities bearing deregulated interest rates, the proportion of variable interest rate loans (so-called 'spread banking') can be expected to increase.

On the one hand, financial innovation, deregulation and reform may result in negative effects on bank profits, such as increases in interest payments, and in management risks, such as interest rate risk, liquidity risk, credit risk and foreign exchange risk. For instance, as observed in table 10.7, banks that have mismatched short-term liabilities and long-term assets would face increasing interest rate risk and liquidity risk. On the other hand, certain positive results can also be expected, such as an accelerated increase in deposits caused by higher competitiveness resulting from liberalization of interest rates on deposits; stabilization of profit margins as a result of spread banking; reduction in the various types of implicit interest rates triggered by non-interest rate competition under conditions of regulated interest rates (for instance, increases in commission income and decreases in personnel- and non-personnel-related expenses); and increased opportunities to generate profits, reduce costs and diversify risks as a result of liberalization and internationalization of banking activities (economies of scope).

TABLE 10.6 Changes in profits of all banks in Japan[a]

Fiscal year	Distribution percentage of current revenues					Distribution percentage of current expenditures									Current profits
	Current revenues	Interests on loans	Dividends and interests on negotiable securities received	Other interests received	Commission	Current expenditures	Interest expenses				Transferred to reserve for possible loan losses	Operating expenses			
							On deposits	On bank debentures	On CDs	On call money and bills sold			Personnel expenses	Non-personnel expenses	
1977	6.0	67.3	17.6	6.6	3.5	5.4	64.4	10.9	—	4.9	1.0	28.2	16.9	9.2	0.6
1978	5.5	61.7	19.6	8.3	4.2	5.0	61.0	10.9	—	4.5	1.1	38.7	17.4	9.3	0.6
1979	6.2	58.8	16.4	14.1	3.8	5.9	61.9	8.5	3.0	6.1	0.4	21.9	13.3	7.1	0.3
1980	7.5	61.5	13.8	17.1	2.9	7.1	52.6	7.3	3.9	7.4	0.2	18.0	10.8	6.0	0.4
1981	7.7	54.7	13.0	25.1	3.1	7.3	56.0	6.2	5.0	7.5	0.1	15.9	9.4	5.3	0.4
1982	7.2	54.5	13.8	24.9	3.1	6.7	54.4	6.6	4.6	8.0	0.9	16.8	9.7	5.4	0.5
1983	6.5	56.7	14.6	21.7	3.2	6.0	53.6	7.7	4.9	7.4	0.6	17.8	10.3	5.8	0.5
1984	6.8	53.2	14.0	25.7	3.0	6.3	55.2	7.0	5.9	7.3	0.6	15.5	8.8	5.2	0.5

[a] Current revenues, current expenditures and current profits shown as fiscal year-end percentage of total outstanding assets.
Source: Federation of Bankers' Associations of Japan, 'Analysis of financial statements of all banks in Japan'.

TABLE 10.7   Terms of assets and liabilities of city banks at the end of Fiscal year 1984 (distribution percentage)

Term	Loans	Deposits
Under 1 year	65.4	76.3
Over 1 year, under 3 years	7.6	23.7
Over 3 years	27.0	0

It is difficult to predetermine which of these factors will be stronger – the positive or the negative. Judging from experiences in the United States, where the deregulation of interest rates has progressed further than in Japan, the liberalization of deposit rates will not necessarily result in the deterioration of bank profits. There is, however, no doubt that innovation and deregulation will intensify competition at home and abroad. Under these circumstances, the management skill of each bank will be more clearly reflected in its profits than in the past, and this will increase differentials in profits among banks.

Impact on the Stability of the Banking System

Innovation, deregulation and the resultant reforms of Japan's financial markets will have both positive and negative effects on the stability of the banking system. On the positive side, they will encourage the expansion and diversification of banking activities. Because of economies of scope, banking will become more sound, which will, in turn, increase the stability of the banking system. Also, liberalization of the financial markets will probably accelerate the weeding out of unsound banks. Although this weeding-out process may initially destabilize the banking system, in the long run it will serve to stabilize it.

Various negative effects may also be expected. In an environment of intensified competition, differentials in profits among individual banks will probably widen because of increases in various forms of management risk. Under these circumstances, it is reasonable to conclude that bank failures may increase.

Which of the two effects – the positive or the negative – will be stronger will depend on whether we are discussing long-term or short-term effects. At least during the transition period it is likely that problems will become much more acute than in the past. In the longer run, however, when most of the inefficient institutions have been weeded out, the financial system will become more efficient and stable. In the meantime, it is imperative to devise measures to guard the system. The monetary authorities are now considering ways to consolidate safety devices, such as introducing portfolio regulations and strengthening bank surveillance and the deposit insurance system.

IMPLICATIONS FOR MONETARY POLICY

Financial innovation and deregulation has affected, and will continue to affect, the central bank's intermediate targets and the transmission channels of monetary policy effects in Japan in a number of ways.

Structural Shifts in Money Velocity and Money Demand

The Bank of Japan has emphasized the money stock as an intermediate target of monetary policy since 1975; but, the velocities of money and near-moneys, and the demand functions relating the money stock to nominal GNP and market interest rates (Hamada and Hayashi, 1985), have shown the following structural shifts.

As shown in figure 10.4 the velocity of M1 had been declining until 1973. It subsequently remained somewhat stable until 1980, and followed an upward trend thereafter. This trend resulted from the economization on cash currency and demand deposits made possible by financial innovations such as credit cards, payment of salary through bank remittance, automatic transfer of taxes and charges, installation of cash dispensers and ATMs (see table 10.4) and the introduction of deposit combined accounts and cash management services, as previously described.

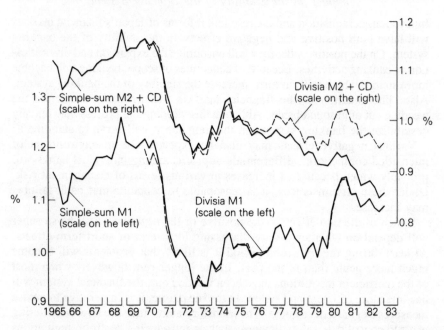

FIGURE 10.4 The velocities of Divisia and simple-sum M1 and M2+CD

Figure 10.4 also shows that the velocity of M2+CD has been declining until recently. But Divisia M2+CD stopped declining in 1973, and has remained fairly stable thereafter. Here, Divisia M2+CD is compiled as a weighted average of the components of M2+CD, using their corresponding degrees of moneyness as weights (Barnett and Spindt, 1982; Ishida, 1984). This observation suggests that within M2+CD, the share of components whose interest rates are high and responsive to variations in open market interest rates, and whose degrees of moneyness are low, has been increasing.

Table 10.8 shows the results of estimating separate money demand functions for the period up to the first quarter of 1977, when open markets remained underdeveloped, and for the subsequent period since the second quarter of 1977, when these markets began to develop. The short-run income elasticity of demand for M1 and the short- and long-run interest elasticity of demand for M2+CD and M3+CD declined after 1977 (Suzuki, 1984a). The reasons behind these changes are similar to those behind the shifts in the velocities. For M1, the changes resulted from the economization on cash currency and demand deposits as financial innovation progressed. For M2+CD, they were caused by the increasing share of components whose yields were sensitive to open market interest rates.

The result of estimating the money demand functions using Divisia monetary aggregates is also shown in table 10.8. Compared with the functions based on simple-sum monetary aggregates, the parameters of the income terms are more significant, the long-run income elasticity comes closer to 1 and the fits are somewhat improved (Ishida, 1984). In other words, despite financial innovation, the relationship between Divisia money stock and nominal GNP seems to be relatively stable.

This paper has noted how, as financial innovation has progressed, the velocities of money and the money demand functions have shown structural shifts. In Japan, however, these structural shifts were not so drastic and unpredictable that they obscured the optimal quantity of money consistent with the appropriate aggregate demand. Specifically, structural shifts in income elasticity did not greatly alter our estimates of the optimal quantity of M2+CD, the principal indicator used by the Bank of Japan. Whether Divisia M2+CD is useful in determining the optimal quantity of money deserves further study in the future.

Changes in the Transmission Channels of Policy Effects

Nevertheless, the fact that in the M2+CD demand function the interest elasticity has declined, suggests that the transmission channels of monetary policy have been changing. The effect of changing interbank interest rates on bank lending depends on the stickiness of the lending rates. The rise of financial disintermediation also depends on the rigidity of interest rates on deposits, bank debentures, money trust and loan trust. As interest rate

TABLE 10.8 Results of estimating the Divisia and simple-sum money demand functions

	Explained variables	Explanatory variables					R^2 (s.e.)	DW (ρ)	Long-run GNP elasticity	Long-run interest elasticity
		Constant	LAG (−1)	GNP	R	r				
70/IV − 77/I	Simple-sum M1	0.2675 (4.3021)	0.7663 (9.0995)	0.2635 (1.8853)	−0.1191 (−4.2048)		0.9726 (0.0366)	1.8797 (0.0732)	1.128	−0.510
	Simple-sum M2+CD	0.2274 (5.0714)	0.7489 (10.211)	0.3008 (2.5332)	−0.1682 (−5.5825)	0.0816 (2.0384)	0.9989 (0.0111)	1.8667 (0.1420)	1.198	0.607
	Simple-sum M3+CD	0.3676 (3.8064)	0.6332 (4.8368)	0.5729 (2.5664)	−0.2496 (−2.5792)	0.0918 (1.5618)	0.9860 (0.0115)	2.1460 (0.3578)	1.562	−0.680
77/II−83/I	Simple-sum M1	0.1871 (4.9824)	0.9497 (11.066)	0.1308 (1.9956)	−0.0971 (−4.7928)		0.9581 (0.0196)	2.1634 (−0.5615)	2.600	−1.930
	Simple-sum M2+CD	0.0243 (2.3118)	0.7836 (8.4164)	0.3680 (2.5301)	−0.0001 (−0.0487)	−0.0067 (−1.6034)	0.9978 (0.0080)	2.1094 (−0.3140)	1.701	0.001
	Simple-sum M3+CD	0.0576 (5.1716)	0.8742 (15.558)	0.2665 (2.5578)	−0.0491 (−4.8852)	0.0230 (2.7130)	0.9993 (0.0057)	2.2940 (−0.5243)	2.118	−0.390

	α_0	α_1	α_2	α_3	α_4				
Divisia M1	0.1620 (4.7718)	0.8359 (17.661)	0.1052 (2.1542)	−0.0702 (−4.5884)		0.9874 (0.0207)	2.0001 (−0.1910)	0.641	−0.428
Simple-sum M1	0.1709 (4.6724)	0.8250 (16.813)	0.1051 (2.1711)	−0.0748 (−4.5210)		0.9833 (0.0213)	1.9859 (−0.1223)	0.600	−0.427
Divisia M2+CD	0.1356 (4.4676)	0.7855 (12.219)	0.2247 (2.8275)	−0.0822 (−2.7311)	0.0284 (0.8626)	0.9929 (0.0148)	2.0031 (0.0912)	1.048	−0.383
Simple-sum M2+CD	0.1244 (3.5127)	0.8171 (10.174)	0.2244 (2.0010)	−0.0830 (−2.9384)	0.0372 (1.1729)	0.9908 (0.0126)	2.1867 (0.4122)	1.216	−0.453
Divisia M3+CD	0.1233 (4.0888)	0.7819 (10.453)	0.2627 (2.5128)	−0.0347 (−1.2233)	−0.0187 (−0.8669)	0.9949 (0.0137)	2.0043 (0.1178)	1.204	−0.159
Simple-sum M3+CD	0.1170 (3.4478)	0.8626 (10.261)	0.2015 (1.4188)	−0.0265 (−0.9133)	−0.0208 (−0.9168)	0.9942 (0.0113)	2.2242 (0.4566)	1.467	−0.193

(Sample period: 70/IV–83/I)

Note: The money demand functions are estimated in the form: $\log(M/P) = \alpha_0 + \alpha_1 \log(M/P)_{-1} + \alpha_2 \log(GNP/P) + \alpha_3 \log R + \alpha_4 \log r$

where M = Divisia or simple-sum M1, M2 + CD, and M3 + CD

GNP = nominal GNP

R = benchmark rate, that is, interest rate on the substitute of money. Instead of the commonly used call rate, *Gensaki* rate or yield on interest-bearing telegram and telephone bond (*Dendensai*), the benchmark rate used in compiling the Divisia index is adopted here in conformity with the theory of Divisia aggregates. For the sake of convenience, it is taken as the average of the firms' benchmark rate R^f and the households' benchmark rate R^h.

r = 'own rate', that is, the interest rate on money. For M1, it is taken to be 0 (excluded from the estimated equation) and for M2 and M3, it is taken as the interest rates on time deposits and fixed amount postal savings, respectively.

regulations are relaxed, allowing lending rates and yields on near-moneys to move flexibly in line with the open market rate, these channels will probably decline in importance.

On the other hand, the interest rate effect on spending will become more important. This is because, as interest rates on loans, deposits, bank debentures, money trust and loan trust etc. become as flexible as open market interest rates, both the opportunity costs for the fund surplus sector and the financial costs for the fund deficit sector with respect to spending will also become more flexible. Since the interest elasticity of spending in Japan is high, the effectiveness of monetary policy as a whole will be maintained (Suzuki 1983a, 1984b).

The fact that the effectiveness of monetary policy is becoming more and more dependent on the interest rate effect rather than on the changes in the volume of bank lending or the money stock suggests the following. First, that the time lags between changes in the volume of bank lending or money stock and the changes in nominal GNP that follow them will shorten; eventually they will fluctuate simultaneously. Secondly, as diversification takes place in the channels of raising and using funds, and as the mobility of capital between domestic and foreign markets increases, selective financial control of specific sectors will become more difficult. The effectiveness of window guidance will decline. As long as the yen-denominated monetary base as a whole is properly controlled, however, the effectiveness of monetary policy through interest rates will remain.

Nevertheless, two factors that may harm the effectiveness of monetary policy in the future deserve further discussion. The first is the settlement of domestic transactions among residents using foreign currencies (perfect currency substitution), and the second is the accumulation of yen-denominated assets by non-residents, which disturbs the yen-denominated monetary aggregates held by residents. The first factor is, and should be, forbidden by the Foreign Exchange Law. Monetary policy in Japan would otherwise lose its independence. As for the second, as long as control of yen base money by the Bank of Japan remains firm, yen-denominated monetary aggregates held by residents will basically be controlled (although they will perhaps be subject to some time lags or random fluctuations caused by Euro-yen flows).

REFERENCES

Barnett, W. A. and Spindt, P. A. 1982: Divisia monetary aggregates: compilation, data, and historical behavior. Federal Reserve Board, *Staff Studies* 116 (May).
Economic Planning Agency 1984: *Keizai Hakusho* (White Paper on Economics) (Japanese).
Goto, S., Kure, B. and Hizume, R. 1983: *Nihon no Kin'yu Kakumei*. (Financial innovation of Japan) (Japanese). Yuhikaku Sensho.
Hamada, K. and Hayashi, F. 1985: Monetary policy in postwar Japan. In A. Ando et al. (eds), *Monetary Policy in Our Times*. Massachusetts: MIT Press.

Ishida, K. 1984: Divisia monetary aggregates and demand for money: a Japanese case. Bank of Japan, *Monetary and Economic Studies* 2, No. 1 (June).

Kure, B. and Shima, K. 1984: *Kinri Jiyuka* (Liberalization of interest rates) (Japanese). Yuhikaku Business.

Royama, S. 1983: *Nihon no Kin'yu Shisutemu* (Financial system of Japan) (Japanese). Toyo Keizai Shimpo Sha.

Suzuki, Y. 1980: *Money and Banking in Contemporary Japan.* New Haven, Conn.: Yale University Press.

Suzuki, Y. 1983a: Interest rate decontrol, financial innovation, and the effectiveness of monetary policy. Bank of Japan, *Monetary and Economic Studies* 1, No. 1 (June).

Suzuki, Y. 1983b: Changes in financial asset selection and the development of financial markets in Japan. Bank of Japan, *Monetary and Economic Studies* 1, No. 2 (October).

Suzuki, Y. 1984a: Financial innovation and monetary policy in Japan. Bank of Japan, *Monetary and Economic Studies* 2, No. 1 (June).

Suzuki, Y. 1984b: Monetary policy in Japan: transmission mechanism and effectiveness. Bank of Japan, *Monetary and Economic Studies* 2, No. 2 (December).

Suzuki, Y. 1986: *Money, Finance, and Macroeconomic Performance in Japan.* New Haven, Conn.: Yale University Press.

11

The Private ECU Market: A Case of International Financial Innovation

ENRICA GUGLIELMOTTO and GIUSEPPE PASSATORE

INTRODUCTION

Any financial innovation can be explained as a byproduct of a particular set of circumstances. However, a more general model has been developed[1] which provides a microeconomic framework for financial innovation. According to this, new financial instruments or practices are introduced in order to lessen the financial constraints imposed on utility maximizing economic agents. In other words, the rising costs of adhering to existing constraints stimulates the search for new financial products which can obviate those constraints.

The success of the European currency unit (ECU) during the past few years can be usefully analysed within the above framework. It is important to note, however, that the ECU was not designed primarily within a framework of financial innovation. The 1979 agreement setting up the European Monetary System (EMS) assigned the ECU important functions that were, however, limited to transactions between central banks belonging to the European Monetary Cooperation Fund (EMCF),[2] in other words to what is often called

---

1 William L. Silber, 'Towards a theory of financial innovation', in Silber (ed.), *Financial Innovation*. Lexington, Mass.: D. C. Heath, 1975.
2 Apart from acting as the numeraire for the exchange rate mechanism and as a reference point for the divergence indicator, the 'official' ECU was attributed a more substantial role as the denominator for operations in both the intervention and the credit mechanisms and as a means of settlement and a reserve asset of EMS central banks. Hence the introduction of the well-known EMCF transfer mechanism via swap

the 'official use' of the ECU. Thus, the ECU was first of all an instrument of central banks, rather than commercial ones, and it was created by governments, rather than by the market.

In spite of this, the ECU has experienced its greatest success in the market, with public and private agents using the European currency for both short- and long-term financial assets and liabilities. The process has developed to such a point that, in the debate on the performance of the ECU, the success of the 'private circuit' of the European currency is often favourably compared to its less developed 'official circuit'. In fact, a substantial private ECU market has rapidly developed: its size has now overtaken the volume of ECUs issued by the EMCF, the latter being approximately equal to 53–4 billion. If measured in terms of market activity, size and frequency of transactions etc., the greater vitality of the 'private circuit' is even more striking.

However, simply to contrast the success of the private ECU to the less brilliant performance of the official one is not very fruitful. Essentially, we believe that the success of the ECU as a new financial instrument depends on certain particular characteristics of the European currency and above all on the relative stability it has boasted in the past and potentially may continue to possess in the future. This stability is a vital property in a period characterized by major uncertainties about the future behaviour of monetary and financial variables and it has made the ECU particularly appetizing to agents seeking

---

operations using 20 per cent of central banks' dollar and gold reserves for which they received ECU in exchange. Nevertheless the use of the official ECU has been less extensive in the EMS's first six years for numerous reasons. Not the least of these has been the fact that the crossed transfer of reserves between EMCF and the central banks is still conducted on the basis of quarterly swaps rather than being definitive. Other factors operating against the use of the official ECU in the exchange market have been partly overcome by the recent agreement between the central banks of the EMS ratified by the EEC's Council of Economic and Finance Ministers in April 1985.

Among other things the agreement envisages:

1 The temporary mobilization of part of their ECU reserves by central banks needing dollars or EMS currencies for intramarginal exchange operations.
2 Under circumscribed conditions, central banks that have a net debtor position in ECUs and are simultaneously creditors in the very short-term financing arrangement must accept 100 per cent of their net claim in ECUs.
3 The calculation of interest rates applied to central banks' net ECU positions deriving from very short-term loans on the basis of the market rates of the component currencies.
4 ECU transfers by EMS central banks to the central banks of non-member countries closely linked to the EEC or international monetary institutions.

Hence the measures announced tend to favour the use of the official ECU both by making it more attractive (because it is more remunerative and more liquid) and by extending the range of its regulated utilization.

protection against both exchange rate and interest rate risks. In the presence of volatile and unpredictable foreign exchange fluctuations, companies have to learn to hedge and to protect their costs as well as their revenues and profit margins as efficiently as possible. They must avoid losses on sales or purchases in foreign currencies and they must not lose, as a consequence, their share in the international markets. At the same time, investors need to choose the components of their portfolios in order to obtain the 'best' risk–reward solution.

The interest rate on an ECU asset or liability and the exchange rate of the ECU consist of weighted averages of the corresponding rates of the component currencies. As such they present a relatively higher degree of stability than those rates applicable to individual currencies and therefore appeal to the rest of risk-averse borrowers and investors. However, the institutional background, i.e. the fact that the ECU is not simply a privately created basket of currencies, but rather a product of the EMS agreement, has played an equally crucial part in creating the conditions that have made the ECU so attractive to individual operators. Thus, a more useful way to analyse the performance of the ECU as a financial innovation consists of taking the microeconomic as well as the macroeconomic and institutional levels into account. Their interaction and the predominance of one rather than the other have determined the characteristics and respective performances of the two – official and private – ECU circuits. The same dualism provides a useful reference point for an analysis of the problems to be faced in the near future and will help us to decide whether or not we have the potential means to overcome them.

The first section of this paper analyses the features of the ECU's exchange and interest rates as they emerge from *ex post* data and compares them to those of the other major international currencies. The way in which exchange rate fluctuations affect the level, but also and more importantly, the volatility of foreign currency borrowing costs or investment returns is considered particularly. In general, it appears that if we exclude the domestic currency, the ECU has performed very well, especially in terms of stability. The claim can thus be made that ECU denominated assets/liabilities represent a feasible instrument with which to diversify and, in particular, to protect foreign currency positions against the exchange rate risk.

The second section tackles the problem by analysing the role placed by the institutional back-up in fostering the growth of the private ECU market. Further, some interesting insights will be derived by looking at the break-even exchange rates over the next year. For currencies belonging to the EMS exchange rate agreement, a useful comparison may be developed between break-even rates and the range of values within which various currencies are allowed to fluctuate.

The following section outlines ways in which the ECU is contributing to create a more efficient financial environment in Europe. The final section concludes by presenting the problems to be resolved and outlining some potential lines for future development.

THE ECU AS A STABLE CURRENCY: LEVELS AND VARIABILITY OF
INTEREST AND EXCHANGE RATES

In a world characterized by efficient foreign exchange and capital markets,
free of restrictions on capital movements, arbitrage tends to equalize *ex ante*
the expected total costs/yields (i.e., interest rate plus currency depreciation or
appreciation) of comparable instruments denominated in different currencies.

If expectations were always realized, any one currency would do as well
as any other as a means to denominate borrowing/investment transactions.
This is not the case, however, in reality, and especially after the introduction
of the flexible exchange rate system, unexpected fluctuations in exchange rates
have tended to produce huge and erratic discrepancies between *ex post* total
costs/yields of different currencies, making the foreign exchange risk a major
concern for decision-makers operating in the international environment.

Thus, an economic agent's decision about the currency or, more probably, set
of currencies in which to denominate his/her payables and receivables will
essentially depend on two factors: the relative cost/yield of each currency (or
set of currencies) and the degree of risk due to the possibility that *ex post* total
costs/returns will differ from their *ex ante* expected values. The latter obviously
cannot be known beforehand, though they can be estimated on the basis of fore-
casts for future interest and exchange rates. There is, however, some room for
error in such estimates and any agent will have doubts when the time comes for
portfolio decisions. Such doubts have, of course, increased dramatically since
fixed exchange rates were abandoned. Analysis of the level and volatility of
the total costs/yields of the various currencies can be developed at two levels:

1 Using *ex post* data as the best proxy for what will happen in the future.
2 Taking into account other economic and monetary factors which may add
   more specific hypotheses about the future performance of interest and
   exchange rates.

This section will tackle the problem on the basis of information supplied by
ex post data.

To examine what emerges from *ex post* data, we simulated a one-month
investment/borrowing transaction and, for each currency and base country,
calculated the total rate, i.e. the rate determined by both the one-month interest
rate and the variations in the exchange rate during the one-month period. The
data utilized were the end-of-month exchange rates and the average between
bid and offer Eurorates.[3] The considered period runs from January 1980 to
September 1985. Some subperiods were considered too, in order to check
whether, after the March 1983 EMS realignment, European currencies showed,
on average, more stability among themselves.

As for the variables to be analysed we took into account the average 'total rate'

3 For a detailed description of the adopted methodology, see the Appendix.

over the different periods, as well as its breakdown into 'interest rate effect' and 'exchange rate effect'. To have a proxy for risk, we used two measures of volatility based on the dispersion of observed values around their mean: the standard deviation and the coefficient of variation.

The first will vary in relation to the 'dimension' of the variable concerned, yet we feel its utilization in this context is justified for two reasons. First, because the mean values of the effective rate for each currency and country are not so quantitatively different as to invalidate the indications we are able to deduce from a comparison of standard deviations. Secondly, because in the case of cost/yield of a financial operation, the absolute value of the deviation between the expected (here represented by the mean) and the observed value is as important if not more important than the amount of that deviation expressed in units of cost/yield. In analysing currency choices it is therefore useful to refer to both indicators.

It is worth specifying that the use of mean values and their volatility as a tool for ranking currencies according to some trade-off between return (cost) and risk is an approximation. Such ranking depends, in fact, on the utility function of the borrower/investor and, in particular, not only on the variables that enter it but also on the functional form of the utility function. For instance, a ranking done according to the value of the return/risk ratio assumes that the investor is indifferent whether he/she has a low return/low risk asset or a high return/high risk one, which may not be true if the investor is very concerned about the absolute value of his/her risk.

The analysis presented here is based on two basic hypotheses. We assume that the national currency is the agent's preferred monetary habitat and that he/she is averse to risk. We also describe the choices of a 'generic' economic agent interested in the level of variability of the total rate for currency operations. In a real situation we would have to develop a more complex typology, which would not only distinguish between short- and long-term decisions but which would also introduce specific cases like that of exporting and/or importing companies. Essentially, such companies have to bear in mind the need to cover themselves against the exchange risk. Thus their choices of financing and investment currency may be conditioned by the invoicing and settlement currencies used for trade contracts.

Finally, to make comparisons between alternative portfolios, we consider currencies individually. In real life, agents handle currency portfolios in which the mean effective rate depends on the weighted mean of the component currencies' effective rates, but the total variability is a function of the correlation between the interest and exchange rates of the currencies themselves. In such a case, a negative correlation between currencies has a damping effect on the variability of the portfolio's total effective rate and vice versa. The empirical analysis of alternative sets of currency portfolios is much more complex. For this reason, our analysis is based on individual currencies while remembering that recourse to a particular currency never implies the denomination of *all* one's assets and liabilities in that currency but merely the inclusion of the currency in a basket of other currencies.

Interest Rate Levels and Variability

Tables 11.1 and 11.2 show that over the period 1980–5 the interest rates of a number of countries showed a considerable degree of divergence. In fact, their average values ranged from a minimum of about 5.3 per cent for the Swiss franc to a maximum of about 19.6 per cent for the Italian lira and currencies could be grouped either as 'low interest rate' currencies (the yen, the Swiss franc, the deutschmark and the Dutch florin) or as 'high interest rate' currencies (the US dollar, the pound sterling, the French and Belgian franc, the Italian lira). The ECU interest rates could be considered in a middle position, because of the ECU's link with the weighted average of ECU component currencies rates, although closer to the second group of currencies. By breaking-down the period into two sub-periods it is, however, possible to observe that as various countries' inflation rates decreased and moved closer to each other, the range of interest rates significantly narrowed down too. While during the first sub-period average interest rates range from 6 to 23 per cent, during the more recent sub-period, they range between 4.4 and 15 per cent.

As far as interest rate variability is concerned, this can be measured by looking at both the standard deviation and variation coefficient. Reported data (see table 11.2) refer to both the period as a whole and its two sub-periods. However, because most currencies present a strong trend and we work on raw data, it seems more appropriate to look at the two sub-periods alone. In this way volatility measurements are less influenced by deviations of observed values from their mean induced by the trend effect and they can be more appropriately interpreted as an indicator for discrepancies between 'expected rate' and their observed *ex post* values.

By comparing the two sub-periods, two elements may be noticed. First of all, there has been a consistent decrease in interest rate volatility over time: during the period 1983–5 both the standard deviation and the coefficient of variation present lower values for all the ten currencies considered. Secondly, in spite of the fact that ranking the currencies by their interest rate variability leads to somewhat different results over time, depending on which variable we use as a measure for variability, the ECU consistently shows a very good ranking: its interest rate is the least volatile during the period 1980–3 and it is only slightly more variable that the yen interest rate (yen and deutschmark if we look at the standard deviation) during the period 1983–5.

The Exchange Rate Effect

Interest rate levels and volatility are very important; indeed, they would be the main variable to look at in the context of fixed (or somehow very stable) exchange rates. However, this has not been the case for more than a decade now, i.e. since the collapse of the Bretton Woods system. Since then the potential foreign exchange gain/loss from currency movements has had a dominant effect over total returns/costs of investment/borrowing transactions.

The predominance of exchange rates in determining both the level and the volatility of total return/cost can be seen from tables 11.3 to 11.12. For most

TABLE 11.1 Eurocurrencies one month interest rates (end-of-month, bid-offer average)

	US $	Yen	SFR	UKL	DM	FF	HFL	BFR	LIT	ECU
1980 – Jan.	14.25	8.00	4.81	18.19	8.31	12.25	11.25		21.37	14.81
Feb.	16.06	10.19	4.19	18.37	8.69	13.25	12.00		18.00	12.31
Mar.	20.25	14.62	6.31	18.62	9.31	13.62	10.75		15.75	12.03
Apr.	13.37	11.69	5.69	17.56	9.31	12.72	10.50		16.75	12.91
May	10.62	13.37	5.69	17.25	9.56	12.69	11.25		16.75	12.09
Jun.	9.62	13.44	5.72	17.59	9.59	12.50	10.62		36.50	12.91
Jul.	9.81	13.12	5.19	17.25	8.97	11.87	9.75		25.75	13.16
Aug.	11.50	11.62	6.06	17.00	8.75	12.00	10.66		25.50	13.22
Sep.	13.56	11.87	5.25	16.37	8.81	12.37	9.91		22.25	12.44
Oct.	13.00	10.25	4.19	17.31	8.87	11.75	9.22		19.50	12.25
Nov.	19.50	10.37	6.37	14.50	9.69	10.37	9.37	12.56	18.25	11.16
Dec.	19.06	7.87	4.94	14.91	9.12	10.31	9.12	12.00	16.75	11.47
1981 – Jan.	17.62	8.31	5.81	14.31	9.37	10.62	9.12	11.87	19.50	11.50
Feb.	16.75	8.69	8.81	13.94	15.00	13.00	11.00	12.81	17.50	14.09
Mar.	14.12	7.87	7.44	12.56	12.56	13.00	9.62	26.50	19.50	13.06
Apr.	17.87	6.81	9.19	12.50	12.19	13.56	10.87	16.75	19.00	13.28
May	18.06	7.25	9.62	12.09	12.31	22.62	12.16	16.62	23.00	15.56
Jun.	18.12	7.00	9.31	11.97	12.25	26.00	11.75	15.69	24.25	16.19
Jul.	20.12	6.81	8.62	14.37	12.06	22.00	13.75	26.00	29.50	16.50
Aug.	18.00	7.25	8.44	13.69	12.31	32.00	13.87	21.50	36.12	18.75
Sep.	16.62	7.25	10.75	16.37	12.00	36.00	12.87	27.00	39.12	18.69
Oct.	15.00	6.44	9.94	16.25	11.19	16.31	12.87	19.00	21.12	14.62
Nov.	11.75	7.50	9.31	15.25	10.62	16.12	11.19	16.12	21.56	13.56
Dec.	13.12	6.19	8.81	15.44	10.50	15.06	10.75	22.37	22.62	14.31

1982 – Jan.	14.25	6.12	8.25	14.50	10.06	15.12	10.00	17.00	22.37	13.44
Feb.	14.62	6.37	7.06	14.09	10.00	14.62	9.56	14.50	21.00	12.94
Mar.	15.50	6.87	4.62	13.56	9.22	30.00	8.31	17.00	32.25	16.06
Apr.	15.00	6.94	3.81	13.56	9.00	22.75	8.81	16.50	25.25	14.25
May	14.25	7.19	3.75	13.37	8.62	29.50	8.50	16.25	25.25	16.00
Jun.	15.37	7.31	4.06	13.00	8.94	15.50	8.75	16.75	22.06	12.31
Jul.	12.31	6.81	3.25	11.91	8.81	15.37	9.00	14.12	20.37	11.81
Aug.	10.87	7.25	3.25	11.06	8.19	20.00	7.94	13.87	22.06	13.12
Sep.	11.00	7.06	3.81	10.69	7.69	16.50	7.69	12.25	18.12	11.19
Oct.	9.69	6.75	3.06	10.00	7.06	19.50	6.62	12.87	21.56	11.56
Nov.	9.44	7.56	3.94	10.50	7.19	18.75	6.69	12.75	23.37	11.87
Dec.	9.12	6.69	2.87	10.62	5.87	23.00	5.25	16.50	33.75	12.69
1983 – Jan.	9.12	6.69	2.62	11.56	5.81	16.75	5.06	13.50	20.44	10.31
Feb.	8.69	6.87	3.00	11.44	5.44	23.25	4.50	13.37	21.00	11.06
Mar.	9.44	6.44	3.87	10.75	4.94	12.56	3.81	9.75	17.50	8.69
Apr.	8.87	6.19	4.44	10.37	4.94	12.37	5.94	10.25	14.69	8.44
May	9.12	6.37	4.87	10.31	5.00	12.37	5.81	9.75	15.06	8.37
Jun.	9.50	6.50	4.62	9.69	4.94	12.44	5.00	8.75	16.25	8.25
Jul.	9.87	6.56	4.75	9.62	4.94	12.75	5.50	8.69	15.62	8.19
Aug.	10.00	6.75	4.25	9.66	5.31	13.12	6.06	9.12	17.37	8.87
Sep.	9.37	6.69	3.75	9.69	5.62	12.62	6.00	9.50	17.00	8.81
Oct.	9.50	6.19	3.50	9.22	5.62	12.00	5.87	8.75	16.50	8.69
Nov.	9.75	7.44	4.06	9.09	6.22	12.25	6.06	10.75	16.37	8.94
Dec.	9.81	6.25	2.44	9.19	5.81	12.25	5.87	10.50	16.12	8.75

Table 11.1 continued on following page

TABLE 11.1　continued.

	US $	Yen	SFR	UKL	DM	FF	HFL	BFR	LIT	ECU
1984 – Jan.	9.56	6.12	3.19	9.22	5.75	12.25	6.37	10.75	16.87	9.16
Feb.	9.87	6.69	3.44	9.22	5.69	15.75	6.06	13.75	17.25	10.03
Mar.	10.50	6.25	3.50	8.81	5.56	12.87	6.06	12.25	16.37	9.34
Apr.	10.69	6.03	3.44	8.62	5.47	12.12	5.81	12.00	14.87	8.97
May	11.00	6.37	4.00	9.19	5.87	12.12	6.00	12.00	15.00	9.03
Jun.	11.81	6.06	4.31	8.91	5.62	12.00	5.94	11.50	15.25	9.09
Jul.	11.56	6.19	4.81	12.28	5.47	11.37	6.19	11.37	14.50	9.41
Aug.	11.81	6.37	4.50	10.97	5.37	11.00	6.12	11.25	14.00	9.09
Sep.	11.12	6.19	4.75	10.75	5.50	11.06	6.06	10.75	15.50	9.66
Oct.	9.81	6.22	4.94	10.69	5.62	10.56	5.81	10.62	15.37	9.56
Nov.	8.87	6.59	5.12	9.75	5.69	10.81	5.62	11.00	14.25	9.22
Dec.	8.44	6.16	4.56	9.62	5.56	10.81	5.75	10.75	14.00	9.28
1985 – Jan.	8.44	6.22	5.37	13.19	5.94	10.44	6.19	11.00	14.75	9.91
Feb.	8.87	6.53	5.69	14.06	5.87	10.69	6.75	10.62	14.37	9.97
Mar.	8.69	6.28	5.31	13.69	5.75	10.75	6.75	10.50	14.75	10.12
Apr.	8.37	6.19	5.00	12.81	5.75	10.37	7.06	9.37	12.25	9.50
May	7.62	6.37	5.19	12.69	5.56	10.19	7.12	9.00	13.25	9.37
Jun.	7.62	6.25	5.19	12.44	5.50	10.56	6.81	8.87	13.87	9.44
Jul.	8.09	6.31	4.44	11.56	4.75	14.25	6.12	11.00	11.25	9.00
Aug.	8.00	6.50	4.50	11.94	4.56	10.37	5.81	9.37	12.50	8.12

Abbreviations: SFR, Swiss franc; UKL, British pound sterling; FF, French franc; HFL, Holland (Dutch) florin; BFR, Belgian franc; LIT, Italian lira.
Source: *ECU Newsletter* based on *Financial Times* data.

TABLE 11.2 Eurocurrencies one month interest rates (end-of-month, bid-offer average)

	US $	Yen	SFR	UKL	DM	FF	HFL	BFR	LIT	ECU
Period: 01/1980–09/1985[a]										
Average value	12.104	7.523	5.289	12.670	7.757	14.967	8.108	13.407	19.552	11.510
Standard deviation	3.489	2.039	1.989	2.810	2.539	5.607	2.518	4.363	5.890	2.619
Variation coefficient	0.288	0.271	0.376	0.222	0.327	0.375	0.311	0.325	0.301	0.228
Min. value	7.625	6.031	2.437	8.625	4.562	10.187	3.812	8.687	11.250	8.125
Max. value	20.250	14.625	10.750	18.625	15.000	36.000	13.875	27.000	39.125	18.750
Period: 01/1980–02/1983[a]										
Average value	14.133	8.429	5.996	14.304	9.560	17.438	9.762	16.574	23.074	13.405
Standard deviation	3.377	2.350	2.348	2.476	2.014	6.419	2.205	4.305	5.669	1.976
Variation coefficient	0.239	0.279	0.392	0.173	0.211	0.368	0.226	0.260	0.246	0.147
Min. value	8.687	6.125	2.625	10.000	5.437	10.312	4.500	9.219	15.750	10.312
Max. value	20.250	14.625	10.750	18.625	15.000	36.000	13.875	27.000	39.125	18.750
Period: 03/1983–08/1985										
Average value	9.534	6.376	4.394	10.600	5.474	11.837	6.012	10.452	15.092	9.109
Standard deviation	1.152	0.272	0.739	1.569	0.383	1.236	0.602	1.188	1.523	0.533
Variation coefficient	0.121	0.043	0.168	0.148	0.070	0.104	0.100	0.114	0.101	0.059
Min. value	7.625	6.031	2.437	8.625	4.562	10.187	3.812	8.687	11.250	8.125
Max. value	11.812	7.437	5.687	14.062	6.219	15.750	7.125	13.750	17.500	10.125

[a] Data relative to the Belgian franc refer respectively to the periods 11/1980–08/1985 and 11/1980–02/1983.
Abbreviations as in table 11.1.
Source: ECU Newsletter based on *Financial Times* data.

TABLE 11.3 Total yield cost of one-month investment/indebtedness: base country – the United States

Currencies	Average			Standard deviation			Variation coefficient		
	Interest rate	Exch.rate return/loss[a]	Total yield/cost	Interest rate	Exch.rate return/loss	Total yield/cost	Interest rate	Exch.rate return/loss	Total yield/cost
Period: 2/80–9/85									
Euro-$	12.104	.000	12.104	3.489	.000	3.489	.288	.000	.288
Euro-Yen	7.523	2.512	10.066	2.039	44.223	44.945	.271	17.606	4.465
Euro-SFR	5.289	-4.356	.928	1.989	46.917	47.539	.376	10.771	51.227
Euro-UKL	12.670	-7.693	4.919	2.810	43.631	44.823	.222	5.671	9.113
Euro-DM	7.757	-6.853	.854	2.539	42.210	42.388	.327	6.159	49.625
Euro-FF	14.967	-11.467	3.348	5.607	42.900	43.532	.375	3.741	13.004
Euro-HFL	8.108	-7.227	.834	2.518	41.824	42.250	.311	5.787	50.675
Euro-BFR[b]	13.407	-10.802	2.470	4.363	43.141	43.440	.325	3.994	17.584
Euro-LIT	19.552	-13.617	5.715	5.890	35.359	36.413	.301	2.597	6.372
ECU	11.510	-9.046	2.375	2.619	39.394	39.793	.228	4.355	16.753
Period: 2/80–3/83									
Euro-$	14.133	.000	14.133	3.377	.000	3.377	.239	.000	.239
Euro-Yen	8.429	1.042	9.505	2.350	51.028	52.054	.279	48.983	5.476
Euro-SFR	5.996	-6.882	-.898	2.348	47.015	47.909	.392	6.831	53.357
Euro-UKL	14.304	-12.911	1.272	2.476	35.363	36.961	.173	2.739	29.059
Euro-DM	9.560	-9.818	-.337	2.014	39.689	40.047	.211	4.042	118.937

Euro-FF	17.438	-17.498	-.298	6.419	40.974	42.563	.368	2.342	142.591
Euro-HFL	9.762	-10.482	-.799	2.205	38.497	39.110	.226	3.673	48.973
Euro-BFRᵇ	16.574	-18.182	-1.843	4.305	39.511	40.786	.260	2.173	22.129
Euro-LIT	23.074	-17.692	5.076	5.669	35.597	37.770	.246	2.012	7.441
ECU	13.405	-13.266	.000	1.976	35.631	36.376	.147	2.686	172952.200
Period: 4/83–9/85									
Euro-$	9.534	.000	9.534	1.152	.000	1.152	.121	.000	.121
Euro-Yen	6.376	4.374	10.775	.272	35.591	33.849	.043	7.680	3.141
Euro-SFR	4.394	-1.155	3.241	.739	46.595	46.965	.168	40.328	14.491
Euro-UKL	10.600	-1.084	9.538	1.569	51.505	52.777	.148	47.500	5.533
Euro-DM	5.474	-3.097	2.363	.383	44.922	45.135	.070	14.504	19.104
Euro-FF	11.837	-3.827	7.966	1.236	44.053	44.301	.104	11.511	5.561
Euro-HFL	6.012	-3.105	2.901	.602	45.357	45.838	.100	14.610	15.798
Euro-BFRᵇ	10.452	-3.914	6.496	1.188	45.198	45.410	.114	11.547	6.990
Euro-LIT	15.092	-8.454	6.524	1.523	34.362	34.602	.101	4.065	5.304
ECU	9.109	-3.701	5.384	.533	43.108	43.554	.059	11.648	8.089

[a] -/+ indicate exchange rate appreciation/depreciation of the base country's currency.
[b] Belgian franc data refer respectively to the following periods: 12/80–9/85, 12/80–3/83, 4/83–9/85.
Methodological note: see Appendix.
Abbreviations as in table 11.1.
Source: ECU Newsletter.

TABLE 11.4   Total yield cost of one-month investment/indebtedness: base country – Japan

Currencies	Average			Standard deviation			Variation coefficient		
	Interest rate	Exch.rate return/ loss[a]	Total yield/ cost	Interest rate	Exch.rate return/ loss	Total yield/ cost	Interest rate	Exch.rate return/ loss	Total yield/ cost
Period: 2/80–9/85									
Euro-$	12.104	-.921	11.186	3.489	43.167	44.102	.288	46.863	3.942
Euro-Yen	7.523	.000	7.523	2.039	.000	2.039	.271	.000	.271
Euro-SFR	5.289	-6.251	-.971	1.989	41.203	42.010	.376	6.591	43.254
Euro-UKL	12.670	-9.283	3.303	2.810	45.730	46.671	.222	4.926	14.130
Euro-DM	7.757	-8.612	-.904	2.539	40.125	40.676	.327	4.659	44.993
Euro-FF	14.967	-13.283	1.526	5.607	39.153	40.266	.375	2.948	26.394
Euro-HFL	8.108	-8.965	-.912	2.518	40.343	40.906	.311	4.500	44.852
Euro-BFR[b]	13.407	-10.911	2.384	4.363	39.685	40.689	.325	3.637	17.067
Euro-LIT	19.552	-15.271	4.055	5.890	36.362	38.185	.301	2.381	9.417
ECU	11.510	-10.776	.641	2.619	38.009	38.795	.228	3.527	60.536
Period: 2/80–3/83									
Euro-$	14.133	1.080	15.232	3.377	49.976	50.813	.239	46.282	3.336
Euro-Yen	8.429	.000	8.429	2.350	.000	2.350	.279	.000	.279
Euro-SFR	5.996	-6.763	-.770	2.348	49.090	50.163	.392	7.259	65.126
Euro-UKL	14.304	-12.508	1.670	2.476	45.993	47.160	.173	3.677	28.235
Euro-DM	9.560	-9.569	-.073	2.014	45.672	46.497	.211	4.782	638.737

Euro-FF	17.438	-17.364	-.142	6.419	44.216	46.274	.368	2.546	325.668
Euro-HFL	9.762	-10.189	-.501	2.205	45.932	46.633	.226	4.508	93.144
Euro-BFR[b]	16.574	-13.806	2.611	4.305	46.252	47.981	.260	3.350	18.377
Euro-LIT	23.074	-17.435	5.362	5.669	42.531	45.311	.246	2.439	8.450
ECU	13.405	-13.012	.271	1.976	42.499	43.669	.147	3.266	160.847
Period: 4/83–9/85									
Euro-$	9.534	-3.456	6.062	1.152	32.381	33.032	.121	9.371	5.449
Euro-Yen	6.376	.000	6.376	.272	.000	.272	.043	.000	.043
Euro-SFR	4.394	-5.604	-1.226	.739	28.196	28.510	.168	5.032	23.258
Euro-UKL	10.600	-5.199	5.371	1.569	45.065	45.962	.148	8.668	8.557
Euro-DM	5.474	-7.400	-1.957	.383	31.531	31.777	.070	4.261	16.238
Euro-FF	11.837	-8.113	3.638	1.236	30.829	30.901	.104	3.800	8.494
Euro-HFL	6.012	-7.414	-1.433	.602	31.821	32.214	.100	4.292	22.479
Euro-BFR[b]	10.452	-8.208	2.172	1.188	32.142	32.427	.114	3.916	14.930
Euro-LIT	15.092	-12.530	2.399	1.523	26.310	26.450	.101	2.100	11.025
ECU	9.109	-7.944	1.109	.533	31.185	31.552	.059	3.926	28.458

[a] −/+ indicate exchange rate appreciation/depreciation of the base country's currency.
[b] Belgian franc data refer respectively to the following periods: 12/80–9/85, 12/80–3/83, 4/83–9/85.
Methodological note: see Appendix.
Abbreviations as in table 11.1.
Source: ECU Newsletter.

TABLE 11.5   Total yield cost of one-month investment/indebtedness: base country – Switzerland

Currencies	Average			Standard deviation			Variation coefficient		
	Interest rate	Exch.rate return/loss[a]	Total yield/cost	Interest rate	Exch.rate return/loss	Total yield/cost	Interest rate	Exch.rate return/loss	Total yield/cost
Period: 2/80–9/85									
Euro-$	12.104	6.171	18.348	3.489	45.933	46.848	.288	7.443	2.553
Euro-Yen	7.523	7.709	15.290	2.039	41.356	41.951	.271	5.364	2.744
Euro-SFR	5.289	.000	5.289	1.989	.000	1.989	.376	.000	.376
Euro-UKL	12.670	-2.603	10.054	2.810	38.430	39.415	.222	14.762	3.920
Euro-DM	7.757	-2.175	5.562	2.539	20.109	20.003	.327	9.246	3.597
Euro-FF	14.967	-6.758	8.085	5.607	24.239	23.284	.375	3.587	2.880
Euro-HFL	8.108	-2.554	5.531	2.518	18.993	18.942	.311	7.436	3.425
Euro-BFR[b]	13.407	-6.544	6.775	4.363	25.098	25.072	.325	3.835	3.701
Euro-LIT	19.552	-8.654	10.740	5.890	25.156	25.456	.301	2.907	2.370
ECU	11.510	-4.268	7.193	2.619	20.792	20.693	.228	4.871	2.877
Period: 2/80–3/83									
Euro-$	14.133	8.754	22.986	3.377	46.568	47.237	.239	5.319	2.055
Euro-Yen	8.429	8.832	17.337	2.350	49.446	50.186	.279	5.598	2.895
Euro-SFR	5.996	.000	5.996	2.348	.000	2.348	.392	.000	.392
Euro-UKL	14.304	-4.857	9.420	2.476	44.160	45.550	.173	9.093	4.836
Euro-DM	9.560	-2.947	7.030	2.014	22.228	21.830	.211	8.901	3.105

Euro-FF	17.438	−10.141	7.093	6.419	28.420	27.304	.368	2.802	3.849
Euro-HFL	9.762	−3.146	6.580	2.205	21.096	20.843	.226	6.705	3.168
Euro-BFR[b]	16.574	−10.766	5.642	4.305	31.286	31.401	.260	2.906	5.565
Euro-LIT	23.074	−10.186	12.670	5.669	27.193	27.409	.246	2.670	2.163
ECU	13.405	−5.806	7.525	1.976	23.849	23.703	.147	4.108	3.150
Period: 4/83−9/85									
Euro-$	9.534	2.899	12.472	1.152	44.902	45.680	.121	15.490	3.663
Euro-Yen	6.376	6.287	12.698	.272	27.860	28.050	.043	4.431	2.209
Euro-SFR	4.394	.000	4.394	.739	.000	.739	.168	.000	.168
Euro-UKL	10.600	.251	10.858	1.569	29.373	29.870	.148	117.002	2.751
Euro-DM	5.474	−1.766	3.701	.383	17.041	17.236	.070	9.647	4.657
Euro-FF	11.837	−2.472	9.341	1.236	16.604	16.784	.104	6.718	1.797
Euro-HFL	6.012	−1.804	4.201	.602	15.905	16.118	.100	8.816	3.837
Euro-BFR[b]	10.452	−2.603	7.832	1.188	16.495	17.109	.114	6.337	2.184
Euro-LIT	15.092	−6.712	8.295	1.523	22.159	22.506	.101	3.301	2.713
ECU	9.109	−2.321	6.772	.533	15.895	16.081	.059	6.849	2.375

[a] −/+ indicate exchange rate appreciation/depreciation of the base country's currency.
[b] Belgian franc data refer respectively to the following periods: 12/80–9/85, 12/80–3/83, 4/83–9/85.
Methodological note: see Appendix.
Abbreviations as in table 11.1.
Source: ECU Newsletter.

TABLE 11.6 Total yield cost of one-month investment/indebtedness: base country – Britain

Currencies	Average			Standard deviation			Variation coefficient		
	Interest rate	Exch.rate return/loss[a]	Total yield/cost	Interest rate	Exch.rate return/loss	Total yield/cost	Interest rate	Exch.rate return/loss	Total yield/cost
Period: 2/80–9/85									
Euro-$	12.104	9.289	21.503	3.489	42.332	43.343	.288	4.557	2.016
Euro-Yen	7.523	11.149	18.746	2.039	46.789	47.219	.271	4.197	2.519
Euro-SFR	5.289	3.862	9.179	1.989	39.093	39.674	.376	10.123	4.322
Euro-UKL	12.670	.000	12.670	2.810	.000	2.810	.222	.000	.222
Euro-DM	7.757	1.424	9.192	2.539	35.968	36.362	.327	25.267	3.956
Euro-FF	14.967	-3.262	11.684	5.607	35.576	37.184	.375	10.905	3.182
Euro-HFL	8.108	.979	9.094	2.518	33.061	33.421	.311	33.778	3.675
Euro-BFR[b]	13.407	-.322	13.092	4.363	35.619	36.632	.325	110.647	2.798
Euro-LIT	19.552	-5.163	14.330	5.890	36.205	38.080	.301	7.012	2.657
ECU	11.510	-.872	10.635	2.619	29.195	29.801	.228	33.473	2.802
Period: 2/80–3/83									
Euro-$	14.133	14.123	38.420	3.377	36.026	36.548	.239	2.551	1.286
Euro-Yen	8.429	14.497	23.028	2.350	48.056	46.416	.279	3.315	2.102
Euro-SFR	5.996	6.543	12.589	2.348	45.182	45.928	.392	6.905	3.648
Euro-UKL	14.304	.000	14.304	2.476	.000	2.476	.173	.000	.173
Euro-DM	9.560	3.633	13.218	2.014	39.334	39.580	.211	10.827	2.994

Euro-FF	17.438	−4.189	13.224	6.419	39.120	41.355	.368	9.338	3.127
Euro-HFL	9.762	2.870	12.649	2.205	35.025	35.161	.226	12.202	2.780
Euro-BFR[b]	16.574	1.701	18.300	4.305	40.097	40.929	.260	23.574	2.236
Euro-LIT	23.074	−4.245	18.788	5.669	37.906	40.299	.246	8.930	2.145
ECU	13.405	.040	13.452	1.976	31.286	31.918	.147	779.758	2.373
Period: 4/83−9/85									
Euro-$	9.534	3.165	12.741	1.152	48.484	49.283	.121	15.320	3.868
Euro-Yen	6.376	6.907	13.322	.272	44.777	45.077	.043	6.482	3.384
Euro-SFR	4.394	.465	4.860	.739	29.284	29.367	.168	62.932	6.043
Euro-UKL	10.600	.000	10.600	1.569	.000	1.569	.148	.000	.148
Euro-DM	5.474	−1.375	4.092	.383	30.961	31.081	.070	22.515	7.595
Euro-FF	11.837	−2.088	9.734	1.236	30.459	30.999	.104	14.590	3.185
Euro-HFL	6.012	−1.417	4.591	.602	30.223	30.488	.100	21.325	6.641
Euro-BFR[b]	10.452	−2.210	8.231	1.188	30.740	31.335	.114	13.910	3.807
Euro-LIT	15.092	−6.327	8.682	1.523	33.892	34.245	.101	5.357	3.944
ECU	9.109	−2.028	7.066	.533	26.262	26.454	.059	12.951	3.744

[a] −/+ indicate exchange rate appreciation/depreciation of the base country's currency.
[b] Belgian franc data refer respectively to the following periods: 12/80−9/85, 12/80−3/83, 4/83−9/85.
Methodological note: see Appendix.
Abbreviations as in table 11.1.
Source: ECU Newsletter.

TABLE 11.7 Total yield cost of one-month investment/indebtedness: base country – Germany

Currencies	Average			Standard deviation			Variation coefficient		
	Interest rate	Exch.rate return/ loss[a]	Total yield/ cost	Interest rate	Exch.rate return/ loss	Total yield/ cost	Interest rate	Exch.rate return/ loss	Total yield/ cost
Period: 2/80–9/85									
Euro-$	12.104	8.375	20.580	3.489	41.972	43.016	.288	5.012	2.090
Euro-Yen	7.523	10.047	17.646	2.039	40.801	41.502	.271	4.061	2.352
Euro-SFR	5.289	2.516	7.828	1.989	20.105	20.994	.376	7.990	2.682
Euro-UKL	12.670	-.341	12.346	2.810	36.149	37.320	.222	106.044	3.023
Euro-DM	7.757	.000	7.757	2.539	.000	2.539	.327	.000	.327
Euro-FF	14.967	-4.578	10.297	5.607	14.872	13.200	.375	3.249	1.282
Euro-HFL	8.108	-.344	7.764	2.518	6.543	7.504	.311	19.006	.967
Euro-BFR[b]	13.407	-4.720	8.627	4.363	13.663	13.846	.325	2.895	1.605
Euro-LIT	19.552	-6.508	12.930	5.890	14.162	14.841	.301	2.176	1.148
ECU	11.510	-2.082	9.404	2.619	6.288	8.182	.228	3.981	.870
Period: 2/80–3/83									
Euro-$	14.133	11.246	25.517	3.377	40.443	41.285	.239	3.596	1.618
Euro-Yen	8.429	11.452	19.981	2.350	47.039	47.927	.279	4.107	2.399
Euro-SFR	5.996	2.917	8.946	2.348	22.309	23.543	.392	7.649	2.632
Euro-UKL	14.304	-2.340	11.970	2.476	39.273	40.836	.173	16.781	3.412
Euro-DM	9.560	.000	9.560	2.014	.000	2.014	.211	.000	.211

Euro-FF	17.438	−7.642	9.637	6.419	19.178	17.453	.368	2.510	1.811
Euro-HFL	9.762	−.601	9.161	2.205	8.391	9.473	.226	13.963	1.034
Euro-BFR[b]	16.574	−8.898	7.556	4.305	18.064	19.047	.260	2.030	2.521
Euro-LIT	23.074	−7.727	15.190	5.669	14.467	15.135	.246	1.872	.996
ECU	13.405	−3.306	10.057	1.976	9.901	9.839	.147	2.993	.978
Period: 4/83−9/85									
Euro-$	9.534	4.739	14.326	1.152	43.562	44.332	.121	9.193	3.095
Euro-Yen	6.376	8.266	14.688	.272	31.065	31.289	.043	3.758	2.130
Euro-SFR	4.394	2.009	6.413	.739	16.893	17.126	.168	8.408	2.671
Euro-UKL	10.600	2.192	12.822	1.569	31.573	32.314	.148	14.406	2.520
Euro-DM	5.474	.000	5.474	.383	.000	.383	.070	.000	.070
Euro-FF	11.837	−.697	11.132	1.236	2.915	2.801	.104	4.181	.252
Euro-HFL	6.012	−.019	5.993	.602	2.769	2.893	.100	144.905	.483
Euro-BFR[b]	10.452	−.820	9.626	1.188	4.986	5.476	.114	6.078	.569
Euro-LIT	15.092	−4.964	10.066	1.523	13.610	13.943	.101	2.742	1.385
ECU	9.109	−.529	8.577	.533	5.215	5.280	.059	9.867	.616

[a] −/+ indicate exchange rate appreciation/depreciation of the base country's currency.
[b] Belgian franc data refer respectively to the following periods: 12/80−9/85, 12/80−3/83, 4/83−9/85.
Methodological note: see Appendix.
Abbreviations as in table 11.1.
Source: *ECU Newsletter.*

TABLE 11.8 Total yield cost of one-month investment/indebtedness: base country – France

Currencies	Average			Standard deviation			Variation coefficient		
	Interest rate	Exch.rate return/loss[a]	Total yield/cost	Interest rate	Exch.rate return/loss	Total yield/cost	Interest rate	Exch.rate return/loss	Total yield/cost
Period: 2/80–9/85									
Euro-$	12.104	13.134	25.393	3.489	43.220	44.402	.288	3.291	1.749
Euro-Yen	7.523	14.740	22.367	2.039	39.718	40.347	.271	2.695	1.804
Euro-SFR	5.289	7.304	12.638	1.989	25.008	25.876	.376	3.424	2.047
Euro-UKL	12.670	4.342	17.080	2.810	36.054	37.284	.222	8.304	2.183
Euro-DM	7.757	4.789	12.582	2.539	15.583	16.232	.327	3.254	1.290
Euro-FF	14.967	.000	14.967	5.607	.000	5.607	.375	.000	.375
Euro-HFL	8.108	4.416	12.558	2.516	14.834	15.515	.311	3.359	1.235
Euro-BFR[b]	13.407	.977	14.405	4.363	17.741	19.154	.325	18.157	1.330
Euro-LIT	19.552	-1.838	17.698	5.898	14.704	17.001	.301	8.002	.961
ECU	11.510	2.633	14.174	2.619	12.156	13.170	.228	4.617	.929
Period: 2/80–3/83									
Euro-$	14.133	19.231	33.594	3.377	42.607	43.357	.239	2.216	1.291
Euro-Yen	8.429	19.307	27.881	2.350	45.189	45.816	.279	2.341	1.643
Euro-SFR	5.996	10.933	17.002	2.348	29.547	30.550	.392	2.703	1.797
Euro-UKL	14.304	5.495	19.893	2.476	39.499	40.886	.173	7.189	2.055
Euro-DM	9.560	8.014	17.635	2.014	20.104	20.165	.211	2.509	1.143

Euro-FF	17.438	.000	17.438	6.419	.000	6.419	.368	.000	.368
Euro-HFL	9.762	7.363	17.183	2.205	19.072	19.269	.226	2.590	1.121
Euro-BFR[b]	16.574	2.155	18.773	4.305	25.104	26.465	.260	11.648	1.410
Euro-LIT	23.074	.085	23.169	5.669	15.684	17.533	.246	183.701	.757
ECU	13.405	4.576	18.037	1.976	15.421	16.084	.147	3.370	.892
Period: 4/83–9/85									
Euro-$	9.534	5.412	15.005	1.152	42.754	43.528	.121	7.900	2.901
Euro-Yen	6.376	8.956	15.382	.272	30.485	30.720	.043	3.404	1.997
Euro-SFR	4.394	2.706	7.112	.739	16.550	16.759	.168	6.116	2.357
Euro-UKL	10.600	2.881	13.517	1.569	31.086	31.791	.148	10.789	2.352
Euro-DM	5.474	.705	6.182	.383	2.932	2.981	.070	4.160	.482
Euro-FF	11.837	.000	11.837	1.236	.000	1.236	.104	.000	.104
Euro-HFL	6.012	.684	6.700	.602	3.627	3.729	.100	5.300	.557
Euro-BFR[b]	10.452	-.123	10.329	1.188	4.215	4.600	.114	34.363	.445
Euro-LIT	15.092	-4.273	10.767	1.523	12.957	13.408	.101	3.032	1.245
ECU	9.109	.171	9.281	.533	4.778	4.759	.059	28.022	.513

[a] −/+ indicate exchange rate appreciation/depreciation of the base country's currency.
[b] Belgian franc data refer respectively to the following periods: 12/80–9/85, 12/80–3/83, 4/83–9/85.
Methodological note: see Appendix.
Abbreviations as in table 11.1.
Source: ECU Newsletter.

TABLE 11.9 Total yield cost of one-month investment/indebtedness: base country – the Netherlands

Currencies	Average			Standard deviation			Variation coefficient		
	Interest rate	Exch.rate return/loss[a]	Total yield/cost	Interest rate	Exch.rate return/loss	Total yield/cost	Interest rate	Exch.rate return/loss	Total yield/cost
Period: 2/80–9/85									
Euro-$	12.104	8.725	20.934	3.489	41.533	42.600	.288	4.760	2.035
Euro-Yen	7.523	10.418	18.018	2.039	40.947	41.622	.271	3.931	2.310
Euro-SFR	5.289	2.862	8.174	1.989	19.054	19.916	.376	6.658	2.436
Euro-UKL	12.670	-.060	12.627	2.810	33.381	34.500	.222	556.770	2.732
Euro-DM	7.757	.380	8.139	2.539	6.590	6.957	.327	17.329	.855
Euro-FF	14.967	-4.226	10.653	5.607	14.152	12.337	.375	3.349	1.158
Euro-HFL	8.108	.000	8.108	2.518	.000	2.518	.311	.000	.311
Euro-BFR[b]	13.407	-3.926	9.427	4.363	13.798	13.788	.325	3.514	1.463
Euro-LIT	19.552	-6.144	13.296	5.890	14.426	14.830	.301	2.348	1.115
ECU	11.510	-1.730	9.758	2.619	6.745	6.282	.228	3.899	.644
Period: 2/80–3/83									
Euro-$	14.133	11.844	26.122	3.377	39.275	40.125	.239	3.316	1.536
Euro-Yen	8.429	12.092	20.624	2.350	47.093	47.928	.279	3.895	2.324
Euro-SFR	5.996	3.529	9.560	2.348	21.265	22.444	.392	6.025	2.348
Euro-UKL	14.304	-1.839	12.473	2.476	35.234	36.740	.173	19.162	2.945
Euro-DM	9.560	.660	10.223	2.014	8.455	8.384	.211	12.804	.820

Euro-FF	17.438	−7.031	10.254	6.419	18.172	16.181	.368	2.584	1.578
Euro-HFL	9.762	.000	9.762	2.205	.000	2.205	.226	.000	.226
Euro-BFR[b]	16.574	−7.277	9.190	4.305	18.633	19.109	.260	2.561	2.069
Euro-LIT	23.074	−7.100	15.821	5.669	14.464	14.473	.246	2.037	.915
ECU	13.405	−2.695	10.673	1.976	7.707	6.951	.147	2.860	.651

Period: 4/83−9/85

Euro-$	9.534	4.775	14.363	1.152	43.912	44.686	.121	9.197	3.111
Euro-Yen	6.376	8.296	14.718	.272	31.356	31.585	.043	3.779	2.146
Euro-SFR	4.394	2.016	6.419	.739	15.774	15.982	.168	7.824	2.490
Euro-UKL	10.600	2.193	12.823	1.569	30.726	31.434	.148	14.010	2.451
Euro-DM	5.474	.025	5.500	.383	2.768	2.866	.070	108.562	.521
Euro-FF	11.837	−.673	11.157	1.236	3.617	3.592	.104	5.375	.322
Euro-HFL	6.012	.000	6.012	.602	.000	.602	.100	.000	.100
Euro-BFR[b]	10.452	−.799	9.648	1.188	4.875	5.465	.114	6.105	.566
Euro-LIT	15.092	−4.934	10.097	1.523	14.287	14.658	.101	2.896	1.452
ECU	9.109	−.507	8.598	.533	5.022	5.082	.059	9.904	.591

[a] −/+ indicate exchange rate appreciation/depreciation of the base country's currency.
[b] Belgian franc data refer respectively to the following periods: 12/80−9/85, 12/80−3/83, 4/83−9/85.
Methodological note: see Appendix.
Abbreviations as in table 11.1.
Source: ECU Newsletter.

TABLE 11.10 Total yield cost of one-month investment/indebtedness: base country – Italy

Currencies	Average			Standard deviation			Variation coefficient		
	Interest rate	Exch.rate return/loss[a]	Total yield/cost	Interest rate	Exch.rate return/loss	Total yield/cost	Interest rate	Exch.rate return/loss	Total yield/cost
Period: 2/80 – 9/85									
Euro-$	12.104	14.845	27.119	3.489	36.016	37.233	.288	2.426	1.373
Euro-Yen	7.523	16.616	24.255	2.039	37.428	38.133	.271	2.253	1.572
Euro-SFR	5.289	9.269	14.616	1.989	26.180	27.180	.376	2.825	1.860
Euro-UKL	12.670	6.302	19.063	2.810	36.862	38.179	.222	5.849	2.003
Euro-DM	7.757	6.717	14.523	2.539	14.642	15.369	.327	2.180	1.058
Euro-FF	14.967	2.021	16.997	5.607	14.764	14.638	.375	7.304	.861
Euro-HFL	8.108	6.357	14.514	2.518	15.003	15.848	.311	2.360	1.092
Euro-BFR[b]	13.407	2.604	16.041	4.363	18.292	19.042	.325	7.024	1.187
Euro-LIT	19.552	.000	19.552	5.890	.000	5.890	.301	.000	.301
ECU	11.510	4.575	16.131	2.619	12.816	13.434	.228	2.802	.833
Period: 2/80 – 3/83									
Euro-$	14.133	19.059	33.427	3.377	36.658	37.614	.239	1.923	1.125
Euro-Yen	8.429	19.272	27.853	2.350	43.967	44.789	.279	2.281	1.608
Euro-SFR	5.996	10.920	16.995	2.348	28.299	29.625	.392	2.592	1.743
Euro-UKL	14.304	5.470	19.873	2.476	38.207	39.773	.173	6.985	2.001
Euro-DM	9.560	7.958	17.585	2.014	14.914	15.541	.211	1.874	.884

Euro-FF	17.438	.116	17.538	6.419	15.445	15.578	.368	132.685	.888
Euro-HFL	9.762	7.324	17.152	2.205	15.023	15.860	.226	2.051	.925
Euro-BFR[b]	16.574	.776	17.372	4.305	21.777	23.154	.260	28.069	1.333
Euro-LIT	23.074	.000	23.074	5.669	.000	5.669	.246	.000	.246
ECU	13.405	4.558	18.018	1.976	12.317	12.960	.147	2.702	.719
Period: 4/83–9/85								
Euro-$	9.534	9.508	19.129	1.152	34.454	35.158	.121	3.624	1.838
Euro-Yen	6.376	13.251	19.699	.272	26.578	26.793	.043	2.006	1.360
Euro-SFR	4.394	7.178	11.602	.739	23.052	23.379	.168	3.211	2.015
Euro-UKL	10.600	7.355	18.038	1.569	35.055	36.032	.148	4.766	1.998
Euro-DM	5.474	5.146	10.644	.383	14.134	14.231	.070	2.747	1.337
Euro-FF	11.837	4.435	16.312	1.236	13.472	13.321	.104	3.038	.817
Euro-HFL	6.012	5.132	11.173	.602	14.888	15.189	.100	2.901	1.359
Euro-BFR[b]	10.452	4.311	14.798	1.188	14.079	14.053	.114	3.266	.950
Euro-LIT	15.092	.000	15.092	1.523	.000	1.523	.101	.000	.101
ECU	9.109	4.596	13.741	.533	13.422	13.641	.059	2.920	.993

[a] −/+ indicate exchange rate appreciation/depreciation of the base country's currency.
[b] Belgian franc data refer respectively to the following periods: 12/80–9/85, 12/80–3/83, 4/83–9/85.
Methodological note: see Appendix.
Abbreviations as in table 11.1.
Source: ECU Newsletter.

TABLE 11.11 Total yield cost of one-month investment/indebtedness: base country – Belgium

Currencies	Average			Standard deviation			Variation coefficient		
	Interest rate	Exch.rate return/loss[a]	Total yield/cost	Interest rate	Exch.rate return/loss	Total yield/cost	Interest rate	Exch.rate return/loss	Total yield/cost
Period: 2/80–9/85									
Euro-$	12.104	12.386	24.636	3.489	43.753	44.916	.288	3.532	1.823
Euro-Yen	7.523	14.027	21.648	2.039	41.487	42.096	.271	2.958	1.945
Euro-SFR	5.289	6.528	11.863	1.989	24.485	25.564	.376	3.751	2.155
Euro-UKL	12.670	3.578	16.308	2.810	36.063	37.308	.222	10.080	2.288
Euro-DM	7.757	4.002	11.791	2.539	13.671	14.458	.327	3.416	1.226
Euro-FF	14.967	-.642	14.292	5.607	16.943	16.334	.375	26.376	1.143
Euro-HFL	8.108	3.638	11.777	2.518	13.624	14.499	.311	3.745	1.231
Euro-BFR[b]	13.407	.000	13.407	4.363	.000	4.363	.325	.000	.325
Euro-LIT	19.552	-2.560	16.953	5.890	17.580	18.968	.301	6.866	1.119
ECU	11.510	1.872	13.401	2.619	12.380	12.911	.228	6.615	.963
Period: 2/80–3/83									
Euro-$	14.133	17.755	32.102	3.377	42.876	43.702	.239	2.415	1.361
Euro-Yen	8.429	17.899	26.464	2.350	47.424	48.056	.279	2.649	1.816
Euro-SFR	5.996	9.443	15.513	2.348	28.998	30.348	.392	3.071	1.956
Euro-UKL	14.304	4.018	18.401	2.476	39.341	40.822	.173	9.791	2.218
Euro-DM	9.560	6.496	16.110	2.014	17.342	17.674	.211	2.669	1.097

Euro-FF	17.438	-1.258	16.120	6.419	22.336	21.317	.368	17.756	1.322
Euro-HFL	9.762	5.864	15.678	2.205	17.383	17.964	.226	2.964	1.146
Euro-BFR[b]	16.574	.000	16.574	4.305	.000	4.305	.260	.000	.260
Euro-LIT	23.074	-1.316	21.728	5.669	20.099	20.932	.246	15.276	.963
ECU	13.405	3.108	16.546	1.976	15.555	15.736	.147	5.005	.951
Period: 4/83–9/85									
Euro-$	9.534	5.585	15.178	1.152	43.908	44.649	.121	7.862	2.942
Euro-Yen	6.376	9.121	15.547	.272	31.773	32.013	.043	3.483	2.059
Euro-SFR	4.394	2.835	7.241	.739	16.412	16.630	.168	5.790	2.297
Euro-UKL	10.600	3.020	13.656	1.569	31.416	32.119	.148	10.404	2.352
Euro-DM	5.474	.842	6.319	.383	4.977	4.954	.070	5.914	.784
Euro-FF	11.837	.137	11.976	1.236	4.199	4.417	.104	30.558	.369
Euro-HFL	6.012	.819	6.835	.602	4.876	4.902	.100	5.955	.717
Euro-BFR[b]	10.452	.000	10.452	1.188	.000	1.188	.114	.000	.114
Euro-LIT	15.092	-4.137	10.904	1.523	13.579	13.966	.101	3.282	1.281
ECU	9.109	.306	9.417	.533	6.047	5.983	.059	19.743	.635

[a] −/+ indicate exchange rate appreciation/depreciation of the base country's currency.
[b] Belgian franc data refer respectively to the following periods: 12/80–9/85, 12/80–3/83, 4/83–9/85.
Methodological note: see Appendix.
Abbreviations as in table 11.1.
Source: ECU Newsletter.

TABLE 11.12 Total yield cost of one-month investment/indebtedness: base country – Denmark

Currencies	Average			Standard deviation			Variation coefficient		
	Interest rate	Exch.rate return/loss[a]	Total yield/cost	Interest rate	Exch.rate return/loss	Total yield/cost	Interest rate	Exch.rate return/loss	Total yield/cost
Period: 2/80–9/85									
Euro-$	12.104	11.050	23.285	3.489	41.467	42.624	.288	3.753	1.830
Euro-Yen	7.523	12.688	20.302	2.039	39.127	39.776	.271	3.084	1.959
Euro-SFR	5.289	5.222	10.549	1.989	21.505	22.535	.376	4.118	2.136
Euro-UKL	12.670	2.315	15.031	2.810	35.540	36.760	.222	15.351	2.446
Euro-DM	7.757	2.703	10.481	2.539	7.853	8.810	.327	2.906	.841
Euro-FF	14.967	-1.930	12.987	5.607	13.370	12.379	.375	6.928	.953
Euro-HFL	8.108	2.348	10.476	2.518	8.962	10.007	.311	3.818	.955
Euro-BFR[b]	13.407	-1.246	12.146	4.363	10.444	11.363	.325	8.381	.936
Euro-LIT	19.552	-3.859	15.628	5.890	12.972	14.226	.301	3.361	.910
ECU	11.510	.590	12.105	2.619	8.189	8.618	.228	13.880	.712
Period: 2/80–3/83									
Euro-$	14.133	15.294	29.616	3.377	40.344	41.272	.239	2.638	1.394
Euro-Yen	8.429	15.406	23.956	2.350	44.398	45.147	.279	2.882	1.885
Euro-SFR	5.996	6.978	13.032	2.348	24.161	25.545	.392	3.462	1.960
Euro-UKL	14.304	1.637	15.993	2.476	38.347	39.866	.173	23.420	2.493
Euro-DM	9.560	4.053	13.647	2.014	9.133	9.678	.211	2.254	.709

Euro-FF	17.438	-3.682	13.664	6.419	17.152	15.849	.366	4.659	1.160
Euro-HFL	9.762	3.436	13.231	2.205	10.973	11.852	.226	3.194	.896
Euro-BFR[b]	16.574	-2.756	13.785	4.305	13.681	14.958	.260	4.964	1.085
Euro-LIT	23.074	-3.754	19.241	5.669	12.792	13.660	.246	3.407	.710
ECU	13.405	.695	14.107	1.976	9.371	9.557	.147	13.489	.677

Period: 4/83–9/85

Euro-$	9.534	5.673	15.266	1.152	42.239	42.959	.121	7.445	2.814
Euro-Yen	6.376	9.246	15.673	.272	30.856	31.081	.043	3.337	1.983
Euro-SFR	4.394	2.997	7.403	.739	17.319	17.515	.168	5.779	2.366
Euro-UKL	10.600	3.174	13.813	1.569	31.608	32.559	.148	9.959	2.343
Euro-DM	5.474	.993	6.471	.383	5.377	5.338	.070	5.416	.825
Euro-FF	11.837	.289	12.131	1.236	4.870	5.278	.104	16.832	.435
Euro-HFL	6.012	.969	6.987	.602	5.111	5.220	.100	5.273	.747
Euro-BFR[b]	10.452	.163	10.617	1.188	5.668	5.998	.114	34.801	.565
Euro-LIT	15.092	-3.992	11.051	1.523	13.195	13.598	.101	3.305	1.230
ECU	9.109	.457	9.570	.533	6.384	6.414	.059	13.956	.670

[a] −/+ indicate exchange rate appreciation/depreciation of the base country's currency.
[b] Belgian franc data refer respectively to the following periods: 12/80–9/85, 12/80–3/83, 4/83–9/85.
Methodological note: see Appendix.
Abbreviations as in table 11.1.
Source: ECU Newsletter.

currencies and base countries the exchange rate percentage change (expressed on an annual basis) is almost as large as the corresponding interest rate; even more importantly, its volatility is many times greater than interest rate volatility. This can clearly be seen by comparing the interest rate and exchange rate variation coefficients. No matter what the investor's (borrower's) base country and what the currency, we consider the volatility of the exchange rate effect to be 'the' relevant one: over the period 1980–5 its variation coefficient takes on values that usually range between 2 and 10 (even if in a few cases they are significantly higher), while the interest rate variation coefficients have values much lower than that (around 0.2–0.3).

Total Cost Return

The first factor affecting the mean value of total cost/return is the trend in the US dollar, and to some extent the yen, exchange rate, a trend that has been moving constantly upwards in recent years, the only exception being the recent weakening of the US dollar. As a result, both these currencies have produced a mean total cost/return far higher than others, both for US and Japanese agents and, to a greater extent, for everyone else. However, assessments of the relative advantage of investing (disadvantage of borrowing) in dollars or yen cannot ignore the degree of uncertainty that exists about the future total rate of such an operation undertaken today. *Ex post* data shows quite a high degree of volatility. In fact, for the *totality* of countries hereby considered, the US dollar and the yen present the highest standard deviation. The variation coefficient takes on lower values because the standard deviation is normalized in it by using the average values and the latter are much higher for the dollar and the yen. However, as was said at the outset, risk-averse agents set a great deal of importance on the absolute deviations from the mean, in addition to normalized deviations. To take just one example, let us consider a Swiss investor: over the period February 1980 to September 1985 he/she would have obtained an average return equal to 18 per cent on a US dollar investment and equal to 7 per cent on an ECU investment. The volatility, measured by the variation coefficient, was similar for the two assets, but standard deviation was more than double for the US dollar than for the ECU,[4] leading to the conclusion that the investor might have preferred a lower return/lower risk asset to a high return/high risk one.

   This is the story that *ex post* data can tell. However, uncertainty about the future, and in particular about the possibility of a strong turnaround in the dollar exchange rate, seems to play an even more important role than *ex post* variability. The US dollar is still the major international currency, but the elements of uncertainty related to it have induced not only non-US agents, but also US ones, to differentiate their net currency position. This is certainly

---

4   Maximum and minimum values of total returns over the period were respectively −124%/+122% for the dollar asset and −48%/+62% for the ECU asset.

one explanation for the recent success of ECU bonds on the US market with both private and institutional investors.[5] In fact the inclusion of the ECU in their portfolios appears to answer their need to cover themselves against the risk of a decline in the trend of the dollar exchange rate. Thus, they invest in a currency with a larger yield than the deutschmark or the Swiss franc and potentially lower variability. The data reported in table 11.3 are quite interesting in this respect. For instance, the April 1983 to September 1985 period shows an average total return for the ECU equal to 5.4 per cent, i.e., much higher than the 3.2 per cent of the Swiss franc and 2.4 per cent of the deutschmark. At the same time, ECU return volatility was lower, as measured both by the standard deviation and the variation coefficient.

We shall now focus on the situation for European currencies and, particularly, for the ECU *vis-à-vis* the other major currencies.

Tables 11.3 to 11.12 show that generally the ECU presents a higher total cost return than currencies whose nominal domestic rates are low (the deutschmark, Swiss franc and Dutch florin) and vice versa for the other currencies (French franc, lira, British pound).[6] This 'regularity' holds for all base-countries – including the United States and Japan – and across time too. It is, however, interesting to notice that the 'regularity' has been much more pronounced in recent years (see the April 1983 to September 1985 period). This could be put down to the fact that the EMS exchange rate agreement has been more stringent since the March 1983 realignment, allowing currencies to fluctuate only within a narrow band. The 'regularity' has often led people to identify the ECU as an investment currency for countries with low interest rates and a borrowing currency for the other countries. In fact, the issue is not as straightforward as this. The reason lies again in the greater stability of the ECU's exchange and interest rates and hence its 'total rate', which may make the ECU particularly appealing to risk-averse investors/ borrowers wishing to diversify their exposure to the exchange rate risk.

We might take an Italian operator as a typical example. In the period in question, an Italian company with no particular currency structure with regard to its costs and revenues that might incline it towards one currency rather than another, would have paid less on debts in Swiss francs or deutschmarks than on debts in ECU. However, the risk of divergence between expected and *ex post* effective cost would have been higher with the former than with the ECU.

Tables 11.3 to 11.12 show that apart from domestic currencies, the standard deviation of the ECU is relatively small compared to that of alternative

5   The first issue, worth 200 million ECU and launched by the EEC in November 1984, was successfully followed between March and September 1985 with issues by Hercules (50m ECU), the French Crédit Foncier (150m ECU), the Kingdom of Denmark (150m ECU) and Banque Nationale de Paris (150m ECU).
6   Return/cost of the Belgian franc – a high interest rate currency behaves somewhat more erratically and return/cost are often lower than those of the ECU.

currencies. The same goes for its normalized variability. As expected, this is particularly evident for EMS based economic agents, but can apply to others as well. It is also more evident during the February 1980 to March 1983 period, when the ECU was really 'the' currency whose total cost/return had the lowest variability.

Although to a lesser extent, the same comment applies to the most recent period when ECU variability has still been low, even though for each base country it is possible to find one (or more) particular currency whose exchange rate is more strongly correlated to the national currency, producing a lower volatility of total cost/return. This does not invalidate, however, the general statement that over the years the ECU has been a suitable currency for the diversification of assets and liabilities.

The points made about volatility are illustrated graphically in figures 11.1 to 11.16. Figures 11.1 to 11.8 present the behaviour over time of the total yield/cost levels for each base country. The US dollar and the yen can be seen to account for most of the peaks, reaching values sometimes as high as +/−100 per cent. Figures 11.9 to 11.16 present the distribution of frequency of total cost/yield values for the ECU and US dollar denominated transactions. Concentration of values around their mean suggests a higher probability that *ex post* total return/cost will not differ widely from its *ex ante* expected value, as approximated by the mean. As expected, the ECU presents a lower dispersion than the US dollar for all the EMS countries. However, results are in favour of the ECU for Swiss agents, too.

So far we have examined reasons why economic agents might have preferred the ECU by looking at the choice of the currency (currencies) available to denominate their investments and/or debts. The same approach could be extended to analyse the commercial use of the ECU and, in particular, the use of it for invoicing and settling foreign trade transactions. This is another sector where the greater stability of the ECU compared to that of other currencies, especially the US dollar, is particularly valuable. This is why, even if up to now there has been little ECU invoicing, a consistent expansion of it is foreseeable.

THE ECU AS THE EMS CURRENCY

The ECU's ex ante Predictability

The previous section analysed the behaviour over time of costs/returns related to foreign exchange transactions, and it was pointed out that volatility, mainly induced by exchange rate fluctuations, is the most important element to be taken into account by decision-makers acting in the context of uncertainty. In this respect one important feature of the ECU is its greater stability compared to that of other major international currencies.

We also said that suggestions emerging from *ex post* data can tell only one part of the story because of difficulties inherent in the process of forecasting future exchange rates. At the same time, when undertaking any foreign exchange investment/borrowing transaction, decision-makers need to have in mind some hypothesis about future spot exchange rates as well as the probability of their having made the 'wrong guess'. One variable to be considered in this respect is the forward exchange rate. The latter represents, in general, the break-even exchange rate, i.e. the exchange rate which equates the return/cost of transactions denominated in different currencies. The forward exchange rate may be interpreted as the best guess of the *market* as a whole on future spot rates. As such each economic agent may use them as a benchmark to compare to his/her subjective expectation of future spot rates.

A useful exercise could be developed by comparing forward rates to future spot rates with the aim of checking how well the former can predict the latter. The degree of error between the two is another measure of the volatility, and hence of the degree of predictability, of various currencies. This is an elaboration we do not intend to present extensively here, but it is, however, useful to stress that data derived from divergences between actual spot rates and corresponding forward rates confirm the wider predictability of the ECU *vis-à-vis* the US dollar.

The basket nature of the ECU is often claimed as the explanation for the European currency's stability and hence the favour it has found with operators. Other basket currencies, the most important being the SDR (Special Drawing Right), have developed no private market. One common reason given for the SDR's failure to take off is that the dollar takes too big a share in it for the SDR to be a useful instrument for currency diversification. In this sense the composition of the ECU basket does offer particular advantages over the SDR. As several US or multinational companies have emphasized in commenting on their position as 'takers' of the European currency, ECU borrowing can offer effective hedging not only in respect of ECU assets but also in the more common case of assets denominated in a set of European currencies. In this case the basket of currencies contained in the ECU does not correspond exactly to the basket of currencies in which the company's assets are expressed. Nevertheless, as a 'synthetic' currency, the ECU can, on average, guarantee satisfactory coverage and also costs less to manage than multi-currency hedging.

The ECU, being a weighted average of the component currencies, certainly plays a role in damping exchange rate fluctuation; it is not, however, the only, nor probably the most important, reason for that property, which should rather be attributed to the fact that the ECU is the weighted average of exchange rates *whose reciprocal fluctuations are not free but regulated by the EMS agreement*. Thanks to its mechanisms of intervention and the pursued policies of adjustment, the EMS has been able to guarantee a greater internal stability of exchange rates. Indeed, in spite of the many weaknesses still present in it, the 'experiment' has proved to be a successful alternative to the floating exchange rate system and as such it has been drawn into the recently renewed debate on the opportunity and/or possibility of improving the functioning of the international monetary system.

TABLE 11.13 EMS: ECU central rates[a]

	13 Mar. 1979	24 Sep. 1979	30 Nov. 1979	23 Mar. 1981	5 Oct. 1981	22 Feb. 1982	14 June 1982	21 Mar. 1983	21 May[b] 1983	22 July 1985
Belgian/Luxembourg franc										
Units of national currency per ECU	39.4582	39.8456	39.7897	40.7985	40.7572	44.6963	44.9704	44.3662	44.9008	44.832
Percentage change from previous central rate		0.98	-0.14	2.54	-0.10	9.66	0.61	-1.34	1.20	-0.15
Percentage change from initial central rate		0.98	0.84	3.40	3.29	13.28	13.97	12.44	13.79	13.62
Danish krone										
Units of national currency per ECU	7.08592	7.36594	7.72336	7.91917	7.91117	8.18382	8.2340	8.04412	8.14104	8.12857
Percentage change from previous central rate		3.95	4.85	2.54	-0.10	3.45	0.61	-2.31	1.20	-0.15
Percentage change from initial central rate		3.95	9.00	11.76	11.65	15.49	16.20	13.52	14.89	14.71
Deutschmark										
Units of national currency per ECU	2.51064	2.48557	2.48208	2.54502	2.40989	2.41815	2.33379	2.21515	2.24184	2.2384
Percentage change from previous central rate		-1.00	-0.1	2.54	5.31	0.34	-3.48	-5.08	1.20	-0.15
Percentage change from initial central rate		-1.00	-0.1	1.37	-4.01	-3.68	-7.04	-11.77	-10.71	-10.84

French franc

Units of national currency per ECU	5.79831	5.85522	5.84700	5.99526	6.17443	6.19564	6.61387	6.79271	6.87456	6.86402
Percentage change from previous central rate		0.98	−0.14	2.54	2.99	0.34	6.75	2.70	1.20	−0.15
Percentage change from initial central rate		0.98	0.84	3.40	6.49	6.85	14.07	17.15	18.56	18.38

Italian lira

Units of national currency per ECU	1,148.15	1,159.42	1,157.79	1,262.92	1,300.67	1,305.13	1,350.27	1,386.78	1,403.49	1,520.60
Percentage change from previous central rate		0.98	−0.14	9.10	2.99	0.34	3.46	2.70	1.20	8.34
Percentage change from initial central rate		0.98	0.84	10.00	13.28	13.67	17.60	20.78	22.24	32.44

Irish pound

Units of national currency per ECU	0.662638	0.669141	0.668201	0.685145	0.684452	0.686799	0.691011	0.71705	0.725690	0.724578
Percentage change from previous central rate		0.98	−0.14	2.54	−0.10	0.34	0.61	3.77	1.20	−0.15
Percentage change from initial central rate		0.98	0.84	3.40	3.29	3.65	4.28	8.21	9.52	9.35

Netherlands guilder

Units of national currency per ECU	2.72077	2.74748	2.74362	2.81318	2.66382	2.67296	2.57971	2.49587	2.52595	2.52208
Percentage change from previous central rate		0.98	−0.14	2.54	−5.31	0.34	−3.49	−3.25	1.20	−0.15
Percentage change from initial rate		0.98	0.84	3.40	−2.09	−1.76	−5.18	−8.27	−7.16	−7.30

[a] Positive sign indicates depreciation relative to the ECU.
[b] Technical adjustment induced by a variation in the pound sterling 'notional' central parity.
Source: Commission of the European Communities.

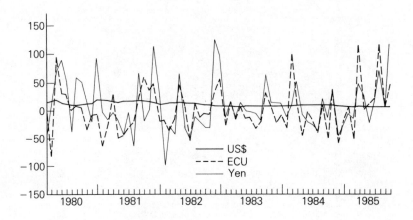

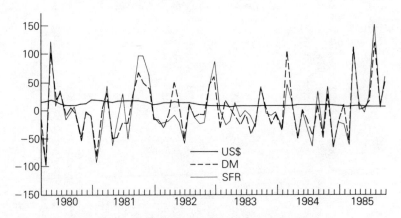

FIGURE 11.1 Total cost (return) of one-month debt (investment).
Base country, United States; period, 2/80–9/85.
Source: ECU Newsletter.

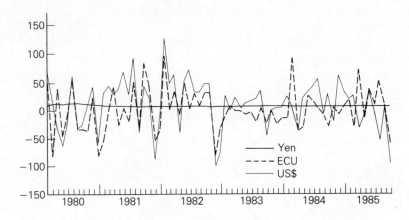

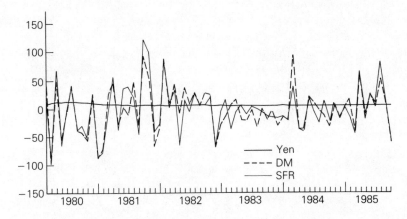

FIGURE 11.2 Total cost (return) of one-month debt (investment).
Base country, Japan; period, 2/80–9/85.
Source: ECU Newsletter.

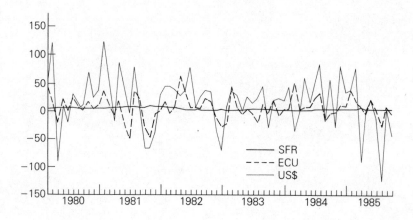

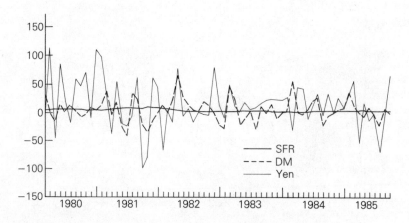

FIGURE 11.3 Total cost (return) of one-month debt (investment).
Base country, Switzerland; period, 2/80–9/85.
Source: ECU Newsletter.

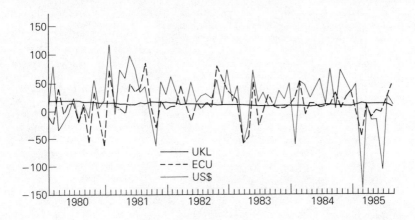

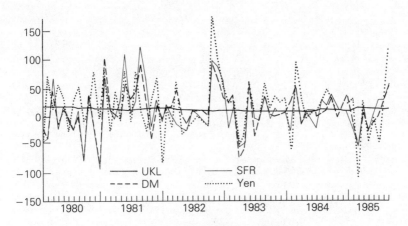

FIGURE 11.4 Total cost (return) of one-month debt (investment).
Base country, Britain; period, 2/80–9/85.
Source: ECU Newsletter.

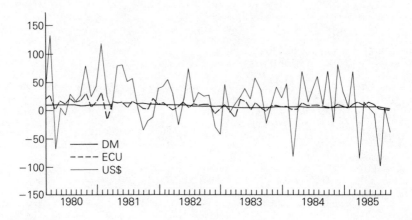

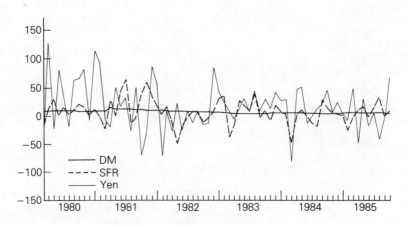

FIGURE 11.5 Total cost (return) of one-month debt (investment).
Base country, Germany; period, 2/80–9/85.
Source: ECU Newsletter.

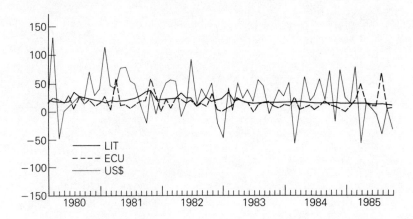

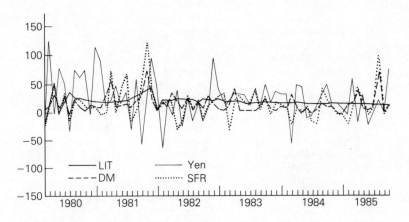

FIGURE 11.6 Total cost (return) of one-month debt (investment).
Base country, Italy; period, 2/80–9/85.
Source: ECU Newsletter.

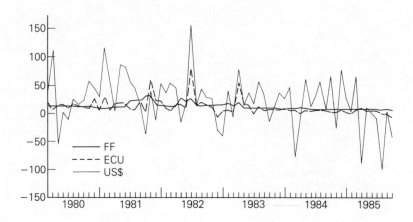

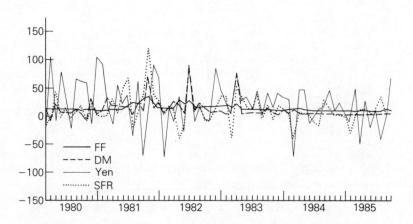

FIGURE 11.7 Total cost (return) of one-month debt (investment).
Base country, France; period, 2/80–9/85.
Source: ECU Newsletter.

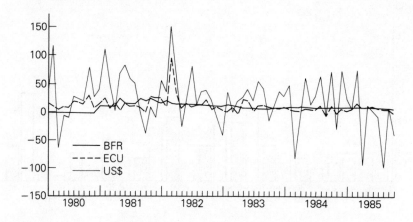

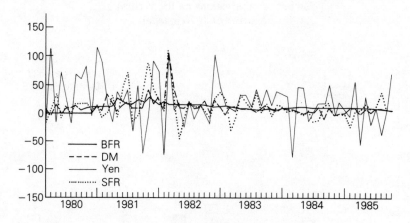

FIGURE 11.8 Total cost (return) of one-month debt (investment).
Base country, Belgium; period, 2/80–9/85.
Source: ECU Newsletter.

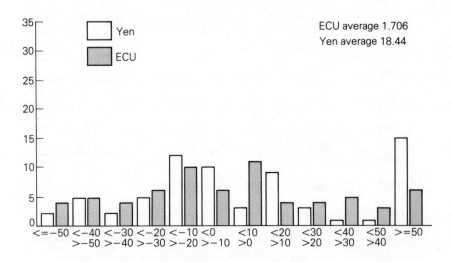

FIGURE 11.9 Total cost (return) of one-month debt (investment).
Distribution of frequency over the period 2/80–9/85; base country, United States.
Number of observations on the vertical axis.
Source: ECU Newsletter

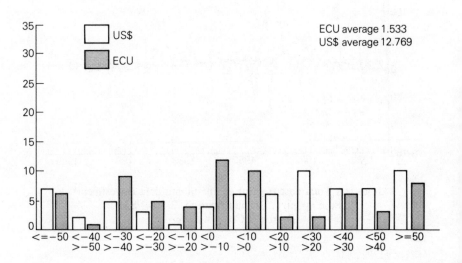

FIGURE 11.10 Total cost (return) of one-month debt (investment).
Distribution of frequency over the period 2/80–9/85; base country, Japan.
Number of observations on the vertical axis.
Source: ECU Newsletter.

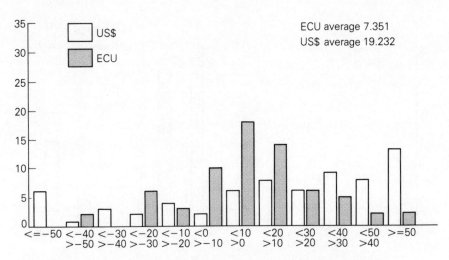

FIGURE 11.11 Total cost (return) of one-month debt (investment).
Distribution of frequency over the period 2/80–9/85; base country, Switzerland.
Number of observations on the vertical axis.
Source: ECU Newsletter

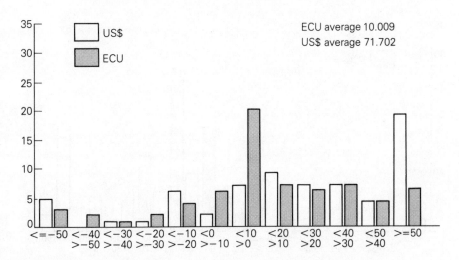

FIGURE 11.12 Total cost (return) of one-month debt (investment).
Distribution of frequency over the period 2/80–9/85; base country, Britain.
Number of observations on the vertical axis.
Source: ECU Newsletter.

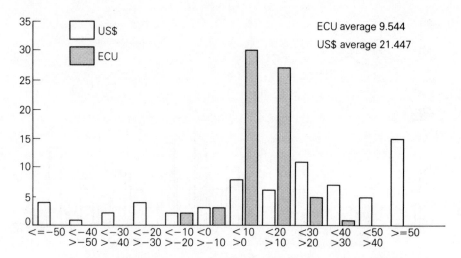

FIGURE 11.13 Total cost (return) of one-month debt (investment).
Distribution of frequency over the period 2/80–9/85; base country, Germany.
Number of observations on the vertical axis.
Source: ECU Newsletter

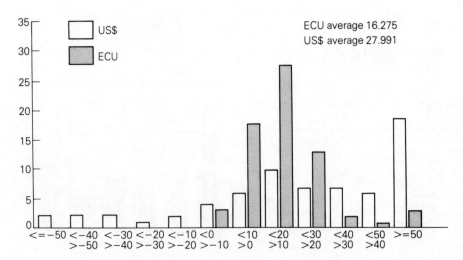

FIGURE 11.14 Total cost (return) of one-month debt (investment).
Distribution of frequency over the period 2/80–9/85; base country, Italy.
Number of observations on the vertical axis.
Source: ECU Newsletter.

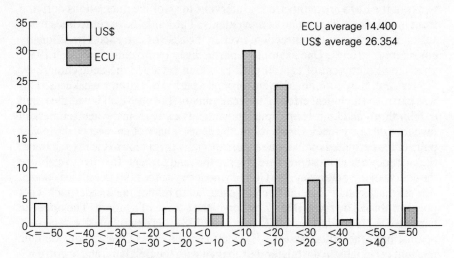

FIGURE 11.15 Total cost (return) of one-month debt (investment).
Distribution of frequency over the period 2/80–9/85; base country, France.
Number of observations on the vertical axis.
Source: ECU Newsletter

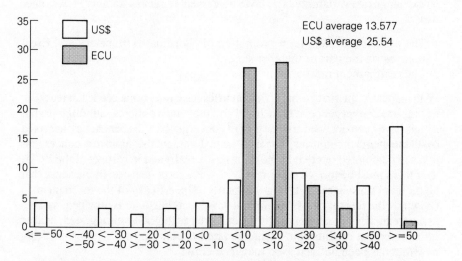

FIGURE 11.16 Total cost (return) of one-month debt (investment).
Distribution of frequency over the period 2/80–9/85; base country, Belgium.
Number of observations on the vertical axis.
Source: ECU Newsletter.

The EMS agreement works in three ways. First, margins are established for the exchange fluctuations between any two component currencies. The central banks of the EMS are authorized to intervene to stabilize fluctuations deriving from imbalances or speculative movements. The banks have sometimes made substantial moves in this direction, even in the case of currencies traditionally considered 'strong'. One example is particularly interesting. In March 1983, after the realignment of central parities which revalued the deutschmark by 5.5 per cent, the deutschmark went through a period of extreme weakness. This was partly the technical effect of the realignment, but above all it was the result of both short- and long-term capital movements away from the deutschmark in favour of other currencies. As a result, the deutschmark often reached the lowest point of the permitted oscillation range, especially in relation to the French franc, the currency under most pressure prior to the realignment. In order to stabilize the course of their currency, the German monetary authorities purchased enough deutschmarks on the foreign exchange market to reduce the Bundesbank's net position abroad by some DM 17 billion in the course of a month. The opposite happened the following year. In fact, in early 1984, the deutschmark was gaining against both the dollar and the EMS currencies. This created considerable tension, especially in the bilateral exchange with the Belgian franc, a currency that even earlier had been very weak inside the system. Following the measures taken to support the Belgian franc–deutschmark exchange rate, the Bundesbank's net position abroad improved by over DM 4 billion during February and March of 1984.[7]

These examples are indicative of the stabilizing effect of the EMS agreement on exchange rate variability. The EMS agreement regulates stability in two other ways:

1 The medium- to long-term promotion of coordinated monetary and fiscal policies on the part of member states.
2 The realignment mechanism.

With respect to the first point, EMS countries have not yet succeeded in reaching a complete convergence of their fiscal and monetary policies, although partial results have been obtained and the goal of convergence is the benchmark accepted by all the member countries. As far as the realignment mechanism is concerned, it has to be pointed out that if one currency is realigned in respect of the ECU, the others must be too. In other words, this is a joint decision in the sense that all partners must agree to changes in parity. The efficacy of the mechanism is shown by the fact that the EMS has not developed into a 'crawling peg' system as the frequency of realignments in the early stages might have suggested, neither into a fixed but readjustable exchange rate system, but rather into something new that has been defined as a 'managed crawl'.[8]

7 See Bundesbank annual reports for 1983 and 1984.
8 This is the definition given by G. Magnifico, in the paper 'The EMS and the ECU', presented at the European Banking Conference in April 1984. According to Magnifico:

Data presented in table 11.4 show that the EMS has had a twofold stabilizing effect. On the one hand it has reduced the variability over time of the individual EMS currencies' exchange rate in relation to the totality of the currencies participating in the system. On the other, it has made the EMS currencies less variable than those outside the system.

So, the existence of an exchange rate agreement between EMS currencies in an international context of flexible rates often subject to erratic and unpredictable

TABLE 11.14　Exchange rate variability (percentage values)

	March 79–March 83		April 83–March 84	
	Average % change[a]	*Mean s.d.*[b]	*Average % change*[a]	*Mean s.d.*[b]
Vis-à-vis the main international currencies[c]				
Dollar	0.099	1.10	0.033	0.80
Yen	0.007	1.37	0.180	0.91
Deutschmark	0.046	0.73	−0.015	0.43
Pound sterling	−0.009	1.20	0.068	1.08
French franc	0.097	0.82	−0.063	0.40
Italian lira	−0.103	0.71	−0.104	0.41
Dutch guilder	0.010	0.64	−0.018	0.38
Vis-à-vis EMS currencies[d]				
Deutschmark	0.099	0.53	0.051	0.17
French franc	−0.070	0.64	−0.017	0.18
Italian lira	−0.075	0.54	−0.062	0.23
Dutch guilder	0.038	0.42	0.030	0.13
Pound sterling	0.039	1.13	0.131	1.06

[a] Geometric mean of weekly percentage changes over the period.
[b] Weighted average of mean standard deviations of bilateral exchange rates' percentage changes.
[c] The 14 currencies used by the Bank of Italy to compute the effective exchange rate.
[d] To make the calculation only currencies that participate in the exchange rate agreement were considered. Pound sterling is reported as a memorandum item only.
Source: Bank of Italy, annual report for 1984.

'The EMS has been managed by a system it would be appropriate to describe as a ''managed crawl'' since the decision to realign is not triggered mechanically by the indication of certain strategic variables but rather by an intensified process of comparison and analysis applied to the monetary, budget and economic policies of the member states and their effects on economic developments.'

fluctuations endows the ECU with one highly appealing property, i.e., the greater stability and predictability of its exchange rate.

What we have just said is consistent with the comments developed previously by looking at *ex post* data. However, it also provides us with an important piece of information for the evaluation of the ECU's future exchange rate volatility. By means of the divergence threshold, the EMS agreement in fact sets ceilings and floors to the fluctuations of the EMS currencies' exchange rates. It is interesting to put them in relation to the break-even exchange rates.

Table 11.15 contains spot exchange rates observed on 30 September, 1985, which were used, together with the corresponding interest rates, as a basis for the calculation. It also shows the break-even exchange rates over periods of one, three and six months, and one year, and, finally, the minimum and maximum fluctuation margins with respect to the ECU.

Under the assumption that *no realignment* will take place during the period considered, table 11.15 supplies decision-makers needing to select an investment (borrowing) currency with two interesting sets of additional information. The first consists of ceilings to the currency gain/loss, i.e. the currency-induced error with respect to the 'expected' total return/cost as measured by the break-even exchange rate. As we have already said, the latter is the 'best' market guess about the future spot exchange and, as a consequence, the *expected* return/cost for all currencies is equal, but borrowers/investors are concerned about the error they may make in selecting one currency rather than another in case their expectations turn out to be wrong. With freely fluctuating foreign exchange rates there are no limits to such errors and, in fact, we saw earlier how big such errors have often been, especially in relation to currencies such as the US dollar. The EMS exchange rate agreement puts bounds on such errors, through its fluctuation band. Table 11.15 is an example of that.

Consider a Belgian investor, in doubt as to whether he/she should invest in assets denominated in the national currency or in ECU. Over a one-year investment horizon a Belgian asset would yield 9.6 per cent, an ECU asset would have the same expected yield, that is, about 9 per cent (the value is expressed on a 365 day basis to make it comparable to the Belgian franc rate) plus the Belgian franc percentage depreciation towards the ECU. Due to the Belgian franc's fluctuation band, *ex post* returns on the ECU could fluctuate between about 10.6 and 7.28 per cent.

The second type of information supplied by table 11.15 concerns currencies which, in the absence of realignment, will present a cost/yield certainly different from the 'expected' one. This is, for instance, the case of the deutschmark or the Dutch florin. To produce the 'expected' return/cost both currencies should appreciate more than the EMS exchange rate agreement allows them to do.

TABLE 11.15 Break-even exchange rates

Currency	Spot rates 30 Sep. 85	Break-even exchange rates				EMS divergence threshold	
		1 mth	3 mth	6 mth	1 yr	Min. value	Max. value
DM/ECU	2.2124	2.205	2.190	2.168	2.128	2.2129	2.2642
FF/ECU	6.7515	6.760	6.786	6.823	6.908	6.7709	6.9584
HFL/ECU	2.4941	2.488	2.477	2.457	2.420	2.4841	2.5606
BFR/ECU	44.8802	44.901	44.971	44.975	45.112	44.1458	45.5289
LIT/ECU	1494.3599	1500.000	1512.100	1526.000	1562.000	1458.470	1582.730

Abbreviations as in table 11.1.
Methodological note: see Appendix.
Source: ECU Newsletter based on EEC and *Financial Times* data.

Institutional Back-up for the Private ECU Market

The often emphasized contrast between 'the success of the private ECU' and 'the partial failure of the official ECU' is therefore the result of over-simplification. Undoubtedly there is a difference in the utilization of the ECU in the two circuits. However, the private ECU would not have been a success without the institutional back-up provided by the EMS.

We have seen how exchange rates are handled; other elements also confirm the importance of the ECU's institutional and official framework. First, the fact that the ECU is not simply a private unit of account but a currency officially launched by EMS members has a positive psychological effect on the confidence of private operators about the future growth of the European currency. In this respect it is quite interesting to recall the debate that developed in the early days of the private ECU market about the opportunity to use the 'open basket' rather than the 'closed basket' formula. Some issuers and bank managers believed that bonds, loans, deposits and all sorts of ECU contracts should be pegged to the basket as it stood at the time the contracts were defined. So if the official composition of the ECU changed before the maturity date, the value of the ECU repayment should be computed according to the original composition of the basket. Supporters of this approach felt that a 'closed basket' would offer them greater independence of political decisions, and would hence offer greater security. On the other side, there were those in favour of the 'open basket' formula, so that the private ECU would automatically be adjusted whenever the official ECU changed in value. Their main contention was that, if they did not operate with the 'open basket', there would be a serious risk of different types of ECUs. This would have created many difficulties by reducing the ECU's liquidity and impeding the development of a wide secondary market.

As is well known, almost everyone opted for the 'open basket' solution and this decision has proved to be successful if we look not only at the size and vitality the ECU market has reached, but also at the way in which the market reacted to last year's basket redefinition.[9]

So the ECU, being a currency officially launched by the EMS countries, turned out to have a positive influence on the growth of the private ECU market. Even more important is the fact that Europe's public agents themselves, governments as well as publicly-owned bodies and EEC institutions, are increasingly resorting to the private ECU market.[10]

In more general terms, however, the influence (positive or negative) of the institutional back-up on the success of the ECU depends on the status

9 On this particular subject see 'The ECU basket redefinition', *ECU Newsletter*, No. 10 (September), 1984, pp. 4–12.
10 Examples are the numerous bonds issued by the Irish government, the Italian CTEs, the Danish issues on both the domestic and the US markets, not to mention the many bonds issued by publicly owned agencies or guaranteed by EEC states.

such back-up confers on the currency. We may say that any currency will be in one of four situations:

1 Not recognized as a foreign currency.
2 An 'ordinary' foreign currency.
3 A 'privileged' foreign currency.
4 A parallel currency.

In various ways, the institutional back-up for the ECU has contributed to the fact that today the European currency has achieved stage 3 in almost all EEC countries (it is at stage 1 in West Germany and stage 2 in Britain) and could well move into stage 4.

There are many examples to demonstrate the way in which the ECU has become a privileged foreign currency, particularly in those member countries where capital movement deregulation is as yet incomplete. France, for example, recently authorized importers to buy ECU in the forward market as a hedge against the exchange risk of contracts invoiced in the European currency and is talking of liberalizing ECU financial futures.

In Italy, numerous ECU securities issued by takers like the European Investment Bank (EIB), the World Bank etc., can be bought by residents without the 25 per cent interest free deposit imposed on other foreign currency investments. A similar procedure was launched in France last January with an EIB issue.

Finally, it is worth remembering the May 1985 resolution by the Italian Interministerial Committee for Economic Planning (CIPE) which outlines the ways in which Italy can promote the use of the ECU at both financial and commercial levels. Among other measures, the resolution, in fact, suggests that monetary authorities study the possibility of residents being authorized to hold financial positions in ECU. Insurance contracts in ECU are also envisaged, as is the use of the European currency to settle Post Office and transportation accounts between the various countries instead of the dollar or other currencies.

THE ECU AS AN EFFICIENT FINANCIAL INSTRUMENT

In the first part of this paper we explained the strong success of the ECU with both private and public agents by pointing out how its greater stability and predictability make it a more efficient instrument to hedge against exchange rate risk. However, the ECU's contribution to a move towards a more efficient financial environment can be traced out in other elements too. One of them is the role played by the European currency as a vehicle to spread financial innovation.

The ECU's stability, together with the particular characteristics that derive from its institutional back-up in the EEC member countries, have enabled the Community currency to expand to a point where it is now one of the major

The Private ECU Market

Eurocurrencies.[11] Even more important, those elements have made the ECU not only a successful financial innovation in itself, but also a good vehicle to spread financial innovations in the Euromarket as well as in individual national markets.

As far as the international market is concerned, the ECU has been used for a complete range of financial instruments: bonds (traditional fixed rate bonds, but also floating rate notes, zero coupon bonds, *titres participatifs*, bonds with interest rate caps, convertible bonds); loans, including multi-currency loans with ECU tranches; floating rate CDs; current accounts; fixed deposit accounts; travellers cheques; trade bills; note issuance facilities and revolving underwriting facilities. Furthermore, currency options and futures on the ECU/US dollar exchange rate will soon be widely available. Official trading of ECU options should begin in December 1985 at the European Option Exchange in Amsterdam. However, at the time of writing, not less than four US exchanges and another two European exchanges have announced their intention to trade ECU/US dollar futures or options.[12]

Meanwhile, the first offering of over-the-counter one year put and call options was made in September 1984 by Solomon Brothers and a growing number of bonds denominated in dollars with warrants allowing the conversion of them into ECUs have now been issued. The ECU has also made its appearance on domestic markets, through both international issues specifically targeted to some national markets and securities directly issued on the domestic markets. With regard to the latter line of development, the most frequently quoted examples are the ECU bonds launched in the US domestic market by the EEC, Hercules, Crédit Foncier de France, Kingdom of Denmark[13] and BNP respectively, as well as the recent placements in Tokyo.

There are other less well known but equally interesting examples. One of them is the launch on the Dutch domestic market of ECU '*bankbrieven*', the

11　The ECU's success may be shown with very little data. Bond issues began in 1981 and by the third quarter of 1985 there had been 246 of them, worth over 19 billion ECU. Comparison with the other main currencies also confirms the success of the ECU, which became the third most important currency of bond denomination in only four years. Data supplied by BIS on foreign and domestic assets and liabilities of European reporting banks also show the significant growth in ECU bank positions. Though still notably lower than dollar assets, by the end of 1984 ECU assets and liabilities had passed all non-dollar Eurocurrencies except for the deutschmark, the Swiss franc and the yen. (For further quantitative information see *ECU Newsletter*, Istituto Bancario San Paolo di Torino, various issues.)

12　See 'ECU futures and options: what they are, where they are going to be traded, who is going to use them?', *ECU Newsletter*, No. 14, (October), 1985.

13　It is worthwhile mentioning the set-up of Denmark's ECU 150m FRN: for each quarterly interest period, the interest rate on the notes will be equal to 70 basis points above the 91-day Treasury bills rate and will be hedged into ECU utilizing the spot and the three-month forward US dollar–ECU exchange rate. A similar set-up has been utilized to determine the interest rate of the more recent BNP issue.

name for bonds issued by Dutch banks on a continuous, tap basis with the issue price reset from time to time to take account of interest rate developments. The two issues recorded up to now represent the only non-guilder *bankbrieven* offering. By the same token, one may emphasize that the ECU was the currency chosen to denominate the French Compagnie de Saint-Gobain issue of *titres participatifs*, which are perpetual, non-voting securities bearing remuneration partly based on group consolidated net profits.[14]

The quoted examples seem to support the idea that the wide range of facilities available for the ECU, together with its status as a 'privileged' foreign currency, make the European currency a potential vehicle for spreading financial innovations in national markets too, thus contributing to the efficiency of the European financial environment. Talking of efficiency, one more point is worth mentioning, i.e., the relationship between the ECU market and competition. At present there are at least five European financial centres that compete for ECU business. They are Brussels, Luxembourg, Paris, Milan and London. A sixth one, Frankfurt, could shortly join the list. The widespread distribution of ECU business centres is related to an aspect of the development of the European currency that has been pointed out by David Lomax.[15] According to him, all banks in Europe, and for that matter banks outside Europe as well, play on a 'level playing field' when they are funding themselves in ECU. This means that, as far as competitiveness is concerned, the ECU is in a different situation from that of other currencies. In other words, many more banks can compete for ECU business than is the case when funding is done in national currencies, where the national banks usually have a competitive advantage. In Lomax's view, which we completely share, this must provide customers throughout the community with a better and more competitive service than if they had to rely on the existing hard currency possibilities.

CONCLUSIONS: THE PROBLEMS TO BE RESOLVED

The growth of the private, monetary and financial ECU market has responded to a variety of needs: governments looking for a less erratic alternative to the dollar; companies seeking less uncertainty in their production and financing programmes; savers wishing to minimize the risk of yields that do not correspond

14   In fact, the remuneration is based on a semi-annual coupon which will be equal to half the yearly rate calculated by adding: (i) a fixed rate of 7.5 per cent applicable to 60 per cent of the principal; (ii) a variable rate consisting of two elements applicable to 40 per cent of the principal: one element is based on group consolidated net profits, while the other is based on the mean of the last four weekly long-term average ECU Eurobond yields, published by the Luxembourg SE.
15   See 'The Time is Ripe', The European Monetary System, the ECU and British Policy. Report of a Federal Trust Study Group. Rapporteur, David F. Lomax. London, Federal Trust for Education and Research, Nov, 1984.

to their expectations; institutional investors seeking diversification but also in search of yields; and banks wishing to maintain a position in the international market. Furthermore, a commercial role for the ECU is now emerging. The practice of invoicing in ECUs is now being adopted by some medium-sized as well as large companies.

There is thus no lack of microeconomic stimuli to a growing utilization of the European Community currency. However, at a macroeconomic and institutional level, we have to create the conditions for the private ECU market to continue to expand and, above all, to expand in an orderly manner. Measures must therefore be taken to tackle potential imbalances, whether endogenous (i.e., imbalance between supply and demand originating either in the money market or in the capital market and its effect on interest rates) or exogenous (i.e., capital movements from the dollar to the ECU or the deutschmark, strong movements and tensions on exchange rates).

On the question of endogenous tensions, we have to ask ourselves how long the private use of the ECU can expand at the current rate without the creation of tensions and difficulties either in the Euromarket or in the individual national markets. If the banks continue to operate as rationally as they have done to date, the ECU market will still have plenty of room for expansion. Increasingly, however, we are realizing the need to 'officialize' some of its structures. Two significant examples are the need for the creation of a clearing system and the regulation of the bond market.

Failing a central bank to act as a clearing system, in 1981 the most active commercial banks began to open reciprocal deposit accounts and credit lines through which to offset their ECU transactions. Four years since those original agreements were made, the market is now too big for this bilateral clearing system to be adequate. The growing need for an official, supranational clearing system to which all banks operating in ECU can apply, is, however, producing good results. The ECU Banking Association (EBA) was officially set up in September 1985 with the aim of promoting the use of the ECU and, in particular, concluding the agreement with the Bank for International Settlements (BIS), which will act on the EBA's behalf as the common clearing bank. The new system, which will become operational in 1986, presents some interesting features, including the fact that each clearing bank will be required to keep at the BIS a minimum balance of non-interest-bearing deposits. Banks which go below that minimum level will have to borrow ECU funds from those banks with surpluses. In this way, a structure very similar to that of the US federal funds will develop and produce ECU interest rates which move in response to the liquidity of the market.

The second situation that we mentioned concerns the bond market. Now that bond issues are so large and so frequent, simple self-regulation by banks operating in the market is no longer sufficient. We need more official control of the market to regulate both the scheduling of issues and the technical forms these may take, as is the case for all other Eurobond currencies. Official control could avoid problems such as the destabilizing effect on interest rates of issues being crowded too closely together, or the potentially negative impact of financial formulae that (in the attempt at catching a bigger share of the market) present an excessive level of fancifulness to the detriment of clarity in evaluating yields/costs and risks of the issue.

Finally, we come to the question of handling exogenous shocks originating in the exchange market. This is a topic made even 'hotter' by recent events, such as the September 1985 New York Meeting of the Group of Five, which agreed on central bank intervention to weaken the US dollar exchange rate, or the new emerging proposals to reform the international monetary system by moving towards target zones. In this respect, whether the ECU or the deutschmark will play the role of the 'third' currency together with the yen and the US dollar, is very important for the future stability of the European area, and of the system as a whole. But to 'impose' the ECU as the third currency, European countries need to reach sufficient agreement to strengthen the EMS. As Helmut Schmidt has pointed out,[16] the crucial problem is whether we can strengthen the EMCF and its power to use ECUs to intervene in the exchange rate market. Here too, despite existing difficulties, there are signs of new openings.

Given that central banks act as private agents on the international markets, it is not surprising that there has been competition between the private and official ECU. The attractiveness of the former in terms of interest rate, liquidity and transferability have made it increasingly attractive to central banks as depositors; furthermore, borrowing in the private ECU market by public entities in France and Italy has provided a substitute for the use by these countries of the EMS credit mechanisms. One consequence of this competition was the recent agreement between central banks to increase the return on official ECU deposits to market levels, and to enhance their transferability by allowing non-EMS central banks to hold them. Central banks may also want to diversify out of the dollar in the coming months – who will provide the ECU deposits, the official or the private market? Some central banks outside the EEC have begun to hold private ECU in their reserve assets (for example, the Central Bank of Norway and possibly the USSR's Bank for Foreign Trade). As far

16 Schmidt's proposals for the strengthening of the European Monetary System appeared in full in *ECU Newsletter*, No. 12 (April), 1985. The part relating to FECOM may be summarized as follows:
1 Role of the European Fund for Monetary Cooperation (FECOM)
  to oversee the control of the maximum quantity of ECU in circulation in both official and private transactions;
  to coordinate exchange market operations;
  to activate ECU swap lines with the Federal Reserve System and other central banks;
  to guarantee the phase of transition towards currency liberalization.
2 Modifications to FECOM function
  weekly meetings of the Fund's council of governors;
  appointment of a permanent staff guided by a director.

as the institutional framework is concerned, the recent agreement made by central banks has given the European Monetary Cooperation Fund power to decide which institutions outside the EMS should be allowed to hold official ECU and, more importantly, has allowed the BIS to participate in the official ECU system.

APPENDIX: METHODOLOGICAL NOTE TO TABLES

Tables 11.3 to 11.12: The total cost/yield of one-month investment/ indebtedness has been determined *ex post* taking into account the one-month interest rate in the various currencies, adjusted for the appreciation or depreciation of the debtor's (investor's) national currency *vis-à-vis* the currency of the indebtedness (investment) over the one-month period. It is assumed that the operation ends at the end of each month indicated in the table and starts at the end of the previous month.

Columns 1 to 3 show average values over the period of the following variables:

1 One-month interest rate referred to the beginning of the indebtedness/ investment period considered. Data are end-of-month and bid-offer averages.
2 Percentage appreciation (negative sign) or depreciation (positive sign) of the base country's currency during the one-month period, expressed on an annual basis (i.e., multiplied by 12) to make it comparable to the interest rate dimension.
3 Values, on an annual basis, of the total yield/cost derived as follows:

$$\text{total yield/cost} = \frac{e_1(1 + \frac{i_0}{12}) - e_0}{e_0} \times 100 \times 12$$

where: e_0 is the exchange rate at the beginning of the transaction period
e_1 is the exchange rate 1 month later
i_0 is the 1-month interest rate at the beginning of the period.

That formula can easily be written as:

$$\text{total cost/yield} = \left[\left(\frac{e^1 - e_0}{e_0} \right) + \frac{i_0}{12} + \frac{i_0}{12} \left(\frac{e_1 - e_0}{e_0} \right) \right] \times 100 \times 12 =$$

$$= \left[12 \left(\frac{e_1 - e_0}{e_0} \right) + i_0 + i_0 \left(\frac{e_1 - e_0}{e_0} \right) \right] \times 100$$

where: $(i_0 \times 100)$ is the interest rate reported in column 1

$$\left[12 \left(\frac{e_1 - e_0}{e_0} \right) \times 100 \right]$$

is the exchange rate effect reported in column 2.

Table 11.15: The break-even exchange rate has been computed as follows:

$$F^t_{x/y} = \frac{E^0_{x/y} \left(1 + i_x \frac{gg}{yr}\right)}{\left(1 + i_y \frac{gg}{yr}\right)}$$

where: $F^t_{x/y}$ is the break-even rate of the currency x with respect to the currency y, at time t

$E^0_{x/y}$ is the spot exchange rate at time t_0

i_x is respectively the 1, 3, 6-month and 1-year interest rate of the currency x, at time t_0

i_y is the 1, 3, 6-month and 1-year interest rate of the currency y, at time t_0

gg is the number of days between t and t_0

yr is equal to 360 for all currencies but the BFR, in which case yr is 365.

The EMS divergence threshold is defined as follows:

$$0.75 \times \beta \times (1 - P_i)$$

where: β = 2.25 for all currencies, 6.0 for the Italian lira

P_i = ith currency's weight calculated as the ratio of the quantity defined on 17 September 1984 and its central parity with the ECU determined on 21 July 1985.

Index

Indexed by Jacqueline McDermott

Terrence R. Keeley
Vice President

PaineWebber International Trading Inc.
1 Finsbury Avenue
London EC2M 2PA
(01) 377 0055
Telex: 297361

74¢

31¢

PaineWebber

1.34 − 1₿

150 ¥ − 1₿

Aus ¥ 10 yr ⇒ 13½%

Jap ¥ 10 yr ⇒ 4¾%

1158.6

A$: Y_0 $746.27

Y_{10} $2647.600

×3.55

2367.8

J¥: Y_0: $666.66

Y_{10}: $1035.30

×1.55

2.367

.67

150

What can I do that I am not doing? What should I
not do that I am doing?

PERSONAL

- I know Jane is not for me. I will not marry her. I do not
need to see her; it might be better if I did not see her at
all. I will see her if she really wants to see me.

- If there is a "right" woman, she is ① loving ② bright, aware +
ambitious ③ attractive.